whereby the ſ ... anſ
act may be ev ... menuer man rorreit the
sum of FIVE HUNDRED POUNDS for every ſuch
offence, and ſhall become incapable of any office or employment, civil or military ; and every perſon who ſhall
give, offer or promiſe, any ſuch bribe or reward, or ſhall
contract, agree, or treat with any perſon, ſo authoriſed
as aforeſaid, to commit any ſuch offence, ſhall forfeit
the ſum of FIFTY POUNDS.

And be it further enacted by the authority aforeſaid,
That the forfeitures and penalties inflicted by this act
ſhall and may be proſecuted, ſued for, and recovered, and
be divided, paid and applied, in like manner as other
penalties and forfeitures inflicted by any act or acts of
parliament relating to the trade or revenues of the Britiſh colonies or plantations in America, are directed to
be proſecuted, ſued for, or recovered, divided, paid and
applied, by two ſpecial acts of Parliament, the one paſſed
in the fourth year of his preſent Majeſty (entituled, An
act for granting certain duties in the Britiſh colonies
and plantations in America, ; for continuing & amend-
ing, and making perpetual, an act paſſed in the ſixth
year of the reign of his late Majeſty King George the
ſecond, entituled, An act for the better ſecuring and encouraging the trade of his Majeſty's ſugar colonies, in
America ; for applying the produce of ſuch duties, and
of the duties to ariſe by virtue of the ſaid act, towards
defraying the expences of defending, protecting, and ſecuring, the ſaid colonies and plantations ; for ex-
plaining an act made in the twenty-fifth year of the
reign of King Charles the ſecond, entituled, An act for
the encouragement of the Greenland and Eaſtland
trades, and for the better ſecuring the plantation trade ;
and for altering and diſallowing ſeveral drawbacks on
exports from this kingdom, and more effectually prevent-
ing the clandeſtine conveyance of goods to and from the
ſaid colonies and plantations, and improving and ſecuring the trade between the ſame and Great-Britain) the
other paſſed in the eighth year of his preſent Majeſty's
reign (entituled, An act for the more eaſy and effectual
recovery of the penalties and forfeitures inflicted by the
acts of Parliament relating to the trade or revenues of
the Britiſh colonies and plantations in America.)

And be it further enacted by the authority aforeſaid,
That every charter party, bill of lading, and other contract for conſigning, ſhipping, or carrying any goods,
wares, and merchandiſe whatſoever, to or from the ſaid
town of Boſton, or any part of the bay or harbour thereof, deſcribed as aforeſaid, which have been made or entered into, or which ſhall be made or entered into, ſo
long as this act ſhall remain in full force, relating to any
ſhip which ſhall arrive at the ſaid town or harbour, after
the firſt day of June, one thouſand ſeven hundred and
ſeventy-four, ſhall be, and the ſame are hereby declared
to be, utterly void, to all intents and purpoſes whatſoever.

And be it further enacted by the authority aforeſaid,
That whenever it ſhall be made to appear to his Majeſty,
in his Privy Council, that peace and obedience to the
laws ſhall be ſo far reſtored in the ſaid town of Boſton,
that the trade of Great Britain may ſafely be carried on
there, and his Majeſty's cuſtoms duly collected, and his
Majeſty, in his Privy Council, ſhall adjudge the ſame to
be true, it ſhall and may be lawful for his Majeſty, by
proclamation, or order of Council, to aſſign and appoint
the extent, bounds and limits, of the port or harbour of
Boſton, and of every creek or haven within the ſame, or
in the iſlands within the precinct thereof ; & alſo to aſſign
and appoint ſuch and ſo many open places, quays and
wharfs, within the ſaid harbour, creeks, havens and
iſlands, for the landing, diſcharging, lading, and ſhipping of goods, as his Majeſty, his heirs or ſucceſſors,
ſhall judge neceſſary and expedient ; and alſo to appoint
ſuch and ſo many officers of the cuſtoms therein, as his
Majeſty ſhall think fit ; after which it ſhall be lawful for
any perſon or perſons to lade or put off from, or to diſcharge and land upon, ſuch wha ...
places, ſo appointe ...
other, any goods, ...

Provided always ...
chandiſe, ſhall be l ...
landed upon, any o ...
places, ſo to be app ...
ſhip, boats, and o ...
the horſes, or other ...
the ſame, and the ...

... knowingly
come, ſhall ſuffer all the forfeitures and penalties impoſed by this or any other act on the illegal ſhipping or
landing of goods.

Provided alſo, and it is hereby declared and enacted,
That nothing herein contained ſhall extend, or be con-
ſtrued, to enable his Majeſty to appoint ſuch port, harbour, creeks, quays, wharves, places, or officers, in the
ſaid town of Boſton, or in the ſaid bay or iſlands, until it
ſhall ſufficiently appear to his Majeſty that full ſatisfaction hath been made, by or on behalf of the inhabitants
of the ſaid town of Boſton, to the united Company of
Merchants of England trading to the Eaſt-Indies, for
the damage ſuſtained by the ſaid Company, by the de-
ſtruction of their goods ſent to the ſaid town of Boſton,
on board certain ſhips or veſſels as aforeſaid ; and until
it ſhall be certified to his Majeſty, in Council, by the
Governor, or Lieutenant-Governor, of the ſaid province,
that reaſonable ſatisfaction hath been made to the officers
of his Majeſty's revenue, and others, who ſuffered by
the riots & inſurrections above mentioned, in the months
of November and December, in the year one thouſand
ſeven hundred and ſeventy-three, and in the month of
January, in the year one thouſand ſeven hundred and
ſeventy-four.

And be it further enacted by the authority aforeſaid,
That if any action or ſuit ſhall be commenced, either
in Great-Britain or America, againſt any perſon or perſons, for any thing done in purſuance of this act of
Parliament, the defendant or defendants, in ſuch action
or ſuit, may plead the general iſſue, and give the ſaid
act, and the general matter, in evidence, at any trial to be had thereupon, and that the ſame was done in
purſuance and by the authority of this act : And if it
ſhall appear to have been ſo done, the jury ſhall find for
the defendant or defendants ; and if the plaintiff ſhall
be nonſuited, or diſcontinue his action, after the defendant or defendants ſhall have appeared ; or if judgment
ſhall be given upon any verdict or demurrer, againſt
the plaintiff, the defendant or defendants ſhall recover
treble coſts, and have the like remedy for the ſame, as
defendants have in other caſes by law.

Also by Nick Bunker

Making Haste from Babylon:
The Mayflower Pilgrims and Their World

An

EMPIRE

ON THE

EDGE

An

EMPIRE

ON THE

EDGE

How Britain Came to
Fight America

NICK BUNKER

THE BODLEY HEAD
LONDON

Published by The Bodley Head 2015

2 4 6 8 10 9 7 5 3 1

First published in Great Britain in 2015 by
The Bodley Head
20 Vauxhall Bridge Road,
London SW1V 2SA

A Penguin Random House company

www.penguinrandomhouse.com

www.vintage-books.co.uk

Frontispiece: Published in London in September 1774, this print engraved by the Irish artist
John Dixon uses the image of a horse throwing its rider on the road between Boston and
Salem, Massachusetts, to symbolize colonial resistance to Great Britain, with the
horseman representing the imperial government. *Library of Congress*

A CIP catalogue record for this book
is available from the British Library

ISBN 9781847921543

Printed and bound in Great Britain by Clays Ltd, St Ives plc

This book is dedicated to my wife, Sue Temple.

The rulers of Great Britain have, for more than a century past, amused the people with the imagination that they possessed a great empire on the west side of the Atlantic.

—ADAM SMITH, *The Wealth of Nations* (1776)[1]

Contents

PROLOGUE
  One: THE FINEST COUNTRY IN THE WORLD — 3
  Two: THE OLD REGIME — 13

Part One: THE EMPIRE OF SPECULATION

  One: THE TIGER'S MOUTH — 31
  Two: "THIS DARK AFFAIR": THE *GASPÉE* INCIDENT — 50
  Three: A BANKRUPT AGE — 70
  Four: THE UNHAPPINESS OF LORD NORTH — 85
  Five: IGNORANCE AND BAD POLICY — 104

Part Two: THE SENDING OF THE TEA

  Six: THE EAST INDIA CRISIS — 127
  Seven: WHIGS, WEST INDIANS, AND THOMAS HUTCHINSON — 139
  Eight: MASSACHUSETTS ON THE EVE — 162
  Nine: THE BOSTON TEA PARTY: PRELUDE — 187
  Ten: THE BOSTON TEA PARTY: CLIMAX — 206

Part Three: DOWN THE SLOPE

  Eleven: THE CABINET IN WINTER — 239
  Twelve: "BOSTON MUST BE DESTROYED" — 256
  Thirteen: THE REVOLUTION BEGINS — 281
  Fourteen: AN ELECTION IN ARCADIA — 310

Fifteen: THE ARMING OF AMERICA   326
Sixteen: THE FATAL DISPATCH   343

Epilogue: THE NOBLE DEAD   366

Appendix One: The Meaning of Treason   373
Appendix Two: The Value of Money in the 1770s   377
Sources and Further Reading   379
Notes   381
Acknowledgments   413
Index   415

An
EMPIRE
ON THE
EDGE

PROLOGUE

One

THE FINEST COUNTRY
IN THE WORLD

Let the savages enjoy their deserts in quiet.

—THOMAS GAGE, COMMANDER IN CHIEF OF
THE BRITISH ARMY IN AMERICA[1]

In the summer of 1771, the Mississippi River marked the western boundary of the British Empire.

A few miles from the water's edge, in the furthest corner of what is now the state of Illinois, a traveler brave enough to venture overland from the east would come to a tall, rocky bluff, pitted with caves and crevices among the trees. Reaching the top he would look down across a wide and muddy tract of land filled with corn and ripe tobacco. Beyond the fields and just before the river, his gaze would fall upon a line of battlements built with limestone quarried from the ridge. They belonged to a fort with platforms for cannon at each corner and a British flag flying above it. As the traveler crossed the plain, more details would emerge from out of the haze. He would see a moat, a sloping earthwork, and a row of huts near the fort, with the smoke from kitchen fires hanging in the sunshine.

Overleaf: The North American interior as the British saw it in the 1760s, in a map drawn up for George III after the defeat of France in the Seven Years' War. All the newly conquered territory west of the Appalachians was set aside for the Indians. The shading from north to south along the mountains represents the Proclamation Line, beyond which settlers were not supposed to pass. Fort de Chartres was located on the Mississippi, to the right of the *V* in Virginia, about forty miles south of St. Louis. *British National Archives, Kew*

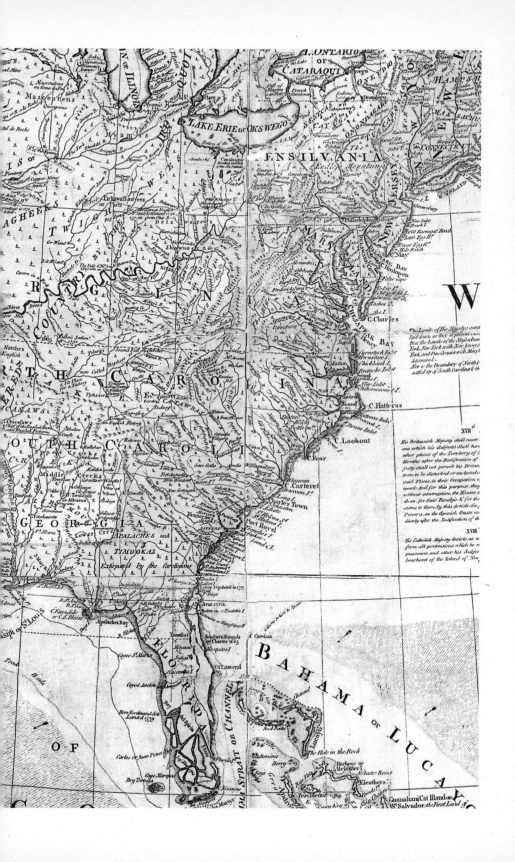

From a distance the fort's defenses seemed solid enough, but the traveler would soon identify odd traces of neglect. Nobody had cut the tall grass by the gate. Heaps of rubble lay beside the track, all that was left of a village or a few abandoned farms. Some broken fences remained, but the cattle they corralled had vanished long ago; the corn was running wild; and many years had passed since a field hand took a harvest of tobacco leaf. In the dusk, the traveler might exchange a greeting with the redcoats who stood sentry in this corner of the wilderness. They would offer him some rum and show him around the back of the fort, where he would find more evidence of decay. Close to the walls, the riverbank dipped away steeply in a cliff of yellow sand. From time to time parts of it crumbled and fell, to be carried off by the Mississippi in the night.

Far away at army headquarters in New York, the base by the river was officially listed as Fort Cavendish, after an English general of noble blood who never found time to cross the Atlantic. On the frontier, the redcoats chose to keep the name the French had given to the place. To a Frenchman, the post was known as Fort de Chartres, mispronounced by the British as Fort Charters. By the early 1770s, it was slipping into ruin like the rest of the imperial system to which the base belonged. From the French, the British had inherited a post constructed on moist, low-lying ground, close to a bayou and next to a swamp, in a site so exposed that the walls needed constant repair until at last they fell apart entirely. Handsome to look at but far too costly to maintain, the fort was built on weak foundations, the British had acquired it without a cogent plan for its future, and in time it was bound to collapse. In other words, the post symbolized Great Britain's plight in North America as a whole, a continent she did not comprehend and could not hope to rule in its entirety.

In theory, Fort Charters controlled a long line of communication from Lake Michigan down to the Gulf of Mexico. In practice, the authority of King George III stretched no further than a field gun could fire six pounds of iron from the ramparts. Much the same was true in the rest of his American dominions, where his position would soon become almost as untenable as the fort.

In the story of what happened to the British in Illinois, we can find a parable about the vanity of empire. It was a tale of error and misunderstanding, of ideas only half thought out, of neglect and delay and occasional corruption. The occupation of Fort Charters would end in failure after a pitiful waste of lives and money: a foretaste of what was to come when, soon afterward, the British lost not only the Mississippi valley but also the loyalty of their old colonies along the eastern seaboard, as the American Revolution started to unfold.

The British involvement in the far west had begun in 1763, by the stroke of a pen at a conference in Paris. A treaty negotiated at the Louvre put an end to the Seven Years' War, a conflict fought out on three continents between France, Spain, and Austria on the one hand, and Great Britain and its Prussian ally on the other. In exchange for peace the French king Louis XV ceded away a string of islands in the Caribbean and all his possessions on the frontier from Quebec to Alabama. Suddenly the British acquired a vast new domain beyond the Appalachians: a territory so immense that two more years passed before they could hoist their colors above every post the French had surrendered.[2]

Caring nothing for the politics of Europe, soon after the signing of the peace of Paris the native tribes rose in rebellion, forcing the British to fight the bloody campaign known as Pontiac's War. Even when it ended, not in outright victory but in a fragile truce, the redcoats could not occupy Fort Charters immediately. First they had to send envoys with liquor and ammunition to win over the local chieftains who had never joined the uprising or been parties to the armistice. And when at last a deal was struck, the British still had to find a way to reach the Mississippi, a journey the army had never made before.

To undertake the mission, they chose the Black Watch, a Scottish regiment used to empty stomachs and hard fighting in the rain. From their nearest camp on the Ohio River it took eight weeks by boat for the Highland soldiers to reach Fort Charters to collect the keys from the ragged platoon of Frenchmen who formed its garrison. That was in the autumn of 1765. At first, the redcoats were enthusiastic, finding the geography superb. Since every British officer either came from the landowning classes or aspired to join them, they appraised the landscape as though it were a vast estate at home, with ample capabilities for pleasure and for profit. It was, said one lieutenant, "the finest Country in the known World," with its rich soil, its bears and buffalo, and a multitude of deer to stalk. But while the British admired the wildlife, they could not abide the people they met. Soon their letters east began to carry warnings that the fort could not be held.

"Your excellency knows the French," the base commander wrote. "You will sooner imagine than I can describe the trouble they give me." In the

Illinois country, King Louis had left behind hundreds of settlers, men and women from Quebec who inhabited their own little world by the river, growing wheat for the West Indies and drinking wine made from wild grapes. Unwilling to remain among the redcoats, most of the French soon disappeared across the water into Spanish-held territory, taking with them their cows and their Jesuit priest. Those who remained were defiant, demanding their own laws, free exercise of their religion, and their own elected assembly.[3]

If the French were difficult, the native people were impossible. In the spring they would gather at Fort Charters, hoping for gifts of food to tide them over until their own harvest of corn. This was part of a system the French had created to keep the peace without using force, but the British found it hard to feed even themselves. Unable to keep the old French bargain with the Indians, the Scotsmen were soon encircled by hostile clans more ruthless than any cattle raider from Loch Ness. One year, a war party silently entered the cottages outside the ramparts and slaughtered a British soldier and his wife in bed. A month later they took more scalps from a community of peaceful Indians who lived nearby. Too few to fight back, the redcoats could do nothing but send another weary letter to headquarters.

Of all their adversaries, the most destructive was the Mississippi. When the snows melted far to the north, the river would begin to rise, sending a tide of brown water surging around a bend until the bastions at each angle of the fort began to shift and crack. After finishing their tour of duty the Black Watch had gone, to be replaced by Irishmen who tried to strengthen the walls by ramming stones into the bank in winter, only to see the spring floods wash them away. And when at last in late summer the river fell, it left stagnant pools filled with mosquitoes, from which disease crept up to infect the barracks and the married quarters. In a single month in 1768, fever killed sixty men, women, and children, leaving only a few dozen soldiers fit to hold a musket. "We Carried out in a Cart four and five a day," wrote an ensign. "The poor little Infant Orphans following."[4]

As each season went by, new tales of woe flowed back to New York to reach the desk of Thomas Gage, the British commander in chief. The dispatches made sorry reading for the officer who had drawn up the original scheme for occupying the frontier. After the truce with Pontiac, General Gage had planned to secure the wilderness with a series of posts like Fort Charters, slung like an iron chain around the *pays d'en haut*, the high country, between the Great Lakes and Tennessee. Further east, the British hoped to keep the peace with their old treaties with the Iroquois, which

left the tribes free to enjoy their ancient hunting grounds safe from inter-
ference by settlers from the colonies along the coast. Between them, the
forts and the treaties would give the British control of the fur trade, the
only kind of wealth Gage believed the wilderness could yield.

From Manhattan the strategy might have seemed plausible, but it rested
on foundations as flimsy as those of the fort. For their supplies and trading
goods, the British in Illinois had to rely on shipments from Philadelphia,
a thousand miles away, coming by a route so costly that they could rarely
turn a profit from dealing in skins. How much easier it would have been
if the knives and blankets could have sailed upriver from New Orleans;
but when the British signed the Paris treaty, they misread the map, giving
the king of Spain all the open channels from the Mississippi to the gulf.
And meanwhile, closer to home the old British deal with the Iroquois
amounted to another bargain they could not guarantee. It would only survive while Gage maintained the flow of gifts and gunpowder and kept his
promise that Pennsylvania and Virginia would leave the tribes unmolested.
With each year that passed, these conditions grew harder to fulfill.

Gage could not even trust his own subordinates. Rumors began to circulate about bullying, fraud, and embezzlement in the Illinois country:
this was a way of life in the British army, where for years the officers went
on claiming pay for men who were long since dead, but on the frontier
the colonels and the majors plumbed new depths of scandal. Embarrassing, expensive, and impossible to manage, the western wilderness swiftly
became a luxury that General Gage could not afford.

Across his whole command from Nova Scotia to the Bahamas, he could
deploy only fifteen battalions of foot. He had no cavalry at all. Including their engineers and their artillery, the redcoats in North America
amounted to fewer than six thousand men, half as many as the British kept
in Ireland. With such a small army and a budget that never seemed to be
enough, the general could not police a continent. Although he was rarely
a bold commander in the field, Thomas Gage understood the logistics of
his army, and he kept careful accounts of every shilling he spent. Soon he
bowed to the inevitable and began to plan the evacuation of the frontier
barely two years after his soldiers had arrived in Illinois.

By the spring of 1767, the general's letters home about the frontier had
become essays in despair. Repeatedly, he made the case for abandoning
it entirely, not only the post at Fort Charters, but also Pittsburgh and
Detroit and all the others in the wilderness. Time and again, he met with
little more than procrastination. As early as 1768, Gage's new strategy of
withdrawal from the frontier received the backing of the relevant minister,

Lord Hillsborough, the colonial secretary, a pessimist about the prospects for America, but Hillsborough could not make the rest of the British cabinet see sense. Compared with the affairs of Europe or the endless maneuvers for power at home, the Mississippi valley seemed too trivial to bother with. Decisions about it were continually deferred.

Even the experts in London disagreed about the role the wilderness should play in the empire's destiny. None at all, said some, because, according to a royal proclamation, dating from the same year as the peace of Paris, the American colonists were supposed to remain firmly behind the Appalachians, hugging the seaboard as docile subjects of the Crown. Allow them to cross the mountains, and they would provoke another Indian war like Pontiac's. Worse still, the settlers might shake off their loyalty to the king and begin to build workshops and factories on the frontier to compete with those of England. But while the official doctrine reserved the interior for the tribes, others took a different view, lobbying hard for expansion in the wilderness as a way to make money for the king or for themselves. Adrift between competing opinions, the British preferred to do nothing about the region, as though somehow or other the problems it posed would resolve themselves.

And then at last, in the autumn of 1771, a moment came when a decision about the Illinois country could no longer be postponed. Sent out by General Gage, an officer of engineers arrived at Fort Charters, surveyed the post, and then under cover of night slipped out by canoe to avoid an Indian ambush. After many detours he made his way back to New York with the damning evidence that Gage required. By now, only a few yards of solid ground remained between the river and the walls. Another spring flood would cause the fort to collapse.

Keen to concentrate his army on the eastern seaboard to deter the colonists from disobedience to the Crown, Gage relayed the report to London, where, in November, it reached Lord Hillsborough, who immediately took it to the cabinet and the king. Reluctantly, they gave the order to evacuate. The following spring, as the walls of Fort Charters began to slide into the Mississippi, the redcoats left the post for good. On the rim of the empire the army gave up one fort after another, but the orderly withdrawal that General Gage intended soon became a rout, as even bases that he meant to keep fell apart for lack of money to maintain them.

At Mobile, Alabama, the barracks were beyond repair, and so they collapsed as well. Far to the north on Lake Erie, the British army's fleet of boats simply rotted away. Even in Boston the troops had to inhabit an island in the harbor, Castle William, living in wooden sheds ankle-deep in water from November until March. In the valley of the Hudson, guarding the trail to Canada, the redcoats manned a fort called Crown Point whose fate was especially humiliating. Someone forgot to sweep a chimney. Somebody else lit a fire in a grate too close to the gunpowder store. In 1773, the magazine exploded, and the fort was blown to bits.[5]

Everywhere the fabric of the empire was beginning to unravel, and not only from the army's point of view. On the frontier, no one could fail to see that the British were losing their grip, as settlers flowing westward threatened to cause the Indian war that Gage and the government in London so wanted to avoid. Elsewhere, in the old colonies from Maine down to Georgia, the process of decay might be less obvious, but it was occurring nonetheless, with the debacle by the Mississippi only one symptom of a far wider malaise.

By the time the British abandoned Fort Charters, their authority in North America was already fading away irreversibly in one field of activity after another. It had never been very robust to begin with, and now it began to evaporate entirely, in the realm of ideas, in the courts of law, in the meetinghouses of religion, and along the coast. Sometimes the collapse of British power was brutally obvious, as it was on the night of the Boston Tea Party. But often their loss of control took a form so stealthy that the British did not even see it taking place until it had become impossible to prevent. As Benjamin Franklin put it at the time, "a great Empire, like a great Cake, is most easily diminished at the edges." Because the events in question were occurring on the fringes of their world, the authorities in London sometimes had only the vaguest idea of their significance.[6]

Although their senior officials were diligent and conscientious, during the decade before the American Revolution the king and his ministers made little effort to study or to analyze the continent they claimed to rule. Only when they learned of the destruction of the tea did the British begin to see the situation in America as it really was. Even then they hoped that the discontent they had aroused could be confined to New England. It took nearly another year until, at the end of 1774, it became apparent that Massachusetts had risen in outright rebellion, with the rest of the colonies in danger of doing the same. Soon afterward, the government gave the orders that sent the redcoats out to fight the rebels and led to America's war for independence, a war the British should never have allowed themselves to fight.

From a British perspective, this book will explain how and why the government in London permitted this tragedy to occur. It will tell the story of the last three years of deepening anger on both sides of the Atlantic, between the evacuation of the wilderness and the affrays at Lexington Green and Concord Bridge, not far from Boston, where the revolutionary war began in the spring of 1775. At home in England, it seems that no one kept a final tally of all the casualties their army and navy suffered in the fighting that lay ahead, until the war ended in 1783; but on the British side at least twenty thousand soldiers and sailors lost their lives in America, the West Indies, or at sea, in battle or dying in their own filth from wounds or disease, with rarely a stone to mark the grave of anyone below commissioned rank. Black Watch, Irishmen, and English privates alike, they fought to save an empire whose time had passed: an odd and fragile empire that no one had designed and very few people could claim to understand.[7]

Two

THE OLD REGIME

This country pretends to be our sovereign.

—BENJAMIN FRANKLIN, WRITING FROM LONDON, JULY 1773

It was always eccentric, the British Empire on the mainland of America, a system as loose and baggy as many of the British were themselves. And to tell the truth, the old colonial regime never really amounted to an empire at all, in the way that a Russian tsar or Queen Victoria might understand the word. From the time of Jamestown and the *Mayflower*, almost every colony came into being by means of private enterprise. They were small, experimental ventures in search of profit or in search of God. Each one was a painful exercise in trial and error, with seldom a firm guiding hand from London.

In the case of the earliest plantations in Virginia, New England, and Barbados, the reason was simply this. Before the English Civil War, the monarchy suffered from a chronic fiscal crisis, so deep that it could not hope to build an empire overseas. Rarely able to turn to Parliament for taxes, for reasons that would fill another book, the first king James could not afford imperial adventures on the far side of the ocean. The same was true of Charles I, his son. Occasionally, the Stuarts had to intervene, as they did in 1624, when they made Virginia a royal colony because the company that ran it was on the brink of failure. Even so, for lack of money they could never rule Massachusetts or the Chesapeake simply by royal decree. For better or worse, the monarchy relied on private citizens to take the risks of settlement and discovery.

Some of the settlers were Puritans, hoping to find salvation on the beaches of Cape Cod. Others simply wanted land or beaver skins. Sometimes they had motives so mixed that historians will argue forever about exactly what they were; and many went unwillingly, as convicts or indentured servants, shipped out to the west by magistrates or kinfolk eager to be rid of them. By the time the civil war began in 1642, the British in America numbered about fifty thousand, strung out along the coast and in the Caribbean and mostly governing themselves with their own laws and customs. It was a very untidy empire—"extensive and detached," said Edmund Burke, the Irish orator—but it was loyal, it was productive, and merchants and investors could finance its expansion: three very good reasons for leaving the system as it was.[1]

Only once did a Stuart king make a sustained attempt to enforce a rigid system of control. During his brief period on the throne, the Catholic king James II tried to rule his American possessions as though they were a fiefdom of the Crown. After three inconclusive wars against their rivals the Dutch, the British had at least secured the island of Manhattan as their own. To cut a long story short, King James appointed a viceroy, Sir Edmund Andros, to combine New York with New England in what amounted to a royal dictatorship. More than just a footnote in the history books, the episode left bitter memories, especially in Massachusetts, but soon enough it ended. In 1688–89 the Glorious Revolution toppled James from the throne and restored the Protestant succession. In America the old colonial system returned, modified and tightened but still nothing close to despotism.

After that, with the Stuarts in exile Britain gradually became a more stable place, controlled more efficiently from above and less fanatical about religion. By 1714, when the first king George arrived from Hanover, the state had begun to resemble a modern government, with a standing army, reliable revenues, and a central bank, the Bank of England. For most of the next twenty years the nation was at peace. But even then, when they might have changed the way they ran their empire, the British kept the old privatized model that had seemed to serve so well.

They took it for granted that the colonies were worthwhile for their timber, their sugar, their tar, and their tobacco or as a means to keep the Spaniards and the French from annexing the Atlantic. But why waste public money on a horde of royal officials when the new Americans, who were Protestant and patriotic, could run their own affairs? Of course there had to be *some* royal appointees and rules by which each colony had to abide. Every new plantation required royal approval. Each one had a charter or a patent, issued with a dangling seal from Whitehall Palace, setting out the limits of its territory and what could be done inside it. But although they were long and full of legalese, the charters allowed for a wide degree of freedom.

Each colony had an assembly to make laws and raise local taxes, and each one had its own militia. Besides going to war with each other, only two things were entirely forbidden by the British: the laws Americans passed must never clash with those of England, and the colonies must never harm its economic interests. Otherwise the empire would have served no purpose. Every colony had to obey the Navigation Acts, laws passed in Great Britain between 1651 and 1696 that obliged their commerce to travel on British or colonial ships and pass through British harbors; but other than that they could do as they pleased. To watch over their assemblies, most colonies, including Virginia and Massachusetts, had a royal governor, sent out from England to serve a term in office and to line his pockets if he could. Others had a governor they elected. In two unusual places, Maryland and Pennsylvania, the post descended through a family at home in England, the Calverts and the Penns. The system was confusing, but it seemed to work, so long as you were white and Protestant and free.

And so in the first half of the eighteenth century, control from London was usually quite loose. Except in time of war, the British kept their distance and simply watched America unfold. Left to themselves, the colonies acquired their own momentum and readily gave Great Britain what it had wanted all along: a new and fertile source of wealth from overseas. By the end of the 1740s, perhaps as many as two million people, including the slaves, lived in British North America, and all of them were workers or consumers, with the potential to add value to the empire.

Every so often the authorities would reckon up the numbers and create a balance sheet for their dominions. The figures were crude and hard to interpret, but nobody could fail to see how rapidly America was growing, not only its population, but also the wealth that it generated on both sides of the pond. Tobacco, rice, indigo, and molasses: all of them flowed back across the sea. In return Great Britain sent the colonies the goods its workshops made. Woolen clothing, clocks, and guns and bullets, steel from Sheffield, furniture from London, and books and ironmongery and silk: off they traveled to America, in quantities ever larger as each decade went by, a rising tide of British trade that paid dividends and wages in the mother country.

Only one thing was strikingly absent. From the tobacco shipped home from Maryland and Virginia, the king and his Parliament received a splendid stream of revenue by way of the duties levied on British smokers and takers of snuff, but as for the colonists themselves they paid the empire only a tiny quantity of tax. Was this a flaw in the system? Some might say it was, since it cost hundreds of thousands of pounds to protect the shipping lanes with the Royal Navy; but most of the time the issue was regarded as obscure and technical. So long as the ships sailed back and forth and trade with the colonies went on expanding, the empire was functioning as it should. However indirectly, the wealth it created enriched the government as well, as increasing prosperity in England helped the king's domestic revenues to grow. That was good enough to make the empire well worth having. Like the universe imagined by Sir Isaac Newton, the system ran like clockwork, and all the more smoothly because the Americans seemed to be so loyal.

Every so often, a statesman at home might have his doubts about that if he succumbed to a fit of zeal and actually read the colonial mail. There he might find some traces of sedition, most obviously in New England. In the 1720s, the working people of Boston had a political leader, Elisha Cooke junior, who invented the party caucus as a way to win elections. Occasionally, after some drinks in the tavern—or so it was said—Cooke would be heard railing about independence; and in the years that followed, a spy from London would have found more examples of the same kind of thing, mostly in Massachusetts but sometimes in the South.

Old Puritan ideas about rebellion and self-rule always found advocates among Americans who knew their history. At moments when the empire seemed too intrusive, they remembered the authoritarian Edmund Andros, and told each other tales of persecution by the Stuarts. Sometimes they might even follow Cooke's lead and murmur about discarding their allegiance to the king. Reported back to London, this talk of colonial independence would cause a flutter of alarm, but not for long. The likes of Cooke could usually be written off as mavericks with a taste for rum and discontent. Everyone knew that the Americans were anti-Catholic and mostly Anglo-Saxon: features of their makeup that would keep them friendly and reliable, as they always were in time of war.

Grumble as they might about the cost, the colonists would always turn out to do their bit against the Spanish or the French. The Americans came out to fight for the same patriotic motives that inspired their kinsmen in the mother country. Best of all, Americans in arms were very good at doing battle, even when their tactics were irregular. The wars they fought ended well, making a profit by way of plunder and more land, and the empire proceeded calmly on its way.

Or so it seemed to the British authorities, until about halfway through the reign of King George II. At that point, like the oil paintings the British collected, the imperial landscape took on a more subtle mixture of light and shade. In the 1740s, a few officials in Great Britain started to imagine a new kind of colonial system, tighter and more unified. At home Parliament had gradually made itself supreme across the British Isles, doing away with local customs and privileges that appeared to stand in the way of progress. For the sake of efficiency, it seemed to make sense to do the same thing overseas.

In wartime, the slack old methods in America sometimes hindered the effort to defeat the enemy. Even in peacetime, the colonies occasionally found themselves at loggerheads with London about some local issue where the governor could not see eye to eye with his assembly. These points of disagreement might concern finance, the choice of officials, the Indian frontier, or the colonies' habit of debasing their currency with a flood of paper money. And so the British began to adjust the system to give the governors more power to make the colonies fall into line.[2]

But only very gradually: because, while the king's ministers wished to be more assertive in America, Parliament remained vague and hesitant about affairs across the ocean. And then, in 1754, another great conflict with France began out in the Ohio valley. By 1756, it had escalated to become a global war that raised new questions about every element of British policy toward the nation's empire. By the time the Seven Years' War drew to a close, the future of America had become an urgent question, and reform of the colonial system had come to seem essential. The war had cost a fortune, and in London it was felt that the colonies had to pay their fair share. Fought out in Asia and Germany, as well as in the West and Canada, the war led to the doubling of Great Britain's national debt. By 1764, it had reached more than £130 million, a colossal sum, greater by a fifth than the annual output of the nation's economy.

Even so, the kingdom remained entirely solvent, with little likelihood of fiscal crisis or default. Huge though their borrowings were, the British could always service them, because interest rates were low and much of the national debt was undated, meaning that it never had to be repaid, so long as the government paid the coupons on its bonds. By long experience, His Majesty's Treasury also knew how to slash the military budget as soon as peace was declared. But although for the time being its finances were sound, the kingdom dared not be complacent. The Treasury had to think about the *next* war and the burden it might impose, rather than the contest that had just ended in victory.

During the seven years of fighting, taxes had risen steeply until, at their peak, they consumed about 9 percent of the nation's income. By twenty-first-century standards this was a small and manageable figure, but in the 1760s—when the laboring classes lived so close to destitution, and nobody believed in big government—taxes could not be permitted to rise any more for fear of unrest in Parliament and on the streets. During the war the duties on beer and wine and gin had climbed to new peaks. When George III went to see a play at Drury Lane, he was heckled from the gallery about the price of ale; and when his ministers tried to put a new tax on cider, the protests that followed were too alarming to ignore.[3]

And so, led by George Grenville, the king's chief minister, the British tried to rearrange their sprawling American empire. The nation had to rebuild its capacity to borrow so that when the time came, it could again defeat the Bourbon powers. In the task of fiscal reconstruction, America must come first, for a very simple reason. While at home the army and the navy were cut to the bone, in the colonies the situation was entirely different. Before the war, the British made do with fewer than a thousand soldiers in America. After it, the first estimates called for ten times as many, to patrol the frontier and keep Quebec from rising in revolt. It would all cost a very large sum of money, and everybody had to make some sacrifice.

Starting in 1764, Grenville introduced a series of colonial reforms, which he believed were reasonable and mild. With Parliament fully behind him, he appointed new officials, new judges, and a new customs board, based in Boston, to ensure that the colonies paid every penny they owed in duties on sugar and molasses. Gradually, he introduced new taxes too; and to protect the interests of British creditors, he imposed strict new limits on the issue of paper money.

From Grenville's point of view, he really had no choice. At the time, a British statesman had two principal duties: to defend the realm, chiefly with the navy, and to defend the revenue that kept the ships afloat. He never expected Americans to meet the whole of the bill for the expanded military on their shores. Even the most hawkish men in London never dreamed of that. But Grenville wanted the colonies to make *some* contribution; that was only right and proper. And all the time he had another agenda, so obvious that no one tried to conceal it.

With their new colonial laws and regulations, Grenville and his colleagues hoped to make America resemble Ireland: a conquered dominion where, although the inhabitants had their own laws and their own peculiar faith, everyone knew where authority ultimately lay. Despite their poverty, the Irish were obliged to pay for the army stationed in their midst: and although this led to frequent wrangling with London, the system remained set in stone. Ever since the Tudors, the last word in any Irish argument had always belonged to Westminster, with a British lord-lieutenant in Dublin to ensure that the country remained subordinate. To leave no room for doubt, in 1720 the British Parliament passed a statute, the Declaratory Act, which made the position absolutely clear. When the need arose, they could make laws for the Irish of whatever kind they chose, and Ireland had to obey.

That was the way things were in theory. But even in Ireland, so close and yet so distant, the British could not crack the whip and expect to be obeyed without dissent. In every decade, Irish writers kept up a barrage of complaint about unfairness from Great Britain, inspired by the brilliant example of Jonathan Swift. Time and again after 1760, the Irish rose in small rebellions, sometimes with a pike or with a gun and sometimes peacefully in their own assembly by the Liffey, where, although no Catholic could take a seat, the spirit of opposition survived. Every few years, the Irish House of Commons would rattle the bars of its cage to delay some unwelcome initiative from London or to demand the economic concessions they so badly needed. In America, where the colonists watched Ireland attentively because its situation had a likeness to their own, protest and resistance of the same kind had a much greater chance of success.

On the western side of the Atlantic, the British scarcely had a whip to crack. In the towns along the coast, George III could call upon barely a handful of salaried officials, even after Grenville's reforms. In Virginia, the largest colony, besides the customs service only seventeen men held office from the king. Massachusetts had even fewer royal servants, to the dismay of conservatives who knew how easily a latter day Elisha Cooke could outflank them. Here and elsewhere in America the British authorities could only do what Americans allowed. Like the Irish, but more effectively, the colonial assemblies caused no end of trouble. Filled with lawyers and fired up by the press, armed with local precedent and local knowledge, they threw dust in the eyes of any British governor who tried to call them to order. Before the revolution, the assemblies used these tactics with the utmost ingenuity, not because they wanted to leave the empire, but because they liked it as it had been before George Grenville.[4]

From Boston down to Georgia, it was impossible to compel Americans to do anything against their will. The British *tried* to do so, and that was the problem, since a policy of confrontation simply could not work. How could it, at a distance of three thousand miles, without a far larger army and many more royal officials? And each time compulsion failed, the colonies became still harder to control. Time and again, the British made empty gestures of authority, which only served to antagonize American opinion. At best, the British would appear to be aloof and incompetent, while at worst they could be portrayed as enemies of freedom as devious as any Stuart king.

And so, like the army's plan to hold the Mississippi, Grenville's project of colonial reform was doomed to failure. In 1765, the House of Commons passed his notorious Stamp Act. His boldest attempt to tax Americans directly, with a levy on legal papers and other documents, it gave rise to a storm of opposition. There were riots, most severe in Boston, New York, and Rhode Island. Up and down the coast the colonies imposed a boycott on imports from Great Britain, and on both sides of the ocean the newspapers prophesied the empire's imminent demise.

By the end of the year, Grenville had fallen from power after a personal quarrel with the king. George III never liked his chief minister, who treated His Majesty like a schoolboy who had failed to do his homework. A new administration took office, the Whigs, led by the Marquess of Rockingham, a party of aristocrats who saw themselves as the natural leaders of the nation. With what they thought were the best of intentions, they tried to correct what they saw as Grenville's mistakes, but they swiftly made an error of their own.

Alarmed by unrest in the colonies and the effect it might have on the economy at home, the Rockingham Whigs abolished the stamp tax. To do so, they needed to win debates in Parliament, where victory was far from guaranteed among lawmakers reluctant to give in to colonial blackmail. Everyone knew the American slogan: "No taxation without representation." Abolish the stamp tax, and you would admit that the Americans were justified in saying that a Parliament they did not elect had no right to tax them. To save face and win the vote for repeal, the Whigs were compelled to pass another law, a declaratory act for the colonies, modeled on the Irish law of 1720.

Passed early in 1766, the Declaratory Act insisted that Parliament remained entirely sovereign in every corner of North America. While the stamp tax had gone, the principle survived that Great Britain reigned supreme, with the right to impose other taxes in the future, much as the marquess hoped to avoid that painful necessity. In the eyes of the Whigs, this seemed to be a sensible compromise: repeal the Stamp Act, but make a plain statement of authority. But far from ushering in a new period of harmony, they merely sowed the seeds of new divisions in the future.

From that moment, a chasm opened up in British politics between two opposing attitudes toward America. On one side stood those parliamentarians who voted to abolish the stamp tax; on the other, their opponents who denounced its repeal as a craven act of surrender. Because Parliament debated colonial affairs only rarely, most of the time this chasm was invisible. Nevertheless, it continued to exist as a permanent feature of the political geography. Sooner or later, those with hawkish views about America would regain the upper hand, and when they did, they might try to revive George Grenville's program.

In their turn the Rockingham Whigs fell from office, much to the relief of George III. The king had given his consent to their liberal stance toward America, but only with deep misgivings. Little more than a year later, another British government attempted to lay another round of taxes on the colonies. Known as the Townshend duties, they were levied on a list of articles—paper, lead, paint, glass, and tea—that the Americans imported from England. Again the new taxes aroused a storm of protest and another boycott of trade with the mother country. In the face of what seemed to be anarchy in Boston, Lord Hillsborough sent in the army in the autumn of 1768 to occupy the town and keep whatever peace there was.

Eighteen months later, in March of 1770 and with the snow still six inches deep, an altercation occurred between a British sentry and a Boston crowd. A guard of redcoats turned out and fired their muskets, leaving five men and boys dying in the slush. However we choose to describe the victims of the Boston massacre—rioters, bystanders, or American patriots— the incident had been a catastrophe. For Boston radicals like Samuel Adams, the spiritual grandson of Elisha Cooke, the massacre became a symbol of tyranny and resistance, to be remembered every year like the *Mayflower* or the Glorious Revolution. Running scared of a local civil war, the British withdrew the army from the town.

And so we approach the point at which this book begins. After many years of turmoil in politics at home—where, said Frederick the Great of Prussia, the king of England changed his cabinet as often as his shirts—at last George III had found a loyal servant whom he could trust. The gentleman in question was Lord North, a stalwart of the British Treasury. He took office as prime minister early in 1770, just before the Boston Massacre. And although he admired George Grenville and always voted for his policies, it seemed for a while that North had found a new accommodation with the colonies.

Looking again at the Townshend duties, he did what appeared to be the pragmatic thing. Because the yield in revenue was always likely to be small,

Lord North abolished them, except for the most important, the tax on tea. After that, tempers cooled down in America, or so it seemed. A period of calm began, but it was deceptive and soon broken. On the frontier the British were in full retreat; and in the towns and the farming country near the coast discontent had never really ceased but simply lay dormant, waiting to flare up again when the moment came.

The Shifting Sands

All the time, the same old problem lingered on. In America the British had only a make-believe empire, a loose mosaic made from tiles without a pattern. Assembled piece by piece when opportunities arose and wars were won, the colonies were never laid out with a plan in mind. They never had a despot at the helm, benevolent or otherwise, to conceive a vision of the system as a whole. Instead, the colonial system remained what it had always been, not so much an empire as a league or a confederation, scattered and diverse.

America consisted of many provinces and sections, each with its local agenda, its local economy, and its cast of characters. Thirteen colonies would eventually rebel, each one was different, and they disagreed about their boundaries, about religion, and internally about who should run their affairs. Seen from Great Britain, each colony seemed to be full of tiresome controversies between rival factions squabbling for power and status. If only there had been a heroic statesman at Westminster, ready first to immerse himself in the details of America, but then to rise above them to produce a wise new program of imperial reform to replace George Grenville's flawed proposals, a new order might have been created, fiscal and military: but no such hero could be found.

In the early 1770s, the political elite in London rarely thought about America. That much is clear from the newspapers they bought, which enjoyed a relationship with politicians as intimate then as it is today. Entirely commercial, the British press sought to give its readers what they wanted. And so the papers watched avidly every intrigue in Europe but gave few column inches to the colonies. A dangerous asymmetry came into existence, with the Americans following news from England with fascination, always looking for clues about the government's thinking, while the British only read about America when a sensation of some kind compelled them to do so. Despite the crisis over the Stamp Act and then the controversy about the Townshend duties, the king and his ministers rarely saw any reason to delve deeply into American affairs. Their eyes were turned elsewhere, to Europe and to Asia as they surveyed a world that filled some observers with optimism, while others saw only danger and uncertainty.

As the final crisis in America drew near, the optimists in Great Britain found an eloquent spokesman in Edward Gibbon, the historian, a personal friend of Lord North's: Gibbon would enter the House of Commons himself in 1774 and vote for the harshest sanctions against New England. At the time he was preparing the first volume of his ironic narrative about the fall of Rome. Much of it was skeptical, and some of it was shocking— Gibbon had no time for Christian piety—but the book contained an essay, "General Observations on the Fall of the Roman Empire in the West," in which the author wrote a happy tale of progress and prosperity.

For Gibbon in the comfort of his study, the future held no terrors, and the British Empire would not go the same way as the Roman. Everywhere he looked, the scholar beheld the fruits of wisdom and improvement. He saw them spreading out to every corner of the globe, encompassing the Old World and the New alike. In the arts and in the sciences, in industry, in commerce, and even in diplomacy, Gibbon saw no limit to what humanity could achieve, led by the England of King George III. Above all, he believed in what he called "the law of nations." While Europe often seemed to be a troubled place, Gibbon had no doubt that ultimately reason would prevail. In every kingdom, and especially his own, he saw enlightened people who shared his belief in peace and moderation. A balance of power had come to exist in which no single European nation held the whip hand. With Britain standing by with its navy on the side of justice and fair play, Gibbon felt a glow of confidence about the years to come. He reached what he called "a pleasing conclusion," and it was this: "Every age of the world has increased, and still increases, the real wealth, the happiness, the knowledge, and perhaps the virtue, of the human race."[5]

Here was a brilliant, erudite man, writing from the heart of the elite. In his stately syntax, he conveyed a vision of serenity and hope. But Edward Gibbon was a man of letters, with twenty years of leisure in which to write his book. For Lord North and the British cabinet, practitioners of business and affairs, the future did not seem so promising. In their happier moments they could sympathize with Gibbon's optimism, and like him they believed that Britain stood for progress. But most of the time their mood was very different, as they surveyed a global scene of lawlessness and strife.

In the early 1770s, North and his colleagues felt that beneath their feet

With George III asleep on his throne at the far right, Catherine the Great and her Prussian and Austrian allies carve up the kingdom of Poland between them in this cartoon from 1772 satirizing Britain's waning influence abroad. *Library of Congress*

the ground was shifting, and they could not say how things would end any more than they could chart the currents of the Mississippi. Beyond the English Channel, the king and his ministers had few friends whom they could trust but many enemies and rivals. Everywhere they heard dark voices prophesying war. In Bengal the British had acquired another empire, operated on their behalf by the East India Company, but at best the company's tactics were dubious, and at worst they were corrupt and self-defeating. Without far-reaching reform of the company's management, the British cabinet feared that one day India might be lost entirely to hostile maharajas in alliance with the French. And nearer home in Europe they saw only confusion.

Far from being stable and secure, the balance of power appeared to be breaking down. France could never be trusted, and neither could the Spanish, while Austria remained a potential foe. To the east the cabinet saw new military nations, the Russians and the Prussians, with expansionist ambitions of their own. In British eyes, the feudal powers beyond the Elbe displayed attitudes to international law that were cynical or even wicked. Another war in Europe might lie just around the corner, and if the British had to intervene again in Germany, the Baltic, or the Mediterranean, the outcome might not be another victory. While at sea the Royal Navy reigned supreme, on land Great Britain could not match the armies of its opponents.*

At home the situation contained perils of its own. Ireland was rebellious again, this time in its northern province, with farmers in Ulster up in arms against their landlords. In London there were factions, feuds, and riots, fomented, it was thought, by atheists and libertines. Meanwhile, the price of corn was rising steeply, causing alarm in the cabinet as well as among the poor. An economic upheaval had just begun, the long, slow, and complicated process that today we call the Industrial Revolution. Nobody used that term to describe the economic changes that were under way, but they were occurring even so, and North and his colleagues felt their early consequences. In its wake, the birth of modern industry in Great Britain brought vast opportunities, exciting and life enhancing, but it also caused unsettling peaks and troughs in the economy, with periods of misery and trauma.

Against this background, the politicians in Whitehall had to come to terms with the unrest in the colonies. However dearly they wished to be as confident as Gibbon, they could not rise above the flux of events and take a calm, judicious view of the American crisis. And because the colonies were far away, it was all too easy to forget about them during the intervals when they appeared to be tranquil. Distracted by so many other issues, the British failed to see just how fragile their position was in North America. Inertia took the place of statesmanship until the machinery of empire had corroded beyond salvation. And when at last the Boston Tea Party obliged them to stare directly at the colonies, they did so not with Gibbon's optimism but with its opposite: a pessimistic vision of anarchy and treason. In the end, their perception of the world as a troubled, lawless place would lead them to the use of force against New England.

This book will amount to a sympathetic study in failure, seen chiefly from the standpoint of British politicians and the British public, whose minds we have to try to enter. Without taking sides, it will try to explain how and why Great Britain stumbled into the war that began at Lexington. Among the British, there will be two leading characters. One is Lord North, while the other is his friend and kinsman William Legge, Lord

---

* The British navy was certainly the strongest in the world, but in 1774 the British army numbered only 27,000 men, while Russia had about 290,000. In 1782, the British reached a maximum strength of 150,000 soldiers under arms, of which only 35,000 were stationed in America. Accurate military statistics for France are hard to come by, but in peacetime its army was about 150,000 strong, and in time of war it was much larger.

Dartmouth, his minister for the colonies. Neither man was dishonest. By the standards of the age they were paragons of virtue, their private lives untainted by a single peccadillo. Far from being unprofessional, Lord North possessed a mastery of politics that few statesmen in his period could equal. But for all his qualities he could not hope to understand the American challenge that lay ahead. As everybody knows, the chain of events that led to war began in an odd or even a comical way, with a quarrel about an item so mundane that almost no one at the time expected it to provoke a revolution.

The item was tea. When Lord North did away with most of the Townshend duties but left the tax on tea in place, he merely postponed another great collision with the colonies. Levied at threepence on a pound of leaves from China, the tax came to symbolize the British claim to complete supremacy. Sooner or later, the tea tax was bound to cause another crisis as severe as the one that followed the Stamp Act, and this time one that could not be resolved by peaceful means.

The British East India Company controlled the nation's trade in tea, but by the summer of 1771 it was approaching a calamity of its own. Loaded down with tea leaves it could not sell, the following year the company came near to bankruptcy. With the connivance of Lord North, eventually it tried to rescue its affairs by shipping the surplus tea to America. Even at the time, a few astute members of Parliament shook their heads, warning about the fury this would cause if the tea still carried the tax; and then, a few months later, the moment of truth occurred in Boston Harbor at the hands of a crew of working men and intellectuals. In December 1773, the people of Boston dumped the company's tea in the water. Angry and appalled, the British government replied with a package of new laws and penalties designed to teach the colonists a lesson in obedience. By the end of the following year, New England had risen in revolt.

None of this was accidental, and least of all the role performed by tea. However bizarre it might seem that tea could cause a revolution, the Boston Tea Party took place as a consequence of fundamental flaws in the system that the British had created. The British really had two overlapping empires: not only the official, political empire, with its garrisons and governors, but also a commercial empire, private and informal and financed with debt. While there were a few politicians who simply wanted power, and the more of it the better on a global scale, in the eighteenth century the British took a far more serious interest in money. Profit was the goal of almost everything they did overseas, and so in reality they valued their commercial empire more highly than the flags they had planted on the map.

At the heart of this commercial empire lay the booming trade in commodities, not only the tea that the East India Company brought home from China, but also rice from Charleston and wheat or tobacco from the Chesapeake, not to mention cotton from India and sugar from the Caribbean. A global system of exchange had come into being, dealing in these items and others more exotic, but in the two decades after 1750 the volume of trade soared to reach a remarkable new peak. By 1772, soft commodities of such a kind accounted for nearly half of the goods imported into Great Britain. In the pursuit of financial gain, the British had created a trading system that resembled a giant hedge fund, investing in items grown by African slaves and Chinese peasants. Complex and dynamic, it was run from London, Liverpool, Bristol, and Glasgow and fed by a myriad of factories and farms, spread out across the globe from Maryland via Calcutta to Canton.

For Lord North and the Treasury, the hedge fund had come to be an essential source of imperial revenue. The global trade in commodities accounted for a quarter of the taxes they collected; for merchants and planters, it was immensely lucrative; and it filled the holds of hundreds of ships in the North Atlantic and the tropics. But by its very nature this great trading system was hazardous and volatile. Men and women borrowed heavily to bet on the price of tea and sugar and tobacco or to buy the land where they were grown. Exposed to many dangers, natural and man-made, dealing in commodities could lead to ruin as easily as riches. If and when a crash occurred, the system might come tumbling down entirely.

Of all the players in the game, the East India Company was the largest, the most aggressive, and the one most addicted to risk. As speculators do, the company's directors pushed their luck too far, until at last the company toppled over under the weight of its own ambition, leaving Lord North to pick up the pieces. In the process he made a series of fatal errors that brought about the revolution in the colonies. Through the eyes of a British sea captain approaching the shores of Asia, we can start to see how the debacle began to take shape.[6]

Part One

The Empire of Speculation

Chapter One

THE TIGER'S MOUTH

China is located in the centre of the earth, and surrounded by seas.

—A CHINESE GEOGRAPHER, IN THE REIGN
OF THE EMPEROR QIANLONG[I]

They reached the coast of China in a squall of rain. It was August, a season when the monsoon turns the sky to indigo, and the crossing from Sumatra had been swift but arduous. As if to chase her even faster, all the way over thunderstorms followed the ship, the *Calcutta*, soaking her planks and deafening the crew like the sound of artillery.

A new ship, fresh from a yard in the Thames, she had a young man for her master by the name of William Thomson, at the helm of his first command. In wide tacks, he swung the *Calcutta* away from the shores of Vietnam and up the very middle of the South China Sea. Although at this time of year it was by far the safest course, even so the route contained a host of hidden perils: sunken atolls, shoals, and reefs, known by the names of English ships whose wrecks lay on the sand beneath them. Each evening at sunset, Thomson would gaze at the horizon, in search of clouds the color of copper, the only warning he would have that a typhoon was approaching.

At last, early in the afternoon of August 20, 1771, through the wet he saw a line of rocks, resembling a row of jagged teeth. With a heavy swell running from the east, making the hull of the ship roll like a pig, an island appeared from out of the spray, and then another, with the Chinese mainland close behind. He found a landmark he knew from his earlier voyages to the region and looked at his chart: sixty miles down the coast was the port of Macao. Seven months had passed since they left England: not the fastest voyage of the season, since there had been accidents, deckhands had died, and they had been forced to stop in Java for repairs. Even so, Thomson brought his ship safely to Canton in search of tea and porcelain and profit.[2]

It was a frantic year, the peak of a boom in the eastern trade, a boom that had lasted nearly a decade and would end in something close to catastrophe. Thirty ships made the long haul from Europe to China, two-thirds of them British, flying like Thomson the flag of the East India Company. Of all the craft in that busy season, his would be the busiest of all. The following spring, when the *Calcutta* left for London, she carried the largest cargo in a European fleet that brought home nine thousand tons of tea. Why did they drive their ships so hard to bring it back in such enormous quantities? Because for the British tea had become far more than a bland, familiar drink for the breakfast table.

Instead, tea had acquired a more exalted status, as a prize to be fought for by powerful and ambitious men. It was one of a handful of commodities that served the wider purposes that crude oil and copper fulfil today, purposes that far exceed their utility in daily life. Traded across the globe, they set all kinds of wheels in motion, as objects of speculation, as a source of jobs and revenue for nations, and as a kind of currency themselves. To take the economic pulse of the modern world, we need only follow the ups and downs in the price of base metals and petroleum.

Much the same was true of tea, tobacco, and sugar in the 1770s. In the British Parliament the point was made emphatically by Edmund Burke. "Tea is perhaps the most important object, of any in the mighty circle of our commerce," he declared, and Captain Thomson would have agreed entirely. In his career and in the adventures of his ship, we can see in miniature all the defining features of British enterprise in Asia, not only its hardships and its vices, but also its virtues of expertise and courage, and above all its economic motives.[3]

The *Calcutta* had left the Thames at the end of 1770, resting for a while at Portsmouth, where, still in sight of England, Thomson lost part of his crew to the Royal Navy. Rumors were rife of an imminent war with Spain, arising from a quarrel about the Falkland Islands. So a boat from a warship came alongside and pressed eleven sailors for the service of His Majesty. A few months later, in the South Atlantic, some of the crew began to brawl and shirk their duties. Order was swiftly restored, with a few men flogged and the rest set to work picking oakum and washing the gun deck time and again, but throughout the voyage the atmosphere remained edgy and bad-tempered.

On they went to the south past the Cape of Good Hope, running fast with the wind behind them until, with the temperature falling, the ice drew near and a storm began to gather. The top of the mainmast cracked and split, a heavy sea ruined their stores of pork and biscuits, and four months out from home scurvy began to take its toll. At last Thomson dropped anchor at Jakarta, pausing briefly for repairs, before the *Calcutta* swung north on the final leg of the journey, losing four sailors swept overboard or dead from disease. But beneath the hatches sealed with tar, his cargo remained intact: English marble, lead, woolen cloth, and, most important, the bullion required for doing business at Canton. The ship carried chests of Spanish silver dollars from Peru with a value in sterling of £30,000.

Two views of an East India Company ship, the *Princess Royal,* painted by John Cleveley the Elder before she sailed to China in 1770.
© *National Maritime Museum, Greenwich, London*

Beating against the current, from her point of landfall the *Calcutta* took a week to reach the Pearl River, where at last she turned a corner and left Macao to port. Passing a battery of Chinese guns, she entered a strait called the Bocca Tigris, or the Tiger's Mouth. From the moment they passed the Bocca, seafarers from the West entered an unhealthy little enclave where months of boredom and alcohol lay ahead. Beneath a stifling canopy of cloud, Thomson made for the haven at Whampoa Roads. There a line of wooden stakes for fishing nets peeped out above the water, marking a limit his ship was forbidden to pass.

As the *Calcutta* dropped anchor, two Chinese boats closed in around her and remained clamped to her sides until she left. In the distance, Thomson and his crew saw the Chigang Pagoda, crimson against the gray of the sky; and, in the foreground, wide, flat islands of mud, the only place where they could take a walk or play a game of cricket. Here they would bury their dead, slaughter pigs for the journey home, and keep their stores and canvas in sheds they made from rushes and bamboo. Around them lay rows of European ships, and Thomson carefully noted their colors. They were Dutch and Swedish, there was one from Denmark, and the French were on their way, but mostly they were British sister ships of his. From time to time a sampan would approach the *Calcutta* filled with harlots, waiting to bribe the police for permission to sell their bodies on the deck.

When the officers went upriver to Canton, to the compound where the East India Company did business, their every move was watched. Sometimes a fracas would occur between the police and a tipsy sailor. On one occasion in 1769 a seaman lost his temper, shooting a mandarin, and the Chinese took reprisals, staking out some English crewmen in the sun. Bored and angry, the deckhands talked of mutiny and hatched a plan to take Canton by storm. To nip any trouble in the bud, the captains had to keep their discipline as tight as ever. And so when a drunkard tried to sell a pile of cannonballs to the locals, Thomson flogged the man severely. Every master in the fleet kept a log filled with incidents like this. All those that survived the journey home were filed away in London, where they remain today, mostly unread since the days when they were written.

Such were the harsh realities in the European foothold on the coast. Somehow a deceptive glamour has come to surround the East India Company: an entity still occasionally remembered by historians with too much respect, as though it served some great, farsighted purpose. In the eighteenth century, the company had visionaries in its service—navigators, a few scientists, or the greatest of them all, Sir William Jones, who translated the Hindu scriptures into English—but they were few and far between. At home there were ideologues and pamphleteers, armchair patriots who gloried in the name of empire. When the army or the navy defeated the French, victory led to a surge of national pride in a kingdom that believed it was born to rule the waves. But when we meet the Britons who actually went abroad, their letters and diaries tell a story far simpler and less chauvinistic.

Courageous though they were, they sailed to Asia for one reason only: to make a profit as quickly as they could and get out again before they died from fever, drink, or syphilis. In China the company could buy a pound of tea for silver worth eleven English pennies and sell it at home for more than three times as much. Dealing for themselves, mariners like William Thomson did the same. With so such money to be made, a dash for growth took place. In the peace that followed the defeat of France in 1763, the tea trade between Great Britain and Canton doubled in size in the space of eight years.

At home demand for the product had risen by leaps and bounds. Of course nobody really needed tea, a point often made by old-fashioned moralists who saw tea drinking as a form of decadence. The French hardly drank it at all, except as a medicine. Neither did the Germans or the Spanish. Only the British and their American cousins had come to see it as something they could not do without. We could ruminate forever about the reasons this was so and why each country differed in its taste. But for a man like Captain Thomson the question was irrelevant. From his point of view, all that mattered was this: that tea had become embedded in the British way of life. And people drank tea in ever larger quantities because the price kept falling, despite the taxes loaded on the product.

When it first arrived in London in the 1650s, tea had been scarce and precious, with a flavor very different from the mild, warm beer the British drank with every meal. For nearly seventy years it remained an expensive status symbol consumed by the elite. They called the principal variety Bohea, a mangled English name for the Chinese hills from whence it came. With its dusty black leaves that smelled like scorched grass, it was a crude form of tea. No connoisseur would drink it today, but to begin with, it was all the British had. As late as 1712, Bohea was still rarefied enough to figure as an object of satire for the poet Alexander Pope. But as the century wore on, the beverage ceased to be so scarce. The turning point came in the 1720s, a prosperous time in Britain. China seemed to have unlimited supplies of tea, which arrived in England in quantities undreamed of hitherto. Once it was commonplace, Bohea lost its cachet and became a drink for tradesmen and their wives. As markets do, the market for tea grew wider and became more differentiated, with the wealthy turning to green, aromatic varieties, where the price was higher and the taste more delicate.

By the 1740s the official figures showed that the British were drinking four times as much as they had two decades earlier. If we count the growing black market as well, made up of tea that was smuggled in, the rate of increase was probably still greater. By the time the Seven Years' War began, the trade was so large that the East India Company was sending nine ships to the Pearl River each year.[4]

During the war the tea trade stagnated for a while because of the risk of meeting French warships at sea. When peace returned, the floodgates opened wide. Another boom began, the boom that carried Thomson to Whampoa. For the investors who owned the East India Company's stock, the profits were enormous. In 1771, the richest noblemen in England, the Dukes of Bedford and Devonshire, enjoyed an annual income of about £50,000 each from the rents their tenants paid. That same year, the company made a profit of six times that sum from its trade in China tea alone. Between them, the East India Company and its Chinese hosts had engineered a business model with apparently endless potential, but one that was far too good to be true.[5]

Between the hills where the tea was grown and the drinkers in the West, there lay a long chain of dealers and agents, each of them keen to take a cut as the stuff passed down the line. At each step, the system encouraged those involved to deal in ever larger volumes of tea, and to borrow heavily in the expectation of reward. But ultimately they all relied on the consumers, chiefly in Great Britain. So long as they continued to buy all the tea that returned from Asia, the China trade would thrive, but if their thirst for tea ever slackened, the consequences would be dire.

By intervening in the trade, the government had made the system all the more unstable. From the moment tea was introduced to England, the state began to tax it, with at first a modest duty of just 5 percent. But each time Britain fought a war with France, the taxes rose, on alcohol, tea, and tobacco alike, until they reached a peak in 1765. By then, tea sold in London carried seven separate duties, a combination of customs and excise, amounting to 40 percent of the retail price, enough to tempt even the most honest housewife to dabble in contraband. Above the counter, a pound of premium tea would cost her six shillings. If she knew a smuggler or his mate, in the capital or near the coast, she could get the stuff for less than four.

In Europe in the eighteenth century, from Connemara to the Urals there always existed an immense illegal economy, thriving in the shadow cast by indirect taxation. Every monarch fought a losing battle with the smuggler of salt or alcohol or tea, but tea leaves were one of the easiest products to carry and conceal. By the end of the 1760s, nearly a third of the tea arriving from China was destined for the hands of smugglers by way of friendly ports in Europe. From there it crossed the sea to Britain or America. Keen to undermine the revenues of George III, the king of France connived at the illicit trade, and the Dutch did much the same. Ceasing to be a small affair, the work of little bands of criminals, smuggling became a great enterprise of its own, run by commercial syndicates and financed by banks, an enterprise so large that it might wreck the legal trade entirely.

By the time Thomson left Whampoa Roads for England early in 1772, a crisis of such a kind was rapidly approaching. The price of tea was about to collapse, as the supply of it far exceeded the amount that Europe could absorb. From time to time a glut had occurred before, but nothing on quite the scale of the one that appeared in the early 1770s. It arose not only because of greed, but also because the tea trade had become as complex and as volatile as the global trade in oil today. It had its downstream and its upstream, its producers, brokers, and refiners and a horde of hungry mouths to feed. This intricate chain of industry and speculation began in the China of the emperor Qianlong.[6]

The Emperor and the Hongs

At this moment in history the Chinese empire, not the British, could rightfully claim to be the greatest in the world. For nearly four decades Qianlong had occupied the throne, reaping the rewards of prosperity and war. To pacify his dominions, he had fought six great campaigns. In Tibet and central Asia, his army had crushed the last elements of resistance. Even though Burma and Vietnam remained free and independent, his borders had come to be secure.

Safe in his domain and almost entirely self-sufficient, the emperor imposed the strictest limits on foreigners who hoped to disembark on his shores. Every port except Canton was closed to them. The interior was completely out of bounds. If all Westerners were suspect and inferior, the British were seen as the worst of all, because in the north of India and in Nepal they were threatening to trespass on his borders. In the late 1750s, a few English ships ventured up the Chinese coast toward Zhejiang, the commercial heart of the empire, a thousand miles north of Macao. The experiment ended badly when a merchant named James Flint tried to petition the emperor, complaining about officials who demanded exorbitant bribes. While Flint was deported, his Chinese contacts were locked up, tortured, or beheaded.

After that the Europeans found themselves ever more tightly confined to Whampoa Roads or to their compounds in Canton. Here, in the prov-

ince of Guangzhou, the emperor had a viceroy, Li Shiyao, who drew up
a set of rules for the Westerners, called the "five limitations on barbar-
ian merchants." Some could be bent in exchange for bribes, but the basic
principles were never compromised. The rules allowed the foreign merchants to buy tea, porcelain, silk, and a few other textiles, but nothing else.
Imports of weapons and opium were banned. To prevent the foreigners
from gathering intelligence about his country, the viceroy's edict kept their
contact with his people to a minimum, even barring Europeans from hiring Cantonese servants.[7]

From the Chinese point of view the Europeans were merely temporary guests, welcome only for the sake of their money. On arrival at the
Bocca the ships paid not only a toll, the first of many, but also charges for
mooring, loading, and unloading and for pilots and translators, and there
were "presents" to be given to the mandarins. The largest levies were the
customs duties on exported tea. To ensure that they were never evaded,
Li Shiyao insisted that the Europeans deal with a small, exclusive group
of nine merchants, known as the Hongs, who collected the taxes on the
emperor's behalf. The richest and most adventurous was a man the British
called Puankhequa.

Since corruption was rife, not all the tea duties found their way to Bei-
jing. Even so, each year a million ounces of silver traveled up by porter and
pack animal to reach the Forbidden City. This represented only a small
fraction of the emperor's income, most of which came from a land tax on
his peasants, but an extra tranche of silver always had its uses. The export
trade in tea helped finance China's military machine; it oiled the wheels of
commerce with hard currency; and it brought a new source of prosperity
to the countryside. As Qianlong knew full well, his empire rested on the
backs of Chinese farmers and the crops they grew. In places where rice
and grain could never flourish, they needed a substitute, and tea served this
purpose to perfection.[8]

In the southeastern corner of his empire, facing the island of Taiwan,
the emperor had a remote, secluded province called Fukien, small by Chinese standards but not by those of Europe. Although its rugged shores
were beaten by typhoons, and although hills and forests filled the land and
the soil was thin and poor, about twelve million people lived there, one
million more than the population of the British Isles.* Fukien was never

---

* To put these figures in perspective: in 1771, the Chinese empire had a population of about
270 million; Bengal, about 50 million; Great Britain, about 7.7 million, with about another
3.2 million in Ireland; British North America, about 2.5 million.

rich: but deep in its northern interior, where the mountains rose as high as seven thousand feet, the warm, wet climate was ideal for growing tea. Known as Wu Yi, the region produced the leaves the British called Bohea. In the sixteenth century the farmers adopted a tactic called *panshan*— "challenging the peaks"—and began to fill the misty slopes with terraces for tea and indigo. Much of the land belonged to monasteries, Taoist and Buddhist, that smiled on this new departure, which had the blessing of successive emperors as well.

But despite its ideal climate and geography, it took many decades for Wu Yi to begin to fulfill its potential. New tea plants took four years to reach maturity, with dikes and drains needed to protect the soil from erosion by summer rains, and at harvest time the farmers required an army of helpers. Once the raw leaves were picked, they had to be processed, first by wilting in the sun and then by a stir fry and careful drying before the tea was fit to drink. And then, to reach the outside world, it had to travel by porter and river barge to Canton, a journey of seven weeks. To finance all of this, the planters needed capital and credit, but only in the 1730s did it begin to arrive from the West in the quantities required, coming mainly from the British, whose prosperous textile trade with India gave them the wherewithal to invest in China. These were the years when a mass market

Factories occupied by foreign merchants at Canton, with the English and the Dutch on the right, painted by William Daniell in 1806 but still much as they were thirty years earlier. *Yale Center for British Art*

for tea developed in Great Britain, and the East India Company stood ready to grasp the rich opportunity that Fukien made available.

Gradually, the company assembled a new trading system that allowed their business to grow as never before. In its factory at Canton the East India Company kept twelve agents, the supercargoes, whose job it was to haggle with the Hongs. Each February, the supercargoes would bid for the next season's tea and pay a cash advance in silver amounting to about two-thirds of the price they had agreed. The remainder fell due in the autumn, when ships like Captain Thomson's arrived from the West. Meanwhile, the Hongs took the cash advance and lent it onward into China along a chain of middlemen and shippers until eventually it reached the farmers on the mountains.

With so much capital at hand they could build more terraces, plant more tea, and recruit the seasonal labor they needed. By 1771, nearly three-quarters of the tea the British drank came from Wu Yi or thereabouts, and with each passing year the price they paid for it in China had fallen as the output of the region soared. But simple though it sounds and successful though it was, the system contained a fatal weakness. With tea so cheap and plentiful, the British supercargoes always tried to buy every ounce they could afford. At some stage the British would go too far and ramp the business up to a level that was unsustainable. Because of the way the East India Company chose to reward its employees, no one wished to call a halt to an enterprise so lucrative.[9]

Instead of a salary, a British supercargo at Canton earned a commission, averaging 4 percent of the value of the goods they bought and sold. Taking so high a cut, he could make £4,000 from a single season in the factory, almost enough to buy a gentleman's estate in the heart of England. If he were brave and fit enough to remain ten years or more, he might come home very rich indeed, with a chance of a seat on the company's board or in Parliament. For reasons such as these the job of supercargo was sought after avidly. Only members of established merchant families in London could hope to be appointed to a post so promising. In choosing candidates, the directors gave first preference to their own relations. The best job of all was that of chief supercargo at Canton, because he took a cut of 10 percent. In 1771 the man in question was, of course, the son of a veteran member of the board.[10]

Paid by commission as they were, the East India Company supercargoes always urged London to send as many ships to China as it could find, and here again the system contained a flaw. Rather than own its ships outright, the company hired them from contractors for a handsome fee per ton. As time went by, the shipowners bought stock, joined the East India Company's board, and formed a powerful lobby, the so-called shipping interest, who established a monopoly on the supply of vessels and the appointment of commanders. In order to inflate their own profits, the shipowners in their turn twisted the arms of their fellow directors to commission an ever expanding fleet. Their kinsmen stood to benefit as well since the shipowners gave their sons and nephews the best careers available at sea. Indeed, this was how William Thomson came to command the *Calcutta*. His father had been an East India captain before him, his uncle led the syndicate of investors who owned the ship, and Thomson's brother sailed with him to China as first mate. Once there, the brothers dealt on their account in Hyson, the costliest brand of tea, four times more expensive than Bohea, bringing home more than a hundred chests for private sale in London. And if he ever tired of his hazardous life at sea, William Thomson could retire, selling his rank to the highest bidder for a going rate in the 1770s of £10,000.[11]

With so much money to be made in so many different ways, whether they were British or Chinese, every player in the China trade wished to raise the stakes and see the business grow more swiftly. The same was true of the British East India Company's principal competitors, the French and the Dutch, who had developed their own effective business tactics. Instead of paying for tea with silver, the Dutch often used tin and pepper, sourced from their network of contacts in Malaya. Striking deals with local sultans for the supply of both, they found a ready market in China, where the devout appeased the gods by burning paper coated with tinfoil, and this meant that the Dutch could give the Hongs terms better than those the British could offer. Meanwhile, at home in Amsterdam, the largest banking houses dealt eagerly in tea, feeding it to smugglers at Dunkirk and Ostend for the short trip across the Channel to the English coast. Further south the French did much the same.

Returning from China, their ships would dock at Lorient in Brittany, where the tea was sold at auction, but very little ever reached the streets of Paris. From Lorient the tea sailed to Guernsey in the British Channel Islands, a perennial hive of corruption where the local magistrates doubled as smugglers themselves. From there the tea traveled to Devon and Cornwall along with brandy and tobacco, coming ashore in coves and creeks for sale all over the west of England.[12]

And so for all its size and energy, the British East India Company saw its share of the tea trade ebb away as its European rivals fed the booming black market at home and in America. Of course the company begged the government to help by cutting the taxes that gave the smugglers their competitive advantage. For five years, starting in 1767, the British Treasury suspended the largest excise duty, slashing the retail price of tea by a shilling a pound. For a while the smugglers lost ground and the law-abiding traders regained the upper hand. But this concession was due to end in 1772, and so the company hit upon another tactic for protecting its status at Canton. To prevent the foreigners from becoming too powerful, the viceroy had banned them from lending money to the Hongs, except by way of the cash advances paid when deals for tea were struck. Quietly, the British disobeyed. As a way to give themselves first choice of all the tea that China grew, they offered the Hongs generous overdrafts until their debts were vast, with Puankhequa alone owing the company the enormous sum of £60,000.[13]

By now the system had become highly unstable; and by flooding the Hongs with credit, the British tipped it entirely out of equilibrium. If the export business lost momentum, the Hongs would be unable to repay what they had borrowed, and so again the supercargoes had to order tea in still larger amounts each season, regardless of the state of the market at home. If, for whatever reason, demand in England began to falter, the result would be a crash. Twice a year the East India Company held auctions in London, where it sold the leaf wholesale to a few dozen expert dealers. Highly experienced, with their own shares of the company's stock, they knew the score: huge cargoes coming home, the tax break due to finish, and the smugglers poised to make another killing. All the dealers had to do was wait, and the price of tea would plummet.

Until the March sale in 1771 the auctions went well, with the company disposing of all the tea it had. But then, between May and August, thirteen ships reached the Thames, carrying nine million pounds of the stuff, three million more than the amount the British market usually took each year. At the auction in September the dealers slashed their orders, leaving two-thirds of the tea without a buyer. For a while the price held firm, but with so much tea in the warehouse, and Thomson and his friends about to leave Canton with even more, at the sales due in 1772 the market was sure to collapse.[14]

Even now the East India Company might have avoided a crisis on the scale that was about to occur. It would have taken foresight and humility, and some discreet negotiations with the Bank of England, but the company's directors might have found a way to solve a problem that had not yet crystallized. Sadly, they had every reason to conceal the truth about their situation. A clique of talented but headstrong financiers had recently come to dominate the board, and prudence was the last thing on their minds.

COMPANY MEN

Time and again in the course of the company's long history, ambitious men had quarreled for control of its affairs. Given the size of the business, the contracts it awarded, and the jobs it had to offer, a seat on the board was always worth a fight. But during and after the Seven Years' War, the East India Company underwent a transformation that made its leadership an even richer prize.

When it started life in 1600, with the granting of its royal charter, the company acted solely as a trading venture importing oriental luxuries. So it remained until the middle of the eighteenth century. As well as the factory at Canton, the company occupied bases in India, at Calcutta, Madras, and Bombay. Apart from that, it did not look for land or prestige. Content to rent space, do business, and no more, it stuck almost entirely to its old vocation, enjoying its monopoly on sales in England of silk and tea and spices. In the 1750s all of this began to change. During the war between Britain and France, the company became a territorial power in its own right. To cut another long story short, the East India Company saw an opportunity to acquire its own dominions in the richest part of India. With the blessing of the government in London, keen to forestall the French, the directors built their own empire in the valley of the Ganges.

Step by step, by way of force, bribery, and maneuver, the British crept up the river from Calcutta to devour the rest of the province of Bengal. In doing so, the company also found a new source of profit, far larger, or so it thought, than any it had seen before. Spanning a fertile crescent, eight hundred miles across, from the edge of Burma to the Hindu holy city of Benares, the province seemed to be immensely valuable, richly endowed with weavers of silk and farmers of rice and grain. Best of all from a conqueror's point of view, Bengal paid an annual land tax to its rulers. Each village had a council and a headman—in Hindi, a *patel*—whose duty it was to collect the revenue. The proceeds were potentially enormous from a territory bigger than the whole of France.

In theory, the land tax belonged to the Mughal emperor in Delhi, but he was a long way off, and he mattered less and less. As each decade went by, his authority faded a little more as he fell victim to invasions by the tribes from Afghanistan. From about 1740 control of the land revenue had passed entirely to the viceroy of Bengal, known as the nawab; and by

1756 the nawab in question was Siraj-ud-Daula, a young man keen to free himself from outside influence. Angry with the British, whom he accused of fraud, he decided to evict them from his territory.

The nawab took Calcutta with its British residents; many of them died in the Black Hole, a complicated incident whose true story may never be entirely known, and for a while it seemed that the British had lost Bengal. To recapture the town and rescue the survivors, the company sent a force of soldiers up the coast from Madras, under the command of Robert Clive. Betrayed by his own allies, the nawab lost a battle by a mango grove, close to the Tropic of Cancer at a little town called Palashi, and then he died of poison. With Siraj-ud-Daula out of the way, Clive replaced him with a puppet. After that the company began its creeping annexation of the province, taking possession of the land tax as it went. It started just around Calcutta, in a region prowled by tigers and known as the 24 Parganas. As time went by, the British expanded to the north until their empire stretched as far as the Himalayan foothills.

The bulk of Bengal's land revenue arose from two locations: the region known as Bihar, centered on the city of Patna; and the district, filled with paddy fields and silkworms, around the still larger city of Murshidabad, next to the modern border with Bangladesh. It took eight years and another military campaign before the British could legally acquire these territories, but at last the deed was done in 1765. Defeated in battle, the emperor signed the Treaty of Allahabad, giving the East India Company the *diwan*, meaning the right to collect all the taxes Bengal produced.[15]

At that moment the British became the greatest power in India, with the prospect of still greater gains in the future as the Mughal Empire died away. Up to a point, the treaty can be compared to its counterpart in the West, the Paris treaty that gave Great Britain the wilderness beyond the Appalachians, but the Ganges far surpassed the Mississippi as a prize. While the American wilderness did nothing for Great Britain, other than drain its resources of soldiers and money, the *diwan* was an asset of the most tangible kind. Just like the Chinese at Canton, the nawabs insisted on taking their revenue in silver, and the British did the same. Before the treaty the company's share of the land tax had amounted to only £600,000, far too small a sum to cover the cost of the army it needed to defend itself. After the *diwan*, its income from Bengal increased to more than £2.5 million. A quarter of that could be taken as a profit in hard cash, while the rest went to pay for salaries and soldiers.

And so when word of the treaty reached London, the reaction was euphoric. When Clive's dispatch arrived in the spring of 1766, the price of the company's stock began to soar in the hope of ample dividends to come. The stock leaped up by more than 50 percent, and since the China trade was booming too, the price went on climbing the following year as well. By the spring of 1768, the company's stock was trading at nearly £280, the highest price that it would ever attain.

Everyone could see that the East India Company had done an excellent deal, but the burden of expectations became ever more demanding. Speculators bought the story, in the fond belief that the company's earnings would grow in perpetuity. If anything happened to disappoint them, the fall would be all the more steep, because the rise had been so sharp. And if things began to go wrong, the directors might be inclined to hide the truth or try to rig the market to keep the stock price from collapsing: which is exactly what they did. In the late 1760s, the company's board fell under the control of three especially aggressive traders, John Purling, Laurence Sulivan, and Sir George Colebrooke, each one taking his turn as chairman or deputy chair. Far from being members of a privileged, hereditary elite, they owed their success to intelligence and hard work, but each one also possessed an appetite for risk exceptional even by the standards of the age. Between them they led the company to the brink of failure.

Sulivan, the oldest of the three, had emerged from obscurity in Ireland, making his way to Bombay as a trader before joining the company's staff in 1741. Returning to England with a fortune, he became a director, thanks to his unrivaled knowledge of the company's activities in India. His friend Purling, born about 1720, began his career as an ordinary seaman, but as the fleet expanded he rose to the rank of captain, sailing twice to China. Like Sulivan, he used the money he made to buy a seat in the House of Commons. Born in 1729, Colebrooke came from a banking family but his grandfather had been a tailor. An avid speculator in commodities of all kinds, he acquired his riches first by winning military contracts during the war with France and then by insider dealing in government bonds at the time of the peace talks in Paris.

None of the three could allow the company's headlong expansion to cease. During the excitement that followed the grant of the *diwan,* both Sulivan and Colebrooke borrowed heavily to buy the company's stock, with Purling among their creditors; and this, and Purling's close ties to the shipping lobby, left him equally eager for growth at any cost. Like the supercargoes in Canton, the triumvirate had to keep the business on the boil or risk the loss of more than they had won.[16]

And then, in the spring of 1769, the letters home from India began to carry bad news. Despite its successes in Bengal, the company remained

exposed to enemies in the south. Another war broke out, with the kingdom of Mysore, a war that seemed to threaten the loss of Madras. Worse
still, it was rumored that the French were poised to intervene, with an
army waiting on the island of Mauritius. When word of all this arrived
in London, the price of the company's stock began to drop. Even when it
emerged that the reports were false, the price did not recover, and so Colebrooke and his friends looked for a way to support it. Every six months,
the company met to declare a dividend. So they kept on increasing it,
until the company was paying its investors nearly £400,000 each year. To
meet the cost of doing so, the directors sent ever more ships to Canton,
expecting their sales of tea in London to supply the cash they required.

With the China trade doing so well and the yield from the land tax in
Bengal increasing year by year, the company's earnings rose in 1771 to a
peak of more than £1 million. But enormous though they seemed to be
on paper, the bulk of these profits arose in India, and the hard currency
that flowed home to London came to a far smaller sum. And while the tea
trade appeared to be thriving, it absorbed huge quantities of silver from
Cádiz: this was a problem too. Inevitably, the price of bullion had risen
in Spain, threatening to erode the profit margins on which the company
relied. In response, Sulivan and his friends thought of yet another cunning
but disastrous plan.

With what appeared to be brilliant ingenuity, the directors had found
a new way to make India yield up its treasure. In the late 1760s, as a way
to obtain bullion in Bengal they began to allow their managers in Calcutta
to write out IOUs to local English merchants, most of whom worked for
the company itself and had accumulated their own private hoards of silver.
From Calcutta the bullion sailed to China, while the IOUs came home to
London to be redeemed when the tea was sold. For the people of Bengal,
this stratagem could only lead to hardship, draining wealth from the province that might have gone to finance tools, livestock, and irrigation. But
for the British, the plan seemed to be ideal. The scheme gave the company
the working capital it needed and allowed its traders to send money back
to England in what seemed to be a cheap and efficient way. But what if
the officials in Bengal were tempted to go too far by issuing IOUs on a
scale the East India Company had never foreseen? This is precisely what
occurred.

On the plains of India, everything depends on the monsoon; but in
the summer of 1769 the rains came too late to the valley of the Ganges.
In places they never fell at all. Even before the drought, the economy had
begun to wither under the blight of the land tax. Eager to strip every rupee

they could from Bengal, the British had also driven up the price of food by stockpiling scarce supplies of grain to be sold at a profit. By the end of October, a famine had begun. It continued far into the following year. The victims filled the streets of Calcutta, where, it is said, nearly eighty thousand people died.

By the time the famine had run its course, the East India Company believed that ten million people had lost their lives. Modern estimates point to a far lower figure, but one that still runs into millions. And the suffering was worst in precisely those locations, in Bihar and around Murshidabad, where so much of the land revenue arose. So the receipts from the tax began to dwindle, while the company continued to spend heavily. Once again, there was talk of war, not only in the south, but also against a new enemy, the Marathas in the west. Running scared of simultaneous attacks on Bombay and Madras, the company's men in India scrambled for cash to hire more sepoys and pay for fortifications.

In the summer of 1770, as they saw the riches of Bengal vanishing before their eyes, they sent grim letters home, warning the directors about their dire predicament. It would be at least a year before they could expect a reply. In the meantime, they took the only option available, and drew even more heavily on the company's credit. At the end of that year, the managers in Calcutta issued a mountain of new IOUs, which came to be known as the Bengal bills. Hoping for the best, they borrowed more than £1 million and charged it all to their superiors in London.[17]

It took another six months for the shareholders in England to learn that something was badly awry. At first, the reports were vague, but in the middle of 1771 they reached the ears of a Scottish investor called William Crichton. As we shall see, Crichton would later play an essential part in the events that led to the Boston Tea Party, but at this stage it seems that he was simply nervous about the value of his portfolio. Among the company's shareholders, there was a small but vocal group of dissidents, of whom he was one, who had begun to ask awkward questions. In June, after hearing rumors about the Bengal bills, Crichton raised the issue with the board, only to be brushed aside. And then at last, after the holidays, the story leaked into the press, presumably from him. The price of the company's stock began to fall. For the directors, so deeply in debt, it was too late to turn back. On September 25, the shareholders were due to meet to hear the board recommend a dividend. The latest tea auction had been a disaster, as we saw, and that, coupled with the huge liabilities that were building up in India, should have made them opt for caution. But with so much at stake, instead the directors chose to tough it out.

Their chief accountant drew up a misleading statement of the company's affairs, choosing a balance sheet date that allowed him not to include the full cost of the Bengal bills. Armed with these dubious figures, Purling and Colebrooke persuaded the meeting to approve the payment of the dividend at its old high level. And then, a week later, over dinner at his home in Piccadilly, Sir George organized a covert operation to support the company's stock. Hiding their identities by dealing through a Dutch bank, he and his friends began to buy it secretly on the Amsterdam exchange.

For a while Crichton and his fellow dissidents withdrew, and the fuss about the balance sheet died down. The shares continued to trade above £200. But by the end of 1771 it was only a matter of time before the reckoning arrived. For as long as the company made a handsome profit from the tea it sold, it could fund its debts, redeem the Bengal bills, and continue to pay a generous cash return to investors. But when the price of tea collapsed, as it was bound to do, the game would be up, and the company would sink beneath the weight of its indebtedness. Meanwhile, in America, the brief period of calm that Lord North seemed to have created was already drawing to a close. An attack upon the king's authority was about to occur, and one which arose from the same oceanic trade in tea.

Six thousand miles from Bengal, the British Empire encompassed another dominion where men and women dealt greedily in commodities: Rhode Island, the little province in New England founded in the seventeenth century by the most original of all the Puritans, the remarkable Roger Williams. Here an incident occurred in 1772 that foreshadowed the great schism between King George III and his subjects in America. Its origins lay in the international trading system which the British had brought into being.

From China to the Caribbean the British operated a private economic empire far too reliant on tea, tobacco, indigo, wheat, and rice, a system built on debt and therefore a system inherently prone to volatility and occasional episodes of panic. Politically their position was equally insecure. On the western side of the Atlantic, they had wayward colonies they could not control, each one with local habits of dissent. Sooner or later these two elements of instability in the empire, political and economic, were sure to compound together in a crisis too deep for the king and his ministers to overcome. This was what happened in Boston Harbor in December 1773, but eighteen months earlier the Tea Party had been preceded by something quite as striking in Rhode Island.

Used to sailing to Africa and the West Indies, where they bought and sold slaves, the people who lived by Narragansett Bay earned their living mostly from the seaborne traffic in rum, sugar, molasses, tea, and a host of other items, much of which was legal but a great deal of which was contraband. If the British dared to interfere decisively to stamp out smuggling in Rhode Island, the outcome was likely to be violent, and all the more so because the culture of Providence and Newport left no room for compromise. Of all the American colonies, Rhode Island was the freest, the most radical, and the one least inclined to follow royal instructions.

And so it was here that the countdown to war began. Early in 1772, with the East India Company heading toward its nemesis, a flood of illegal tea came surging across the ocean from Holland and Scandinavia, where the glut from China had filled the storerooms until they overflowed. Much of the tea looked for American landfall on the coast between Cape Cod and Long Island Sound. When the Royal Navy heard of what was going on, it tried to put a stop to this pernicious activity. In response, the region's mariners fired the first shots of the revolutionary crisis.

Chapter Two

"This Dark Affair":
The *Gaspée* Incident

Rhode Island, Mr. H., is a strange form of government.

King George III, speaking to Governor
Thomas Hutchinson of Massachusetts[1]

I t was a dreadful winter: the coldest, it was said, for two generations. In
New England the temperature fell to forty below, and storms caused
a host of shipwrecks up and down the coasts. In Virginia a blizzard left
three feet of snow in George Washington's backyard, while in Boston on
Christmas Day a citizen could clamber across the harbor on the ice. But
even while the freeze continued, the season for contraband began.

The British ran a network of spies in Europe whose latest bulletins
carried word of unusually large sales of tea in Denmark and Sweden.
Transmitted by the Admiralty in London, the reports arrived in America
in the fourth week of January to be read by the British naval commander
in Boston. No sooner had he passed the word to his officers on patrol
than evidence appeared confirming what the spies had said. In the middle
of February the admiral learned of a Dutch ship moored off the coast of
Maine, full of tea bound for Boston. Ten days later he received news of
another smuggling vessel, this time from South America, carrying rum and
sugar. Soon afterward informers told him that yet another Dutchman was
approaching with still more smuggled tea, and hourly expected somewhere
close to Salem.[2]

It was organized crime on an enormous scale, calling for stern measures
from the navy. Rear Admiral John Montagu rose to the occasion with
alacrity. Many Bostonians loathed Montagu—John Adams spoke of his

"brutal, hoggish manners"—partly because they thought he owed his post to nepotism; but that, you may be sure, was a wicked Yankee libel against a sailor whose career had been exemplary, despite his cursing, his swearing, and his taste for claret.

Born into the landed gentry, he counted among his many cousins the Earl of Sandwich, the First Lord of the Admiralty. In his thirties the young captain Montagu had sat for a while in Parliament as a silent member for a constituency his relative controlled. But Lord Sandwich worked immensely hard, he did not care for fools, and he would not give a rank so senior to a stooge, even one from his own family. Since Montagu joined the service in his teens, he had fought in two wars against the French, commanded eight battleships, and shot by firing squad a fellow officer. In Admiral Montagu we behold a man who understood the meaning of duty. Before he left England, he received strict orders to keep his squadron at sea as much as possible in order to enforce the laws of trade. The admiral kept a daily journal, which displays the diligence with which he tried to do so.[3]

To cover the coast from Labrador to Florida, the navy gave him two dozen ships, most of them small and built to hug the shore. Under constant insult from the ocean their hulls and rigging needed frequent repairs, but his budget allowed for only one dockyard, up north at Halifax, Nova Scotia. As if he were playing a vast game of chess, Montagu shuttled his captains back and forth, in and out of refit, constantly urging the shipwrights to work more swiftly.

One of the ships he moved most often was a schooner called the *Gaspée*. Her role was to cruise to and fro across the bays where smugglers might lurk. By the autumn of 1771 she was bruised and battered after a long spell at the mouth of the Delaware. So the *Gaspée* took a rest at Halifax before spending November in the Gulf of Maine. In the depths of winter she hunted around Cape Cod, returning to Boston just in time for the reports from Europe about an upsurge in the volume of smuggled tea. On January 25, 1772, Admiral Montagu ordered the *Gaspée* out to sea again to watch the most suspect section of the shore. In the eyes of the navy the worst of the smugglers came from Martha's Vineyard or Rhode Island, where the nooks and crannies of the coast supplied the best kind of cover. So off went the *Gaspée* under the command of a keen young Scotsman called William Dudingston.

Later, when he achieved his fifteen minutes of fame, opinions would differ about Lieutenant Dudingston. While an American called him "a very dirty low fellow," the first official British history of the Revolutionary War took a very different view, praising him as an officer "vigilant and active, in the execution of his duty." The Scotsman had every reason to enforce the law severely. While in peacetime most naval officers kicked their heels at home on half pay, he belonged to the happy few with a command on active service. Aged thirty-one, the son of a laird on the coast of Fife, he came from a family crippled by debt, and Dudingston himself had borrowed heavily. An officer of his rank earned only four shillings a day, but in colonial waters he could double or treble his salary if he found guilty ships to seize.[4]

He had a host of targets from which to choose. Along the American coast hundreds of vessels made thousands of voyages each year, often breaking the law, knowingly or not, because the British had put in place an impossibly complicated tariff of customs duties and an equally complex set of regulations to ensure that they were paid. Some of the rules had existed for many decades, like the Navigation Acts, which obliged the trade of the colonies to pass through British ports. Others were new, mostly dating from Grenville's abortive plan to pull the colonies into line. Of all the recent measures, the threepenny Townshend tax on tea caused the most resentment, but many others were almost as irritating. Even the smallest coasters were obliged to carry official papers showing the origin and destination of their cargoes and proving that all the duties had been paid. So complex were the rules and so liable to lead to friction that even some officials in London had begun to despair about the system, arguing that while it produced little money, it damaged the empire by angering honest traders who might be tempted to rebel as a result.

Just how little did the taxes yield? Only one produced a significant sum, the penny duty on a gallon of molasses. Even in the best year in the 1770s the tax revenue from America came to a total of only £47,000, a small fraction of the empire's running costs. General Gage had bills to pay, so did the Royal Navy, and the customs service needed their salaries too. So did the governors, the judges, and the rest of the small cohort of officialdom. Add everything up, and the total came to roughly £400,000 each year. Even if we include the revenues the British government received from the tobacco trade, another £200,000 in duties paid by consumers at home, the outcome is the same: the colonies never came close to meeting the cost of their defense and their administration.[5]

That being so, why bother to tax them at all? Why not scrap all the duties and all the red tape? Do that and trade would thrive along the coast and up the rivers that led inland. Freed from its task of patrolling the coast, the navy could come home or cruise the Caribbean instead, while the colonials spent the extra money in their pockets on English hardware and woollen cloth. But the British had yet to fall in love with free trade, something that would have to wait until after the war with America was lost, when Adam Smith acquired his admirers in high places. Besides, every politician knew that sooner or later the British would have to fight the French again. Only the previous year the Falklands crisis had very nearly led to war, and it was taken for granted that one day the king of France would try to reconquer the possessions he had lost. If so, the British would need every penny they could find.

And so the taxes and the regulations remained in place, with all their tiresome bureaucracy. So much the better for a young lieutenant with debts to pay in Fife. If William Dudingston caught an American vessel without the right papers, he would not only receive a share of the proceeds when the boat and her cargo were sold. He would also know that he had served the empire well. During the last war with France, when the Americans openly traded with the enemy, the British armed forces had come to regard almost every local merchant as a smuggler and a cheat.

In Great Britain this became an article of faith among the nation's leaders. When they asked themselves why America rose in revolt, they often traced the cause to contraband and nothing else. When in 1794 the British published their official history of the Revolutionary War, written by an American Loyalist, Charles Stedman, the book made the point emphatically, accusing the people of New England of a multitude of what the author called "illicit practices," with six long pages devoted to the details. In search of hard currency to pay for all the things they needed, including guns and bullets, they sailed off to the Caribbean to flout the law by selling their wares to the Dutch, the Spanish, and the French. In return, they brought home cargoes of tea, molasses, and rum, as well as silver from Mexico, or paper IOUs they could turn into ready money in Lisbon. When the British tried to eradicate the smuggling trade, the Americans rose up in arms, and that, said Mr. Stedman, was how the revolution began.[6]

Or so many people in London believed: a very simple analysis, which contained a grain of truth but little more. Nobody doubted that smuggling was rife. No one in America seriously denied it. For simple economic reasons, the contraband trade had come to be woven into the fabric of everyday life, just as it was in Europe and the British Isles, with the only difference being that in the English Channel cognac took the place of rum. But while smuggling certainly played its part in the revolutionary story, the British displayed an obsession with the topic that obscured other motives for rebellion.

It was an obsession that might wreak havoc if a greedy officer took it too far. By 1772, Dudingston had a reputation for doing exactly that. From Virginia northward the press ran stories about his foul mouth and his freedom with his fists, and in Rhode Island he provoked the confrontation that gave him his place in history. The *Gaspée* incident, as it was known, would reveal in miniature all the forces driving Great Britain and its colonies apart. Too often dismissed as merely a riot by a mob, the affair needs to be taken very seriously indeed, because in London—and especially at the Admiralty—the incident caused deep and abiding anger, while in America the lieutenant's behavior left an equally dire legacy of distrust. The incident would take place in June, after more than four months of tension between the Scotsman and the people of the coast.[7]

The feud began when the weather cleared in the first week of February, allowing the *Gaspée* and another naval vessel, the *Canceaux*, to keep a close watch on the creeks and inlets of Buzzards Bay. Because drifting floes of ice made the entrance to the bay especially perilous, the navy sent in a small boat, under the command of an officer called Christie. Not far from Newport he sighted a sloop, lying low in the water and heavily laden: the *Swanzey*, bound for Boston, or so her master claimed. Armed with an act of Parliament and an order from the Privy Council in Whitehall, the navy had the law behind it if it stopped a craft that looked so obviously suspect. When Christie boarded the *Swanzey*, he found rum and sugar sourced from the Dutch West Indies but without the necessary papers. So he put the sloop under armed guard for the trip back to base; but night was closing in, and Christie dared not venture over the shoals around Cape Cod. Running for cover to Martha's Vineyard, he found a place of safety beneath a whaling village called Holmes Hole.*

With the wind picking up and snow falling hard, Christie waited with his prize until, in the early hours of February 7, four boatloads of armed Americans came swarming over the side. When the newspapers picked up the story, they said the men were dressed as Indians. Seizing the crew, they stripped them of their weapons, cut the *Swanzey*'s cable, and made off toward the open sea, pausing only to dump Christie and his men in a dinghy to paddle their way back to shore in the bitter cold.[8]

The following morning Dudingston appeared nearby with the *Gaspée*. Picking up Christie, he mustered a boarding party and sent them off in search of the *Swanzey*. They set off up a creek that led inland toward the road to Edgartown, the sloop's most likely hiding place. Finding no trace

---

* Now called Vineyard Haven.

of the sloop, they rowed back, only to hear a volley of shots from the village. A crowd of three hundred had gathered onshore, and they launched their boats to intercept the British sailors. The navy opened fire with small arms, the whaling men retreated, and both sides backed away from a battle neither could win. Even so, the incident did lasting damage. As word traveled along the coast, to be followed by more confrontations between the *Gaspée* and American seafarers, the lieutenant became a marked man, incurring the hatred of all those whom he met.

For Admiral Montagu the affair was utterly outrageous. If smuggling was a felony, here was something close to treason: outright contempt for the British flag and two violent assaults on his sailors. Although he was new to America, the admiral knew that incidents like this had taken place before. Three years earlier, at Newport, a crowd had taken a customs sloop and destroyed her by fire. Sometimes naval officers came under attack when they tried to press Americans into the king's service. But while these earlier incidents could mostly be dismissed as isolated affairs, spontaneous and unplanned, in 1772 the violence seemed to take a more sinister shape, resembling an organized conspiracy. Montagu soon came to believe that the harshest measures were needed to drag New England back within the rule of law.

In the meantime, the *Gaspée* carried on with her mission, seizing another American sloop, bound in from Haiti and loaded with sugar. Taking her into Newport for prosecution as a smuggler, Dudingston went to introduce himself to the governor of Rhode Island. There followed a brief and awkward exchange of courtesies that, in due course, would become yet another source of angry disagreement. The governor inquired about the *Swanzey* affair, and then the Scotsman hurried back to his ship.

In the middle of February, when at last the ice started to melt in Narragansett Bay, the *Gaspée* began to probe inland along the chain of coves that led to the Providence River. For what happened next, we have conflicting sources, British and American, a common problem with the revolution, disagreeing about the precise date and location and about the rights and wrongs of what took place. Fortunately, they agree about the gist of what occurred and the identity of the Americans whom Dudingston offended.

On February 17—or the nineteenth, depending on which source we read—the *Gaspée* spotted a sloop called the *Fortune* close inshore, with small boats moored on the tidal flats and again a crowd assembled on the beach. Off went another boarding party to seize the sloop, with the rum and sugar she carried. Later the Americans claimed that the *Fortune* was merely a coaster making a routine voyage when the navy stopped her without a reason. According to the lieutenant, the sloop fired on his men, and the rum was smuggled from the Dutch Antilles. Unwilling to trust a local judge, he sent the *Fortune* round to Boston, a step of doubtful legality that only made matters worse. Unwittingly, the *Gaspée* had antagonized a family of Rhode Islanders who embodied all the values for which the colony stood.[9]

The rum belonged to the Greenes, Quakers with a farm or two, a sawmill, and a forge for making anchors. The navy had not the slightest idea who they were or why it might be unwise to upset them. But one of the men who owned the cargo was Nathanael Greene, who would soon shed his Quaker beliefs to become the youngest general in George Washington's army and his closest aide from Bunker Hill to Yorktown. As Greene wrote soon after the arrest of the *Fortune*, the loss of her cargo created "such a Spirit of Resentment that I have devoted almost the whole of my time in devising measures for punishing the offender." In saying that, Greene spoke for many other people in a province deeply attached to its distinctive way of life.[10]

When it seized the *Fortune*, the *Gaspée* collided not only with the Greenes but with an entire society, with an alien culture the navy viewed with disdain. Although factors such as these are notoriously hard to quantify, already the values and the attitudes of Britons and Americans had drifted far apart. While they spoke what seemed to be a common language, the words it contained—like "God," "liberty," "patriotism," and "law"—had acquired different meanings on each side of the ocean, so that as they slid toward war often each nation simply misunderstood what the other was saying. Here was another reason why the rift between them became impossible to mend.

Like their colleagues in the army, Dudingston and Montagu came from the British landed gentry, rural oligarchs of a traditional society built from bricks of deference. In Rhode Island they came up against a very different environment for which they felt no sympathy. By 1772 the province had already become one of the most advanced societies of its time, and one over which Whitehall exercised almost no control. Here by the sea a visitor could taste the flavor of avant-garde America, chiefly in the thriving town of Providence.

A LIVELY EXPERIMENT

Although we think of Rhode Island as a little place, its small dimensions were a source of strength. Only sixty thousand people lived there, barely a fifth as many as in Massachusetts, but they were tightly clustered around the rim of the bay, not scattered across a hundred miles of farms and forest. One in four of its people lived in sizable towns, making this the most urban province in America. And so information traveled fast in the columns of two newspapers or on the weekly stage from Boston. Of all the colonies, Rhode Island was also the one where the ocean entered most deeply into the lives of the people, and this made the province all the more open and more extrovert.[11]

Thanks to hard work, a little luck, and its geography, it had already built a free republic, albeit one that fell far short of perfection. Elections were rigged; the courts were political; and a gulf of inequality divided the rich from the poor, with the top 10 percent of the population owning two-thirds of the wealth. And yet by the shores of Narragansett Bay a visitor would find democracy in action, and very successfully so.

A singular place, Rhode Island liked to flaunt its achievements. Go to Providence today, and in the eighteenth-century buildings that remain you will see the evidence of enterprise and flair. Some might even call it arrogance. Just before the revolution the town reinvented itself with a new town hall, a brick schoolhouse, a covered market, and of course the College of Rhode Island, later to become Brown University, all of them still to be seen along a grid pattern of streets first marked out in the year of the *Gaspée*.

One edifice towers above all the rest: the First Baptist Church, begun just after the Boston Tea Party and finished a few weeks after Lexington. A handsome building, painted white, with an illustrious wooden steeple, it climbs up the hillside above the inner harbor, with a bold design that symbolized the ambition of the town. When the church held its first Sunday service, the worshippers filled only the first five rows of pews in a huge interior that could accommodate several thousand, a sign of their confidence about the town's future. In the previous twenty years, while the town of Boston stagnated, hardly growing at all in the decades before the revolution, the population of Rhode Island had risen by 50 percent, with Providence advancing especially rapidly.

To trace the origins of its prosperity, a new arrival in Providence had only to follow his nose along the waterfront, to enjoy the fragrance left by cocoa, molasses, charcoal, apples, and rum. Nearby at a place called Tockwotton, he would encounter the most distinctive smell of all, oily and full of the sea. Sprawling across eleven acres, a factory made candles from the wax inside the heads of whales. It sold the best candles in America, wrapped in blue paper, for shipment up and down the coast and off to England.[12]

An industrial town of artisans as well as mariners, turning out iron, cider, and chocolate as well as candles and liquor, Providence bore at least a passing resemblance to seaports in the mother country, and especially in the eastern neighborhoods of London, such as Stepney and Wapping. There you might have found the same combination of ships, wharves, and factories, and the same dissenting attitudes in matters of belief as well as politics. In London behind the docks you would see chapels for many different kinds of Christians, even the least orthodox. In just the same way, in Providence and Newport the people played many variations on the theme of God. In Rhode Island, at least five Christian denominations vied with each other for believers, led by the Quakers and the Baptists, followed closely by the Congregationalists and the Episcopalians. Close behind came the Presbyterians, not to mention the Jews at Newport, and free thinkers like Nathanael Greene who were swiftly abandoning any formal creed.

And yet, despite some vague affinities with parts of London, there was nothing in the old country that really compared with Rhode Island. King George could hardly fail to raise his eyebrows when he thought about the way the colony chose its leaders. Even by American standards it was an extreme case of popular government; and ironically enough, this was partly the legacy of an earlier monarch. In the 1630s, Rhode Island came into being as a haven of religious freedom, thanks to Roger Williams. In due course, after the English Civil War the Puritans lost the mother country, and King Charles II regained his throne. At that moment, we might have expected the sovereign to draw the colony firmly back within the pale. In fact he did the reverse. In 1663, the king gave Rhode Island a charter that protected the system Williams had created: "a lively experiment," as the charter put it, "with a full liberty of religious concernments." At the same time, the king upheld its other liberties as well, with the charter making every public office an elected post, including the governorship.[13]

Only adult males with property could vote, but the electorate still came to about a quarter of the population. In May, they picked sixty-four deputies to form their assembly for the following year. In turn the assembly chose the governor and his deputy and the judges, who sat in the five

Left: Narragansett Bay and the coast of Rhode Island, with Providence at top left and Newport at the bottom, from the first scientific British naval chart of the region, published in 1777. Gaspée Point, where the schooner ran aground, is on the western side of the Providence River immediately above the topmost fold on the left. © *National Maritime Museum, Greenwich, London*

county courts. Then they picked the local justices, the sheriffs, and the captains of militia, all elected too. Each town had its own council, while committees met to build bridges or schoolhouses or manage the lotteries that paid for them. The same principle of democracy extended to matters of faith, but perhaps the most radical feature of the colony was the way it ran its courts of law.

To the British then and now, the very idea of an elected judge seems absurd, a recipe for bias and misconduct. But although in Rhode Island the judges were often amateurs, and their decisions sometimes blatantly one-sided, the system had its merits, providing not only a degree of openness that England could not match but also an element of originality. On the bench a justice chosen by the people might develop ideas a professional jurist dare not express.

A case in point was the political boss of Providence, a man of sixty-five named Stephen Hopkins. At the time of the *Gaspée* he served as chief justice, as he always did, with a veto over anything the governor might decide. A farmer but also an industrialist, he owned ships and dealt in iron, he read the poetry of Pope, and he drank a lot of liquor: but as far as we can tell, Hopkins never endured a day's formal tuition in the law. Near the town's new college, he lived in a clapboard house from which he pulled strings and mentored the young, keeping in close touch with the patriots in Boston and writing for the *Providence Gazette*. Amateur though he was, Hopkins fashioned a powerful doctrine that helped to inspire the campaign against the *Gaspée*. As early as 1757, he told his friends that "the King & Parliament had no more Right to make Laws for us than the Mohawks." Again, it was the sort of thing a man might say in a pub, but it was entirely consistent with Rhode Island's charter.

As a way to maintain some influence over the colony, the king had included in the charter a phrase saying that Rhode Island could pass no laws "contrary and repugnant" to those of England. But although these words might seem clear enough, the following clause introduced a caveat that opened the way for radicals to interpret the document as something close to a manifesto for independence. The statutes of Rhode Island must be "agreeable" to English laws, the charter said, but only after taking into account what it called "the nature and constitution of the place and people." From words like these, so rich in ambiguity, a lawyer might forge a revolutionary creed. He might take them to mean that only the people of Rhode Island, and nobody else, could decide what laws they lived by.[14]

It seems that Stephen Hopkins read the clause in precisely that way, and then, during the 1760s, he went further still to become a theorist of liberty for all the colonies, and not merely his own. Given his background, naturally he began by opposing the new Grenville taxes on sugar and molasses. To start with, Hopkins's arguments did not seem new or unusual: like many other Americans he merely cited an ancient principle of English law, dating back to King Edward I in the thirteenth century. By virtue of a statute enacted in 1297, taxes required the consent of those who had to pay them; and consent took the form of a vote by their representatives in Parliament. It would never have occurred to George III to question such a hallowed tradition, and he never did. Americans, including Hopkins, simply pointed out that since they sent no elected delegates to Westminster, they could not have given their consent to Grenville's taxes, including those levied under the Stamp Act: hence their refusal to pay them.

So far, so familiar; but by itself, the colonial critique of imperial taxation need not have led to outright rebellion. It was perfectly feasible—in fact, it was commonplace—for a colonist to object to taxation by the British while remaining loyal to the Crown in every other way. To legitimize a revolution, Americans required a far more radical ideology, which Hopkins began to develop as early as 1764. According to him, *every* action taken by the British government in America, fiscal or not, required the consent of the people, given locally in Rhode Island or its sister colonies. And if you wished to know if any particular law was valid, you had to ask the local judges. If their opinion differed from that of the king and Lord North, so much the worse for the British, since the local colonial view should always prevail.

For the time being, Hopkins did not wish to secede from the empire. Rather like Benjamin Franklin, he came to see it as something akin to a gentlemen's club. The empire was old-fashioned, it was pompous, and many of the rules were silly, but membership offered some benefits that Americans preferred not to lose. Although the laws of trade could be irksome, at least they gave the colonies free access to the British market for the goods they sold. It was also worth belonging to the club for the sake of the Royal Navy: provided the admirals desisted from harassing honest traders and kept to their proper vocation of sinking the French.

But none of this amounted to a ringing endorsement of loyalty to Great Britain. If Stephen Hopkins believed that Whitehall had no constitutional right to overrule a judge in Newport, and if he owed allegiance to the king only so long as he was given something in return, he had already strayed halfway down the road to independence. And by 1769 at the latest, we can find the *i* word being freely discussed in the circles in which Hopkins moved. When the new college at Providence held its first graduation day, it marked the occasion with a debate between two bright students. The question they discussed was this: "Whether British America can, under her present circumstances and consistent with good policy, affect to become an independent State." We do not know which speaker received the most applause; what matters is the fact that they held the debate at all. Long before the *Gaspée* incident, Hopkins and his friends had already begun to equip an arsenal of ideas with which to justify the stiffest of resistance to the navy.[15]

By the early 1770s, animosity between the colony and the Crown had come to be almost routine. The British complained about Hopkins for ignoring directives from London and for refusing to compensate victims of the riots against the Stamp Act. For their part, the Rhode Islanders demanded compensation of their own, to pay for their efforts to defeat the French ten years earlier. Worse still, a waterfront gang in Newport had nearly beaten to death an English customs officer, Charles Dudley. Causing outrage in London, the affair led to a swift rebuke and a warning of reprisals if it happened again. The British did not specify what form they might take, but one measure would have been by far the most effective. Sooner or later, Parliament might decide that the colony's seventeenth-century charter was an eccentric throwback and take steps to revoke it. It might also do the same in Massachusetts. Before the Boston Tea Party, the British made no firm plans to do so in either colony, but both sides saw it was a possibility. This helped to darken the atmosphere in London and New England alike.

Ironically enough, the terminal crisis in the relationship between Rhode Island and the British arose not from a slump in the local economy but from its very opposite. In Rhode Island and the other colonies the first half of 1772 marked the peak of a business cycle. The volume of shipping rose sharply to reach the highest level of the century so far, as Americans shared in the maritime boom that extended all the way to China, a boom that explains that year's acceleration in the smuggling trade. With more money in their pockets, men and women bought more tea, brandy, and rum. At home in England, the files of His Majesty's Treasury showed a sudden, alarming increase in all kinds of illegal traffic there as well, and across the ocean the shipping boom had a powerful effect on the little port at Providence.[16]

It enriched the harbor's most dynamic family, the famous commercial brotherhood called Brown. Allies of Hopkins, they shared his political views, and they led the rebuilding of the town. Joseph Brown designed the new Baptist church; his brother John supervised the work; and their sibling Nicholas paid for the bell. Like so many others in Rhode Island the Browns owed their wealth to the old, primary trade with the Caribbean, exchanging meat, fish, and tobacco for sugar and molasses. But since the end of the war with France in 1763, the Browns had begun to spread their wings, leading the way in the ventures that made the colony more diverse, including the ironworks and the candle factory. When the *Gaspée* first hove into view, they were expanding again, making new connections in the mother country with London and the textile mills of Lancashire.

Of all the family, the most reckless was John Brown, aged thirty-six, small but abrasive, a trader in slaves, and another man ready to gamble in pursuit of profit. If the Royal Navy posed a threat to his thriving business, he would have to stop it, by force if necessary. As the ice melted and word spread about the *Fortune,* John Brown prepared to meet the Scottish lieutenant head-on.[17]

Fire and Sword

With the *Fortune* taken into custody, the *Gaspée* continued to prowl inshore in pursuit of more cargoes to seize. On February 20, Dudingston found another prize in the form of a boatload of molasses. Four days later the *Newport Mercury* appeared, sounding the alarm about what it called a "piratical schooner," heavily armed, attacking poor but honest traders. "Americans take CARE of your PROPERTY!!" the newspaper shouted. While some people said the ship belonged to the Crown, with heavy irony the newspaper doubted that this could be so. The navy existed, said the *Mercury,* to defend the empire and surely not to plunder the honest seafarers of the coast.

It was a fine piece of journalism: forthright, timely, and even accurate, more or less. As the revolution drew near, the press played an essential role, as a reporter but also as a catalyst, driving forward the process of disobedience. Swiftly, the column in the *Mercury* found a wider audience in Boston and Philadelphia. Like any good story, it upset the powerful, in this case Admiral Montagu, who sent the article home to London as more evidence of anarchy in New England. Dudingston simply ignored it, heading out to sea to intercept another boat from the West Indies. Then, with the weather growing colder again, he returned to Narragansett Bay. After such a hard winter everything was in short supply, and yet, it was reported, his men stole hogs from local farmers, stripped the shore of firewood, and fired at passing fishermen. Most of these incidents occurred, it seems, around Prudence Island, where the *Gaspée* could cut the route upriver from Newport to Providence. By the middle of March, with more snow on the way, Dudingston had created something close to a blockade that might cripple the colony's economy.[18]

If, as English law allowed, the *Gaspée* searched every craft she met, she might wreck the trade in rum. Despite the Browns' efforts to diversify, this remained the core of their activities, a reliable source of cash from an everyday item. Before the age of bourbon, Americans drank rum in heroic quantities for the charge of warmth and energy it gave. To make it, they needed huge volumes of molasses, the sticky brown fluid from which it was distilled. At least a third of the molasses passed through the hands of smugglers, which meant that if Dudingston patrolled the bay tightly, he would find an endless stream of unlawful goods to confiscate.

Of course the importers could avoid arrest simply by paying the customs duty. But while the sums involved were modest from a British point of view, they amounted to a heavy burden for the local traders. If every gallon of molasses bore the tax, the annual bill for Rhode Island alone would come to £1,000 in sterling, payable in silver, which the colonists did not have. As John Adams once said, molasses was "an essential ingredient in American independence." We can see why the Browns felt obliged to protest even if this meant attacking the Royal Navy.[19]

From the outset a threat of violence loomed over the affair, as it would later in Boston in the weeks before the destruction of the tea. Soon after he arrived, Dudingston heard rumors that the colonists planned to arm a ship of their own against him; and later the British would come to believe that John Brown always intended to resort to force. Initially, however, his tactics were entirely peaceful. In the middle of March nine merchants from Providence signed a petition against the *Gaspée*, with Brown's name at the top. They showed the paper to Hopkins, who wrote his legal opinion on the back. According to him, before a British officer entered the colony's waters, he had to show the governor his orders and his commission from the king. The *Gaspée* had failed to do so, which meant, said Hopkins, that she was little better than a pirate ship herself.

With Hopkins on their side, the petitioners approached the governor, Joseph Wanton, a rich but popular man, genteel and charming. Although he owed his rank to support from Hopkins, he never claimed to be a radical, and later he refused to back the revolution. Here was a dignitary with whom the British should have been able to negotiate. Instead, the navy made an enemy of the one man who might have prevented the clash that was about to occur. In the small world of Rhode Island, Wanton could hardly ignore a petition from John Brown and his allies. Traders to the Caribbean, the Wantons counted the Browns among their friends and business partners, buying from them the tobacco they needed for their own slaving voyages to Africa. Nor could the governor disregard an opinion from his chief justice. When he received the petition, Wanton wrote a firm letter to the lieutenant asking for sight of his papers.[20]

At this point Dudingston should simply have complied with good grace, since he had the necessary documents. Instead, he reminded Wanton of their earlier meeting in February and questioned his authority to ask for anything more. An angry reply came back from Wanton, which the lieutenant sent straight to Boston. With reports arriving of more Dutch ships with illegal tea, the admiral had no time for a lecture from Rhode Island. On the contrary, Montagu had already sent a bigger warship, a sloop called the *Beaver*, to seal the entrance to Long Island Sound. Two weeks later the admiral wrote Wanton a rude letter of his own, wrecking any hope of compromise. Calling the governor insolent and ridiculous, he threatened to hang any man who tried to oppose the *Gaspée*.

By the middle of May the situation had reached a deadlock far beyond diplomacy. Cruising in and out of Narragansett Bay, the *Beaver* and the *Gaspée* stopped boat after boat, traded insults with the crews, and seized a few cargoes of coffee, wine, and rum. Meanwhile, the locals ran their own campaign of obstruction, refusing to sell the British any stores and harassing the navy with lawsuits in the local courts, led by Nathanael Greene and his brothers.

The assembly convened in an angry mood, with five men called Greene among their number. They instructed Governor Wanton to write to London about the *Gaspée*, which he did, but the admiral refused to alter course. Fearing the worst but unable to climb down, he kept his ships in place but warned his officers to be on their guard against attack. At last it came in the early hours of Wednesday, June 10. Some of the details are open to debate, but nobody can quibble about the central element of what occurred. The seafarers of Rhode Island took up arms and committed an act of treason.[21]

Tuesday, the ninth, had begun cold and dull. Close to Newport the *Beaver* and the *Gaspée* lay at anchor until noon, when Dudingston set off toward Providence, thirty miles away, to pick up some new crewmen. Although this should have been a routine errand, the wind was against him, and his route contained hazards of which the lieutenant knew nothing. Under orders to save money, the navy would not pay for coastal pilots, and so the *Gaspée* had to find her course unaided. The first twenty miles were easy enough, in deep water across the bay, but beyond that the land closed in on either side. A long spit of sand curved out from the western shore, marking the point where the bay ended and the Providence River began: a watery corridor lined with marshes, shoals, and shallow coves where without warning the current would suddenly rip around a headland.

Somewhere out in the bay, at about three o'clock that afternoon, Dudingston spotted a vessel called the *Hannah* and gave chase. Later, when he was court-martialed for losing his ship, he preferred not to mention this detail, but American sources gleefully describe what happened next. A mile inside the river, close to a promontory called Namquit Point, the skipper of the *Hannah* suddenly changed course and veered toward the shore. Dudingston did the same, hit a sandbank, and settled in two feet of water. The *Hannah* vanished around a bend, arriving in Providence in time for supper. There was nothing the *Gaspée* could do except wait for the tide to float her off the next morning. The lieutenant ordered his crew over the side to splash around the hull and scrape its bottom, and they sent out a boat to take some soundings. As night fell, they turned in, leaving only one seaman on the deck.

The moon dropped below the horizon soon after midnight, and so it was almost entirely dark when, at about 12:45, the lookout noticed what he took to be some rocks between the *Gaspée* and the shore. As the rocks came closer, the crewman realized that they were six or seven longboats, each one filled with men. When they ignored a challenge, he tried to shoot, but his musket failed to fire. Hurrying below, he roused the lieutenant.

Before he came aloft, Dudingston paused and ordered his midshipman to open the ship's chest full of guns. The chest was locked, and no one could find the key or matches to light the lamp. Armed only with his cutlass, the lieutenant reached the deck and leaped up on the starboard bow. The line of boats was fifty yards away and making straight for the *Gaspée*. The lieutenant called on them to halt.

An American voice swore loudly out of the dark. "God damn your blood, we have you now," he said, or something like it, and the lieutenant swore back. As the two men hurled insults at each other, the midshipman broke open the box and slung an armful of weapons up through the hatchway. The British had time to fire only a few pistol rounds before the first of the raiders clambered over the bows. Still in his shirtsleeves, Dudingston raised his sword to strike, and a musket shot rang out. The lieutenant fell back, with bullet wounds in his arm and in his thigh.

As he staggered toward the stern, a second wave of raiders appeared over the port side. The crew tried to hold them back in a fight with fists and handspikes, but they were outnumbered by three to one. Lying in a pool of blood, Dudingston told his men to surrender. The Americans carried him into his cabin and gave him first aid with scraps of linen. They tied up the crew, rifled through the *Gaspée*'s official papers, and, the British said, the raiders even stole her silver spoons.

That accomplished, their business was done with the navy. They bundled the *Gaspée*'s crew into small boats and tossed them out on a beach nearby. The lieutenant was too badly wounded to stand up, and so the Americans released five crew members, who carried him over the side in a blanket. As Dudingston was ferried to the shore, from the bottom of the boat he heard a series of explosions. The raiders had set his ship alight. As the flames leaped up in the darkness, they ignited the charges of gunpowder inside its cannon. By the time the sun rose, the *Gaspée* had ceased to exist.

When the midshipman swore an affidavit later that day, he called the raiders a mob. Modern historians sometimes use the same word, but it does little justice to the efficiency with which they acted or the complete success of their mission. At the time nobody came forward to confess, because they knew that they were traitors and might hang; but many years later, when America celebrated half a century of independence, at least four of the raiders were still alive.

On the Fourth of July 1826 they took part in the festivities in Rhode Island, as guests of honor riding in an open carriage. The papers printed the recollections of one of them, Ephraim Bowen, who at the time of the raid had been a medical student from Providence and dressed the lieutenant's wounds. Although his narrative differs from the British sources and from an account by another of the raiders, the points of disagreement are trivial. It is perfectly clear that far from being a mob, the raiders were led by the maritime elite of Providence. Alongside them, in spirit at least, stood the chief justice, Stephen Hopkins, whose legal opinion had justified the onslaught on the *Gaspée*.

Who was the man who swore out of the dark? A master mariner, Abraham Whipple, a frequent sailor to the West Indies on behalf of the Browns. His accomplices included at least three other sea captains and two nephews of the chief justice, while Whipple himself was married to Hopkins's niece. Two of the raiders served as trustees of the new schoolhouse, while another was the son of the town's leading doctor. We can safely assume that the rank and file mainly consisted of seamen, mustered by their skippers, or artisans employed by the Browns. According to another eyewitness, the *Hannah* alerted John Brown to the beaching of the *Gaspée*, and he sent a drummer down the waterfront to assemble the raiders at an inn. We have no reason to doubt that this is what took place.[22]

So the raiders were more than a rabble, and we cannot dismiss the attack on the *Gaspée* as just another riot. A military operation three years ahead of its time, it arose not merely from a private quarrel with a Scotsman but also from a matrix of ideas, formed in the circle that surrounded Stephen Hopkins. From the very start, when Brown wrote out his petition, he made this point emphatically. He did not object to the *Gaspée* simply because its commander was a bully, although of course that did not help. He attacked the ship because the lieutenant was acting *unlawfully* by failing to show his commission to the governor and by ignoring the local judges. For Brown and Hopkins the only law they recognized was theirs, laid down by their assembly and their local courts. They saw no role in Rhode Island for the English laws that gave the navy its authority.[23]

For their part, the British had never seen anything quite like the *Gaspée* affair. At home they were accustomed to riots, they remembered the Jacobite rebellion of 1745, and in Ireland small insurrections were frequent. But with the great exception of the '45 these affairs were hopeless and chaotic, entirely unlike the incident at Namquit Point.

It was the combination that was new. Brown had assembled a new and potent mixture of elements: clear and simple ideas; an economic grievance; and a great deal of raw anger against the wider system of which the navy was a part. Added to that was something else: the sheer audacity with which the men of Providence had behaved. Seven years earlier, during the riots against the stamp tax in New York, a crowd had come close to storming the army's headquarters, but deals were done and the crowd backed off. John Brown and the *Gaspée* raiders acted in a way that made compromise impossible. Like the Boston Tea Party, their attack on the ship amounted to a gesture of absolute denial: a complete rejection of the empire's right to rule.

The nearest royal officials had no doubt that this was so. From Massachusetts the governor, Thomas Hutchinson, warned his superiors in London that the flames of insurrection would inevitably spread to Boston. Recovered from his injuries, the customs officer Charles Dudley wrote a long letter to the admiral, calling the attack "this dark affair," the work of a conspiracy, planned with cool deliberation. Montagu agreed entirely. On the evening of June 10, when the midshipman from the *Gaspée* arrived with the news of its destruction, the admiral swiftly drafted a dispatch and sent it express to England.

If the British government had functioned as governments should, an incident so extreme should have led to a firm official response or even, perhaps, to some deep reappraisal of the way they tried to run the northern colonies. Here was an act of the blackest treason, committed by men whose wealth and status should by rights have made them pillars of society. From an imperial point of view, it should have been clear that New England required thorough reform, but the timing could not have been worse. After five weeks at sea the admiral's dispatch arrived to find the politicians grappling with a crisis of another kind.*

In July the government usually fell asleep, as Parliament ended its annual session and rose for the long recess. But in 1772 its peaceful doze was interrupted by bad news from all sides. From Europe the mail brought word of revolution and upheaval of a kind that might lead to another war with France. At home the price of corn was soaring again, causing agitation and disorder. In the words of James Boswell, looking on aghast from Scotland, it was a year of "confusion, dismay and distress." Worst of all, the financial markets chose that summer to collapse in the most alarming panic since the South Sea Bubble.[24]

---

* Five weeks was a normal journey time for an Atlantic crossing from west to east, while a voyage in the opposite direction usually took about three weeks longer, because of the prevailing winds and currents. These are only averages, however, and often ships would suffer long delays on account of bad weather. Conversely, if conditions were exceptionally good a sailing ship could reach England from America in less than four weeks.

Chapter Three

A Bankrupt Age

Not a day passes but we hear of suicides.

—A Virginia tobacco merchant, writing home
from England in the summer of 1772[1]

As chance or fate would have it, the crash began on the very day that the *Gaspée* met her end. On the morning of June 10, as the schooner burned away toward her waterline, a firm of bankers in London failed to open its doors for business. The banking house was called Neale, James, Fordyce and Down, and its failure could not have been more visible or more disgraceful.

The firm might have seemed safe enough, with a fine new office in Threadneedle Street, close to the Bank of England, but for weeks a few people in the know had been muttering about its plight. While three of the partners were old-fashioned bankers—honest, dull, and easily deceived—the fourth was a trader in stocks called Alexander Fordyce. His name had already become a byword for excess. Another Scotsman, tall and debonair, he lived between a house in Mayfair and a mansion in the suburbs. At the age of forty-three, Fordyce was "the greatest speculator in London," in the words of one contemporary. That morning the city awoke to learn that he had vanished, leaving behind him debts of half a million pounds.[2]

Ever since Christmas his bank had been dying by inches, as each bet he made on the market went badly wrong. Nervously, his partners watched their assets dwindle, while Fordyce kept a secret ledger known as Waste Book Number Five in which he hid the details of his dealings. In desperation, he made one last throw of the dice, staking everything they had left on what seemed to be a certainty of profit.

By now, the city was full of rumors about the East India Company, its mountain of debt from India, and its glut of unsold tea. Sooner or later, the price of its stock would collapse, and so Fordyce did what any trader might. In the spring he sold the company's stock short, betting that the price would fall, but as the weeks went by, instead it simply drifted sideways and then it even began to rise. By early June, his straits were dire, and his brokers were after him for cash to cover his losing position. Fordyce hurried around the city, looking in vain for help, until at last, on the evening of the ninth, he knew that all was lost. One final, hopeless session with his clerk, poring over the accounts by candlelight; and then, in the early hours, he drove home to his splendid house at Roehampton in Surrey, where his splendid wife was entertaining guests.

Wild-eyed with Madeira, Fordyce ranted and raved, ate greedily, drank his best champagne, and gave the servants Burgundy with which to toast his health. Then off he scurried into hiding, looking for a chance to slip away across the English Channel. "The blow was struck, the bubble burst," one of the guests would remember. "The speculation so replete with ruin had failed, altogether failed; Alexander Fordyce was a bankrupt and a beggar."[3]

Had this been an isolated incident, a simple case of fraud by just another rascal, his name would swiftly have been forgotten. But when the Fordyce bank went down, it took with it ten more in the capital and another nine in Scotland. Twelve days after he disappeared, a run came close to wrecking every bank in London. As the months went by, the crisis spilled over into Holland and then across the ocean to America, where in Rhode Island the Browns were left with a heap of worthless IOUs from Amsterdam. Most dangerously of all, the crisis would nearly break the East India Company as well.

Quite apart from the turmoil and the hardship it caused, men and women talked about the Fordyce affair so avidly because it seemed to say so much about the times in which they lived. Soon after his disgrace, he inspired a stage play, a comedy by Samuel Foote called *The Bankrupt*. The era was "a bankrupt age," said the author, with men like Fordyce displaying all its least attractive features. Selfish, corrupt, and a social climber, he played for the highest stakes and lost a fortune, but so did many others far less famous.

"We have become a gambling nation," Lord North told the House of Commons in 1774, as he announced a new public lottery. It was one of the shrewdest comments he would ever make. This was an era when his own half brother, a bishop in the Church of England, had to take up residence in Italy with his wife when her extravagance and gambling debts left the couple close to ruin. The British had always liked to take risks, and gaming was an ancient vice, but in the years just before the crisis in the colonies they acquired a new addiction to chance and hazard. They borrowed money and laid bets on a scale not seen before. At the card table, on the racecourse, and in the world of finance, gaming became a way of life, symbolized by the great wooden lottery wheels, six feet across, kept by the Treasury in a chamber overlooking Whitehall.[4]

When Americans write about the period, sometimes they portray the mother country as a decrepit, tired, and obsolete place, with a powerful navy but a moribund economy. The truth was very different. If the colonies contained dynamic people like the Browns, so did Great Britain, and in much larger numbers. Far from being exhausted or inert, the British were exactly the reverse, an energetic but reckless nation, eager to explore every opportunity for profit.

In about 1760, suddenly the pulse of economic life in the British Isles began to accelerate. With hindsight, we can see that this was so more clearly than anyone could in the eighteenth century. New roads, new mines, and new canals, and scores of patents, filed for new inventions: we can make lists, draw lines on a graph, and show how the nation was starting to change forever, as the Industrial Revolution began. But at the time, although men and women could feel that something new was occurring, they found it strange or unsettling, they found the process hard to quantify, and they could not always tell if it was destructive or benign. They could not see a clear dividing line between wild speculation and sound investment for the long term.[5]

In some eyes, like Edward Gibbon's, Britain seemed to be a beacon of progress, leading the world toward the future. With its pots and pans from Birmingham and its ships with copper bottoms, the kingdom had a great deal to be proud of. It had its spinning jennies and canals and engineers to build fine new machines. It had James Watt, with his steam engine; Josiah Wedgwood, selling his wares as far away as Russia; and a king who loved astronomy and gadgets and every new technique to make the soil more fruitful. But from another point of view, the nation seemed at risk of imminent decline.

Addicted to gambling, luxury, and debt, the British had come to seem like a headstrong and greedy people. According to James Boswell, the crash of 1772 arose from the same assortment of human frailties. The crisis took its origins, he said, from opulence, from carelessness, and from "the desire of being precipitantly rich." It was the kind of tirade that often appeared in an age when writers such as Boswell enjoyed condemning luxury almost as much as they liked spending money themselves. But his economic views were very widely shared, especially in America; and in two different ways, the speculating habits of Great Britain would play their part in its rift with the colonies.[6]

The first was a question of attitudes and perception. In the years before the revolution, a gradual process of alienation occurred, as even Americans fond of the mother country began to lose their patience with the way it functioned. In the case of the banking crash, it took only six weeks for the news to reach Virginia, where the tobacco growers relied on loans from London and Glasgow. For nearly a year, the flow of credit dried up. Although the blight on their business was only temporary, it deepened their exasperation with the empire. American visitors to England sailed home to the colonies with tales of vanity and default. When the *Virginia Gazette* carried long reports about Alexander Fordyce, its readers drew their own conclusions. They decided that the British were a busted flush, decadent and unreliable. Here again we find a cultural divide between the Old World and the New, a divide almost as deep as the one between the Royal Navy and Rhode Island.

Second, the crash and its aftermath were simply too much for the British political system to cope with. As it became the first industrial nation, Great Britain became more volatile, behaving in a manner ever harder to predict. Every year some new problem appeared, worrying the king and his cabinet, whether it be the run on the banks or the rising price of bread. Everywhere they looked, they found the signs of change, but with economic theory in its infancy they could not fit them into a pattern or explain how one thing related to another. When they encountered a crisis, such as the banking crash, all they could do was patch together a solution, with only the dimmest grasp of what its side effects might be.

Across the Atlantic, the unintended outcome of their policies would prove to be calamitous. Behind all of this lay the basic truth: that a new Great Britain was emerging, urban and industrial, harder to understand than the old and also more unstable. As they tried to govern their own complicated country, Lord North and his friends allowed America to slip away.

Splendor and Magnificence

The British adored the art of caricature. If we wished to draw a cartoon of the nation in the 1770s, we could portray it in many different ways, because the country had so many facets. All the time, the British were spinning more cotton and making new machines, but despite the acceleration after 1760 this new economy was still too small to dominate the picture. Instead, a cartoonist who looked at the kingdom purely from a narrow, statistical point of view might have portrayed it as an ancient cart horse, trudging along with a wagonload of baggage from the past.

Estimates are hard to make, but the best suggest that although Britain had already become a nation of shopkeepers, its wealth was still increasing only very slowly. Taken as a whole, its gross domestic product was merely inching forward, growing by significantly less than 1 percent each year. Perhaps as many as two-fifths of the population still earned their living either close to the soil, farming or working in trades that relied in one way or another on agriculture, or as domestic servants. Their output changed only modestly from one decade to the next. For more than a century the yield from the land had risen steadily, thanks to the reclamation of wasteland and bog or to new farming methods copied from the Dutch, but then, for thirty years or so after 1740, the rural economy stood still or in places even shrank. And because it was still so large within the British scheme of things, if farming output did not grow the kingdom as a whole could not advance swiftly.[7]

But that was only part of the story; and if we left it at that, we would come away with a travesty of Britain at the time. Nobody likened the country to an old gray mare. On the contrary, observers often saw something very different: an economic nation that had lost its balance, with deepening divisions between widespread poverty and pockets of rapidly increasing affluence. However sluggish the countryside might be, in London and many other towns and cities a visitor would find Europe's most highly paid workers and all the usual signs by way of lavish consumption that a boom was occurring. In the decade before the American crisis, a handful of people made very large fortunes indeed in those sectors of the economy that were on a roll.

The most exciting growth took place in the trade in commodities brought home from the colonies or from Asia. While the tea trade was roaring ahead, the flow of tobacco from Maryland and Virginia also reached a new peak on the eve of the American Revolution, having doubled in the space of thirty years. Much the same was true of Caribbean sugar, where volumes had grown by 30 percent since the early 1760s. But precisely because these sectors were doing so well, it was hard, if not impossible, for outsiders to join in. In the case of tobacco, a tight little circle of merchants in Glasgow and London had locked up much of the importing business. As for sugar, the price of land in the old core of the British West Indies— Barbados, Jamaica, Nevis, and Antigua—had risen to levels that kept newcomers at bay. In principle, tea was rather different—anyone with money could buy the East India Company's stock or bid for tea at its sales—but, as we have seen, in fact the business was tightly controlled by another small coterie. And so, for the most part, the ambitious had to go elsewhere for opportunities.

A few hoped to profit from the latest advances in science and technology. In this respect, the period supplied two excellent role models in the shape of the potter Josiah Wedgwood and his friend and neighbor Matthew Boulton, the factory master and engineer from Birmingham who financed James Watt. Their long careers defy any attempt at a brief summary, but, putting it very simply, we can say that they were innovators in design, in marketing, and in techniques of mass production, making objects of high quality at a price consumers could afford. They were also very unusual.

Both men were in their prime, their names familiar to anyone who read the press, but Boulton and Wedgwood had few imitators, and neither would have featured on a list of the period's richest tycoons. Instead, the businesspeople who prospered the most were not the pioneers of industry but the speculators: men who dealt in paper assets or in real estate. While the commodity trade grew so explosively, the financial sector experienced a boom of its own, fed by falling interest rates and bankers eager to lend money. By 1772, this boom was nearly ten years old, with origins that lay in the last great war against the French. The conflict left a damaging legacy, not only in America, but also at home. Of course, the Seven Years' War had cost an enormous sum, and taxes had to rise, but the economic injury that it caused was more profound than simply the huge increase in the national debt.

The problem arose from the way the war was won. The British might have relied on the navy, which was relatively cheap and cost-effective, but instead they committed ground troops in Europe as well. By 1761, when the British had 100,000 men in Germany, where supplies were scarce and expensive, the army's annual budget had reached nearly £10 million, double the amount spent on the fleet. Huge contracts were awarded for the supply of food, forage, and munitions, and the military contractors, men like Sir George Colebrooke, did very handsomely indeed. So did the bankers, British and Dutch, who procured the bullion the government needed or underwrote the bonds it issued.[8]

When the war ended in 1763, the contracts unwound, and the bond issues ceased, but the effects were lasting. In spending a military budget so immense, the government poured money into the hands of its suppliers, who were either bankers already or swiftly turned to finance after the Treaty of Paris. Looking for ways to reinvest the fortunes they had made, they created a new breed of private banking houses, not only lending money but also trading avidly themselves in commodities and stocks.

In the space of a decade, the number of private banks in London more than doubled, until there were fifty, including the one that Fordyce brought to its knees. The same thing occurred in Scotland, where a dozen new banks appeared, founded by men enriched by military contracts, by sugar, or by tobacco. Before the war, the shires of England had only ten country banks, as they were known; in the 1760s, their numbers began to soar, reaching nearly a hundred by the end of the decade.[9]

By 1770 credit was easy to find, and it was cheap. After seven years of peace, the government had little need to borrow, and instead London lent freely to speculators like Alexander Fordyce. His career was emblematic of the period, not only in the way in which he rose and fell, but also in the motives that led him to behave as he did. The son of a provost or mayor of Aberdeen, he came from a talented family, with brothers who excelled in medicine and in the church, but Fordyce hoped to surpass them all and join the ranks of the aristocracy.

In the words of his sister-in-law, Fordyce aspired to be "the richest commoner in England." In the days after he vanished, people talked about his desperate quest to find a wife of noble blood. "He would have none but a Lady of Quality," it was said, but it was an age of snobbery as well as speculation. Because he had begun his career as a mere clerk in a London bank, Fordyce had to wait until he was forty to find a suitable match: the daughter of a Scottish earl, very young and very pretty. Her husband made sure that her picture could be seen in every print shop in the capital.

People like Fordyce have always existed, but in the reign of George III they found a host of new ways to advance themselves. At the time of the peace talks in Paris, Fordyce was among those, like Sir George Colebrooke, who made a killing from insider trading in government bonds. It was a common practice at a time when, as Colebrooke put it, "every member of the cabinet had relations and friends to serve by a revelation of what he knew." And then in 1766, as the East India Company's earnings rose to new heights, Fordyce made another fortune by trading in its stock.

Only rarely did he buy and sell it directly. Instead, Fordyce dealt in the secret world of derivatives, where brokers created dark pools of risk that only a few professionals could fathom. He placed his bets on the market by way of "contracts for difference," a device used in London and Amsterdam in the eighteenth century to make large profits from small movements in the price of paper assets or commodities. That was how he came to lose so much, when he sold the company's stock short and it failed to drop as he expected. To fund his activities, Fordyce built a network of friendly bankers at home and in the Netherlands. The largest was a firm called Hope & Company, an Amsterdam bank that financed wars, smugglers of tea, and slave plantations in the Caribbean, and liked to consider itself respectable. The Hopes gave him long lines of credit and dealt discreetly on his behalf.[10]

The trader from Aberdeen was an accident waiting to happen, but his exit from the scene would not have caused such a calamity unless the rest of the system was already very fragile. The effects were so severe because so many other people participated in the same culture of debt and speculation, dealing not only in paper but also in property. A boom occurred in real estate, adding the last ingredient required to bring about the crash of 1772.

In the past, newly rich men had simply bought English farmland, as a safe bet and a badge of social status. But over time, rolling acres full of wheat became a little less attractive. For as long as anybody could remember, the price of rural property had risen, but at last a moment came when it was simply too expensive and the future profits were likely to be dull. Bored with the shires, entrepreneurs looked further afield for places to invest the profits they had made.[11]

In Scotland, where the farmers were still backward with their oats and wooden plows, rents were low and the price of land was cheap. So cheap, in fact, that in the late 1760s we find English investors crossing the border to buy tens of thousands of acres of moors and bogs, hoping to improve them with fences and ditches and lime, often turning for finance to a new Scottish industrial bank, Douglas, Heron, founded in Ayr in 1769. With its plans to transform the region with new roads, mills, canals, and factories for linen, it recruited the local aristocracy among its backers. And if investors did not care for the countryside, they could opt for real estate in Edinburgh, where at this moment the city's banking elite began to create the Georgian elegance of the New Town.

Or if they preferred a warmer climate, at last investors could find new prospects in the West Indies. The old British colonies were full, but as part of the Treaty of Paris the French had been compelled to hand over the Windward Islands, far to the south of Jamaica. To help pay down its debts, the British government sold land on the islands to a squad of eager buyers. Speculators hurried to Grenada, Tobago, and Dominica to buy estates and slaves, with money borrowed in London or from Dutch firms including the Hopes.

So much for Scotland and the colonies; but if you wished to find the cutting edge of risk, as always you had to go to the West End of London. When the cost of a mortgage fell below 4 percent, a boom in construction began in the city, the greatest it had ever seen. The traces it left can still be seen by the banks of the Thames, five minutes' walk from the house in Craven Street where Benjamin Franklin lived at the time. Near the Savoy Hotel a flight of steps leads up from the embankment, toward a tall brick building, unmistakably Georgian. With its frieze, its pediment, and its pilasters, the house at 3 Robert Street was designed partly to evoke the memory of the ancient world, and partly to make a great deal of money for Robert Adam, the Scottish architect who brought it into being.

A view of the Thames in about 1772, with Robert Adam's Adelphi project under construction on the right, from a painting attributed to William Hodges. Westminster Abbey is in the background. *Yale Center for British Art*

When historians try to capture the atmosphere of the period, often they turn to poems, or novels, but this emphasis on written texts can be

misleading. Highly educated though they were, the moneyed and political elite took more interest in houses, pictures, pottery, and parties than
they did in literature; and the literary genre they enjoyed the most was the
theater, for its visual appeal as much as the lines the actors spoke. As their
arbiter of style, the elite looked to Robert Adam and his brothers, who
gave them something especially exciting and concrete. Three cabinet ministers lived in homes that he created, and so did the sister of Lord North.
Adam defined the culture of the age in a way that words could never do.[12]

The house in Robert Street survives as a relic of his boldest venture,
the Adelphi, a residential complex built along the waterfront. Anyone who
looked at the plans could see what Adam was trying to achieve: a revival of
the glamour of antiquity. Some people, including Samuel Johnson, found
his work too ornate and overpowering, but Adam's clientele loved every
marble fireplace and every gilded swag of stucco. The movement he led had
a manifesto, composed by his friend John Gwynn, a civil engineer, which
explains the secret of its appeal. "The English are now what the Romans
were of old, distinguished like them by power and opulence," he wrote.
"Our wisdom is respected, our laws are envied and our dominions are
spread over a large part of the globe. Let us no longer neglect to enjoy our
superiority; let us employ our riches . . . by promoting the advancement of
elegance." In defense of luxury, Gwynn spoke of rebuilding the capital to
sweep away the debris of the past. The citizens of London would share
in what he called "Publick Magnificence," their waking hours enriched by
scenes of beauty. To make his point, his book contained pictures showing
the embanking of the Thames, where the mud and squalor were replaced
with fine terraces and colonnades, surpassing those of Rome in splendor
and durability.

Britain's politicians had spent their youth studying the classics, and so
when Robert Adam asked for their consent to build along the riverbank,
they readily gave the Adelphi their blessing. What better way to beautify
the city, in the manner of Augustus? Adam built seventy houses on a slope
leading up to the Strand over cellars copied from vaults he had studied in
the Palace of Diocletian. By the spring of 1772, the buildings were nearly
finished, and the first trophy tenant had arrived: David Garrick, the finest actor of the age. At breakfast time, surrounded by the paintings of
Hogarth, Garrick would receive his guests and recite Shakespeare while
they admired the view. It was precisely the effect that Robert Adam had
striven to create.[13]

It was all very grand, but sadly the Adelphi rested on a flimsy pyramid of credit. To finance the project, the Adam brothers turned to the new private banks, chiefly those from their native land. The new Scottish banks were small, with too little capital, but they found Robert Adam the money he needed by running up their own vast debts to larger banks in London. Altogether the Adams raised about £200,000, which they kept on deposit with the same small Scottish firms, including one owned by John Fordyce, a kinsman of the cheat from Aberdeen. The crash was about to occur, and Robert Adam would become its most famous victim, with the Adelphi another symbol of the British cult of speculation.[14]

THE CRASH OF 1772

It did not come entirely without warning. A man who tried to keep abreast of things, George III took a daily paper, the *Public Advertiser*, where early in April the king would have seen a prophecy of doom. Disaster was about to strike, the writer said, because of what he called "the great Extent, shameful Abuse, and fatal Consequences of CREDIT."

According to the *Advertiser*, the hectic pace of lending had strayed far beyond the boundaries of prudence. It blamed the Bank of England for keeping interest rates too low and giving other banks free access to its funds. The newspaper made a fair point, and privately the central bank had reached an identical conclusion. The very same week, a well-informed reporter elsewhere in the press said that the Bank of England was quietly refusing to grant new loans to the Scotsmen who financed the Adelphi or the Dutch firms like the Hopes who were so close to Alexander Fordyce.[15]

One firm worried the authorities more than any other: the bank from Ayr, otherwise known as Douglas, Heron. In the space of just three years it had outgrown all its rivals, borrowing vast sums in London from bankers including the East India Company's Sir George Colebrooke and laying the money out north of the border. Up to a point Douglas, Heron made for progress, leaving a permanent mark on the southwest of Scotland with new harbors, new highways, and streets of little whitewashed cottages for linen weavers. But its directors were rash and aggressive to the point of fraud, running the bank with what an official inquiry later called "the highest pitch of abuse and irregularity." More than half the bank's loans were suspicious, said the inquiry, unsecured and given to the partners and their friends.

In the words of a hostile observer, the Ayr Bank financed "a black swarm of projects," not only the Adelphi, but also slave plantations in Grenada, bought at the top of the market.* Apparently, it never lent money directly to Alexander Fordyce, but even so it was partly because of Douglas, Heron that the Fordyce affair turned out to be so catastrophic. When Fordyce absconded, the bank from Ayr had huge debts in the capital, all of them due for repayment within ten weeks. In a crisis the Ayr Bank was bound to fail and bring down many others in its wake.[16]

On Wednesday, June 10, when it emerged that Fordyce had vanished, at first the city of London remained relatively calm. As a central bank was supposed to do, the Bank of England stepped in and lent freely to any bankers in distress. But in Scotland the reaction was entirely different. Late on Friday a horseman rode into Edinburgh with the news, and on Monday morning the banks began to collapse.

The first domino to fall was John Fordyce. On the government's behalf, his bank held the proceeds of the Scottish land tax; the authorities were worried that the money might be lost, and so they went to court to get instant payment of what they were owed. When the news leaked out, the townspeople hurried to withdraw their funds. The Fordyce bank locked its doors, and a run began on every bank in the city. On the cobblestones of the Canongate, crowds gathered outside the offices of Douglas, Heron demanding to regain their deposits in gold. For a week or so the management prevaricated, blaming "foolish or malicious persons" for spreading false rumors about its situation. But still the panic went on. Five more banks went down while Douglas, Heron frantically looked for help from London, where another storm was about to break.

Despite the best efforts of the Bank of England, the city was rapidly losing its nerve. The following weekend, the first man killed himself, a trader from the suburbs who cut his throat while his wife slept peacefully beside him. Hearing him choke, she awoke to find the pillows drenched with his blood. Two days later, on Monday, June 22, panic set in. That very day somebody spotted Alexander Fordyce at Dover, boarding a boat for France; and while the villain fled, depositors were laying siege to every banking house in London. By ten o'clock one had gone down to ruin, and the partners of eighteen more had gathered in a frightened huddle at the Bank of England. In the next three days the bank lent them nearly £1 million, but it could not prevent the economic slump that followed.[17]

---

* It seems that the Ayr Bank also dabbled in money laundering. Speaking in the House of Commons in 1774, the poet and politician Richard Glover alleged that its initial capital included £28,000 subscribed by what he called "noted smuggling societies."

At the Adelphi hundreds of craftsmen reported for work as usual, unaware that Robert Adam had lost the money to pay their wages. "When informed of it they came down from the walls in silence," the newspapers said. "They stood for some time in the street in a body, and at last went off one by one, with every regret for the fate of their masters." Work on the project ceased. All across the capital credit disappeared, with tradesmen demanding cash from any customers who crossed their doorsteps. Even George III had lost his nerve, it was said, and withdrawn all his money from his bankers in the Strand. The story was invented, but not the distress that swept away a multitude of lesser beings. By the end of the week it was reported that twenty firms of merchants had failed, with more tales of suicide by razor, by pistol, or by leaping from a window.

It took another fortnight for calm to be restored. The Bank of England went on lending, and at last the crisis produced two saviors, Scotsmen of rank and property, for whom the fate of Douglas, Heron was an affair of honor, like a duel begun with a challenge they could not refuse. Into the breach stepped the young Duke of Buccleuch and his cousin the Duke of Queensberry, proprietors of vast estates between the Solway and the Clyde. Both men had been among the founders of the bank, which grew as swiftly as it did partly because they gave it their seal of approval. Feeling duty-bound to save the bank of Ayr, they pledged their land as collateral. An emergency loan was arranged by the Bank of England, and the firm survived to fight another day. The following year, when things did not improve, Douglas, Heron had to close, but it was wound up in an orderly fashion. By the 1790s, the bank had repaid almost everything it owed, but that was far longer than most of its creditors could wait.

For the time being, the East India Company survived apparently unscathed, with its own line of credit from the Bank of England and a few months left to go until the next tea auctions. The rest of the kingdom sank into a deep recession, which dragged on into the spring of 1773. More businesses failed, and many thousands of workers lost their livelihood. The output of linen collapsed, demand for coal and woolens fell away, and new canals were left half excavated. In the midst of perfecting his new steam engine, James Watt had to lay down his tools when Matthew Boulton lost the cash for the project in one of the insolvent banks. In London, Robert Adam had to hold a lottery, raising the funds to complete the Adelphi by raffling off five of the finest houses in the scheme.

All of this occurred beneath the watchful eyes of visiting Americans, who promptly wrote home with the news. "Were I to recount the many Catastrophes that have happen'd & the many families reduced to want &

Beggary I should fill a volume of incidents," wrote a young man from Virginia who was living in England as a dealer in tobacco. But among all the Americans in London, the opinions of one man about the crash have a special interest and relevance: not Benjamin Franklin, who simply shrugged his shoulders—by now, British muddle and mismanagement came as no surprise to him—but a friend of his, Henry Marchant, the attorney general of Rhode Island. The province had sent the lawyer to England to resolve its disputes with the mother country.[18]

His mission was a failure, but Marchant traveled widely and kept a careful record of everything he saw. Little known and never published in its entirety, his journal gives us perhaps the best American account of the mother country on the eve of the revolution. Other visitors tended to linger in London, but Marchant, a young man of thirty-one, toured the rest of the country as well, inspecting schools and jails, peering down coal mines, and chatting with men and women who spun cotton. With Franklin at his side he marveled at a wonder of the age, the Carron ironworks in Scotland. Returning to the capital, he left his card with David Garrick, who took him backstage at Drury Lane and invited him to join the throng at breakfast time.

Much of what Marchant saw evoked his admiration, but he also came away appalled. His meetings with the government, politicians, and businessmen left him deeply troubled by what he took to be a national malaise. Great Britain, he believed, was greedy, arrogant, and riding for a fall, and the banking crash appeared to prove him right. June 22 found him in London, an eyewitness to the panic in the city. Like James Boswell, he blamed it on moral decline. The crash came about, said Marchant, because of what he called "the Luxury and Folly of the Times; the madness of Paper Credit, and false Appearance of Riches." It was merely a prelude, he believed, to the entire collapse of British power.

Four weeks later the news arrived of the loss of the *Gaspée*. Just along Threadneedle Street from the Fordyce bank, Americans would gather at the New England Coffee House to trade in whale oil, charter ships, and collect their mail. The lawyer from Rhode Island was on the premises on July 17 when word came in about the burning of the schooner. Horrified by what he heard—he called the raid "a mad and foolish act"—Henry Marchant sailed for the colonies filled with a sense of foreboding.[19]

To begin with, the *Gaspée* story made only a few lines in the papers, falsely reporting that Dudingston was dead. But the authorities knew the truth: they had the letter from the admiral. Eleven days later it reached the man who, on the British side, would play the central role in the revolutionary drama. He was the leader of the government, Frederick, Lord North, First Lord of the Treasury and chancellor of the Exchequer.

After nearly two decades in politics, Lord North was apparently a statesman in his prime. Clever and amusing, he enjoyed the respect of his opponents as well as the admiration of his friends. A few weeks earlier, George III had made him a knight of the Garter, the highest rank he could bestow. And yet, for all his prestige and his outward confidence, in private North suffered agonies of self-doubt. The state of the kingdom gave him many reasons to be fretful.*

* As the eldest son of a peer, the Earl of Guilford, he was known as Lord North as a courtesy title. North became a peer in his own right only when his father died in 1790. Until then, he sat in the House of Commons as member of Parliament for the family borough of Banbury.

Chapter Four

THE UNHAPPINESS
OF LORD NORTH

It must always be my wish to be released from a station which is too great for my abilities.

—LORD NORTH, WRITING TO HIS FATHER, MAY 1772[1]

While the winter had been long and bleak, the early weeks of summer were superb. Almost from the moment Fordyce disappeared, the sun began to shine as if to celebrate his downfall. By the end of July nearly two months had passed with barely a cloud in the sky.

To the west of London, at a place called Bushy Park, Lord North had been given the use of a country house, another token of gratitude from his benevolent king. At this time of year North was always exhausted, after many months of arduous work at Westminster. As a way to relax, he laid out a skittle ground for games with his eldest boys, down from Eton College for the long vacation. In the brilliant weather he could reflect on a parliamentary session that, despite its length, had gone extremely well.[2]

George III had every reason to reward his prime minister. Two years earlier, when Lord North first took office, few observers had expected him to survive for long. At that time one great and vexatious issue dominated the politics of Great Britain. In the county of Middlesex, at four separate elections in 1768 and 1769 the voters chose the radical John Wilkes to represent them in the House of Commons. Each time the king and his ministers had to use their majority in Parliament to stop Wilkes taking his seat, on the grounds that he was a convict, incarcerated in the King's Bench Prison on two charges of seditious libel.

But each time the Commons chose to exclude Wilkes from its ranks, public opinion swung a little further in favor of the Wilkesites, and at Westminster the government found its majority ebbing away. If Lord North were to remain in office, he would have to settle the matter once and for all. To everyone's surprise he succeeded. A shrewd tactician, he won over a decisive bloc of voters in the Commons, the landed gentry from the English counties who prided themselves on what they thought of as their independence. With them behind him, Lord North defeated the supporters of John Wilkes and went on to form what seemed to be a strong and lasting administration. For this and for much else, the king was deeply grateful.

By the middle of 1772, North appeared to be invincible. In March, despite more trouble in Parliament, he secured the passage of the Royal Marriage Act, that controversial law, still in force today, by which royal sons and daughters cannot marry without the monarch's prior consent. In one debate his majority had dwindled to as few as eighteen votes. Even so he won the battle, earning the king's thanks once again.

Then, in the spring, North emerged triumphant from his annual ordeal, the presentation of his budget to the House of Commons. For the sixth year in a row, he expected to achieve a surplus, and this time it amounted to more than £1 million. Even the king of Prussia commented on his skill with finance; and since Frederick the Great despised the British, for their duplicity, pride, and hopeless lack of rigor, praise from him was praise indeed.[3]

And so, at the age of forty, Lord North stood at the very summit of ambition. With six children, a circle of close friends, and a wife whom he loved deeply, he seemed to possess every blessing his age could bestow. The only thing missing was money. His father owned a fine estate in Oxfordshire at a place called Wroxton, but much of his property was mortgaged or held in trust for distant relatives, and the family rarely had funds to spare. It was a common predicament among the aristocracy, but North made up for it with intellect and charm. During his own years at Eton his aptitude for Latin took him to the top of his class. In adult life, despite his debts he acquired a reputation for generosity. When a neighbor was down on his luck, North gave him five guineas as they passed each other in the street. Below stairs his servants dined on beef and oysters, while in the drawing room, said Edward Gibbon, Lord North was "one of the best companions in the kingdom."[4]

He turned even his strange appearance to good use. Clumsy and often disheveled, North was plump or even corpulent and so myopic that he

Frederick, Lord North in 1773 or 1774, from the portrait by Nathaniel Dance. *Crown Copyright: U.K. Government Art Collection*

could barely see the opposing side in the debating chamber. His lips were thick, and his tongue seemed too big for his mouth. His eyes had a disconcerting habit of rolling around in all directions. But North made a virtue out of features such as these, with quick, self-deprecating wit that increased his popularity in Parliament. One evening at a party a stranger pointed at a lady and asked, "Who is that ugly woman?" "It is my wife," Lord North replied, "and we are reckoned the ugliest couple in London." Since she adored her husband too, we can safely assume that Lady North did not object.

King George III in military uniform in 1771, from Johann Zoffany's oil painting. *Crown Copyright: U.K. Government Art Collection*

As for his voice, it was deep, loud, and unmelodious, and he spoke with "a blustering kind of elocution," said a fellow member of Parliament. But when the need arose, North could be devastating, with a rare ability to crush an opponent with a well-timed put-down. On one famous occasion, a member of the opposition giving a long and tedious speech remarked that Lord North was asleep. His lordship opened one eye and said, "I wish to God I were."

There were hostile critics who accused him of relying on repartee and jokes at the expense of substance. But during his early period in office, North possessed the great advantage of sheer stamina. In an era when many of his rivals were disabled by alcohol, gout, or promiscuity, North stood out as a political athlete who rose early for breakfast meetings with the king and carefully mastered his brief. During his first four years as leader of the government, he gave eight hundred speeches: a remarkable feat at a time when most members of Parliament, including Gibbon, never uttered a word in debate.[5]

So here we have Lord North at the very peak of his career. He should have been happy, but he was not. His private letters show that even now he was anxious and prone to melancholy. Throughout his working life he would swing back and forth between moods of euphoria and depression.

Even in 1772 he often spoke about resigning. That year, after his triumphant budget speech, North wrote a typical letter to his father, filled with
a sense of inadequacy. Before the speech, he had suffered cruelly from
what he called "distress and agitation." When it was over, all he wanted
was an opportunity to leave office before, as he put it, "I have entirely
forfeited the little reputation I have gained." Much later, during the war
with America, these fits of melancholy became habitual. He fell asleep in
meetings, his memory began to fail, and letters went unanswered, leaving
his colleagues in despair.[6]

Was Lord North a neurotic? Sometimes historians use that phrase to
describe him, but in itself it tells us nothing. His tragedy was this: for
all the talents that he possessed, his were not the gifts required to solve
the deeper problems of the empire. In Lord North the king had found a
master of maneuver and debate, with the personal charm to manage the
House of Commons. But immersed in the minutiae of politics, North
could never rise above them to acquire a wider view of the future of his
nation at a time when this was urgently required. To his credit, he seems to
have known that this was so, and he felt personally to blame.

Even in 1772, at the height of his success, North believed that he had
failed. A deeply conservative man, by temperament but also as the outcome of his education, he never wished to be a visionary. But he knew that
around him the world was changing and that Britain needed new solutions
to the challenges it faced. He simply had no idea what they might be. This
was what the king of Prussia had in mind when he accused the British of a
lack of systematic thought. Publicly, Lord North would deny that this was
so, but in private he felt like a swimmer out of his depth. Even the summer
weather reminded him of the forces he could not control, as the heat wave
ceased to be glorious and became another source of anxiety.

In England it was rare to see a thick haze of dust hanging over the fields,
but this was such a year. Beneath a blazing sun, the soil was ground to
powder, and peas and barley withered in the furrows. "No rain; everything
burnt up; no grass for anything to eat," wrote a society lady in July after an
evening on horseback at Notting Hill. For many miles around the capital,
gardeners saw great swarms of bees and forecast a bumper yield of straw-
berries and honey, but as each day went by, the drought grew more alarming. Streams and ponds dried up, while the men who cut the hay went idle.

Before the holidays, the fashionable world assembled for one last extravagance, a great display of fireworks over the Thames at Chelsea, and then
they left for the country, only to encounter signs of deep distress. For
many years, the harvest had been disappointing, not only in Great Britain,

but across the rest of northern Europe too. After a late and chilly spring, the price of food was already rising steeply. Everyone could see that if the drought continued, something close to famine lay ahead.[7]

With more than two centuries of hindsight, we might think that America should have been the chief concern of British politicians, but in fact the harvest often pushed the colonies to the back of their minds. Eighteen months had passed since Parliament last debated colonial affairs. During the whole of 1772, Parliament never discussed America at all. Even the *Gaspée* raid went without comment on the floor. Until the beginning of 1774, when news arrived of the Boston Tea Party, other issues far more pressing commanded the attention of Lord North. As always, foreign policy came first, with the British cabinet following the ups and downs of politics in Europe, every intrigue and conspiracy, not from idle curiosity but because the consequence might be another war with France. As the months wore on, the financial crisis and the plight of the East India Company came to the fore, but so did the soaring price of bread and meat, a question not only of economics; but also of law and order, which worried the king and his ministers quite as much.

In eighteenth-century England the price of corn swung up and down from year to year, depending on the climate, but from the middle of the 1760s a worrying new trend appeared, as the cost of living rose and went on rising. Every time the price of bread spiked upward, it reached a new peak, so that even in years when prices fell they never returned to the levels men and women remembered from the past. By now, every town of any size had a weekly newspaper, and in the spring of 1772 they ran scores of stories about the scarcity of food. From Worcester, one writer warned the nation that it faced "a real Famine," caused by "Money-loving Landowners." Signing himself "an old-fashioned farmer," he called for an end to enclosing cornfields to rear sheep. In Exeter, according to another correspondent, "the deplorable Condition of the Poor" was "beyond Description; our Markets are kept so thin of all sorts of Provisions, and every Article of Life is so excessive dear."[8]

The politicians could not fail to see the evidence of hardship. Because all the king's ministers owned estates in one county or another, they knew firsthand the effect of rising prices. Unable to measure the speed with which the population was starting to grow—the first national census was three decades into the future—they could not explain why food was becoming so expensive; but in the rural landscape where they spent the holidays, they saw the results. In April, the first signs of unrest appeared in Essex and Suffolk, where the price of a four-pound loaf of bread and a pint of beer cost ten pennies, compared with sixpence a decade earlier. Crowds began to gather, breaking into mills and granaries and seizing meat from butchers. Locally, the leading dignitary was North's colleague the diplomat Lord Rochford, Britain's greatest expert on the international scene. As Lord Lieutenant of Essex, he took personal charge of the situation, rallying the local justices at a country inn and calling out the militia and the cavalry.

Soon afterward, trouble spread to the west country, where it reached the very doorstep of Lord North. His wife came from Somerset, where the family home lay next to the little town of Ilminster. By virtue of his marriage North held the title of lord of the manor, and so he chaired the board that paid relief to the poor. The previous year, to cope with a rising number of claimants, they had set up a workhouse with North as trustee of the funds, but clearly the initiative came too late, because in June, as the *Gaspée* was approaching her end, the laborers began to riot in Ilminster's marketplace. Roaming far and wide, they hijacked cartloads of butter and plundered bakers' shops for flour.[9]

If times were hard in southern England, in Scotland and Ireland they were even worse. Touring both countries twelve months earlier, Benjamin Franklin saw destitution of a kind that even he, a man of long experience, found deeply shocking; he sent his friends bitter descriptions of hungry men and women in rags. In Ulster, despite the harsh winter the landlords demanded a steep increase in their rents. In the spring of 1772, rebels called the Hearts of Steel began an insurrection near Belfast, so violent that five regiments of soldiers were required to put it down. When the uprising was over, a surge in emigration followed. Each year as many as ten thousand migrants left for America, mostly Irish or from the Scottish Highlands, and this diaspora across the ocean reached its peak at precisely this moment.[10]

It was against this background of distress at home that Lord North and his colleagues made their mistakes about the colonies. From all sides, items of bad news would arrive about a crisis in the markets, riots in the countryside, strikes in London, or a spate of highway robberies. Taken in isolation, no single incident of mayhem would cause the government to panic, because the forces of authority were simply far too powerful. Even so, local episodes of disorder fostered a climate of unease among the leaders of a nation given to protest, disaffection, and unbridled free speech, not to mention drink and immorality. Was the nation impossible to govern? So it often seemed. All around them, the king and his ministers saw evidence of men and women flouting the rule of law; and so they looked for remedies. Besides the war with America, the 1770s witnessed the first serious efforts in England to create a uniform national system of work-houses, and even some early steps toward creating a modern police force. On both sides of the Atlantic, the British authorities saw a rising tide of crime and disorder. This colored their perception of the *Gaspée* raid, the Boston Tea Party, and the events that followed.

On July 28, with the capital emptying fast for the vacation, at last Admiral Montagu's dispatch about the *Gaspée* reached the desk of Lord North. Once or twice a week, North convened the small but powerful committee that supervised the kingdom's finances. To underline its senior-ity, the Treasury Board assembled in a lofty chamber above Horse Guards Parade. Lord North would always chair the meeting from the head of a vast mahogany table, its massive legs carved to resemble the paws of a British lion.

Because the session on the twenty-eighth was the last before the sum-mer break, it was unusually long, and all the more tedious because the news was grim. Since the start of the year, the correspondence received by the board had been filled with reports of illegality that posed an urgent danger to the kingdom's revenue. From Dunkirk, news had arrived of smuggling vessels bound for Ireland, armed with cannon and filled with tea and gin. In April, excise officers complained about gangs of smugglers in Kent, ruffians so numerous that Lord North considered calling in the dragoons. In crews of fifty men at a time, the smugglers carried tea and brandy in convoy through the suburbs of south London. In Scotland, meanwhile, the shore was simply too long and too wild to patrol. "All the troops in Britain are not sufficient to prevent smuggling on a coast so universally accessible," said a dismal letter from Edinburgh.[11]

There was nothing entirely new about smuggling, any more than there was about riots for bread or rural unrest in Ireland. But, as we saw, the early 1770s marked a cyclical peak of illegal traffic in the British Isles, alarming not only for the volume of the trade but also because of the violence that went with it. And as far as the Treasury could tell, exactly the same thing was occurring in America. In previous years, sometimes many months went by without the board seeing an item of colonial correspon-dence. When the general in New York overspent his budget, the board would sign a draft to ensure that his soldiers were paid, but apart from that American business was trivial and infrequent. But in 1772 bad news from the west came thick and fast.

Since the previous November, not a penny had arrived from America by way of revenue. So the Treasury wrote to the cashier for the colonies, demanding an explanation. And when the board assembled in late July, the papers spread out on the table painted a picture of willful disobedience. Word had arrived from Falmouth, Maine, about a customs officer held up at gunpoint and forced to reveal the names of his informants. Near Philadelphia, a mob had seized a customs launch, and so the news went on. Another letter told the board that in many of the colonies the local judges flatly refused to issue search warrants for smuggled goods.

The fate of the *Gaspée* fell into the same appalling pattern. On the coast of North America, the rule of law seemed to be breaking down entirely. From the Admiralty, Lord Sandwich sent over a copy of Montagu's letter, which said exactly that. According to the navy, the men and women of Rhode Island were "a set of piratical people, whose whole business is defrauding the king."[12]

From the official point of view in Whitehall, the situation was entirely unacceptable. Although the British had retreated from their most ambitious plan to raise new revenues in America, Grenville's Stamp Act, the Treasury had never abandoned his basic principle: that the colonies had to make a reasonable contribution to the cost of their administration and defense. Nobody in authority in London realistically expected that the Americans should foot the entire bill. Even Grenville and his advisers had never proposed to raise more than about £200,000, half of the colonial budget, by way of the Stamp Act and his other taxes. However, no British government could tolerate a situation where, because of civil disobedience, America paid next to nothing.[13]

On hearing the news of the *Gaspée* incident, Lord North had to face a very uncomfortable truth. It was rapidly becoming impossible to collect *any* of the taxes the colonists were obliged to pay. Of course, the British might choose to return to the old system, the one that existed prior to Grenville, when the customs duties from America were paltry and the colonial assemblies voted their own taxes to pay the judges and the governors. But this was unacceptable too, since North and his colleagues wanted the judges and the governors in America to be salaried from revenues belonging to the British Crown. Only if that were so could they act as wise, impartial representatives of royal authority, unbeholden to the whims of malcontents in places like Boston and Rhode Island.

From the destruction of the *Gaspée*, it should have been clear that New England as a whole was drifting away toward independence, and not only the Providence of the Browns. At this moment, therefore, the British government should have acted firmly and decisively. In the best of all possible worlds, it would have thought again about every aspect of the colonial system, abolishing futile customs duties and laws of trade that could not be enforced. Failing that, the British cabinet might have opted for the other extreme. Send more warships to Boston, blockade the coast from Cape Cod to Connecticut, and revoke the charter of Rhode Island: this would have been the hard-line alternative. Such a strategy would have been expensive, controversial, and fraught with risk, but it might have worked. Faced with a display of force and resolution, Americans inclined to disobey might have beaten a hasty retreat.

In the relationship between Great Britain and America, a choice always had to be made between the liberal policy and the authoritarian. But in the summer of 1772, Lord North and his colleagues showed themselves incapable of making any clear choices at all. At that very moment they were thrown into turmoil by a quarrel among themselves, centering on the minister whose brief it was to supervise the colonies.

An Ulsterman from county Down, with a great estate close to the scene of the recent rebellion, the colonial secretary Lord Hillsborough had seen sedition and disorder many times. Everyone knew that he favored coercion. This was the minister who had sent the army to occupy Boston; it was due to him that the navy had made the town its headquarters, in a vain effort to put a stop to smuggling; and Hillsborough called for the revocation of the charters in Massachusetts and Rhode Island. Although his colleagues and the king were reluctant to take such a drastic step, word of Hillsborough's intentions leaked out in America, where he became an object of hatred and contempt.[14]

According to Benjamin Franklin, he was obstinate, conceited, and wrongheaded, but the most brutal verdict on Lord Hillsborough came from the patriots of Boston. When they wished to punish a lackey of the British, they smeared the man's doors and windows with feces and urine, a mixture to which they gave the name "Hillsborough paint." But even somebody so widely disliked may have a few qualities, and Hillsborough displayed at least the virtue of consistency. Compared with his colleagues, who so often vacillated, the colonial secretary shone out as a beacon of resolution. In response to the *Gaspée* incident, he demanded stern reprisals, but he did so without a hope of putting them into effect. Two days after the news arrived from Rhode Island, he told Lord North that he wished to resign.

Hillsborough fell victim to a rift within the cabinet, an unseemly fracas of a kind that was all too common. At this period, every government of Britain was a coalition, a loose alliance drawn from rival factions, and Lord North's was no exception. At a time when the nation needed clarity of purpose, he was obliged to keep the peace within his own ranks. As it happened, the dispute arose from another American problem: the fate of the Ohio valley, which Hillsborough and General Gage wished to surrender to the Indians.

North called the quarrel about the frontier an "unlucky business," but it was more than just a little local difficulty. The controversy drove a deep wedge between Lord Hillsborough and his cabinet colleagues, who connived against him until he had to go. At their best, they were shrewd, hardworking patriots of their own kind, committed to the service of the kingdom. But the row about the wilderness revealed the British cabinet at its worst, and it made a swift, decisive response to the *Gaspée* raid impossible to achieve.[15]

A Ruling Class

The cabinet resembled a pack of willful hounds. Point them in the right direction, at a common enemy such as John Wilkes or the king of France, and they would work together to take the fox. The rest of the time they were equally likely to run around in circles, snapping at each other's heels. Toss them a bone in the shape of some chance of financial gain, and they would squabble over it, even at the risk of damaging the national interest in which they all believed.

Apart from Hillsborough and North himself, there were four ministers who really counted.* All of them were peers of the realm, members of the aristocracy with a seat in the House of the Lords. Each one had his own obsessions and his own agenda. All four remained in office throughout the American crisis and shared in the errors that were made. In the diversity of their interests, each one also represented a different facet of the elite.

At fifty-four, William Zuylestein, the fourth Earl of Rochford, belonged to the older generation of British politicians, men with a view of the world shaped by the Jacobite rebellion of 1745, when the nation had stood on the brink of catastrophe. When the Young Pretender came within a week of taking London, Rochford and his friend Lord Sandwich were already in their late twenties. During their adult lives, Great Britain had also fought two long wars with France. Both men saw the defense of the realm as their overriding responsibility, and in their different ways they devoted their careers to it.

---

* There was also a fifth man, Lord Dartmouth, who joined the cabinet shortly afterward, replacing Hillsborough as colonial secretary. We shall come to him later.

For Lord Rochford, the secret of national security lay in the balance of power. A fine linguist, he served as ambassador in Turin, Madrid, and Paris. Weak in some respects, in others he was indispensable. The French called him "un homme de plaisir," and so he was. Fond of the theater, and even more of actresses, Rochford made a habit of adultery and spent a fortune he did not possess. Prone to ill health, he would sometimes choose a moment of emergency to take a rural holiday, but his colleagues and the king could not do without him for long. His knowledge of European politics was unrivaled.

On a single sheet of paper, Rochford could distill the most complex problem of foreign policy into simple language. In the cabinet of Lord North, he served as the senior of two secretaries of state. Cheerful, lively, and often indiscreet, given to what another Frenchman called "petites vivacités," Rochford watched over domestic affairs, which chiefly meant law and order, but he also dealt with Britain's strained relationship with France and Spain, the most sensitive task a minister could undertake.

In 1772, one issue occupied the forefront of his mind. Deeply suspicious of the French, Rochford knew that Britain needed allies on the Continent to deter the Bourbon powers from making war again, but none were available. Austria was aligned with France, and the king of Prussia did not trust the king of England. Logically, the British should have forged an alliance with the Russian empress, Catherine the Great, whose army was so much larger than their own. Efforts were made to reach an agreement, but they came to nothing. The empress required a subsidy, paid in sterling, and help in dismembering Poland and the Ottoman Empire. The British would rather have no deal at all than a pact concluded on Russian terms so callous and expensive, and so the empress turned to her distant cousin Frederick the Great. On the eve of the American Revolution, Great Britain found itself isolated, a situation that filled Lord Rochford with alarm. "We have not a single friendly power," he told his colleagues, in an anxious note written that autumn.[16]

Nobody felt more respect for Rochford than his friend John Montagu, the fourth Earl of Sandwich, the minister who presided over the fleet. Equally wary of the French, he took the same pleasure in women and the stage. A keen gambler, always in debt, he gave his name to the sandwiches we eat today, because, or so the story goes, he needed a way to dine without leaving the gaming table. At fifty-three, Sandwich retained all the vigor of early manhood but also some of its clumsiness. Tall but ungainly, he was apt to break the porcelain on entering a lady's drawing room. Only one man in London, it was said, could walk down two sides of the street at the same time, and that was Montagu. Apart from his mistress, a pretty young soprano, Lord Sandwich had three great passions: cricket, the Royal Navy, and the oratorios of Handel. The greatest of these was the navy.

Isolated as it was, the kingdom relied all the more on the fleet. By itself the navy might act as deterrence enough to keep the French at bay, but only if the service was kept in fighting readiness. The minute book of the Admiralty Board survives, with every page showing Lord Sandwich intent on the task, trying to build and repair ships more quickly, with greater firepower, copper hulls, and crews protected by the latest cure for scurvy. The letters that passed between him and Lord North are equally important for what they reveal about Great Britain's situation. Keen to preserve the nation's financial standing so that in wartime it could borrow freely, North favored strict economy in each department. Sandwich, on the other hand, tried his best to defend the navy and squeeze more resources from a parsimonious Treasury.[17]

While Rochford worried about foreign policy, and Sandwich toiled at his desk or toured the dockyards, their colleague the second Earl of Gower chiefly looked after himself. The richest member of the cabinet, aged fifty-one, fluent in speech and dignified in manner, in order of precedence Gower ranked next to North, serving as Lord President of the Privy Council. His name rarely appears in official papers, because Granville Leveson-Gower performed no executive role. He sat in the cabinet not because of what he did but because of who he was. In the old, unreformed parliamentary system, where boroughs could be bought and sold, the king needed the support of plutocrats like Gower, ready to use their resources to keep the government in power.

After selling their stock in the South Sea Company just before it failed, the Leveson-Gowers had bought a great swathe of their home county of Staffordshire. Investing in coal and canals, they made themselves the leaders of their region. And while six members of the House of Commons owed their election directly to the Gowers, his lordship had also formed close ties with the even more opulent Duke of Bedford. Known as the Bloomsbury gang, the faction they led spoke for another thirty seats. If North were to form a lasting administration, he could not do without their loyalty. Their help had been essential in the task of seeing off John Wilkes. But Lord Gower always wanted a great deal in return: a voice in key decisions and endless favors for the Bloomsburyites, commissions in the army, and posts on the Treasury payroll. If North failed to deliver, Gower would plot behind his back until he found another premier who could.

The youngest member of the cabinet was only thirty-three. Genial, modest, and impeccably polite, Henry Howard, twelfth Earl of Suffolk, took on the post of the junior secretary of state with deep misgivings, worrying about his poor command of French, the language of diplomacy. Serving as deputy to Rochford, he oversaw Britain's dealings with the Baltic powers and Russia; and to his own surprise, Suffolk impressed foreign envoys with the speed with which he learned their trade. So crippled with disease that he could barely hold a pen—his ailment was said to be gout, but his symptoms suggest that his heart was weak—he enjoyed the king's friendship and his colleagues liked and trusted him. Just before the American war, Suffolk wrote them a poem in the style of Pope, making fun of the rebels; but however flippant he might be, Suffolk worked as hard as Sandwich. He would be dead before he was forty.[18]

How did the cabinet, besides composing satires in verse, treat the American question? To a man—though Rochford sometimes had second thoughts—they were hard-liners. In their eyes, the king and his Parliament were legally supreme over each and every colony. Using his prerogative, the king had chosen to delegate some functions to provincial assemblies or to local officials, but if any dispute arose, of whatever sort, then Parliament at Westminster had the final word. Gower, Sandwich, and Suffolk never wavered from this principle, and neither did Lord North.

There had been a moment, six years before the *Gaspée* incident, when they had made their views entirely plain. It had occurred early in 1766, during the debates on the repeal of the Stamp Act. In the House of Lords, more than thirty peers had fought a dogged campaign against repeal. Sandwich and Suffolk led the fight, and they nailed their colors so firmly to the mast that they could never change their stance without appearing foolish or dishonest. The same applied to Gower, who voted with them, opposing even the smallest concession to America.*

They saw the repeal of the Stamp Act as a betrayal of everything they cherished. By doing away with the tax, Great Britain had raised a white flag in the face of treachery and riot. Worse still, the repeal of the act endangered the twin pillars of the British constitution: the sovereignty of Parliament and the rule of law. It was the duty of the House of Lords, they believed, to stand up against the mob and to resist democracy wherever it appeared. Only the peers who sat in the upper chamber, high-

---

* Lord North was a backbench MP in 1766, and he played little part in the debates of that year. However, his private correspondence shows that he took the same hard line as Sandwich and his friends.

minded patriarchs who never faced the voters, could be trusted to act in the nation's best interests. In their opinion, the public was inherently capricious, easily misled by troublemakers such as Wilkes or his counterparts in Boston. Abolish the Stamp Act, and you would give them victory. The outcome would be anarchy and the end of empire.

In the future, anyone who did not like a tax would refuse to pay it. According to Suffolk, Americans were "an unfortunate people, misled by factious judges and seditious lawyers." From New England to Georgia, the provincial assemblies had become nurseries of disobedience, openly demanding equality with London. Hand the Americans one concession, and they would ask for more until they won autonomy.[19]

Six years on, this remained the creed in which North and his colleagues believed. After giving voice to it so clearly, they could not abandon it, and they never did. But a creed is what it was: not a practical agenda or a plan of action, but a statement of dogma, rigid and doctrinaire. It was all too tempting to deal in abstract ideas about the sovereignty of Parliament, forgetting that authority and power were two very different things. It was easy to proclaim, as they did, that the king and Parliament possessed an "ancient, unalienable right of supreme jurisdiction." It was far harder to make the decisions required if the British were to give this abstract notion any substance. The dispute about the Ohio country made this very plain.[20]

The Hillsborough Memorandum

The quarrel in the summer of 1772 that spelled the end of Lord Hillsborough had been nearly four years in the making. It could trace its origins to 1768 and a deal between British emissaries and the six nations of the Iroquois. After a conference at Fort Stanwix, the Iroquois sold their rights to an immense territory west of the Appalachians, between the mountains and the Ohio River. Under the Stanwix treaty it became a possession of King George, to be divided between aspiring settlers from Pennsylvania and Virginia, where investors formed syndicates to make bids for the land.

The news reached London, where it horrified Lord Hillsborough. He inherited the treaty from his predecessor, Lord Shelburne, whose views about the wilderness differed entirely from his own. Shelburne had believed that money might be made by asking the settlers to pay rent to the king, but for Hillsborough the risks involved in westward expansion far outweighed any likely reward. He advanced the same old arguments: allow the colonists to cross the mountains, and they would throw off their allegiance to the king. Another great Indian war would break out, of exactly the kind that he wished to forestall. For the next three years, Hillsborough used every tactic of delay to prevent any grants being made.

Gradually, however, he found himself outflanked by rivals more powerful than he. One group of investors had come to the fore: the Grand Ohio Company, run from Philadelphia. With Benjamin Franklin on their side, they hatched the most ambitious scheme of all, offering to buy two million acres in the wilderness we now call West Virginia. Unable to obtain Lord Hillsborough's consent, the investors began a lobbying campaign in London with the aim of circumventing him.

At a time when the business climate was so wildly optimistic, the company soon found backers from the world of finance. As the price of real estate rose steeply in Great Britain and the West Indies, speculators found virgin land in the Ohio valley an irresistible alternative. With cynical good sense, the company also made a direct appeal to Hillsborough's cabinet colleagues. They recruited first Lord Suffolk's father-in-law and then a string of senior officials at the Treasury. They gave free shares to Lord Rochford, who always needed money, and to Lord Gower, who did not refuse. His support was essential because, whatever Hillsborough might say, the final decision lay with the Privy Council, where Gower sat in the chair.[21]

By the spring of 1772, Lord Hillsborough was isolated and almost as unpopular in Whitehall as he was in Boston. For all his rank in Ireland he had no following in London, where his opponents were so influential. It was rumored that Gower wanted to have him dismissed, as a prelude to getting rid of Lord North as well. Even the king dropped hints that Hillsborough was behaving foolishly. At the end of April, Hillsborough decided to bring matters to a head. He sent Gower a long memorandum, firmly rejecting any western settlements at all: the only memorandum, as it happens, that survives from the early 1770s to give us a full account of colonial policy from a cabinet minister's point of view. Filled with long, pessimistic extracts from the letters of General Gage, the document was clear and logically consistent. As plainly as could be, Hillsborough set out the orthodox British conception of the future of America, but in doing so he revealed just how narrow that perspective was.[22]

In Hillsborough's eyes, the empire existed for one purpose only: to create material wealth for Great Britain. The colonies were there, he said, "to improve and extend the commerce, navigation and manufactures of this kingdom, upon which its strength and security depends," and that was all. He listed the ways in which the empire added value to the mother country, and there were only four.

First came the fisheries, from Cape Cod to Newfoundland, which were vast, lucrative, and British, and so they should remain. Because they employed so many ships and seamen, they helped ensure that King George remained the master of the seas. Second, the coastal plain of North America provided a rich supply of raw materials—timber, tar, and hemp—required by the Admiralty to build and rig the fleet. Third, the colonies served as a captive market for goods manufactured in Great Britain. Last, Lord Hillsborough mentioned the role the Americans played in supporting the West Indies. The sugar planters needed food to feed the slaves and lumber for making barrels and sheds. These could only come from the mainland.

Follow these arguments to their conclusion, and you would maintain only a relatively small empire on the coast, a few hundred miles deep at the most. Everything else would be left to the tribes. This was precisely Lord Hillsborough's point: that the purpose of the empire in America could be accomplished entirely within the terms of the royal proclamation of 1763, without expansion into the Ohio country. But by the time he signed his memorandum, it was already obsolete.

With so many migrants arriving in America, driven across the ocean by rising rents and prices, it was impossible to close the frontier. In New England or beside the Hudson River, fertile soil was scarce. And so, regardless of official wisdom, settlers were crossing the hills in a great arc from western Virginia to Vermont. Hillsborough knew this perfectly well: in 1772 the dispatches from the colonies were full of reports of the trouble that westward migration caused. And yet he believed that somehow the tide could be held back. But his strangest miscalculation of all related not to the Ohio valley, but to the plantation colonies of the South. Time and again, the British government failed to understand how weak a grip it had on the region. Anyone who read a newspaper, in London or in Glasgow, could see how swiftly the slave economy was developing: he or she need only glance at the long lists of ships carrying rice, tobacco, and wheat from Charleston or Annapolis. But Lord Hillsborough barely mentioned the South. It did not occur to him that this might be the Achilles' heel of empire, where the colonists were most dangerously outgrowing British rule.

By putting his case against the Ohio venture so firmly, Hillsborough made a fight with his colleagues inevitable. Lord Gower and the Privy Council asked for their own report from an advisory body, the Board of Trade, which heard evidence from the Grand Ohio Company. The result was a foregone conclusion, given the powerful allies that Franklin and the company had recruited. In early July, two weeks before the news arrived about the *Gaspée*, the Board of Trade gave Gower and Rochford what they wanted, coming out in strong support of the Ohio scheme. Meanwhile, the Bloomsbury gang briefed the press with sly little stories that Hillsborough's days were numbered.

Taking the hint, he began to talk about resignation, throwing Lord North into a customary fit of despair. It had taken years of work to assemble a durable government, and now North found his colleagues at each other's throats. "I foresee mischief in any new arrangement," he wrote to Lord Gower on June 30, and the sentence might have served him for an epitaph. The split within the cabinet was the sort of situation North tried to avoid, and it showed him at his least impressive. He could not see how high the stakes had risen. It would be hard to think of an issue more important for the future of the colonies. During its fruitless talks with Hillsborough, the Ohio company had increased the amount of land it wanted, from two million to twenty million acres. Grant the company's request, and a new province would come into being beyond the Appalachians, nearly two hundred miles square, throwing Indian country wide open. Refuse to give the Ohio investors what they wanted, and Americans would view the closure of the frontier as one more act of imperial oppression.

At this point North might have taken the lead and made the future of America a central theme of British policy. But unless he remained in power, there was nothing he could do at all, and so he tried to kick the Ohio valley into the long grass of politics. Keen to avoid an outcome that would strengthen the Bloomsbury gang, for the whole of July North played for time, hoping that the fuss would soon die down. He urged Gower to put off a final decision about the Ohio grant until after the summer recess.

As the weeks went by, even the king began to tire of what he called Lord North's "good nature and love of indecision." The affair was unpleasant, and it could only have one end, regardless of the merits of the case. Coming from Ulster, Hillsborough was expendable, because Ireland sent no members to the British Parliament. His rivals were a very different matter. For the sake of Rochford's talents, and Gower's influence and money, they had to be placated. Under pressure from the king, North reluctantly looked for a new colonial secretary. As a first choice, he picked a Bloomsburyite, Lord Weymouth, but fortunately he declined the post. Breathing a sigh of relief, North offered the department to a friend he trusted implicitly: his stepbrother William Legge, the second Earl of Dartmouth.

Forty-one years old, Dartmouth was loyal, pious, and incorruptible, three qualities for which the era's politicians were less than famous. Surprised to be asked but willing to help, he came over to Bushy Park to be briefed about America, and then he said yes to the offer. Lord Hillsborough resigned. On August 14, 1772, Dartmouth became colonial secretary. With that, Lord North selected the last, and the most important, of the men who would oversee the American debacle.[23]

For nearly a month, the divisions in the cabinet had left it unable to respond to the *Gaspée* raid. It was not too late to be resolute, but the omens for the future were poor. The most senior officials in Whitehall were painfully aware that across the ocean they were impotent.

Chapter Five

IGNORANCE AND BAD POLICY

The British lion has been asleep these four or five years.

—THOMAS HUTCHINSON, GOVERNOR OF
MASSACHUSETTS, SEPTEMBER 1772[1]

Lord Dartmouth took over a small department drooping under the
burden of its duties. His office in Whitehall was delightful, recently
redecorated by Lord Hillsborough; and in theory, his staff of thirty-five
should have been adequate. But ten of them simply drew their salaries and
never turned up for work. Another four merely "attended the king," in the
words of a list drawn up for the new minister. The rest were mostly there
to carry messages, to welcome visitors, to sweep the floor, or to brew the
tea. In practice, the weight of American affairs rested on the bent shoulders of two undersecretaries and seven clerks.

Shortly before he took up his post, Dartmouth received a plaintive note
from the head of the department. "I consider my race as run," wrote John
Pownall, the senior undersecretary. "I have neither spirits nor constitution
to undergo the fatigue of attending to the business." Worn out by the age
of fifty, the nation's leading expert on America was yearning for his pension. He longed to spend his retirement with his collection of Roman
coins and pots, dug from the soil of his native Lincolnshire.[2]

After a lifetime dealing with the colonies, Pownall had every reason
to be exhausted. Since his earliest days as a junior clerk, he had displayed
"abilities, attention and integrity," in the words of his obituary. A gram-
mar school boy, from a family shabby but genteel, he rose through the

ranks by virtue of brains and hard work. Tied to his desk, he never crossed the Atlantic, though his brother Thomas served a term as governor of Massachusetts. Instead, John Pownall tried to run America on paper by reading and writing a mountain of letters.

Every year hundreds of packets arrived from the colonies, each one demanding an urgent reply. All of them were docketed and filed. They survive to this day in the archives in London, bulky and tattered, filled with newspaper cuttings, long lists of numbers, and petitions from people with axes to grind. It would be enough to wear out any official, but John Pownall's career had been especially wearisome because it was so futile.

During the previous decade, he had advised on every British policy toward the colonies. Almost without exception, each one had fallen by the wayside. The Stamp Act came and went, defeated by American resistance. The Townshend duties also failed to survive, apart from the threepence on a pound of tea. So did the plan to keep the West free from British settlers. Ten years earlier, Pownall drafted the royal proclamation that tried to keep the colonists behind the mountains. Now that doctrine lay in ruins, and no new program had emerged to take its place.

John Pownall expected the consequences to be dire, and word soon arrived of settlers killing Indians on the frontier. "Such savage degeneracy of the human heart," he wrote in September, "has brought us to the eve of an Indian war: the most ruinous and expensive that can be waged." This was exactly the outcome that he, like General Gage, had striven to prevent. And when he surveyed the rest of America, Pownall saw signs that the colonies were following the frontier into turmoil.[3]

On the coast, the smugglers had made the collection of taxes all but impossible. Meanwhile, from Lake Champlain to South Carolina the dispatches carried news of other insults to authority. In the valley of Vermont, settlers had built a town called Pownall, named in honor of John's brother. It fell within a tract of virgin land between the Connecticut River and the Hudson, where rival groups of pioneers were at each other's throats. Settlers from three separate colonies—New Hampshire, New York, and Connecticut—laid claim to the area, and by the summer of 1772 something close to civil war appeared to be breaking out.

For the first time, the Colonial Office heard the name of somebody called Ethan Allen, in reports of a skirmish between a magistrate from New York and Allen's gang of vigilantes. A range war began, violent but very local, of the kind that later generations in America would simply take in their stride as part and parcel of life on the frontier. That year the quarrel in Vermont filled scores of pages in the letters sent to White-hall. Whatever ministers might say about the rule of law, the Allen affair showed just how little they could do to enforce it.

John Pownall had not the least idea who Ethan Allen was, or why his name would become so famous. Three years had yet to pass before Allen helped to lead the revolution in New England at the head of Vermont's Green Mountain Boys. But for the British, the stories were already deeply worrisome. As the flow of people westward accelerated, so incidents like this were bound to become more common, but nobody could think of a way to prevent them. In theory, royal officials existed to resolve exactly the kind of boundary dispute that caused the trouble in Vermont. But if nobody would listen while men like Allen openly disobeyed author-ity, what purpose did the empire really serve? And far to the south in the wealthiest corner of British North America, the system appeared to be breaking down entirely.

In Charleston, the planters had an assembly. Keen to run their own affairs, its members saw an ally in John Wilkes. In 1769, believing that Wilkes was friendly to their cause, they sent a donation to help him in his efforts to take his seat in Parliament. From the British point of view, this was illegal, and so Hillsborough issued instructions banning the assembly from making any payments of the sort. The fight that followed, between the royal governor and the assembly, paralyzed the government of South Carolina. No taxes were levied, and no laws were passed. Either the assem-bly would not vote for them, or the governor barred the members from sitting at all. Endless letters passed to and fro between London and the colony, but the dispute was never settled. Only the war put an end to the quarrel.[4]

All around the rim of the empire there were little local crises of this kind under way, just as there were disputes and disorders in Great Brit-ain. Seen from Whitehall, each individual problem might seem trivial, but added together they painted a picture of chaos. The empire had grown too swiftly, in Asia and America alike, partly because of greed and speculation and partly as a side effect of victory against the French. Nobody knew what it meant to be a global power. Nobody put in place the structures such a huge empire required. John Pownall had a deputy named William Knox, the second undersecretary, who never ceased to say exactly this.

Born in Ireland, Knox was another pious man, from a family of Pres-byterian Scots. In his youth he went to Georgia to grow rice, hiring mis-sionaries to convert his slaves to faith in Jesus Christ. Returning home, he married an heiress and penned a stream of essays on American affairs that attracted the attention of the government. He joined the Colonial Office, which needed an eloquent writer to put the empire's case. In public he defended the official wisdom that the colonies were merely humble satellites, orbiting around the king and Parliament. Privately, Knox urged his superiors to reform an imperial system that seemed to be disintegrating. In Georgia, Knox had seen just how hard it was to rule a continent three thousand miles away. This became a constant theme of his career. The colonists, he argued, were hell-bent on independence, while the ministers in London would not take the necessary steps to hold them back. "It was with no small degree of astonishment," he once wrote, "that I perceived a total want of plan or system in the British government." In the history of British North America, he saw nothing but a long, sad chronicle of "neglect, Ignorance, bad Law and worse Policy." While John Pownall was depressed, William Knox felt driven to distraction by a cabinet he saw as timid and effete.[5]

And so he spent his time writing papers to which his superiors paid no heed. Both he and Pownall were struggling, in their different ways, with a basic flaw of the old colonial system. Far from being unified, the empire was split into fragments, with thirty separate colonies on the mainland or in the West Indies, twenty-five of which had their own parliament or assembly. Each one had developed its own constitution, which it was determined to preserve. At the most extreme, there were Rhode Island and Connecticut—"little republics," Knox called them—already independent in all but name. But everywhere else, he saw worrying evidence of what he called "the predominancy of the Democratic Power."[6]

It was all very different from the way the Victorians would supervise their empire. If the British had ruled America in the way they later governed India, they would have installed a viceroy in New York to oversee the whole. He would have been given powers to tax and spend and to borrow money to build roads and drain or irrigate the land. He would have made a code of laws, uniform across the continent. With an army of his own, recruited locally and officered by men like George Washington, he would have defended the frontier. If he were honest and talented and stood up for colonial interests, he might have won the respect of the Americans. Perhaps he might even have kept their loyalty.

Failing that, an English viceroy might have bought off a pampered elite with commissions, salaries, and subsidies, as the British did in Bengal, while leaving the slaves and peasants to toil. But at this stage in the history of the British Empire, a viceroy of such a kind was inconceivable. Each colony jealously guarded its own laws and customs. Each one preferred to pay its own bills and call out its own militia when the need arose. And the very mention of an American viceroy would have caused uproar in London. For Lord North and the lawyers who advised him, authority must always lie with Parliament and the Crown. But as his name implied, a viceroy would be a petty king, and so potentially a rival to Westminster. As far back as 1754, Benjamin Franklin had come close to proposing a viceregal government for America, with his abortive plan for a union between the colonies, devised as a means to organize defense against the French. We cannot really call Franklin's plan a missed opportunity, because the British cabinet apparently never discussed it at all, and his ideas left his fellow Americans equally unimpressed. But without a viceroy or some system for managing America as a whole, the British were left with an empire too diverse to be held.

It would have been hard enough to cope if Pownall and his staff had merely had the mainland to occupy their time. But they had to deal with the Caribbean as well. Time and again, before and during the war, the West Indies fatally diverted the attention of the government. With as many as 1,800 slave plantations producing sugar cane worth £3 million a year, these treasure islands were the brightest jewel in the crown of empire for crude financial reasons that a single tale will illustrate. It concerns the clerical half brother of Lord North. As a young man, Brownlow North struggled to obtain preferment in the Anglican church, and the family had no money to give him an income. At last the king came to the rescue by making the youth a bishop at the age of only thirty. That was in 1771; the very same year, the newly eligible Brownlow married a slave owner's heiress from Antigua. And so the bishop secured his future, until Mrs. North lost so heavily at cards.[7]

For reasons such as this, the sugar islands were simply too valuable to lose, but they were also very costly to keep. Always at risk of a slave revolt or a surprise attack by the French, the West Indies required a garrison and warships standing by, but this depleted the strength of the army and the navy, whose young men died in their hundreds from fever. Every year produced some fresh emergency, and 1772 was no exception. On St. Vincent, British troops were about to fight a small war against what remained of the native people, the Caribs who had risen in revolt. In Grenada, meanwhile, where John Wilkes's brother had gone to grow sugar, the British planters were staging their own peaceful insurrection.

Like the Mississippi valley, the Windward Islands harbored a community of French settlers, all of whom were Roman Catholic. Accustomed to coexisting with Catholics in Northern Ireland—he found the Presbyterians far more difficult—Hillsborough wished to give the French inhabitants seats in the Grenada assembly as a way to retain their obedience. The idea horrified the British on the island, who flatly refused to cooperate with London and allow the Pope's children to participate in government. What was worse, the economy had faltered as well. On Grenada, Tobago, and Dominica, the speculators who bought old French estates had mortgaged themselves to the hilt. As the financial crisis began to bite in 1772 in London and Amsterdam, the new plantation owners found it impossible to pay for more slaves or the supplies they needed from the mainland; and some defaulted on money they still owed the government.

In the face of so much trouble in their western dominions, the British needed a farsighted statesman to set priorities and lay down a clear strategy for the future. For all his virtues, Lord Dartmouth could not rise to that particular challenge; but even a politician of genius might have found the task beyond his powers. To heal a failing organization, a manager requires reliable information, and in 1772 the British did not have it. John Pownall and his colleagues could rarely trust the American messages that they received. True, they had General Gage, who always seemed convincing, in letters concise and beautifully written. But if the dispatches came from the royal governors in each mainland colony, sometimes they were worse than useless.

For all the detail they contained, the governors never quite got to the point. In fact, sometimes their communications were deeply misleading, because the men who wrote them had too many private interests and selfish preoccupations. "You can never manage America well, without having good governors," wrote a wise friend of Lord Dartmouth's, warning him about the trials he would face in office. The information the British received was only as good as the men who sent it, and they were very mixed.[8]

Although the file of letters from Governor Hutchinson in Boston was always full to bursting with reports of naughty goings-on, it failed to convey an objective appraisal of public opinion in the Bay Colony. As Pownall already knew, and as Dartmouth would soon learn, although Thomas Hutchinson was highly intelligent, he could also be arrogant, indiscreet, and confrontational. And although he cared deeply about the fate of Massachusetts and the empire, he worried still more about his family, and in particular about his sons, who needed help with their careers. He pursued their material interests with, as we shall see, disastrous consequences.

Although Hutchinson was ultra-loyal, the British could not trust him: a lethal paradox.

Much the same was true of his opposite number in New York, Governor William Tryon, an even less disinterested public servant. Firm and effective when it came to hanging farmers who led an uprising in North Carolina, he was nonetheless a dupe of his own vanity. To the outrage of the king, Tryon devoted his time in New York to amassing real estate, awarding great slices of public land to himself and his friends. Strategically, his province was essential—in the Revolutionary War, the Hudson valley held the key to North America—but it was also politically divided, and its internal affairs especially hard to understand. But Tryon's dispatches amounted to nothing more than long screeds of self-justification, devoid of the cool analysis that Lord Dartmouth required.

As for the other colonies, some rarely sent dispatches at all: freethinking Connecticut and Rhode Island, of course, but also Maryland, where, unknown to the British, the tobacco farmers were some of the first Americans to think of taking up arms against them. The Maryland file was almost empty. But in Virginia the void of information was most damaging of all. In Lord Dunmore, a Scottish nobleman, the British had chosen a governor keen to see the province expand across the Appalachians. His letters dealt chiefly with Indian affairs. He had no inkling that the tobacco planters of the Old Dominion might, in due course, become perhaps the most fearsome rebels of all. "In the progress of our business, the greatest harmony and most perfect good temper have subsisted, between the different branches of the legislature," Dunmore wrote, just before the *Gaspée* incident, speaking about the colonial assembly in Williamsburg. The governor failed to detect the unrest that already existed in the South as well as in New England. Almost until the last moment before the revolution began, he believed that however outspoken Virginia might be, it would never desert the Crown.[9]

To be fair to John Pownall and his staff in the Colonial Department, they were all too aware of the limits of their knowledge. For all the reams of paper they received, some of the most basic facts eluded them. They did not know how many people lived in America, how swiftly the colonies were growing, or how large a militia each one could put into the field. Without data such as these, it was impossible to tell how serious the threat of independence really was. A year after taking office, Dartmouth sent a long questionnaire to each American governor, itemized under twenty-two headings, asking about his population, revenues, system of government,

and much else. The first question, intended to help resolve boundary disputes, was this: where is your colony? Some of the governors never replied
at all. By the time the answers came back from those who did, the revolution had already started.[10]

As the crisis approached, the authorities in London fell even further
behind the curve. In Boston, Thomas Hutchinson could see that this
was so and he felt the same frustration that afflicted William Knox. For
Hutchinson, therefore, the news of the *Gaspée's* destruction was scarcely
unwelcome. Perhaps the British would at last shake off their lethargy and
act decisively in New England. There were men in Whitehall who agreed,
but the official response turned out to be ill-judged and impractical.

THE KING'S FIRM RESOLUTION

Something must be done about Rhode Island, said Lord Rochford on
August 15, the day after Dartmouth took up his new post. He used the
weary, peevish tone that he always employed about America, but in the
next sentence he admitted that he had no solution to offer. The hard line
recommended by Lord Hillsborough struck him as unrealistic. The civil
servants Knox and Pownall also wanted firm reprisals, but Rochford took
them with a pinch of salt. Their advice had been poor in the past. Instead,
he preferred to act cautiously against the *Gaspée* raiders, even when the
lawyers branded them traitors guilty of treason.

Throughout the American crisis, the British cabinet asked for legal advice
about every decision they made. Invited to give his opinion, the attorney
general, Edward Thurlow, quickly confirmed that burning the schooner
was an act of war against the king. He called that treason plain and simple.
Off the record, he added a rider: the culprits, he said, committed a felony
five times worse than the riots against the Stamp Act. But while the law
was one thing, the realities of power were quite another. If the men who
destroyed the *Gaspée* were publicly deemed to be traitors, then Great Britain
had to bring them to trial and hang them, and this was what made Lord
Rochford so nervous. In the summer of 1772, the British dared not provoke
a confrontation in America from which they might emerge as the loser.[11]

Knowingly or not, John Brown had chosen an excellent time for his private rebellion. The politics of Europe were entering a fraught and alarming phase, with Great Britain cast in the role of a spectator. In the first
week of August, the Russians and their allies in Berlin had finally sent their
soldiers into Poland to divide that unhappy country between themselves

and Austria. France, it was thought, would come to the aid of the Poles, sending its navy to threaten the Russians in the north or in the Mediterranean, where Catherine the Great had placed a squadron of her own. Ominous rumors arrived in London, saying that the French were arming their ships for war; and then, a few weeks later, a still more alarming report of a coup d'état in Sweden. With backing from Paris, or so it was alleged, the young king Gustav had seized control of his country, doing away with his own parliament in Stockholm. This was something Russia would not accept, but if it replied in kind, using force against the Swedes, the British could not stand idly by. In practice it was too expensive to import the bulk of Britain's naval stores from America, and so instead the navy relied on the Baltic for its supplies of masts, rope, and tar. A nation built on its power at sea, Great Britain might not survive the loss of the region, whether to France or St. Petersburg.

And so, fearing that they might be sucked into a war in Europe, the cabinet had no choice but to listen to Rochford and act with restraint in Rhode Island. As a parting shot before he left office, Hillsborough tried to force their hand by writing directly to Montagu, telling him to detain anybody he suspected of taking part in the *Gaspée* raid, but this the admiral simply could not do: the law did not permit the military to arrest civilians on land without a warrant from a judge. When Lord North assembled the cabinet on August 20, they had to begin by recalling Hillsborough's letter. And then they took the first of the long chain of decisions that led to the war; but they did so in the belief that they were being calm and unprovocative.

The legal opinion from Thurlow dealt not only with the nature of the offense, but also with the venue for a trial. No one in Whitehall trusted a jury in America to convict their fellow countrymen of crimes against the king. Witnesses would lie, if they testified at all, and the jurors would be intimidated into making an acquittal. The evidence of that was plain to see in the dispatches that arrived that year. Happily, however, the attorney general confirmed that an English court could try and hang the *Gaspée* raiders, and the cabinet gratefully took a piece of advice supported by what seemed to be the best authorities. Because it was a rare and special felony, a case of treason in Great Britain usually came for trial to Westminster Hall to be heard by the Court of King's Bench. This was what had happened after the 1745 rebellion, and why should the *Gaspée* raiders be treated any differently? Although King's Bench rarely tried a colonial defendant, it certainly had the power to do so if an impartial jury could not be found near the scene of the crime. A judge in Westminster could send his writ anywhere in the empire if justice and the king required it. If this were not so, how could the Crown and Parliament be sovereign? The empire would not be an empire if the royal judges could not enforce the law throughout the king's dominions.[12]

Far more than merely legal subtleties, these questions went to the very heart of the divisions between the mother country and its colonies. By this time, the political debate in North America had far outgrown the narrow subject of taxation. Could the British be trusted to preserve any of the civil liberties the colonies had come to cherish? Or did they mean to do away with them all, including the right to due process of law? If this were so, Americans would have no alternative but the pursuit of independence; a chain of reasoning which, by the end of 1772, had come to seem compelling, in the light of the British response to the *Gaspée* incident. By choosing to bring the raiders home for trial—always assuming that they could be caught—North and his colleagues took these questions out of the realm of theory and made them topics for urgent, practical discussion in America.

In the colonies, it was universally agreed that justice required a trial by a jury made up of one's peers, which could only mean men from the same town or county. It would be a flagrant breach of civil liberties to ship a suspect away to face a hostile English court, packed with loyal supporters of King George. And so, when the newspapers in America revealed that the British intended to do precisely that, the story caused outrage, especially in Virginia, where the news put an end to the peace and quiet that Lord Dunmore had described with such complacency. Two years later, when Thomas Jefferson wrote his first verbal assault against the British, he listed this aspect of their reaction to the *Gaspée* affair among the worst examples of imperial oppression.*

Did the cabinet know how much trouble they might cause? Almost certainly not. At the meeting on August 20, the use of force was mentioned only in passing, and no one suggested revoking Rhode Island's charter. Instead they tried to make the Americans take responsibility for pursuing the traitors. Acting cautiously, or so they thought, the cabinet chose to appoint a commission of inquiry, led by Governor Wanton and composed of the senior judges from Massachusetts, New Jersey, and New

---

* In his *Summary View of the Rights of British America*, written in August 1774. In the Declaration of Independence, Jefferson made the same point even more forcibly, accusing George III of "depriving us ... of the benefits of Trial by Jury ... transporting us beyond Seas to be tried for pretended offences."

York. Nobody would be arrested until the commission in Newport heard all the evidence the navy had gathered about the *Gaspée*'s destruction.

Off went John Pownall to draw up a dispatch to Rhode Island for Dartmouth to sign; but here again the British miscalculated. By the time the letter was ready, two weeks later, another report had arrived from Admiral Montagu, pointing the finger at the Browns of Providence. And so, when the dispatch left England in the middle of September 1772, it was couched in a tone of uncompromising harshness. It was, wrote Dartmouth, "his Majesty's firm resolution" to punish the guilty men with the utmost severity. Worse still, the dispatch contained a threat to send the redcoats into Rhode Island to suppress any riots that might follow an attempt to arrest the raiders.[13]

Knowing little about the internal workings of Rhode Island, the inexperienced Lord Dartmouth meant the letter to be private, as though Joseph Wanton were a royal appointee. Once again, a gulf of ignorance divided the two nations. A man elected to his post, a close friend of Stephen Hopkins's and a partner of the Browns, Wanton could not possibly keep the letter confidential. It appeared in print for every American to read and inflamed the situation still further. By the end of the year Britain's clumsy response to the *Gaspée* affair had backfired and helped to create the atmosphere of deep distrust that produced the Boston Tea Party.

This blunder about the dispatch was one of many errors that Lord Dartmouth would commit. But Americans, including Benjamin Franklin, made their own mistakes that were equally damaging. They began by misreading Dartmouth's character. Franklin once called him "a truly good man," and so he was. William Legge had some detractors, but he made no lasting enemies. When the king asked a Scottish visitor his opinion, he called Lord Dartmouth agreeable, enchanting, and a perfect Christian. On both sides of the Atlantic, it was widely expected that he would take the path of reconciliation with the colonies. His appointment, it was thought, might signify a change of tack and lead to policies intended to bring about a lasting settlement of American grievances. This proved to be a sad illusion.[14]

Lord Dartmouth's benevolence is not in doubt. When a clergyman friend lay dying, he nursed the invalid with ass's milk, and he always gave money freely to support those in distress. The outbreak of the war left him heartbroken. When Dartmouth learned of Britain's Pyrrhic victory at the battle of Bunker Hill, all he could do was mourn what he called "the melancholy loss" of so many officers and men. But for all his piety and kindness, he too retained a core of damaging conservatism.

In order to prevent the final rift with America, Dartmouth would have had to break with his colleagues, with North and with the king, and take an independent path of his own. This was something he could never do because, for all his virtues, Dartmouth remained a captive of the system that had made him what he was. Tragically, this fine and gentle Christian who hated the thought of fighting came to be one of those most responsible for the war. In 1775, Lord Dartmouth wrote the dispatch from Whitehall that sent the redcoats up the road to Lexington and Concord.[15]

A QUIET MAN

From his portrait by Gainsborough, Dartmouth gazes out at us with mild serenity. Slender, almost austere, with a long, thin face and a high forehead, he stands tall and upright, dressed with impeccable neatness. With hands folded over his walking stick, he looks like a connoisseur fresh from his picture gallery or his arboretum. Turned slightly away from the viewer, he also seems oddly shy and distant: a sensitive man, detached from the sordid world of politics.

As the war with America drew near, the colonial secretary wrote a thick bundle of letters to his eldest son, an undergraduate at Oxford. Sent to accompany baskets of food and wine, each one contained wise counsel from a loving father. They give us an intimate picture of Lord Dartmouth. "I want you to be everything that can be desired, in a man & a Christian," he told the boy. Lay down rules for your life, and take them from the very source of wisdom. Pray, and read the scriptures. Be polite, be civil, be methodical, and be exact. Most of all have faith in God. Drink to be sociable but never to excess, and carefully avoid any hint of impropriety: this was his advice. "Be very resolute and steadfast, in shewing your disgust with everything licentious," Dartmouth wrote, as his son prepared to leave for a European tour. "Never think it can be a credit, to deal in ribaldry, profaneness or satire."[16]

These were strange words to address to a young man on his way to Paris. Thirty years later, people would think it normal for a peer of the realm to be devout, when after 1800 religious aristocrats such as Dartmouth came into their own as respected advocates of temperance and charity. In the early years of the reign of George III, he stood out as an eccentric. For the moment evangelical faith remained a minority pursuit in England, despite the best efforts of John Wesley. It was almost unheard of in the peerage. Paying tribute in verse to Lord Dartmouth, his friend the poet William Cowper called him "one who wears a coronet and prays," as if this were

William Legge, second Earl of Dartmouth, painted in 1769 by Thomas
Gainsborough. *The Dartmouth Heirloom Trustees*

unusual, and it truly was. Dartmouth did not fornicate or gamble. In an
era when both sins were routine, people did not know what to make of
him. Talking about him, they dealt in clichés, of the kind we use when we
understand nothing about the person concerned.

When Dartmouth joined the cabinet in 1772, a few opponents of Lord
North grumbled about nepotism, but most observers welcomed the choice.
The newspapers liked the new colonial secretary, but they described him
in generalities of little value. As one writer put it, Dartmouth was "universally acknowledged to be possessed of good abilities, and the firmest

integrity." Sent across the ocean, bland phrases such as these created expectations that he could not meet.[17]

In America it was widely known that he had helped to fund a new missionary school at Hanover, New Hampshire, which later became Dartmouth College. Americans also recalled his spell as a junior minister, with some responsibility for the colonies, in the short-lived government led by the Marquess of Rockingham, which did away with the Stamp Act. Since Lord Dartmouth had voted for repeal, many Americans took him for a sympathetic friend. They simply did not know the man, and because few scholars have looked at him closely, the same mistake has often been repeated. Dartmouth's horizons were very narrow. He could no more devise a lasting way to keep America than he could give away all he possessed and live as a hermit in a cave. Like so many British statesmen down the ages, from all points on the political spectrum, Dartmouth confused the New Testament's teachings with those of his own social class or party.

His most obvious flaw was unworldliness. His father had died very young, and so Dartmouth became a peer in his late teens, inheriting the title from his grandfather. He never endured the salutary rough-and-tumble of the House of Commons. After his marriage in 1755, he spent a decade in seclusion with his wife until his brief period as a minister under Rockingham. That only lasted thirteen months before he retired for another six years until North invited him to join the cabinet. A reluctant statesman, Dartmouth rarely spoke in the House of Lords, and when he did, he made a poor impression: "ill-delivered and formal" was the verdict of one listener. When the storm broke in America, even if he wished to make a case for peace he could not compete with confident hawks like Lord Sandwich.[18]

Another source of weakness was this: the bond of affection that tied Lord Dartmouth so firmly to his stepbrother. Boyhood friends, born just a year apart, William Legge and Frederick North always remained close. At Oxford they composed Latin hexameters beneath the same tutor. They traveled together to Europe to finish their education, and after that they saw each other frequently.* They exchanged a host of messages, worry-

---

* For convenience the two men were usually referred to as stepbrothers, but their relationship was a little more complicated than usual. Dartmouth's father died in 1732, leaving a widow, Elizabeth Legge, Lady Lewisham. Then Lord North's father, Lord Guilford, became a widower when his first wife (North's mother) died in 1734. Two years after that, Guilford became Lord Dartmouth's stepfather, when he married Lady Lewisham. The marriage ended with her death in 1745.

ing about their children and their wives, about toothache, smallpox, and miscarriages. When Lord North married his Somerset heiress, Dartmouth acted as a trustee of the marriage settlement, and he did the same again when Brownlow North found his lady from the Caribbean.

Neither Lord North nor Lord Dartmouth was crudely self-seeking: both had ideals, especially William Legge. Every friendship between men of their rank, however, amounted to a kind of military alliance in pursuit of influence and status. Aristocrats by birth and by vocation—nobility was a career at which men and women had to work—they spent their lives trying to make their families secure at the apex of the social pyramid. Lord Dartmouth and Lord North did so more gracefully than most of their contemporaries, but even so it was still their primary aim. They could never afford to be controversial, because within the hierarchy of the peerage they ranked only in the second or third quartile. Far from being ancient feudal dynasties, the Legges and the Norths had acquired their titles less than a century earlier. In the 1680s North's great-grandfather had made a fortune as a brilliant lawyer and a judge under Charles II, becoming the first Lord Guilford. His son soon lost the family money by living beyond his means and failing in business ventures overseas. By the time he died in 1729, all the North estates were financially embarrassed, not only their principal seat at Wroxton, but other estates they had acquired by marriage. It took another sixty years to clear all the family debts: a long source of worry to Lord North and his father.

As for the Legges, their claim to nobility dated from the same era, a reward for devoted service in the Stuart navy. James II made Admiral Legge a baron, an honor that proved inconvenient when the king fled into exile. The new king William III confined the first Lord Dartmouth to the Tower of London, where he died of an apoplectic fit. Thereafter the Legges chose to keep to themselves, making only brief, inoffensive forays into politics. They owned property in Staffordshire and close to London, at Blackheath and Kentish Town, but they did not figure among the nation's greatest proprietors.

And so when they came home from their European tour in 1754, the two young noblemen had to think very carefully about the future. To rise within the aristocracy, first they had to find partners, but although they married well, they did not marry brilliantly. Anne Speke, the future Lady North, brought with her a gentleman's estate, but rents were low in Somerset, and before the wedding, the pliable Lord North agreed to pay his father a subsidy of more than £2,000 each year, to help fund the family liabilities. With such a burden to support, he was often desperate for cash, obliged at times to scour the streets of London in search of a money lender. Meanwhile, Lord Dartmouth had married Miss Frances Gunter Nicholl, an heiress from Yorkshire, but her fortune was smaller than it seemed. Remote and in need of repair, when combined with his own her estates produced an annual income of only £4,000: comfortable but modest compared with the rent roll of a duke.[19]

As any reader of Jane Austen knows, vexatious matters such as these lay uppermost in the minds of Georgian men and women. A peer might have his title, but without an endowment of wealth he could not hope to thrive. Both North and Dartmouth had to make the best of what they had. North turned to public life, where he strove hard to succeed, not only for the salary he might earn—something he urgently required—but also for the prestige his success might confer. For lack of resources, the Norths could afford to bribe the voters of only one Oxfordshire borough, the parliamentary seat at Banbury, close to Wroxton. Banbury always sent Lord North to the House of Commons without an opponent daring to stand against him; but once elected, he had to learn the deeper art of politics and how to climb the greasy pole without the support of money.

For his part, Lord Dartmouth retired to his estates, which he began to nurse back to health, and here he enjoyed a piece of luck. His country seat was at Sandwell, very close to Birmingham, a town swiftly becoming a hub of industry. As the years passed, Dartmouth made friends with the manufacturers, including Matthew Boulton, using his influence to help them win patents for their inventions. Dartmouth was never an entrepreneur, but he did well enough. As Birmingham and London grew, the price of land around them rose as well, enriching families like the Legges who owned estates nearby.

For both men, however, the arrival of George III on the throne in 1760 proved to be an even greater stroke of good fortune. As children North and the king had played together, at a time when Lord Guilford was close to Frederick, Prince of Wales, who was George's father. In itself, this did not count for much: deeply committed to protocol, George III would not promote a politician simply because of boyhood affection. But for a host of reasons, Dartmouth and North gradually became essential members of the royal entourage. Bright and lively, the young king and queen needed friends like themselves. They preferred the company of well-bred men and women of a particular type. They had to be deferential but not dull, funny but never undignified, and clever but not arrogant, with a deep interest, like the royal couple's, in theater, music, and the visual arts.

Among his closest confidants, the king counted his master of the robes,

James Brudenell, a courtier with exactly those qualifications. A close friend and neighbor of the Norths', and brother of the Earl of Cardigan, Jemmy Brudenell came from one of the wealthiest families in England. In 1760, he married Anne Legge, Lord Dartmouth's sister: a splendid match, which drew the Dartmouths and the Norths into the inner circle of the court. Their own social skills and happy marriages made them all the more acceptable to a sovereign keen to uphold morality as well as taste.[20]

By 1772 their ties to the royal family were very close indeed, with North's political talents making them all the deeper. And in the eyes of George III, both he and his stepbrother possessed another crucial asset. They were faithful sons of Oxford University, which meant that they were equally devoted to the Church of England. A pious man, the king worried endlessly about the danger posed to orthodox religion by free-thinkers, skeptics, Unitarians, and Baptists. In Lord Dartmouth and Lord North, he found two allies in the cause of the established church. Deeply grateful, the king did what he could to reward them. While North's two Treasury salaries, as chancellor of the exchequer and First Lord, totaled £5,600 a year, transforming his financial position and making him all the more determined to remain in office, his half brother Brownlow became a prince among bishops, promoted by the king to one fat diocese after another. And when Dartmouth's younger sister married a Mr. Keene, who was short of funds, the king gave the couple rooms in Windsor Castle. Soon after the *Gaspée* incident, the family achieved another great mark of distinction. At Oxford, the university chose Lord North as chancellor, knowing that he enjoyed the full support of George III.

In London, the Keenes, Legges, Brudenells, and Norths were insepa-rable friends. Their social world was small and held together by mutual esteem and by their loyalty to a monarch who did so much to help them. In a milieu such as this, it would be difficult for anyone to develop original ideas, and especially so for Lord Dartmouth because of the kind of Chris-tian faith he held. It colored every facet of his life, including the decisions he took about America. His religion was sincere and even admirable; but it left him blind to the meanings other people might give to freedom.

What did he believe? Commentators often called him a Methodist, and for a while in his youth that was a fair description. As newlyweds, Lord and Lady Dartmouth fell deeply under the influence of John Wesley's friend and rival, the great evangelist George Whitefield. From Whitefield they acquired two things: an emotional faith in Jesus Christ, intense and highly charged, but also a theology steeped in obedience to the powers that were.[21]

Today, if we remember Whitefield at all, we do so because of his mission to America in the 1740s. Young and dynamic, he traveled up and down the eastern seaboard helping to lead the gospel revival known as the Great Awakening. Later, at home in England, Whitefield began a project to evangelize the nation from above by winning over members of the aristocracy. With Wesley beside him he roamed the salons of London, looking for enthusiastic converts. Their message mostly fell on stony ground, but not with the Dartmouths, who ranked among Whitefield's most devout adherents. Flouting convention, in 1757 they invited him to their summer home at Cheltenham, where, to the outrage of the local parson, the Dartmouths held their own awakening. From the countryside the crowds flocked in, sobbing, fainting, and hysterical. When the parson locked the door of the parish church, Whitefield jumped up on a tombstone to preach from the book of Isaiah.

Technically, this kind of thing probably broke the law; and so despite his sympathy for Methodism, Lord Dartmouth gradually returned to the formal structures of religion. By 1772 he had become the sponsor of a small group of clergymen who formed a new evangelical wing inside the Church of England. With Sunday schools, prayer meetings, and mission work with soldiers and the poor, they built a wide following. With names like Henry Venn, William Romaine, and Martin Madan, these Anglican ministers were regarded as some of the finest preachers of their day. When American visitors came to London, they would hurry down to St. Ann Blackfriars to hear the word of God from Mr. Romaine.

Lord Dartmouth never wavered from the creed these pastors taught. Like his mentor Whitefield, the new evangelicals were Calvinists. In their eyes, human beings were sinful and degenerate, and the English were a nation on the brink of doom. "Beware of the general corruption of the times," wrote a young chaplain, Madan's assistant, who was one of Dartmouth's protégés. Beset by greed and atheism, the kingdom lay abject at the feet of Satan. For Dartmouth, the evidence was plain to see in the whores who thronged the streets of London. Every week he attended the chapel at an institution known as the Lock Hospital. Located near Hyde Park Corner, it cared for prostitutes afflicted by venereal disease, and for child victims of rape. It was an unpopular charity, but Lord Dartmouth sat on the hospital's board of patrons. From the pulpit of the chapel, the clergymen he chose proclaimed the urgent need for a rebirth of the spirit. In his letters to his son, William Legge expressed the very same beliefs. "Your acquaintance with mankind will serve to show you the depravity into which we are fallen," he wrote. Only one thing could rescue the sinner: redemption by the saving power of Jesus.[22]

Long before the phrase came into use, the Dartmouths were born-again Christians. For them, the defining moment in their lives came like a thunderclap when all at once they felt the overwhelming love of God and knew that they were saved. As the years flowed by, so the English upper classes became increasingly receptive to theology of such a kind. By the time Lord Dartmouth died at the turn of the century, the evangelical movement had ceased to be marginal. Instead, it became a powerful force within the Church of England, with William Legge among the men and women who did the most to bring this about.

At its best, the movement could produce a hero like William Wilberforce, the antislavery campaigner. A fellow traveler with Dartmouth, he also knelt in prayer at the chapel of the Lock. At its worst, the evangelical revival merely reinforced a harsh social order based on inequality and coercion. In the eyes of the new evangelicals, men and women sinned the most when they disobeyed the rulers whom God placed above them. Believing as he did that human beings were depraved, Dartmouth stood not only for charity, but also for law and order and the severest retribution for sinners who were unredeemed. Apart from Lord North, his closest friend among the laity was a hanging judge called Baron Smythe, another patron of the hospital for whores. When Smythe sent a thief to the gallows, said the minister who preached his eulogy, he would accompany the sentence with "pious and pathetic exhortations." From the bench, he would remind the felon of the "only Refuge and Hope for a guilty Creature: the blood of Christ."[23]

And so in William Legge we see a complicated Christian full of the contradictions that Christianity so often entails. While Dartmouth believed in humility, and acted accordingly in his personal life, he also enjoyed the benefits of privilege and power. Although he preached a gospel of love, he issued the instructions that began a war. Dartmouth spoke about the majesty of God while enjoying the earthly favor of King George. Deeply committed to Lord North, he could not break with him or with his colleagues. An earl committed to the king's authority, how could he understand a colonial farmer, a Virginian with a rifle and a Bible of his own? From Lord Dartmouth's point of view, Americans who questioned British rule were human souls tainted by the sin of pride. And so, for all his goodness, the ambiguous faith of William Legge helped to shape his disastrous policy toward the colonies.

A moment would come, early in 1775, when Benjamin Franklin suddenly realized that Dartmouth could do nothing more for America. Franklin had been slow to understand the minister, but when at last he saw things as they were, the scientist knew that revolution was inevitable. At that point he left for Philadelphia. But in the autumn of 1772 nobody in London foresaw an American crisis so deep that it would end in bloodshed. Other matters filled the pages of the press and Lord North's agenda.

In November the cabinet's old enemy John Wilkes came close to winning the annual poll to choose a lord mayor: another warning of the dangers of democracy. Meanwhile, the plight of the East India Company cast a still longer shadow. As the company slid toward a precipice, the government was obliged to intervene in its affairs. At the time George III felt that Lord North handled it all rather well.

Part Two

THE SENDING
OF THE TEA

Chapter Six

THE EAST INDIA CRISIS

Money was never so scarce in the metropolis as at this moment.

—A LONDON NEWSPAPER, OCTOBER 1772[1]

For a generation, men and women would recall the long, dry summer of 1772, but at last in late August the weather broke. Torrents of rain began to fall at the worst possible moment, when the crops still stood high in the fields. On the night of September 24 a tempest swept in from the sea across the south of England, breaking roofs and ravaging the orchards filled with apples. Lord North had taken a family holiday at his little country house at Dillington, near Ilminster, but he remained in Somerset for only two weeks before he was recalled to the capital.

It was the custom at the time for Parliament to reassemble in November to begin the new session with the annual vote on the budget for the armed forces. Without any imminent threat of war, North had hoped he might postpone the sitting until after Christmas. By the time he reached Downing Street in the first week of October, he knew that so long a delay would be very unwise. From every side, urgent matters required a response, but they also offered opportunities to steal a march on his political enemies, which North was keen to do. He might be indecisive as regards grand strategy, but no one surpassed him in the art of maneuver. He arrived in London ready to put his skills to work.[2]

"Things both at home and abroad are in a critical situation," wrote one of his opponents in the Commons, Edmund Burke. For once, despite his habit of overstating every case he made with brilliant rhetoric that often hid a lack of rigor, Burke was entirely correct. Thanks to the Bank of

England and the Scottish dukes, the financial panic of the summer had gradually subsided. But while the system had survived the acute stage of the fever, the patient remained very sick. In Europe the price of grain soared to reach levels not seen in fifty years, raising the specter of peasant revolt in Sicily and in the north of France. In Britain the banks were still fragile and the recession had sent the number of insolvencies to new heights. Since a poor harvest took six months or more to make its full impact by way of scarcity, it was likely that 1773 would witness deeper hardship. In the East End of London sailors were threatening to riot against a cut in their wages, and in Scotland the unemployed seemed likely to follow suit.[3]

As more news arrived from Sweden and Poland, Lord Rochford continued to sound the alarm. The French, he said, were still readying their fleet, to defend the Swedes or to strike at India. In either case, Britain would have to reply with force. Politics at home supplied another reason for anxiety. It was election time in London, "this immense, unruly town," as one member of the House of Lords described it, alerting the cabinet to signs of trouble on the streets. North did not worry unduly about that kind of thing: one summer evening the previous year, a mob had marched on Downing Street and smashed his windows, an incident he simply shrugged aside. But this time he could not ignore the evidence of disaffection that might give John Wilkes a sweeping victory at the polls.[4]

No British government wanted to see a political opponent as lord mayor of London. If he wished, a mayor might devote himself to brandy, pomp, and ceremony, but if he chose to defy the king and the ministers, he had the power to do so. From the Old Bailey, the mayor and his two sheriffs administered the criminal justice system, not only for the city proper, the old Square Mile, but also for the surrounding county of Middlesex. Newgate Prison fell under their jurisdiction, and any warrant to arrest or search a suspect required their consent. If John Wilkes was elected as lord mayor, the city would become his fiefdom, with his friends taking turns to serve as sheriffs or succeed him as chief magistrate. Secure in his control of London, Wilkes might try to build a new radical faction in Parliament as well.

In three years' time, in the spring of 1775, a general election was due, and already North was making preparations, meeting likely candidates, and trying to ensure that every safe seat went to his supporters. Lose the metropolis, and by inches he would start to lose his reputation and his usefulness to George III. A new phrase, "public opinion," had entered the language in the 1740s to refer to the prevailing mood of the country. In exceptional circumstances, public opinion could even topple an administration. If members of the press decided that a man was weak or unpatriotic, they could destroy him with a relentless campaign of ridicule and innuendo. In living memory, two chief ministers had fallen in this way.

Might the same fate befall Lord North? Fleet Street could not do without his antagonist John Wilkes, an endless source of mischief and amusement. By 1772 Londoners could choose from among nineteen newspapers, with a daily sale between them of as many as thirty thousand copies and a total readership of perhaps ten times that number. Whatever appeared in the London press was swiftly reproduced in the provinces and then relayed to America as well. It was essential, therefore, to prevent Wilkes from winning victories that, as time went by, would undermine respect for authority. Allow the press to make Wilkes a hero again, and North's own position might become untenable.[5]

Suddenly Wilkes made his play for power. As North arrived back at Downing Street, the electors began to gather at London's Guildhall, holding a series of polls to choose the new mayor. About nine thousand citizens were qualified to vote, making the city of London the nearest thing Great Britain had to a popular government. Often, an inner circle of aldermen found a way to fix the result in favor of a candidate with whom the king and his ministers were happy. So they had done in the past, but for nearly three years, since he lost his fight to take his seat in the Commons, Wilkes had been busy organizing a political machine.

As each vote was taken, his support increased. When the polls closed on October 6, fewer than half the voters had opted for candidates loyal to the king and the cabinet. John Wilkes emerged as the winner. North and the king looked on with gloomy irritation, but as yet they saw no cause to panic. They assumed that Wilkes had won by means of fraud, and so, they believed, his margin of victory would disappear when the aldermen scrutinized the ballot.

This was another miscalculation. A demagogue, an adulterer, and even perhaps a perverted infidel, Wilkes stood for everything that George III feared and despised. Lord North felt the same, but their hatred of the man led them to underestimate his talents as a politician. Nor could they see the breadth of genuine support that Wilkes commanded from thinking people on both sides of the Atlantic. A devious self-promoter who trusted only a few close friends and fell out with many of his allies, Wilkes could never build a lasting political movement. But he did have qualities and gifts—courage, intellect, and a brilliant flair for publicity—that in the short run made him a formidable foe. Even uglier than Lord North, he was fully his equal as a Latin scholar. But as the son of a wealthy distiller from Clerkenwell, Wilkes knew London more thoroughly than any cabinet minister could hope to do. For a few short years, he led a broad urban coalition composed of men and women longing for change.

A year earlier, Wilkes and his entourage had drawn up a program for democratic reform. At its heart lay a fierce critique of Parliament and of the small elite who seemed to hold the reins of power with an iron grip. In fact North never felt like a man in firm control, and his colleagues were too selfish to form an entirely solid bloc. But when Wilkes gave a speech at the Guildhall hustings in 1772 calling Parliament "a Senate composed chiefly of hirelings and slaves," his audience knew what he meant. As a way to cleanse the stable of corruption, the Wilkesites called for annual elections, a law against bribery at the polls, and another law to bar the king's officials from sitting in the Commons. At their most radical, they called for "a full and equal representation of the people." This phrase could mean many things, but it would definitely include an end to tame little boroughs like Lord North's seat at Banbury. It might also imply a wide extension of the franchise and a vote for every householder.[6]

The Wilkesite program had a wide appeal. Shopkeepers voted for Wilkes, but so did skilled artisans, attorneys, West India merchants, and traders who did business with America. Not least, he had the backing of religious dissenters, Baptists, Presbyterians, and the like. While their strongest support lay in the eastern districts of London, from Aldgate out to Hackney and Mile End, the dissenters formed a spiderweb of nonconformity, spun across the nation. They had close ties with like-minded people in seaports and commercial towns, places like Newcastle, Bristol, and even Taunton, in Lord North's own backyard in Somerset, where the dissenters were especially troublesome. These were towns that, like the city of London, might choose to send a Wilkesite to the House of Commons.

Given the way the British system worked, the Wilkesites could not hope to win more than a handful of seats at the general election. But even so, they could cause trouble for Lord North and make him worry for the future. They could also reach out across the Atlantic and help to incite a still more powerful movement of resistance. A bond of sympathy aligned the Wilkesites with the patriot opposition in America, not only in Charleston, but also in Virginia and New England. From the colonies, men and women followed the politics of London with keen attention, and nowhere more so than in Boston, where the radicals held the same attitudes to God and to authority. The patriot leader Samuel Adams—a failure in business, a very incompetent collector of taxes, but a fiery journalist and a superb politician—had two American contacts in London, Arthur and William

Lee from Virginia. Both men belonged to Wilkes's inner circle. An even tighter connection existed between the Wilkesites and Adams's Boston ally John Hancock. As his business agent in London, Hancock used a leading merchant, George Hayley, a man from Presbyterian roots who lived in Aldgate among the chapels of the brethren. Wilkes was his brother-in-law.[7]

Whenever John Wilkes scored a political point, his admirers in America saw it as an extra reason to defy the empire. His every victory, including the mayoral election, echoed around the Boston waterfront. The British cabinet knew that this was so—the press cuttings from the colonies often spoke of little else—but they did not appreciate its full significance. In due course the Lees would act as instigators of rebellion, but this was still two years away. While they were known to the authorities, the extent of their activities would only become fully visible in 1774. In the meantime, Lord North and his colleagues had little inkling of how effective the Lees could be. As far as they were concerned, America remained a secondary issue at the most. At the top of their list of woes lay the East India Company.

DISTRESSED IN POINT OF CASH

For more than a year the market for tea had been nearing the point of collapse. In the autumn of 1772 the moment finally arrived. In July, Captain Thomson had reached the Thames with the *Calcutta* and the tea she loaded in Canton. By the end of August, another nineteen ships lay moored around her in the river, beaten by the weather but still safe. They carried between them ninety thousand chests of tea, twice as much as British drinkers of the legal product consumed in the course of a year. A huge overhang of unsold tea still remained from the previous season. When the auctions began in September, the price of Bohea fell by 20 percent.[8]

Even then the East India Company could still turn a profit from its tea, but not enough to meet all the claims upon it. The company's coffers of cash were all but empty, its debts were enormous, and in the wake of the banking crisis it was impossible to borrow any more. From all sides the company faced demands for cash from its creditors, many of them desperate for money as the recession continued.

The moment the ships dropped anchor, the owners sent in their invoices for wages and transit, but the company could not even pay the bills left over from 1771, let alone meet the expense of the fleet that had just returned, the largest it had ever sent to China. The Treasury, meanwhile, submitted

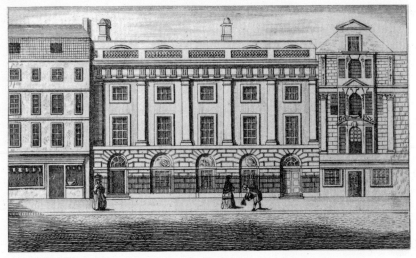

The East India Company's headquarters in Leadenhall Street, on the site now occupied by Lloyd's of London, from an engraving dated 1777.

huge demands of its own for the customs duties owing from the tea sales in the spring. In addition, the government wanted twice as much again to cover another huge liability incurred by the company. In 1766, after the news from Robert Clive about the grant of the land tax in Bengal, the *diwan*, the government had demanded a cut for itself. Reluctantly, the company paid a hefty tribute to the Crown, but as a quid pro quo it asked for some tax relief. And so, for five years, as we saw earlier, the government slashed the duty on tea as a way to beat the smugglers who were stealing the company's business. But the Treasury added a proviso: the company had to promise to make up any shortfall in the revenue owing to the king.

In the autumn of 1772, the bill fell due for that as well. In a normal year, the company would have released a torrent of cash from the auctions in March; but credit was now so scarce in London that the dealers could not pay for the tea they had bought. This was bad enough, but the news from Asia was even worse. The ships coming home from India brought with them the Bengal bills, coming to more than £1 million, payable to bankers, merchants, and old soldiers in London, including Clive, who wanted their money without delay.

To put it bluntly: the East India Company was very nearly broke. The company can be accused of many things, but nobody could fault its record keeping. Its books and ledgers survive, in impeccable calligraphy and bound in red leather, recording every item down to the last penny and rupee. When all the figures are added up, we find that the company needed £3 million to pay all the borrowings due in the next twelve months. Its ready assets, by way of cash, debtors, and stock on the shelves, came to little more than half that sum. In the twenty-first century, we have become accustomed to seeing financial institutions go down to ruin, with liabilities almost beyond comprehension. In 1772 men and women expressed the same outrage and anger.

In the middle of September, while North was still in Somerset, the price of the company's stock began to drop. On the eighteenth the fall became a crash. And then, just before the great gale came in off the Channel, the company assembled its shareholders to break the bad news. The chairman, Sir George Colebrooke, admitted at last that the company was "distressed in point of cash." Even now he would not reveal the numbers: he simply warned of a delay to the next dividend.

A visitor once called the company's shareholders' meetings "the most riotous assembly I have ever seen." The session at noon on the twenty-third lasted four acrimonious hours. From the floor William Crichton leaped up to vilify the board with the relentless eloquence that earned him the title "orator Crichton." Time and again he had warned the company that it was running fast to ruin, and time and again he had been brushed aside. He demanded the creation of a new committee, made up of nine independent men, to investigate misconduct by the board.[9]

The meeting ended with Colebrooke, John Purling, and Laurence Sulivan still in control. Bloody but unbowed, Crichton withdrew to rally support and return to the fray at the next opportunity. During the fierce exchanges, he had won a tactical victory when Colebrooke was forced to reveal that negotiations were under way with the Treasury about a plan to rescue the company with public money. In fact this was another of Sir George's fibs—Lord North was still on holiday, and no talks had begun—but from that moment the plight of the company became a political as well as a financial question.

With each passing day the crisis grew deeper. For working capital between each sale of tea and silk, the East India Company relied on loans from the Bank of England. But the bank itself was under heavy pressure. Since Fordyce disappeared, gold had been draining away from its vaults, as worried men and women asked for bullion in exchange for notes. And while the bank tried to keep credit flowing by lending money to firms it thought worth saving, it became ever more uneasy about its own exposure to East India House.

On Monday, October 5, the Bank of England met the company to discuss its overdraft of £600,000. Wary of Colebrooke and suspicious of the company's accounts, the bank asked for first call on any cash that flowed from its sales of tea. In the future it would only give the company what it called "reasonable temporary assistance," which meant no more than £100,000. The bank set a deadline of December for the rest to be repaid. That evening Lord North wrote another anguished letter to his father, telling him that Parliament had to be recalled. Everywhere, the news was "very unpleasant," he wrote. "There are vexations enough in my office to make me melancholy, amidst all the honours I receive."

The following day, October 6, a deputation arrived from Oxford University to make him its chancellor, but dinner was scarcely over when they heard that Wilkes had topped the final poll for mayor. On the seventh North assembled his inner cabinet to be given Rochford's dire assessment of the risk of war. Keen though they were to avoid hostilities, they drafted a strongly worded note to be sent to Paris, warning the French that if their fleet entered the Baltic, then Britain would send its navy in pursuit.

Next morning Lord North held a first frustrating session with Sir George, who had done so much to wreck the company's affairs. At first glance, it might be thought that North and Colebrooke belonged to the same privileged elite, but in fact they had almost nothing in common. A deep divide of social class and attitudes fell between a peer of the realm and the nouveaux riches of East India House. "The damned East India Company," Lord Rochford called it, speaking for the rest of the landed aristocracy, who rarely owned more than token amounts of its stock.[10]

In an age of gambling, noblemen had many ways to lose their wealth, betting on a horse or on a game of cards, but they usually kept their distance from the company. Only one cabinet member, Lord Sandwich, took a personal interest in its affairs. About a third of the company's stock actually belonged to foreigners, chiefly from the Netherlands. In England, most of the largest holders were merchants in London, old India hands like Clive, or men like Colebrooke, and he was little better than a vulgar parvenu. Sir George ran his own overextended bank, and he was one of those speculators who bought land in Scotland and Grenada at the very peak of the boom.[11]

Like Brownlow North, he married an heiress from Antigua, but his resemblance to the Norths ended at that. Dr. Johnson's friend Mrs. Thrale knew the Colebrookes well, and she drew a fine little sketch of his personality. Sir George was a "pretty little Dapper Man," always dressed in the height of fashion, she wrote; in his green coat and white waistcoat he looked "like a Leg of Lamb & Spinach." Despite his wealth, Colebrooke never seemed to have cash to spare. When he attended a fund-raising party, he had an annoying habit of borrowing a guinea to give away. But the thing that struck Mrs. Thrale most forcibly was the sheer scale of his extravagance: "His Wife was covered with Jewels, his Children harassed with variety of Masters, he bought pictures of great Value, & all was Rapacity, and all was Profusion."[12]

And so Sir George could not expect an ounce of sympathy from the nation's leaders. When American historians describe the events that led to the Boston Tea Party, they sometimes assume that the king and his ministers were keen to help the East India Company, or even that North and his colleagues shared in its corruption. In fact George III disliked the company intensely. A monarch of simple tastes who lit his own fire in the morning, dressed like a country squire, and went to bed by eleven, the king believed that the best parts of the nation were the farmers. In his eyes, speculators like Colebrooke could never speak for an England with honest agriculture at its heart. In language similar to Mrs. Thrale's, the king used the word "rapine" to describe the misconduct that brought the East India Company to its knees. Although Lord North expressed himself more dip-lomatically, he viewed the directors with the same distaste.[13]

Far from being eager to assist them, the king and his friends believed that the company's wounds were self-inflicted. Only with reluctance did they open negotiations about a scheme to save it. At the meeting on Octo-ber 8, Colebrooke bluntly told Lord North that the company could not pay its debts, including, of course, the money it owed the Treasury. In itself, this was not disastrous, because the tax collector in Great Britain always took the first slice of what remained when a company went down. In extremity, Lord North could seize every pound of tea and every yard of silk in the warehouse. However, for a multitude of reasons the cabinet felt obliged to intervene, and not least because India might fall to France.

However woefully the company had administered Bengal, a province so rich in potential could not be abandoned, and a bankrupt company could not sustain the Bengal army. As for the China trade, the taxes levied on the tea it brought home came to about £800,000 a year, about 7 percent of the government's income. If the East India Company went down, En-glish families would still drink the beverage and pay the duty, but once the warehouse was empty, who would finance voyages to Canton? The French and the Dutch might step in, increase their own traffic to the East, and flood Britain and the colonies with still more smuggled tea. Indeed the *Public Advertiser* carried a report from Amsterdam saying that the Dutch were loading naval stores and munitions to be sent to their posts at Cape

Town and in Java. The wider threat to the British economy left the cabinet all the more perplexed. With trade already so depressed, the company's failure might deliver an irreparable blow. With their connections with the mill owners in the Midlands, Lord Dartmouth and Lord Gower knew just how bad things were, as gloomy letters arrived from Matthew Boulton about the blight that afflicted Birmingham.

One last consideration was political. However bleak the situation might appear, at least it gave Lord North an opportunity to force reform on the East India Company. Since the grant of the *diwan*, ministers had come and gone, but each one had followed Indian affairs with increasing anxiety. An enterprise so vital could not be allowed to do exactly as it chose, especially when it scandalized not only the public but also the king. Ever since news arrived of the Bengal famine, the papers had run stories of extortion and suffering in India. Lampooned in the press, Sir George Colebrooke and his friends became objects of hatred, but it was not so easy for the government to intervene.

Because the company had a royal charter, new regulations would require an act of Parliament. Until now, Lord North had been reluctant to try to pass the law required, not least because he might not win the vote. Aloof though the House of Lords might be, fifty members of the House of Commons held the company's stock. Along with the rest of the company's board, Colebrooke sat as a member of Parliament with the power to scatter gifts and favors in the form of remunerative jobs in India. North of the border he did the same. With his new estate in Scotland, Colebrooke aspired to be a local magnate, hovering around the Duke and Duchess of Argyll, who controlled a servile batch of MPs of their own.

In a sense, therefore, the crisis came as a blessing for Lord North, albeit heavily disguised. Gradually, his ideas began to take shape. In return for a loan from the taxpayers, North could defeat Colebrooke and hold the company to ransom. North could demand reform, a say in the running of India, and new directors prepared to listen to Whitehall. But even now, while the Bank of England fumed quietly in the background, Colebrooke prevaricated. Dark rumors had begun to circulate, spread by Crichton and his friends, about the underhand dealings a year before, when the company lied about the Bengal bills and Colebrooke secretly bought stock to keep its price from falling. On October 9, Lord North asked to see all the company's accounts, but it took nearly a month for all the data to arrive.

"Papers are ordered everyday by the Treasury from India House," wrote Edmund Burke, but the figures they contained were confusing and opaque. Twice Lord North had to interrogate the management, at long meetings around the Treasury's boardroom table, before they revealed the truth about their balance sheet. Finally, on November 13, the company came up with a firm number: they would need £540,000 immediately and a great deal more in 1773. By this time, less than two weeks were left before Parliament reassembled on the twenty-sixth, when the company's losses would have to be made public.[14]

Furious with the directors, the king urged Lord North not to compromise about reform. "Any wavering now would be disgraceful to you, and destruction to the public," he told his chief minister. Meanwhile, the atmosphere on the streets had gone from bad to worse. With the price of food still rising steeply, the capital had witnessed another riot, the kind that any rebuff to John Wilkes would inspire. As North and the king had expected, the city aldermen had disqualified enough of Wilkes's votes to stop him from becoming lord mayor. On the evening of November 9, the candidate they chose held his inaugural ball. Led by unemployed seamen, a huge crowd gathered outside the Guildhall. They lit bonfires, stripped the wigs from the heads of guests, and tried to force an entry. "Damn my Lord Mayor for a scoundrel," cried one man. "He has got Wilkes's right, and we shall have him out." The new mayor sallied forth waving his sword while the militia fought back the mob.[15]

As Newgate Prison filled with rioters, the opening of Parliament drew near with the newspapers poring over the company's affairs. Opinion pieces began to appear that advanced ingenious schemes for resolving the crisis. Gradually, they converged around a central theme. Although the company had run out of cash, it had acquired an immense stock of tea, with more due to arrive the following summer. A means must be found to unlock the value of the leaves and release a stream of money to keep the company alive.

From the board, the desperate Laurence Sulivan came up with a plan to float a loan in Amsterdam, with the tea to be used as collateral: a rather lame suggestion, as the largest Dutch banks were also close to failure. An equally hopeless proposal came from Colebrooke, who wanted to ask investors in England for £1.5 million to refinance the business. With money so tight in London this was out of the question. But while these feeble ideas went the rounds, a more practical scheme had begun to emerge. In late September, a writer calling himself "A Fair Consumer" published a letter in the press that made a telling point. In London, wholesale Bohea cost three shillings and four pence a pound. In Amsterdam, where the taxes were tiny, the same packet of tea cost only one shilling and eight pence.

As everyone knew, this situation created the vast black market that ate away at the company's position. The solution was obvious: turn the tables on the Europeans by slashing the price in London to the same low level even if the company took a temporary loss. By flooding the market with cheap tea, the company would drive the smugglers to the wall and cripple its competitors in the China trade.[16]

It was only the germ of an idea, but gradually it evolved into a scheme to send the surplus tea to America. Before it could reach fruition, it would be warped out of shape by intrigue and political maneuver on both sides of the Atlantic. At times the story that follows will resemble an intricate jigsaw puzzle in the style of the rococo, but without it the Boston Tea Party would never have taken place.

Chapter Seven

WHIGS, WEST INDIANS, AND THOMAS HUTCHINSON

It is impossible that I can look with Indifference upon the Prosperity of the East India Company.

—GEORGE III, NOVEMBER 26, 1772[1]

On November 25, George III returned to London from his summer palace at Kew. The following day he opened Parliament. As the weather grew colder, with storms in the Channel keeping the French in their harbors, so the risk of war receded. After such a meager harvest, the government had to find a way to reduce the price of bread—"as far as human wisdom can provide, for alleviating the distresses of the poor," in the words of the king—but the question of India would dominate the session.

Lord North had not yet decided what to do about the company. But politically his hand of cards was strong, and in the months that followed, he would overplay it with a vengeance. For the next nine years, despite his fits of despair, North never lost a debate in the House of Commons on an issue of national policy, whether it concerned India or the colonies or finance. Sometimes a vote would go against him, but never on a subject serious enough to put the government in danger. On the streets the Wilkesites frightened the horses, but in Parliament the official opposition could rarely win a point. They were the Rockingham Whigs. Until the colonies were all but lost, they never broke Lord North's command of the assembly.

At times the Whigs roused themselves to fight with energy and courage, as they did in a series of great debates that preceded the outbreak of the fighting. But those debates took place in 1774–75, after the destruction of the tea in Boston, when perhaps it was already too late to halt the drift to war. Their best chance to prevent this calamity had actually arisen much earlier, in 1773, and their failure to seize the opportunity to do so was a sad reflection of their own deficiencies.

In the three years before the fighting began at Concord, the arithmetic of politics in Great Britain did not change materially. The bottom line is this: while Lord North always had a majority, it existed only because he worked far harder than the Rockinghams to win the political battles of the day. The upper chamber, the House of Lords, consisted of 167 peers of the realm and the compliant bishops of the Church of England, including Brownlow North. But although the king and the cabinet could almost always count on victory in debate, it was here that the Rockinghams possessed their strongest cohort of supporters who—if correctly deployed—might have prevented the sending of the tea to Boston, and then the war.

In the eighteenth century, it was very rare for the Lords to vote down a measure proposed by the government of the day, but it did sometimes happen. During the long debates on abolition of the Stamp Act, the peers had done so on two occasions—in both cases, the peers were supporting Sandwich and Suffolk, in their hawkish stance toward the colonies—and the Rockinghams might have staged their own counterattack in 1773. They could muster as many as thirty votes in the upper house; and since often more than half its members failed to attend debates, this might have been sufficient to mount an effective ambush if and when Lord North made a bad move. The Rockinghams included the rump of the old Whig oligarchy, which, under the first two Georges, had governed the country in alliance with Sir Robert Walpole. Inclined to favor conciliation with the colonies, they were generally far wealthier than the likes of Dartmouth or Lord North. If they wished, the Rockinghams could have used the House of Lords to obstruct an aggressive policy toward America, and eventually they tried to do so: but only when the crisis had already gone beyond repair.

Their weakness lay in their leadership. For a figurehead, the opposition looked to Charles Watson-Wentworth, second Marquess of Rockingham. Six years earlier, in his own brief period as prime minister, he had abolished the stamp tax and passed the American Declaratory Act. As tall and dignified as Lord Gower, the marquess drew a vast income from his Irish estates in county Wicklow and even more from his rolling acres, rich with coal, in Yorkshire and the English Midlands. But at the age of only forty-two he already devoted less time to politics than he did to hypochondria, spending long holidays taking the waters at Bath.*

Best of all Rockingham loved the pleasures of the turf, at the Doncaster races or on the downs at Newmarket, where his horses reigned supreme. But his enemies laughed at his feeble speeches in the Lords—the marquess was, said Gower to Sandwich, a "poor, dumb creature"—while his friends despaired at his lack of energy. A little way behind his fillies and his fox-hounds, he counted Edmund Burke as a favorite companion. But for all Burke's eloquence and Rockingham's money, the Whigs fell at every hurdle that they tried to jump. Led by the indolent marquess, they carried a heavy handicap of snobbery and self-interest. It left them all too slow to react to the early warning signs of more trouble in America, including the *Gaspée* raid: which they scarcely noticed at all.[2]

In the House of Commons, the Rockinghams commanded a smaller following than they did in the Lords. The lower chamber had 558 members, of whom 513 sat for constituencies in England and Wales. The other 45 were Scottish. Behind Lord North and his colleagues from the Treasury there sat a loyal regiment of about 150 men, who would never vote against him on any serious question. They included officers in the army and the navy, other functionaries on the public payroll, and MPs for coastal boroughs where the electors were civil servants, from the post office or the customs. Another 20 belonged to the Bloomsbury gang, sitting for seats where Gower and his friends controlled the votes. Forty more were old allies of George Grenville, recently dead, the architect of the Stamp Act. They would also tend to rally behind the cabinet, partly because Lord Suffolk had been Grenville's dearest disciple.

Put all these together, and North had a base of support of more than 200 members. Add the MPs from Scotland, who were mostly very tame, and the number rose to nearly 250. Or so it did in theory, but in practice Lord North could never rely on them all to attend a debate. Later, when he asked Parliament to ratify some of his toughest policies toward America, more than 40 percent of MPs failed to cast a vote. Given this degree of apathy, a party of opposition might sometimes have a chance to catch the government by surprise if it could bring all its allies to the chamber.[3]

Among the opposition in the Commons a few men—no more than six at the most—advocated radical ideas, akin to those of the Wilkesites.

---

* In Yorkshire, Rockingham inhabited perhaps the finest English country house of the period, the immense Palladian mansion at Wentworth Woodhouse between Barnsley and Rotherham.

Edmund Burke in the late 1760s, just before he turned forty, from a print taken from a painting by Sir Joshua Reynolds. *Library of Congress*

Another group owed their allegiance to a strange old warrior, who in his time had led the military effort against the French. Close to insanity, Lord Chatham—or William Pitt the Elder, to give him his other name—sulked in the wings of politics, every so often emerging like the ghost in *Hamlet* before he returned to silence and the shade. Americans counted Pitt as a friend because of his role in expelling the French from Canada and because he steadfastly opposed the Declaratory Act. In reality, Lord Chatham was another egotist. During the Seven Years' War he had been superb—bold, decisive, and inspirational—but he could not cope with the dull routine and compromise of statesmanship in peacetime. He kept a following in Parliament, but it was very small.

Between them, the radicals and the Chathamites had only about a dozen seats in the Commons. So here again the burden of opposition fell mainly to the Rockingham Whigs. When North took office, they numbered around 120, and in their opinion they spoke for liberty. They even had a manifesto—*Thoughts on the Cause of the Present Discontents*, published in 1770—in which Edmund Burke summed up the beliefs that held them together. According to Burke and the Marquess of Rockingham, the king and his friends—North, Sandwich, and the rest—were engaged in a project to subvert the constitution. They intended to create what Burke called "a system of favouritism" in which, in return for jobs, rank, title, and promotion, Parliament became the willing slave of the Crown.

A master of English prose, Burke conveyed a powerful vision of a world in which justice and freedom were always in danger from conspiracies of powerful men. In saying this, he went almost as far as the Wilkesites, and in America he found many people who agreed with him. His ideas spread widely in the colonies, where they flowed into the rising tide of opposition to the British Crown.* There, too, public opinion had come to believe that North and the king were bent on the destruction of liberty.

But while ideas are fine and splendid things, they matter not a jot in British politics if the people who advance them cannot turn them into votes. Edmund Burke had many friends and admirers, but for all his intellect and skill with words his following did not count where it mattered, in the division lobby. As Lord North scored one victory after another— his budgets and the Royal Marriage Act, for example—the Rockingham Whigs began to lose heart and fall away.

By November 1772, their core vote had dropped to fewer than sixty. Even then, the Rockinghams might have achieved an occasional victory, because the Commons still contained a hundred independent members, mainly landed gentry from the shires. From time to time the country gentlemen would rebel, voting against Lord North. If Burke and his colleagues had made a cogent case against the government, they might have won the day. But as the debates about India would show, the Rockinghams were confused and demoralized. "I never felt more distress on any matters relating to Politicks, than I do at this moment," wrote the marquess a week before Parliament reassembled. He felt too ill to travel to London. The invalid languished in Yorkshire with his dogs and Lady Rockingham, leaving his party to flounder.[4]

Strange as it may seem, there was a case to be made to defend the East India Company against whatever plan of regulation Lord North might propose. The Rockingham Whigs could blame the crisis on the government, accusing it of squeezing too much money from the company and failing to send it military aid. As a matter of principle, they could also stand up for the company's charter, in much the same way that Rhode Island stood up for its own equivalent. Appealing to their old apostle, the seventeenth-century philosopher John Locke, the Whigs might argue

---

* All the more so, because Edmund Burke acted as agent in London for the colony of New York. Within a few months of its publication, the *Providence Gazette* printed a review of his book, and the Boston newspapers quoted Burke frequently.

that charters were close to sacred, as binding contracts between George III and his subjects. And finally, if they wished to be more radical, Burke and his friends could employ their familiar argument against the overweening power of the state. They could denounce North's plans for reform as yet another plot to use the revenues of Bengal to feed his own ambition and the king's.

They *might* make such a case in Parliament, but if they did, the Rockingham Whigs would court political suicide. With public opinion so angry with the company, who would listen to anything they said? "Many men of tender feelings, on the dismal accounts of oppression by the company's servants in Bengal, join the cry that some stop must be put to it," the marquess wrote to Burke. If the Whigs said anything different, the public would assume that they had sordid motives of their own to support the East India profiteers. And then, as the Rockinghams dithered, Lord North played the kind of masterstroke that made him so valuable to the king.[5]

On November 26, after the monarch opened Parliament, North rose to speak himself. He might instantly have introduced a new bill to reform the company, but instead he did something far more effective. He moved for the creation of a small committee of secrecy, composed of members of Parliament with expertise in finance. They would be given confidential access to all the East India Company's most sensitive papers and accounts. Their task was to find reasons for the company's distress and report back to the house by the end of March.

No reasonable person could object to this. When the Rockinghams did so, they went down to a crushing defeat. Edmund Burke "spoke incomparably," said one observer, but his party lost the debate by seventy votes. By the time the session broke for Christmas, the Whigs had fallen into utter disarray: "panic struck, in whatever concerns the East India Company," as one of the Rockingham Whigs put it at the time.[6]

In due course the committee's report turned out to be a model of its kind, lucid and penetrating. In the meantime, the embarrassment of the Whigs had a fateful consequence for the genesis of the American Revolution. With the Rockinghams rendered impotent, the baton of opposition to Lord North passed to another faction, a group of dissidents in London who came up with the scheme for shipping tea straight to the colonies. They were Scotsmen; but far from being mediocre adherents of the Crown, as so many Scottish politicians were, they formed a dynamic little party of their own.

The Scotsmen in question owned shares in the East India Company, they occupied a few seats in Parliament, and they had their own connections in America. In William Crichton they found a combative advocate. From the city of London, Crichton and his compatriots set the agenda for what happened next. They displayed a degree of energy that the Rockinghams could rarely match, but they were outmaneuvered by Lord North.[7]

THE HERRIES PLAN

Not every Scottish businessman teetered on the brink of ruin. At the age of thirty-nine, William Crichton belonged to a group of northern entrepreneurs who were thriving in the booming trade with the colonies. The son of a prosperous maker of saddles from Edinburgh, Crichton had moved south to London, where he became an importer of sugar, an insurance broker, and a player with stocks and shares. Each year the Thames received hundreds of ships from Jamaica and the other Caribbean islands. The merchants who dealt in sugar formed a rich and energetic lobby, with Crichton among them.

He acted as London partner of the most powerful mercantile house in Glasgow, Alexander Houston & Company, whose wealth had originated in the tobacco trade. They would ship stores across the Atlantic—bricks, boots, and Scottish herrings—to the planters in the British West Indies and bring back sugar, rum, and cotton. They also lent the slave owners money on mortgage. When the planters could not pay their debts, the Houstons would foreclose. Over time, therefore, Crichton and his partners became slave owners themselves, with plantations on Nevis and Grenada.[7]

In his leisure hours, Crichton developed political ambitions in the capital, where he later served as alderman and sheriff. Like many other London merchants with interests in the Caribbean, he loosely aligned himself with John Wilkes. He did so, we can reasonably assume, because the Wilkesites were fiercely anti-Catholic and anti-French. For any Briton in the Caribbean, the French in Haiti remained a lingering threat. As we saw, the Wilkesites found natural allies in the colonial assemblies in Grenada and elsewhere. And for another reason the movement led by Wilkes made an obvious home for men like Crichton: he came from outside the landed elite.

By the beginning of 1772, Crichton had become a member of a pressure group called the Society of West India Merchants, which met every month to discuss what favors it might seek from the government. On March 3 it received a deputation from some of London's largest wholesalers in tea. Men who dealt only in the legal product, with all the duties paid, the tea merchants stood to lose heavily from the thriving contraband trade in

New England and elsewhere.* For their part, the West India merchants resented the Dutch, who used their islands in the Caribbean as staging posts for smuggling molasses and rum in and out of North America. The two groups of businessmen had interests in common. So the West India society agreed to lobby Lord North, asking him to help eradicate the smuggling trade by bringing down the price of tea exported to the colonies.[8]

And so when the tea crisis began in the autumn, Crichton had every reason to intervene. He wanted to rescue the East India Company, to keep it free from government control, to protect his partners in the West Indies, and to build his own political reputation. But with the Rockingham Whigs so clearly incompetent, he needed other allies to help him achieve his goals. He found them in the autumn of 1772 in the shape of a vocal little dynasty from his native land. They were a Scottish family called Johnstone, with whom he made common cause in the debates at India House. Together with the Johnstones, Crichton developed the notion that the surplus tea should be sent to America: not as a weapon of imperial oppression, but as a means to fulfill their own business agenda.

On the British side of the water, it is hard to find political heroes from this period of history. From time to time, however, a few activists appeared who, for all their faults, possessed at least the virtue of insubordination. A family of such a kind, the Johnstones came from a distant valley in the county of Dumfries. In the 1745 rebellion, they had allied themselves with the Jacobites, and so for many years they were viewed with suspicion. Their estates in Eskdale were barren moors, fit only for goats and sheep. That being so, the Johnstones were compelled to be creative. A clan with an appealing streak of anarchy, the family gave birth to a hyperactive trio: three brothers called William, John, and George. From Bengal to the Gulf of Mexico, they left a deep and lasting mark on the life of their time. To their credit, they were among the very small number of members of Parliament who foresaw the American Revolution and tried to prevent the war that followed.

Like so many other Scotsmen, John Johnstone had gone to Bengal in the service of the East India Company. Sent to collect the land tax at Dacca, the modern capital of Bangladesh, he did rather too well, making a fortune by diverting the revenue into his own pocket. He came home at risk of prosecution for fraud. With a view to clearing his name, the

* The deputation consisted of two grocers, Monkhouse Davison and Abraham Newman, who were substantial exporters of legal tea to Massachusetts.

family began a long feud with the company's board, led by his abrasive brother George, a former naval officer with a record of reckless bravery at sea. "Irascible, intemperate, violent, he was a warm and zealous friend, but an implacable enemy," said a contemporary. George won election to Parliament, where he could pursue his family's vendetta. There he also enjoyed the rare distinction of knowing the colonies firsthand. Until he was recalled for inciting an Indian war, George Johnstone had served as governor at Pensacola in the new colony of West Florida. On the rare occasions when America was debated, he would always intervene.[9]

Close beside him in the House of Commons sat his brother William, the richest of the three. After marrying an heiress, he took her family name, became Sir William Pulteney, and began to build another fortune as a real estate developer in London and Bath, with Robert Adam as his architect. He also bought land in the West Indies on the islands taken from the French. Like so many other people at the time, Sir William and his brothers played for the highest of stakes, and they saw the financial crash as a splendid opportunity.

As the year drew to a close, the crisis appeared to be entering a new and perhaps an uglier phase, but one which the Johnstones hoped to turn to their advantage. In late November, two days after Parliament reassembled, the press carried word of a devastating hurricane, the most severe in living memory. It had struck the Windward Islands at the end of August before circling back across the Atlantic, carrying the rain that ended the English drought. On Antigua, the storm wrecked every ship in the harbor, whipped the sugarcane to shreds, blew down houses, factories, and sheds, and killed slaves in the fields. The Dutch islands also suffered grievously, and for this the timing could not have been worse. In Amsterdam, the largest banks were still reeling from the shocks that began in June. Some had lent heavily to sugar planters, and now their plight was desperate. In England, with the East India Company's stock down to £160 and still falling, business confidence had begun to ebb away once more.[10]

At this difficult moment the Johnstones stepped forward with their own scheme to rescue the company. The concept came from a close friend of William Pulteney's. A neighbor from Dumfriesshire, he was a wily, controversial financier called Robert Herries. His firm were "damned rascals," said one rival, and they also carried the stigma of old Jacobite sympathies. The Herries family knew the smuggling trade firsthand. Their home, a moorland estate near Lockerbie, lay close to the Solway Firth, an infamous den of contraband, and Robert's elder brother ran a tea-smuggling ring out of Ostend, with Jacobites as partners. Trained in banking in the

Netherlands, Robert Herries made his first fortune in Barcelona in his early twenties, buying brandy for illegal shipment to Scotland via the Isle of Man.

Moving to London he became a banker, and while Lord Sandwich invented the sandwich, Robert Herries invented the traveler's check. By 1772, his firm had a chain of agencies all over Europe where young men away on the grand tour could present a voucher and collect their allowance from home. After coming unscathed through the banking crash, Herries scored a great coup when he won a huge contract from the French government to buy tobacco in Glasgow on its behalf. Rich and famous—the king soon gave him a knighthood—he began to make his name on the political scene.[11]

Early in December, Herries and William Pulteney appeared in Parliament to propose a scheme to help the stricken planters in the Caribbean raise money in London to rebuild their estates. And then, just before Christmas, they published their own manifesto for the reconstruction of the East India Company. On December 21, a pamphlet appeared on the streets of London, under a long and ponderous title that began, *The Present State of the English East-India Company's Affairs*. It opened with a brief but devastating attack on the board of directors and Lord North.

"Shall our fate be national bankruptcy, poverty, oppression and slavery?" the author inquired. Permit the company to fail, and the country would be ruined; but on the other hand, if the government took the revenues of Bengal, then Great Britain and India alike would lie abject at the feet of tyranny. A way had to be found to save the company without relying on help from the government that would come with strings attached.

The pamphlet was anonymous, but anyone who followed the news could tell that it came from the Johnstones or someone very close to them. For weeks, with Crichton in close support, George Johnstone had been appearing at one angry East India Company meeting after another to challenge the board and to organize resistance to Lord North. The brothers had their own motives for defending the company against the Regulating Act for India that North would eventually propose. John Johnstone still lay under a cloud, which they hoped to lift. Intensely ambitious, the Johnstones had risen from almost nowhere, and they wanted to keep the company free as a field for their own endeavors. In order to do so, they had to rebuild its balance sheet.

Halfway through the pamphlet, readers came to a set of proposals to dispose of the company's tea, described as those of Mr. Herries. Whoever wrote the text clearly knew the tea trade intimately, because he filled its pages with facts and figures. Like the "Fair Consumer" in September, the author made the obvious point: that because of the burden of taxes imposed by the government, tea was far too expensive in London. Go to Amsterdam or Lorient, and you could buy it for far less: hence the profit for the smuggler. But if the duties were removed, the tea from England would sweep the board. And so the Herries plan was simply this: Lord North should permit the company to export all its surplus tea directly to Europe, duty-free, and put the continentals out of business. Sell the tea abroad, even at a loss, and the cash would keep the company alive until times improved. If not, the mountain of unsold tea in London would continue to rise inexorably.*

In the weeks that followed, the Herries plan became the talk of the city. Two days after it appeared, the company's shareholders met for another stormy session. Once again William Crichton called for a reduction in the dividend, at last the board agreed, and the dividend was cut in half. Even so the situation remained very grim. With cash running very low and the Bank of England growing ever more impatient, the Herries plan seemed to offer the only hope of financial salvation. With the newspapers snapping at their heels, the directors agreed to discuss it at the first opportunity.

They scheduled a committee meeting for January 5, 1773, to hear not only from Robert Herries but from anyone who objected to his scheme. At this point, we have to cross the Atlantic to New England, where Thomas Hutchinson, the governor of Massachusetts, had his own motives to be worried about the price of Bohea. His family dealt in tea. And when his London agent heard about the Herries plan, he hurried down to India House to lodge a protest on Hutchinson's behalf.

THE FOOLISHNESS OF THOMAS HUTCHINSON

Another tall, thin man, Governor Hutchinson thought of himself as the voice of George III in Boston. An American by birth, from old Puritan stock, he was already sixty-one. Behind him lay a lifetime of public service, and all the bother it brought with it.

A Harvard graduate, highly intelligent, and a fine writer, Hutchinson worked hard and spoke well. Even some of his opponents praised him for his diligence and his commitment to the Commonwealth of Massachusetts. But like Lord North, he suffered agonies in private. Tense and highly

---

* By January 1773, the company's stock of tea had reached 16.8 million pounds by weight, of which they expected to sell only seven million pounds in the British Isles.

Governor Thomas
Hutchinson at thirty,
by Edward Truman.
Bridgeman Art Library

strung, Thomas Hutchinson spent sleepless nights worrying about the
British Empire. He never stopped writing letters to England, often very
indiscreet, and by doing so he caused no end of trouble.

In Boston, his family enjoyed the benefits of rank. They also endured
the envy that power attracts. For that Thomas Hutchinson had only himself to blame. Along with his kinsmen, a family called Oliver, Hutchinson had come to dominate the imperial hierarchy in his colony. While he
served as governor, his brother-in-law Andrew Oliver acted as his deputy,
and Peter Oliver held the post of chief justice. Given the mood in New
England, and the wide support for ideas like those of John Wilkes, at
best it was unwise to concentrate so much power in the hands of a local
oligarchy. Hutchinson's two predecessors had been Britons, sent out to
the colonies to serve a term and then come home. That was a far more
sensible arrangement, since they were better able to remain aloof from
feuds between local factions. At worst the Hutchinson-Oliver axis created
damaging conflicts of interest between their role as representatives of the
king and their need to look after their own families. Just such a conflict
occurred in 1773.

Thomas Hutchinson had many virtues, beautifully described in the
great biography by Bernard Bailyn. In particular he was a loving father, but

this helped to bring about his downfall. After generations of mercantile success, the Hutchinsons owned not only a great slice of the waterfront in Boston, but also a fine estate inland at the little town of Milton. But in colonial New England wealth was more precarious than in Britain. In the mother country, property in land was almost indestructible, and rents very rarely fell. In the colonies, where soil was relatively cheap, wealth depended on the vagaries of commerce. A fortune of that kind was hard to build and apt to vanish, thanks to fire, storm, shipwreck, or a sudden slump in trade. Especially in Boston, where for a generation the economy had been sluggish and bankruptcy commonplace.[12]

In 1765, during the postwar recession on both sides of the Atlantic, an epidemic of insolvencies occurred in Massachusetts. It helps to explain the furious reaction to George Grenville's stamp tax. Keen to protect his family fortune, Hutchinson knew that he needed to find a secure livelihood for his three sons, all of whom were approaching maturity. And so at about this time he decided to set up his eldest son, Thomas Hutchinson Jr., as a dealer in tea. Of course they would need a London supplier, but the family had close friends who could send them all the Bohea they required.

Many years earlier, the governor's kinswoman Abigail Hutchinson had married an Englishman called Palmer from a family of landed gentry in Leicestershire. In 1740, when Thomas Hutchinson visited England on official business, he met the London branch of the Palmers—they were lawyers and merchants—and they became firm friends. The family's members included Thomas Palmer, a grocer who dealt in tea wholesale. By the end of the 1760s, his son William had taken over the family business. He rose to become one of the largest buyers of tea at the East India Company auctions, making money enough to build a fine mansion in Essex, thirty miles from London, where he later served as sheriff of the county. William Palmer shipped tea to the Hutchinsons in Boston in consignments of sixty chests at a time, to be sold by agents as far afield as New Hampshire.[13]

For a while, the enterprise prospered. And then, in 1767, news arrived in America of the Townshend duties, including the threepenny tax on every pound of tea. Boston soon became a very angry town. In the summer of 1768, the people rioted again, to defend John Hancock's sloop the *Liberty* against a raid by customs men in search of smuggled wine. It was this incident that caused Lord Hillsborough to send in the army to patrol the streets and prevent a repetition. From that moment forward, any Bostonian who dealt in legal tea from England became a potential target for insult and abuse. The atmosphere grew darker still in 1769, when Boston led a national boycott of English goods in protest at the Townshend taxes. Imports of legal tea fell away sharply, by about a third. By the autumn of that year, Thomas Hutchinson Jr. was running out of cash and writing to his agent in Portsmouth, complaining about "the unwearied pains of enemies" who were trying to put him out of business.[14]

Four years before the great Tea Party, rumors were already rife that the patriots of Boston planned to destroy all the legal tea they found. Under threat of violence the Hutchinsons abided by the boycott, at least temporarily. But when they resumed their dealings in tea in 1770, the family business found it hard to return to profit. For this the governor blamed the smugglers of tea from the Netherlands. Like the Royal Navy officers in Boston, whom he counted as personal friends, he grew ever more exasperated. In the summer of 1771, Thomas Hutchinson began to bombard Lord Hillsborough with strident letters urging him to intensify the patrols along the coast.

"In New York they import none but Holland tea," he told the colonial secretary. "In Rhode Island it is little better, and in this province the Dutch traders are increasing." According to Hutchinson, the town of Boston consumed three hundred chests of tea each year. For the colonies as a whole the total came to nearly twenty thousand, of which, he reckoned, four out of every five were smuggled in. This estimate closely tallies with the data available from London, where the Treasury made similar calculations.[15]

As time went by, the governor's letters told a story of deepening woe. Despite the best efforts of Admiral Montagu, the smugglers usually evaded detection. Unable to compete, Thomas junior had to slash the price he asked for Bohea. At last, on September 11, 1772, Hutchinson wrote to William Palmer, warning him that their partnership might have to end. Thanks to the inroads made by the Dutch, it would soon be impossible to sell an ounce of English tea. Palmer need not send any chests that autumn: the Hutchinsons had fifty already, which they could not shift. In the governor's opinion, the business was doomed unless either the East India Company or the British Treasury stepped in with a solution. "Nothing will be effectual," the governor wrote, "short of reducing the price in England to the price in Holland." As a loyal servant of the empire, Hutchinson did not wish to see the threepenny Townshend duty abolished: for one thing, the British wished to use the proceeds to pay his salary. But something had to be done, or his son would lose his livelihood.[16]

Even if the voyage from Boston had been unusually long, this letter would have reached William Palmer well before Christmas. And when the

Herries plan appeared in December, Palmer instantly saw that the proposals would destroy his friends' business entirely. According to Herries, the company should flood the market in Holland, France, and Sweden with cut-price tea. But the price was *already* far too low in continental Europe: do as Herries suggested, and it would fall still further. The same cheap tea would cross the Atlantic, leaving the Hutchinsons no option but to sell their own tea at a loss.

Like every wholesale dealer in tea, William Palmer held some stock in the East India Company, giving him the standing to object to a scheme so ill-judged. At the committee meeting on January 5, he did his best to defeat the Herries plan. In the weeks that followed, it underwent a transformation at the hands of Palmer, Crichton, and the Treasury. Between them, they took the plan and bent it into the disastrous form that would lead to the Tea Party.[17]

THE UNDERLINGS OF OFFICE

More banks collapsed, this time in Holland; troops were called out in Scotland to put down riots by the poor; and in London the Countess of Rochford lay dead, leaving her unfaithful husband prostrate with grief and shame. The new year of 1773 began with few rays of light amid the gloom. At India House, it took two full days for the directors to discuss the Herries proposals and to hear from William Palmer. Unable to make up their minds, they opted for caution. They would seek Lord North's permission for a small, experimental shipment of tea to Amsterdam. In the meantime, the company wrote to the Dutch bankers Hope & Company, asking their opinion about the state of the market in Holland.[18]

On January 7, the East India shareholders met again with only one item on their agenda. George Johnstone rose to urge the meeting to support the Herries plan. By now, however, Crichton had clearly heard the objections, voiced by William Palmer and others, and so he leaped up to suggest an amendment. Send all the surplus tea to Europe, and the smugglers would bring it straight back to England. Better, said Crichton, simply to slash the price of tea in London and let anyone buy it who wished to do so, Englishmen and foreigners alike.

Then he added another suggestion. Everybody knew about the smuggling epidemic in America, and the West India lobby to which he belonged shared the government's irritation. So why not ask Lord North to help with that as well? Would it not be simpler for his lordship to remove the threepenny Townshend tax and allow them to send their tea to America

The India-man wrecked. L 12.

free from every duty? At that moment the scheme to send the surplus tea to the colonies was born. An excellent idea, said George Johnstone, who immediately rose to support it. Johnstone drafted a resolution, urging the board to ask for an act of Parliament allowing the company "to export their tea to foreign markets, clear of all drawbacks and duties," including, of course, the Townshend duty. The motion passed unanimously.[19]

Four days later, Sir George Colebrooke went cap in hand to Lord North to reopen their discussions. With its reserves of cash all but exhausted, the East India Company urgently needed to borrow £1.4 million from the Treasury, but in return for his consent North still insisted on reform of the company's affairs. Already, the Secrecy Committee had begun to publish its report in installments—there would be eight in the space of six months—exposing fresh scandals in Calcutta and negligence or worse by the directors. Made to take most of the blame, Colebrooke found himself "pelted at & disavowed by everybody," said a contemporary. Meanwhile, the Bank of England was close to calling time on the company's overdraft.[20]

Even so, the tortuous process of negotiation dragged on until May. It took that long for Lord North to develop his own plan for a new system of government for Bengal, answerable to Parliament. But in one crucial respect Lord North was only too happy to help immediately. As early as January 14, he agreed to allow the company to send tea directly to America. Indeed, somebody—it is not clear whether it was the company or Lord North—proposed a still more radical initiative. In the future, two ships each year would be allowed to sail from China to the colonies, laden with tea, as a way to cut out all the middlemen and make the stuff even cheaper. Whoever suggested this, North gave the concept his full support.[21]

By now it was obvious that the original Herries plan was doomed. It finally died on January 20, killed by a letter from the Hopes. It was ingenious, they said, but utterly impractical—for the obvious reason that so many others had already pointed out. The Europeans liked fine green teas, but they did not care for the company's vast stock of black Bohea and Singlo. Ship it to Amsterdam, and it would simply flow back across the

Left: From January 1773, a cartoon satirizing the plight of the East India Company, with its chairman Sir George Colebrooke—nicknamed Shah Allum, because he lost heavily by speculating in alum, a mineral used in the textile trade—under attack at a shareholders' meeting. The diminutive Colebrooke is being shaken in the air by the tall Scottish dissident George Johnstone. Below, the company is heading for the rocks. *Library of Congress*

North Sea illegally. But even as the Herries plan expired, Lord North and
his colleagues were busy with a variation of their own. Whatever the likes
of William Crichton might suggest, the Treasury had not the least intention of abolishing the Townshend duty. On the contrary: North planned
to leave the threepenny duty very firmly in place. He intended to use the
company's tea to make Americans pay the tax they tried so hard to evade.

Thirty years later, an old, forgotten man living close to poverty, Sir
George Colebrooke wrote a candid set of memoirs. Never intended for
publication—his book was printed only a century later, and copies remain
extremely rare—it gives an insider's view of what followed. Although Sir
George rather liked Lord North—he called him "the best-natured man
that could be"—he took a dim view of his skill with finance. Most tell-
ingly of all, he blamed North for the decision to send the tea to the colonies. A wild and foolish scheme, it was bound to cause violent opposition
because, said Colebrooke, "it was calculated to carry into effect the payment of an obnoxious duty."

According to Sir George, the blame lay entirely with Lord North and
what he called "the underlings of office," whom he accused of using every
devious tactic to make the East India Company do as they wished. Colebrooke did not name the underlings in question, but he must have been
referring to North's two closest aides at the Treasury. One was Charles
Jenkinson, later the first Earl of Liverpool, and the other was John Robinson, a plain-speaking lawyer from the far north of England. While Jenkinson was tall and lean, Robinson was coarse, fat, and untidy. However, both
men were shrewd and cunning, and they worked tirelessly in the Commons
as whips for the government side.[22]

One biographer of Jenkinson describes him as "a born bureaucrat of
restricted sympathies," which certainly did not extend in America's direction. Another protégé of George Grenville's, Jenkinson bitterly regretted
the repeal of the Stamp Act, and he clung to Grenville's dream of raising
a colonial revenue. A man with an eye for detail, he served as the secretary
of the committee investigating the East India Company. When Jenkinson
died, he left behind a huge archive of papers. Among those relating to
Bengal, a document survives that explains the Treasury's thinking as clearly
as could be.

Dated January 18, 1773, the document describes a plan to compel the
Americans to buy all their tea from England. No one signed it. But judg-
ing from the array of figures it contains, and the care with which it was
written, the paper can only be an official memorandum from the Treasury
prepared by Jenkinson and Robinson, with perhaps some help from Wil-

liam Palmer. In six months' time, the writer said, the East India Company should hold a special public auction of nine million pounds of tea. It would be sold at a discount, purely for export to Ireland and the colonies, where the Townshend duty would still have to be paid. The delay was deliberate. It would allow for the auction to be widely advertised on the other side of the Atlantic.[23]

"Very large orders from America may be expected," said the writer, because the price would beat anything a Dutch smuggler could offer. Shopkeepers in the colonies would have no choice but to buy the tea, and so, at a stroke, the plan would accomplish four separate objectives. For the company, it would raise more than £900,000 in cash; it would oblige the Americans to pay the threepenny tax, putting an end to their foolish boycott; it would put the smugglers out of business; and it would raise some revenue for the government.

By the time the tea ships left for the colonies that autumn, the scheme had been revised: William Palmer intervened again, and the idea of an auction in London was dropped in favor of direct export by the company. But the plan's underlying principles remained intact. By the end of January, the Treasury had committed itself to the course of action that led to the Tea Party. As far as it was concerned, it had no alternative. The Treasury had to act firmly to end the crime wave on the coast of America.

The previous summer, Charles Jenkinson had sat alongside Lord North in the Treasury boardroom when they heard the shocking details of the *Gaspée* raid. By the end of January 1773, the commission of inquiry into that affair had only just begun to meet at Newport. But already the navy had written home to London, complaining about the obstruction it met as it tried to find testimony against the Browns. It seemed unlikely that justice would be done in the case of the wounded lieutenant. Meanwhile, the cost of governing the colonies increased with each month that went by. As the price of food rose, the contractors who supplied the garrisons in New York and Boston began to plead for more money. Each dispatch from General Gage carried more warnings about the danger of an Indian war, while in the West Indies fighting had already begun on the island of St. Vincent.

There, the redcoats and the Caribs had been locked in combat since the autumn, and the army suffered grievously as men died in their hundreds from fever if not from wounds in battle. It took six months of fighting, and the deployment of more than two thousand soldiers, before the Caribs laid down their arms. In view of all this, how could the Treasury make concessions to the colonies? With money so tight, how could North abolish the tax on tea? It was simply unthinkable. Besides, Lord North could rely on the House of Commons to support him whenever he revealed the details of the plan.

But for the time being, Lord North still held his hand very close to his chest. In April, the company would choose a new board of directors. Inevitably, Colebrooke and his allies would be voted out, and North hoped to see them replaced by more pliable men who would readily accept all his proposals for reform. In the meantime, he continued to negotiate, but he said little in public. Three months passed in this way. All the while the newspapers eagerly followed the East India crisis, but without an inkling of what the Treasury had in mind. Instead, it was widely assumed that in due course Lord North would give the shareholders what they wanted and allow the company to send its tea to the colonies free from every tax.

One American in London certainly expected that: Benjamin Franklin. Like so many others, he failed to anticipate the crisis that was in gestation. Sixteen years had passed since Franklin came to live in England. There he did a great deal of science and a little diplomacy, as the agent for the colony of Pennsylvania and for the Massachusetts House of Representatives. For most of his time in the metropolis he remained a friend of the empire, and of course he thoroughly enjoyed the intellectual society he found. By 1773, however, his mood had changed to one of weary disenchantment with the British. But rather than seeking to gather intelligence about Lord North's intentions, he gradually lost connection with the politics of the day.

His treatment by Lord Hillsborough had been discourteous and dismissive; the former colonial secretary refused to accept Franklin's credentials to speak for the Massachusetts assembly. However, the change in Franklin's attitude arose from far more than a fit of pique. As he traveled to Ireland and Edinburgh and saw the deepening divide between poverty and wealth, Franklin also grew more skeptical about the mother country. Although he came away unharmed by the financial crash—he was too shrewd to place his money in a British bank—the banking crisis increased his sense of disillusionment. Meanwhile, the endless delays about the Ohio question left him all the more frustrated.

As time went by, Benjamin Franklin gradually became detached from the mainstream of London society. Absorbed in his reading and research and ill at ease with the aristocracy, he chose to spend his evenings with freethinking clergymen, philosophers, and doctors. Clever they might be, but they were mostly radicals and nonconformists, in religion and much else. In an age when the Church of England still commanded the

Benjamin Franklin in
1782, by Joseph Wright
of Derby. *Bridgeman Art
Library*

allegiance, however cynical, of the vast majority of people in public life, Franklin's circle was hardly a fair cross section of opinion in the capital.

From the letters that survive, it seems that Franklin barely knew the Rockinghams at all. He saw nothing of Edmund Burke, with whom he might have collaborated to defend American interests. Unlike the Lees from Virginia, Franklin never dined with Wilkes, whom he did not trust. He also kept his distance from East India House. Of course he read the newspapers, but they were a baffling mixture of truth and falsehood. He rarely entered the drawing rooms of Mayfair or St. James's where the influential gathered. Above all, Franklin misjudged the calibre of Lord North. The two men hardly knew each other: they apparently met only two or three times. Soon after North became prime minister, Franklin attended one of the weekly levees that he held in Whitehall and heard him make a disparaging remark about America. Although Franklin continued to meet other members of the government, henceforth he avoided the politician whom he most needed to understand.*

---

* In fact, Franklin had drifted so far out of touch with politics at Westminster that when at last he tried to write to Edmund Burke, in the autumn of 1774, he sent the letter to an address that Burke had left two years earlier.

Isolated from the court and from high society, all Franklin could see was incompetence. With some arrogance of his own, instead of trying to learn Lord North's secrets he tended to regard the prime minister as a fool. "A fine Hobble they are all got into," Franklin wrote to an American friend, early in 1773, "by their unjust and blundering Politics with regard to the colonies." His comments were not unfair, but in a sense they were naive. Actually, North was a man at the height of his powers. Far from doubting his abilities, the king and his fellow ministers admired the way he managed the East India crisis. And with Hillsborough out of the way and the opposition in the doldrums, at last Lord North was free to devise his own policy for America; but at this crucial moment, Franklin—a scientific genius, but temporarily off his political guard—failed to see that this was so.

Toward the end of March, Franklin went to see Lord Dartmouth, with whom he was never close. It was only their third interview since Dartmouth took office. Their relationship was cordial but no more. Despite his respect for the minister, Franklin came away from the session perplexed by what appeared to be mixed signals. Only a few months earlier, Dartmouth had seemed relaxed, willing to listen to colonial opinion. Even then, in January, Franklin had found that while his lordship was friendly, he was evasive too, speaking in vague clichés. By the spring, the minister's mood seemed to have altered again. While Dartmouth remained an affable host, he showed signs of annoyance with the radicals in New England, their boycott of tea, and their refusal to help bring the *Gaspée* raiders to book. But the colonial secretary gave no clue about his own intentions.

For the time being, Franklin expected the British to climb down and abolish the threepenny Townshend duty altogether. Like so many others, he believed that the next war with France could not be postponed indefinitely. If so, the British dared not lose the support of the colonies, with their naval bases and their reserves of ships and seafarers—or so the argument ran. However, from the spring of 1773, Franklin's letters begin to convey a sense of unease as he found the government's stance increasingly puzzling. As he wrote in a bewildered letter to his son in New Jersey, "All depends upon Circumstances and Events. We govern from hand to mouth. There seems to be no wise, regular Plan."[24]

In all probability, Lord Dartmouth simply did not know Lord North's intentions, and this would explain his vagueness. A ruthless operator when need be, North might very well choose to keep even his oldest friend in the dark until he was ready to spring his own agenda on an unsuspecting House of Commons. Indeed, from the surviving records, it seems that

North never asked the Colonial Office its opinion about his scheme to use the surplus tea as a political weapon. The plan came from the Treasury alone.

Even so, Franklin had rightly detected a change in the political temperature. Thanks to the *Gaspée* incident, a colder wind was blowing from Whitehall, toward another confrontation with the colonies; and meanwhile, three thousand miles away, events were converging toward a climax of their own. At Newport the *Gaspée* commissioners were bringing their futile inquiry to a close. Although they knew that John Brown had organized the raid, they could find no witnesses reliable enough to put before a jury. Their work merely served to deepen hostility and suspicion on both sides of the Atlantic. In the eyes of the British military, the affair simply proved that disloyal Americans would never mend their ways; and among the people of New England a similar hardening of opinion occurred. Since the first news of the Stamp Act arrived nearly eight years earlier, gradually the northern colonies had become estranged from the mother country. In the second half of 1772 this process accelerated and became irreversible.

By the end of January 1773, partly as a result of Britain's bungled attempt to prosecute the *Gaspée* raiders and partly because of other, older grievances, public opinion in New England had swung decisively against the empire. Long before the fighting began at Lexington, a rebellion took place in the mind, starting in Providence and Boston and then spreading outward across the rest of Massachusetts and further afield until eventually it reached kindred spirits in Virginia and Charleston, where many people had already arrived at the same revolutionary conclusions. Some of the ideas they adopted had been current in debate in America for decades, with roots stretching back to the age of Elisha Cooke, if not before, but now they acquired a fresh relevance. As yet, nobody in the colonies had even the slightest suspicion that Lord North intended to send them the company's tea. Even so, in New England rebellious doctrines had already begun to circulate with a new intensity.

Chapter Eight

MASSACHUSETTS ON THE EVE

I have long feared that this unhappy contest will end in Rivers of Blood.

—SAMUEL ADAMS, WRITING TO A FRIEND IN
RHODE ISLAND, JANUARY 1773[1]

The town of Boston stood in urgent need of a change of government, for the sake of its prosperity and for its peace of mind. The same was true of the rest of Massachusetts, where the bonds of obedience were swiftly becoming untied.

Of course, the strength of hostility toward Great Britain varied from place to place in the old Bay Colony. Some districts were far more radical than others; and at least one in five of its citizens never wanted to leave the empire, even long after Bunker Hill. Many others were uncommitted either way. And yet, within a year of the *Gaspée* incident, one thing was already very clear. Impervious to colonial control, Massachusetts contained tens of thousands of men and women, perhaps already forming a majority, who had relinquished all but a token loyalty to the king and Parliament.

Perhaps the closest equivalent in modern times was the end of the Communist regime in East Germany. Of course King George III never had a Stasi. The old colonial system was anything but totalitarian. It was loose, it was flimsy, it dithered and delayed. Its most appalling feature— the institution of slavery—was a private system run by Americans, protected by laws they had passed themselves. Even so, a parallel can still be drawn between the earliest phase of the American Revolution and the fall of the Berlin Wall.

In 1989 it became apparent that the Soviet empire was in full retreat, unable to prevent the Hungarians from opening their frontier to the west. When the East German authorities tried to defend the old order, the first demonstrations began in Leipzig in September. At first only a few thousand people gathered in the main square. As the days passed, the protests grew bolder. The authorities began to waver. The number of people out on the streets increased until they reached as many as seventy thousand. Confronted by the unthinkable, the Honecker regime lost its nerve. A month later the game was up, and the wall that divided Berlin proved to be nothing more than concrete and asbestos.

Something of the kind took place in Massachusetts in the autumn of 1774, with General Gage performing the role of Erich Honecker on horseback. In the space of eight weeks the colony ceased to be British. After a series of episodes of civil disobedience in Worcester, in Salem, and deep in the interior, a provisional government met in October, with John Hancock in the chair.

To outsiders who had never visited New England or the Soviet bloc, these two revolutions appeared to occur with startling speed. But in fact the revolution on the streets could only occur because of an earlier rebellion in the head, gradually unfolding over many years. Long before the events of 1989, the bullies who ran the old East Germany began to lose their grip on the minds of the people. In the cafés a customer could not buy a cup of coffee, and in the restaurants even bratwurst was off the menu. Most families in Leipzig or Berlin lived in cold and damp apartments, shoddily built, from which they could watch West German television and compare a Trabant with a BMW. While Honecker and his comrades spouted nonsense about their achievements, the East German economy faltered and then shrank. By 1988 even an official poll showed that less than a third of the people "were proud to be citizens of a socialist state." A year before the wall came down, the regime was already precarious, as its subjects withdrew the last, grudging degree of respect.[2]

A similar process of alienation occurred in Massachusetts in the decade before the war. By the autumn of 1772 large sections of the population had become convinced, unfairly or not, that Lord North and the king were intent on their enslavement. Even at times when the British did nothing, the divide between the mother country and New England seemed to widen all the more. Long before the fighting started, it became almost routine for men and women at the grass roots to deny the sovereignty of the Crown. Take, for example, a place called Pownalborough, hidden away in the woods in what is now the state of Maine.

At that time it was the seat of Lincoln County, Massachusetts, with a white colonial courthouse still to be seen today. A frontier town built on the site of a military post, Pownalborough grew swiftly after the treaty of 1763 made the area safe against the Indians and the French. By the time of the revolution as many as fourteen hundred people lived hereabouts. Six months before the Boston Tea Party, the townspeople issued their own declaration of independence. "Allegiance is a relative term," they said in a letter to their fellow patriots in Boston. "Our forefathers as soon as they landed here considered themselves as beyond the Supreme Authority of the Crown of England."[3]

If the citizens were so radical in a remote location where people never saw a redcoat, what were they saying in Boston, where the empire was far more conspicuous? At a time when allegedly all was quiet, in fact a visitor would find the most forthright expressions of discontent: for instance, in the *Boston Gazette* of October 5, 1772. The newspaper gave three pages to a tirade against Thomas Hutchinson and the system he represented. "Is it not high Time for the People of this Country explicitly to declare whether they will be Freemen or slaves?" the writer inquired.

For the British, it was tempting to dismiss this kind of thing as empty rhetoric. For many years the *Gazette* had been running outspoken columns by Samuel Adams, full of the same sort of language, which the governor dutifully sent to his superiors. But on their arrival in Whitehall, articles such as these raised difficult questions that historians have been trying to answer ever since. In an age when opinion polls and focus groups were yet to be invented, who could tell what the American people really thought? Were the views contained in the *Gazette* widely held in New England? Or did the newspaper speak merely for a handful of extremists?

The British could not say for sure. It was even harder for them to read the mind of Massachusetts than it was for Benjamin Franklin to understand the cabinet. While a hawk like Lord Sandwich believed that all Americans were rebels by nature, his colleague Lord Dartmouth preferred to give them the benefit of the doubt. In his eyes the revolution arose from a conspiracy by devious men allied with Adams who used the wiles of propaganda to seduce their neighbors into treason. Neither minister considered another possibility, which seems to have been the truth: that even men and women temperamentally inclined to be loyal had begun to see the British Empire as something they could do without.

The sheer size of Massachusetts, with at least 300,000 inhabitants, makes it hard to believe that anyone could fool a majority into disobedience. The speed with which resistance came to a head in 1774 shows that the movement was broad and popular and not a mere conspiracy by

Adams and his friends. There were many reasons why disaffection had become widespread, and sometimes they were very local and specific. In Maine, for example, at places like Pownalborough the farmers resented the way the Royal Navy took their best trees to serve as masts for battleships. But elsewhere, even people without a local grievance ceased to believe in the colonial system. It became ever harder to argue that the empire served a useful purpose.

Like the Honecker regime in East Germany, the king and his ministers lost the respect of their subjects because they failed to honor their side of a bargain. Never a very subtle creed, East German socialism promised to provide equality, security, and material well-being, with—in the long run—a higher standard of living than that of the West. As time went on and capitalism refused to collapse, the pledge made by the Communist state seemed ever more unlikely to be honored. The nation also became more unequal, since only the party apparatchiks could hope to prosper as the economy declined. By 1989 the situation seemed to be terminal, and so respect for the government disappeared entirely. The same thing occurred in Boston during the 1770s. In the eighteenth century, the people of Massachusetts believed that they had their own deal with the British Crown, but by 1772 it appeared to be breaking down. The authorities either could not or would not deliver their side of the imperial bargain.

In Massachusetts the colonists had always seen the empire as a contract between themselves and the Crown: a contract freely entered into by both sides. Far from being abstract or metaphysical, it existed in black and white, written down in the charter of the colony granted eighty years earlier by King William III. Like the similar charter applying to Rhode Island, in places it was loosely worded, leaving it open to rival interpretations. Even so, Bostonians such as Samuel Adams and his kinsman John had no doubt about its fundamental purpose. The charter was supposed to promote their liberty and their prosperity. If the British failed to abide by its terms, the people of Massachusetts were entitled to seek redress by whatever means they chose.

Despite the high-flown language that the Boston patriots often employed, there was nothing rarefied about their view of the empire. In order to fulfill the terms of the contract, the British were expected to provide tangible benefits of four different kinds. Defense came first, economics came second, and the two were closely intertwined. Especially in New England, the Americans relied on maritime trade, but they could not guarantee its safety by themselves. For that they needed the Royal Navy. Second, they expected Great Britain to remain their closest economic partner by keeping its doors wide open to Americans with goods to sell. In both cases, the colonies expected the empire to promote their well-being by making the Atlantic a safe, reliable sea on which to sail.

For similar motives, they turned to George III for a third reason: to provide the gift of justice at times when the colonies required an impartial arbitrator from outside. As they grew, boundary disputes between them became ever more frequent. It was commonplace, and not only in Vermont, for rival claims to land to drive a wedge between one province and another. Here again, the Crown ought to be useful. By supplying wise counsel, surveying the land, and giving an unbiased opinion, perhaps the king or his emissaries could prevent these squabbles from taking a violent form.

Last, the Americans expected Great Britain to give them a guarantee of liberty, civil and religious, of the kind they believed the British enjoyed at home. Again, their concept of freedom had nothing mysterious about it. It was embodied in the Bill of Rights enacted by Parliament in London in 1689 after the Glorious Revolution against King James II. Trial by jury, the right to bear arms, free elections to Parliament, and free speech when it assembled: all of these were made sacrosanct. The monarch could have a standing army, but only if Parliament gave its consent; he could make no laws without its approval, and taxation always required a vote by the House of Commons. It was taken for granted in America that the same rights extended to Americans as well. Indeed, in this respect they were more British than the British. In the colonies people endlessly rehearsed the revolutionary principles of the 1680s, long after the point when in England they had become a tired cliché. Most eloquently, John Adams restated them in the document known as the Braintree Instructions, drawn up as part of the protests against the Stamp Act.

If these were the benefits the colonists expected from the empire, then by 1772 the British seemed unable to supply them. The boundary disputes in Vermont were a case in point. Although Whitehall received long reports about the situation in the valley, the officials could offer no solution. Their dithering about the wilderness placed another question mark over their competence. In Boston the press reported the loss of Fort de Chartres and ran stories from London about the cabinet's disarray. Once again the British had failed to reach a firm decision about the settlement of the Ohio country. Everything was fuzzy and confused, with no sign of a robust policy toward the western frontier.

Nor did the empire's military might appear as awesome as once it had. In the army led by General Gage, desertion was frequent, with nearly 10 percent of each regiment going absent each year. During the opening battles of the war, it would soon become obvious that the British suffered from poor training and indiscipline, but signs of this were already visible during the occupation of Boston between 1768 and 1770. While Americans did not want a standing army on their soil, the one they did have might be too weak to defeat the Bourbons if the need arose. As for the navy, everyone knew that the king had twice as many warships as the French. But after the financial crash, could he afford to keep them afloat?

The crisis in the markets had left a deep impression. In the columns of the press in Boston, it evoked a new skepticism about the mother country. "The resources of this Country are incomparably superior to those of its parent," said the *Gazette* in its diatribe in October. "'Tis matter of notoriety, that the Staples of Great Britain are comparatively few, and that her Commercial Resources are contingent and precarious." Statements such as these were a gross exaggeration—while Britain was in economic trouble, the recession was temporary, and the nation that launched the Industrial Revolution was not a country in decline—but we can see why Americans might form such a view. Benjamin Franklin held the same opinion. In London he counted among his friends the Welsh actuary Richard Price, who believed—honestly, but mistakenly—that Britain's population was dwindling away, as a consequence of poverty, disease, and decadence.*

If that were so, then it was hard to see how Great Britain could indefinitely finance its enormous national debt. In American eyes, the British seemed to face a dismal future. The newspapers in London often said the same thing. And this perception—that the British were weak and all but insolvent while America was going from strength to strength—could only make the colonies more restless.

Above all, the Americans had come to doubt Great Britain's commitment to liberty. Time and again, the king and his ministers appeared to be chipping away at the edifice of freedom. The Stamp Act and the Townshend duties had shown that Parliament had no qualms about imposing taxes in the colonies against the will of the people. When it sent the

---

* A brilliant mathematician, Price was also a nonconformist clergyman, and he kept in close touch with like-minded friends in New England, especially at Yale University. In 1776 he published an outspoken book defending American liberty. His error about the British population arose from what seemed to be convincing evidence: a fall in the birthrate in London, and a decline in receipts from the taxes on windows, ale, and beer. Actually these were statistical blips—in reality, population growth was beginning to accelerate—but his arguments were taken very seriously at the time. In April 1781, Yale conferred honorary doctorates on two men: Richard Price and George Washington.

redcoats into Boston and left them there for eighteen months or more, the government behaved in an overbearing fashion that its own citizens at home would never tolerate. The British reaction to the *Gaspée* raid looked like yet another affront to the principles for which the empire was supposed to stand. By appointing a commission to investigate the affair, with the powers to haul the culprits back to London, Lord Dartmouth appeared to be removing the right to trial by jury. How could a Rhode Islander receive a fair hearing at Westminster in front of a panel chosen for its loyalty to the king? It would set a fearful precedent, one that might make freedom a thing of the past.

And as so often in the northern colonies, men and women feared that religion was in danger. No one in Massachusetts could forget that their colony was founded on the Protestant faith, a form of piety that depended, they believed, on the maintenance of free and equal congregations, without a bishop or a pope to stain the purity of doctrine. Here was another principle to which the British seemed to be indifferent. In America, it was thought that Lord Dartmouth held Christian beliefs closely akin to theirs, but his colleagues were another matter. If they were men of immorality like Lord Sandwich and Lord Rochford, what did they care for religion? It was common knowledge that in the West Indies the cabinet had offered a place in the government to Roman Catholics, simply as a way to keep the peace. Might the British do the same in North America and give the Vatican a bridgehead in the colonies? If such a thing came to pass, it would leave Americans with no option but independence.

As 1772 drew toward its close, opinions like these were expressed in New England with the fervor that precedes a revolution. However unreasonable some of these views might have been, they steadily gained more support. And yet, however much people dislike the system under which they live, it requires more than resentment to turn them into rebels. At least two other preconditions usually have to be fulfilled.

First, they must have a medium of protest. In other words, they need a set of institutions within which they can develop their critique of the old order and create an alternative to take its place. One of the reasons that the revolutions of 1989 in central Europe were so long delayed was just this: that in the late 1940s, the Soviet-sponsored regimes had systematically done away with all the institutions of civil society that might compete with them for power. Second, there has to be a flash point, or rather a series of them: a chain of events that provokes an insurrection, peaceful or otherwise. Both preconditions were satisfied in Massachusetts.

Apart from Rhode Island, it would be hard to think of any corner of the British Empire better educated for self-government. In Massachusetts at least two-thirds of all adult males could vote in the elections to the House of Representatives, the lower chamber of the colony's assembly. In its turn the House chose the upper chamber, the Governor's Council. At a local level, every town held open meetings to run its own affairs. Each one had a militia, more or less well trained. Men and women were used to creating their own enclaves of semi-independence, because that was the way the colony had grown.[4]

By the end of the seventeenth century, the province already had more than eighty towns, each with its own constitution. As the people spilled westward, the number grew to reach nearly two hundred by the time of the revolution. Each new one repeated the process of self-creation, either by staking out virgin soil or by splitting a big old township into smaller units. They fell under some central jurisdiction via the county courts, where the judges sat. The judges were appointed by the governor, who was appointed by the king. And so, in theory, the long arm of the empire reached into the deepest recesses of the countryside. But apart from the judges, it was very hard to find a royal bureaucrat. Although the customs officers policed the waterfront, they did not venture inland. In most parts of the province power lay with the inhabitants, whether sitting on a jury or running a town meeting.

Without their consent, the empire could not function. The revolution took place in the autumn of 1774 when a majority of the people of Massachusetts withdrew their support from the royal authorities. They turned instead to the new Provincial Congress: an institution built from democratic elements—the town meeting and the House of Representatives—that already existed. But this moment of high drama occurred only as the climax of two years of escalation on both sides. Sometimes without intending to do so, British politicians and the people of New England took turns insulting each other until their estrangement was complete. In the end divorce became the only option.

From the British perspective, the *Gaspée* raid was the first step along the road to war. It poisoned the official mind in London. From that moment forth, Lord Sandwich and his closest allies believed they were dealing with rebellion, and eventually Lord North and Lord Dartmouth came to agree as well. But the blame for the next few acts of escalation must lie fairly and squarely in Whitehall. Using his powers at the Treasury, North behaved in a manner that seemed to vindicate all the anxieties that the northern colonies had come to feel. And if he made a terrible error by sending the tea, Dartmouth was equally at fault in another way. Even before the tea had sailed, he permitted Thomas Hutchinson to raise a storm in Boston, a place already scarred by memories of the occupation and the massacre.

When the soldiers withdrew, leaving a small force to hold Castle William, they left behind them an embittered town where the benefits of loyalty to the Crown seemed all but invisible. By the autumn of 1772, seven years had passed since the slump in the middle of the previous decade, but prosperity was still elusive. For many citizens of Boston, life was very hard indeed, and even the wealthy had grounds for discontent.

THE LEIPZIG OF AMERICA

In the eyes of an English visitor, Boston might have seemed familiar, despite its modest proportions. With fewer than seventeen thousand inhabitants, it fell far behind Liverpool or Bristol, which were roughly twice as large, while nearly a million lived in London. But they all had the same winding streets, and they had steeples, wharves, and taverns that looked very similar. Even the Boston slums resembled those of a seaport in England. As he approached the town by sea, a new arrival would initially feel quite at home. But only very briefly: as soon as he stepped ashore, he would start to discover that the town had a culture quite unlike his own.

The British found Boston strange and exasperating. Since the Puritan era when the Bay Colony came into being, their way of life had moved on, as Britain became a nation thoroughly commercial in its values. Old issues of faith and politics that remained alive in Massachusetts had either ceased to fascinate the British, or the debate about them in the mother country had developed in a very different way. Meanwhile, Boston had evolved as well, steering its own distinctive path, until by the 1770s it was almost a foreign town, becoming more un-English with each passing year.

Sadly, the British rarely recorded their physical impressions of the place. Far better accounts were written in the 1780s by French military officers who saw the region with a more friendly eye. In the letters home from Admiral Montagu and other Britons, all we find are complaints: about the locals, about the lack of money and supplies, or about the sorry state of Castle William. As the empire fell to pieces, they had no time for the niceties of observation. But in a happier period ten years earlier a young naval officer came to Boston and painted some fine watercolors. He was Lieutenant Richard Byron, the poet's great-uncle. From his pictures, and from the archives that remain, we can re-create the town and its culture as they would have appeared to a fair-minded Briton just before the war.

The setting was attractive, even beautiful: a blend of the urban and the rural, with meadows, gardens, and orchards reaching deep into the heart of the built-up area. Nature had given Boston the undulating terrain the Georgians loved so much and recorded in their paintings. So Byron produced a study in the picturesque. The town sat on a peninsula, between the harbor and the mudflats of Back Bay, in a basin surrounded by green hills. In 1764, the lieutenant climbed to the top and drew the town from many different viewpoints. A gifted amateur, by luck or by judgment he chose to highlight landmarks that the revolution would make famous.

View of the Long Wharf and Boston Harbor in 1764, by Richard Byron. *The Bostonian Society*

From the heights at Dorchester, he drew the anchorage, crowded with sails. Behind it, Byron showed the curve of the waterfront, two miles long, with its eighty wharves. Somewhere lost among them was Griffin's Wharf, where the tea would be destroyed. Along the water's edge, he added an array of wooden buildings. Behind them, in the middle distance, he cheated a little. The town had seventeen churches—even the navy understood that Boston was devout—and Byron chose to emphasize the point by drawing them taller than they really were. He made the most of three tall steeples, poking up above the roofs and gables. One was the Old North Church, where on the night before Lexington Paul Revere and his comrades hung up the lanterns to say that the redcoats were on the march; another was the Old South Meeting House, where the Tea Party began. Far away behind them, across the Charles River, the lieutenant carefully outlined the slopes of Bunker Hill.

So much for the landscape. Let us imagine that another English visitor arrived in the autumn of 1772, as events began to converge toward the revolution. From the moment he passed the admiral's flagship and landed at the Long Wharf, he would begin to feel slightly out of place in a town that looked familiar but whose way of life was alien.[5]

Because the water was shallow, the wharf was really a pier, stretching a third of a mile out into the harbor. Here, as in Providence or London, he would find the usual smells from ropewalks, distilleries, factories for soap, and scattered heaps of sewage on the mud. Once on dry land, he would see before him a spacious avenue, lined with tall buildings painted white and cream, with signs above their doors that spoke of loyalty. On the right, there was a place to drink coffee called the Crown, and then another, the British Coffee House, further up the avenue. Known as King Street, it sloped up from the waterfront toward the seat of government. Built of red brick, with the royal coat of arms above the door, the old Boston State House might have come from any harbor town in eastern England.

Behind it was a prison, newly built of stone, next to the workhouse: similar to those our visitor knew at home. Around a corner, he would see a church that looked as though it had just flown in from Westminster. When the Bostonians built the Old South, they copied the design from plates in a book by the British architect James Gibbs showing towers and steeples in the empire's capital. Even the layout of the streets resembled London's. Neither place bothered with a neat, rectangular grid, like the one at Philadelphia. Instead, they clung to an old-fashioned model, spilling out on either side of long avenues parallel to the water's edge, with narrow lanes leading down to the harbor and a host of tiny courtyards at the end of alleyways.

Just like London, the town had dense little wards, especially in the North End, filled with artisans and sailors and immigrants and the destitute, like an American version of Limehouse or Wapping. Far into the nineteenth century, Boston still had a few old colonial tenements, spared by the frequent fires that swept away the old waterfront. Photographs survive to show us their appearance. Used as sailors' homes, they looked exactly like old wooden houses by the London docks that served an identical purpose until the Blitz of 1941.

To his relief, the visitor would soon emerge from the labyrinth. A few minutes' walk from the squalor of the North End, he would climb up a steep, grassy slope and find a suburban idyll. There he might pause amid the grazing cows beside a mansion built of granite. It was one of only four stone houses in the town. From the top of Beacon Hill, he could gaze down across the open space of the Common and think about what he had seen. Although Boston had features that he recognized, many things were strangely absent, and the customs of the town seemed very strange.

For example, there was nowhere on the street to cash a check. Boston had not a single bank. In the shops, he saw people buying the latest goods from England, but there was something queer about this as well: they rarely paid the bill with silver coins. It was easy to find a drink—the town had ninety taverns, more or less—but ask for wine and you might be disappointed. Everyone seemed to prefer hard liquor or a pint of ale. In a grocer's store you might find a keg of Madeira, but for some odd colonial reason the price was chalked up not in shillings and pence but by the weight of barley that the merchant wanted in exchange.

All this was bizarre enough, but the newspapers were even more peculiar. The town had no fewer than five, which was strange in itself: an English seaport of the same size would have only one. If he picked up a copy of the *Gazette*, the *Evening-Post*, or the *Massachusetts Spy*, our visitor from England would wonder what eccentric world he had entered. Every London paper filled its front page with advertisements, chiefly of three kinds. They invited the reader to plays, the opera, public balls, or displays of fireworks; they offered him houses for sale or rent; or they listed a regiment of butlers, cooks, and footmen, all of them eager to serve. In Boston, the editors devoted their front page to politics and almost nothing else, bar an occasional sermon. While the British press closely followed the doings of Lord North and his colleagues, often they treated the affairs of state merely as comic relief. The Americans were always deadly serious. Their advertisements were very different too. At the back of a Boston paper you would find "a Negro wench" available for purchase—as much as 10 percent of the inhabitants were black—but you would look in vain for a majordomo or a trained lady's maid. Houses seemed very hard to get as well. The streets were filled with able-bodied men, but no one seemed to be building anything. There was one construction site—a new church, not far from the bourse and assembly room at Faneuil Hall—but apart from that the bricklayers had little work to do.

Everywhere, our visitor would see bookstores, one of them stocked with ten thousand books, but he would look in vain for public amusement. This was a town where a man could be mobbed for playing a flute on a Sunday. Boston had only a single concert hall, in a room above a shop, but the clientele were mostly British naval officers and their friends, there to listen to Haydn and Bach or to throw a party on the queen's birthday. The town would not have a theater for another twenty years.

A visitor from England might simply dismiss the place as a provincial backwater, but if he asked questions, listened to conversations in the street, and kept his eyes open, he would soon find explanations for Boston's peculiarities. Since the historian Cotton Mather coined the phrase in 1702, the people of the town had taken pride in living in what he called "the metropolis of the whole English America." Seventy years later this had begun to sound like empty bravado, and Boston was increasingly frustrated and unhappy.[6]

Like every port in the colonies, the town did well for most of 1772 as a consequence of the economic boom that ended so badly in London. Superficially, Boston appeared to be a busy place, but a glance at the official figures would display a deeper picture of stagnation and decline. Overtaken by other places, chiefly Philadelphia, it was gradually fading into the second tier of colonial harbor towns. Its wharves still saw more traffic than other seaports in America, but much of it was small, coastal stuff. Increasingly, the bigger ships chose to sail elsewhere, to the Hudson, the Delaware, or points further south, where the slave economy was thriving.[7]

Although Boston still made rope and rum and barrels, the trade in cod had moved away to Salem and Plymouth. Very few ships were built. A handful of craftsmen made coaches in the English style; Paul Revere and others did some splendid work with the small quantities of silver available; the town had excellent potters too; and not far inland, there were foundries where iron was produced. Apart from that, Boston manufactured scarcely anything at all. For thirty years, the population had barely grown, despite a constant stream of migrants from outside. Most lingered only briefly until they lost hope of finding a job. Many of the rich had left for bigger houses in the country, and so each year the town became a poorer place. Seven percent of the population was receiving welfare, but many more—perhaps as many people as two in every five—could scarcely pay the rent and keep their heads above water.

With little or nothing to sell to the outside world—certainly no sugar, rice, or tobacco—the townspeople had to struggle all the time. Because the balance of trade was against them, their currency was weak against the British pound, and this was why they had so little silver money. It could only be acquired from overseas, and Boston had little to offer in exchange. A few citizens had some capital, but not enough to put at risk in building factories or digging canals: all of that would have to wait until long after Lexington.

Inland the countryside was comfortable but hardly affluent. If he rode out to Concord or Natick, an English visitor would see how full it was of younger sons and daughters with too little work to do. Within a radius of forty miles or so from Boston, land was in short supply. Try as they might, the farmers could not make their acres grow more corn—their yields had reached a peak some thirty years earlier—and so their incomes did not rise from year to year. Men and women looking for a future on the land were turning away from this part of New England and toward the frontier, far beyond the Connecticut valley, while those who remained had little to spend on goods that Boston might have produced.[8]

The town still had its ships, but so did every other port, from Nova Scotia down to Charleston, not to mention the British themselves, with their large mercantile marine. At sea, competition was fierce for the carrying trade, and Boston no longer had an edge. It was stuck in a groove, economically speaking, something that could never satisfy a man as lively as Paul Revere. To put it bluntly, here was a town that the rest of America was rapidly leaving behind. It was in the wrong place: too remote from the dynamism of Pennsylvania, and too far from the passes over the hills to the west. The town of Boston needed to reinvent itself as the great industrial city it would eventually become after the War of 1812.

Even before the revolution, it contained men and women who understood that this was so. Whatever it lacked by way of banks and silver, Boston never suffered from a dearth of human capital and intellect. On the contrary, the town possessed them in abundance. Apart from its bookstores, it had excellent schools, the rate of literacy was higher than in England, and of course it had Harvard College just up the road. It might be argued that the revolution began in Boston, rather than anywhere else, because its citizens had to solve a chronic problem of unemployment. A town that combined the maximum of talent with the minimum of opportunity, it created far more energy than it could use and too much for the empire to accommodate. In the North End, with its men and boys in search of labor on the docks, this was very obvious, but the problem extended up the social scale.

In every generation Boston gave birth to a surplus of talent, made up of men and women educated beyond the careers available. Many decades earlier the greatest Bostonian of all, Benjamin Franklin, had to leave to seek his fortune elsewhere. By 1772 the problem was acute, as the town failed to grow to absorb the skills its offspring had acquired. What did a boy or a young man do when he left the Boston Latin School or graduated from Harvard? Try as he might, he would find it hard to fulfill his aspirations. Careers might be available in the law, the pulpit, or medicine, but in Massachusetts people lived very long lives by European standards. Every niche was occupied by older men or by the friends and relatives of Thomas Hutchinson.

For artisans like Paul Revere, the same kind of dead end lay in wait, however close he came to perfection in his trade. He could only make so many bowls and flagons for the chapels or for the lodges where Freemasons met. In time he would need a far larger market for a wider range of products, and so would the mechanics who lived nearby. In every stratum of society in Boston, from the very lowest to the wealthy, we can see the same phenomenon: a persistent lack of opportunity.

Too small, too poor, and too reliant on old ways of earning its keep, Boston needed to shake itself loose and kick away the empire. Until it did so, the town could never hope to expand and prosper in the way its people deserved. Under the British colonial system, this could never occur, for two very simple reasons. While the first arose from the dismal science of economics, the second had to do with matters more subtle and more edifying.

As for the economics, the problem was simply this: if Boston and the towns inland were to recover their prosperity, then their future had to lie in manufacturing, because that was the field where ingenuity could achieve by far the best return. It was the only viable option if the Bay Colony wished to spread the benefits of progress among the broad mass of its people, not only the poor in the slums, but also the migrants arriving each year from Europe. But so long as Massachusetts remained within the empire, it could never compete with the British textiles and hardware that flowed in by sea.

At least for a while, the northern colonies would have to throw up a defensive wall of tariffs to protect the industries they needed to create. In the nineteenth century, the federal tariff first established in 1789 would become a source of bitter sectional conflict in America, but it is hard to see what alternative lay open to the early republic. For this reason if no other, there had to be a revolution. Under the old colonial system, tariffs of the kind were entirely forbidden. On the contrary, the British intended to keep America in thrall as a captive market for the goods that only they could make. Far away in Whitehall, Lord Hillsborough had said exactly that.

And so for the sake of its material well-being Massachusetts had to cut itself loose from Great Britain. But in the town of Boston, an astute observer who arrived in 1772 would come across another source of frustration, cultural rather than economic. The novelist Henry James once called it "this unprevaricating city," and so it was. The town displayed an obsession with the most fundamental ideas of right and wrong and liberty and justice. In the course of the eighteenth century, Boston had gradually discarded the Puritan orthodoxies of the past. Like Providence, Rhode Island, with its new college, its newspaper, and the circle who gathered around Judge Hopkins, Boston had created institutions, formal or informal, where free and open controversy was routine.

In effect, debate about political philosophy had become part of the people's way of life; and so it would have been entirely unrealistic to expect Boston to remain content forever within an empire that set rigid limits to innovation. If a visitor from England had gazed down from the top of Beacon Hill, he would have seen a building under construction in a space called Brattle Square. A symbol of autonomy and free debate, the new church rising above the square was one of the civic institutions of Boston in which the revolutionary movement was approaching maturity.

From its origins in 1699, the congregation on Brattle Square had been a citadel of innovation. Tired of old Calvinist dogma, a small group of citizens had assembled to form what they called the Manifesto Church, committed to the principle of open baptism. In other words, anyone could join, without a painful test of morals or belief. In the decades that followed, the church grew and grew, drawing in the town's most highly educated people as well as some of the wealthiest.

If an English visitor in the 1770s had attended its Sunday services, he would have met Abigail and John Adams. Just across the aisle he would have seen the future hero of Bunker Hill, a physician by the name of Joseph Warren. Another member of the congregation was James Bowdoin—rebel, scientist, and friend of Benjamin Franklin's—who drafted the first constitution of the state in which he lived. They sat at the feet of Boston's most influential preacher, Silver-Tongued Sam, or, to give him his proper name, Samuel Cooper, whose brother William held the post of town clerk.

As the numbers grew, the wooden meetinghouse became too small and shabby. And so, in the spring of 1772, it was demolished; in June the first stone was laid for its replacement, in October the carpenters raised the roof, and early in 1773 the pastor gave his first sermon in the new chapel. With 800,000 bricks and a bell shipped over from London, the church on Brattle Square was the largest construction project in Boston in the years just prior to the revolution. At the time of the *Gaspée* incident, when the future looked dark and insecure, the congregation took the risk of building, at great expense, a church committed to a very open form of Christianity.[9]

In a lecture at Harvard, Samuel Cooper poured scorn on what he called "the Romish superstition." Other than that, he made do with very little theology. "The service of Christ requires nothing of us but what is reasonable," Cooper once said. His audience could choose to keep old Puritan ideas if they so wished or toss them in Back Bay if they preferred. In England, even in the established Anglican hierarchy, it was possible to find many clergymen as liberal as Cooper, advocates of a "practical divinity," based on charity and good deeds, rather than on dogma, but English ministers of such a kind could not enjoy in the mother country a social status anything like as eminent as his. Cooper set the tone of faith among the radical elite in Boston.

By the time the new church was erected, civil society in Boston had come to be composed of many institutions—political clubs, Masonic lodges, even the teams of volunteer firefighters—that had developed a habit of freethinking and dissent. Brattle Square was simply one example. All of these institutions existed in complete independence from the official hierarchy of the empire. Like the town meetings out in the countryside, it was only a matter of time before they became the building blocks for a new republic.[10]

Among the worshippers at Brattle Square, there sat a genteel revolutionary called John Hancock, the owner of the granite mansion on Beacon Hill. Always free and easy with his money, he gave £1,000 to build the church, and he paid for the bell. In his career and complex personality, we meet an inverted image of Lord North. While North was typically British, Hancock was typically Bostonian. Like John Wilkes in London, he stood for everything the king and his ministers hated most.

THE PEEVISH PATRIOT

As we did with Lord Dartmouth, we can approach John Hancock by way of a portrait in oils. Hanging today in the Museum of Fine Arts in Boston, it was painted in 1765, when Hancock was only twenty-eight. It came from the brush of John Singleton Copley, another Bostonian who had to leave for greater things. The picture shows us a pale young adult, with an unlined face, sitting at a desk on which stands a vast ledger filled with numbers. His legs are thin, his shoulders are narrow, and the book seems more substantial than the torso. His delicate wrists emerge from beneath a blue frock coat, whose fabric hangs awkwardly over his slender body.

Copley presents John Hancock as a novice, ambitious and diligent, but perhaps unequal to the role society expects him to play. The richest man in Boston, heir to a fortune made by his uncle, he wears gold buttons and

John Hancock in 1765, by John Singleton Copley. *Bridgeman Art Library*

braid, but he looks like somebody for whom wealth is more a burden than a privilege. Is he happy? The set of his mouth, with lips clamped tight, may be a sign of determination, or anxiety, or both. John Adams knew him extremely well—the two played together as boys—and when he wrote down his memories of Hancock, he drew another picture of a highly strung young man.

"Patient," "punctual," "steady," and "industrious": these words sprang to mind, but Adams also recalled John Hancock's struggle with his own emotions. Often confined to bed by some chronic disease whose precise nature is unknown, he suffered from some kind of mental distress as well. According to Adams, Hancock displayed "a certain sensibility, a keenness of feeling, or a peevishness of temper, that sometimes disgusted and afflicted his friends." Because the Hancock papers are scarce and fragmentary, it is hard to say exactly what this means. When he died, heavily in debt, leaving his widow Dorothy all but penniless, most of them were lost, apart from some business records and a few private letters. For his part, Adams believed that John Hancock inherited his anxious nature from his father, a clergyman, gifted but shy, who died young. It may be that as with Lord North the problem lay less with neurosis than with the scale of the challenges he faced.[11]

Hancock's path to rebellion had many twists and turns. Given his rank in society, this was bound to be the case. However sincerely he advocated liberty, he could not easily condone acts of mob rule or an outright attack on wealth and privilege. It would take a long time for John Hancock to make up his mind that the future lay with independence. And so, in 1765, he opposed the Stamp Act, only to take fright when the rioters went wild and ransacked the home of Thomas Hutchinson. In 1768, he became a hero when the customs men seized his sloop the *Liberty*. For a while, he became the leader of the radical party. And then, in 1769, he fell out with Samuel Adams and seemed to be making his peace with the royal authorities.

Given this complicated career, friends and enemies alike often found him hard to read. An opponent called him "Johnny Dupe," a conceited young man or an amateur, all too easily tricked by the likes of Samuel Adams into making political gestures that merely satisfied his vanity. Was he a man of genuine principle? Or simply a merchant and a smuggler, pursuing a selfish agenda of his own? During his lifetime these questions were often asked, and historians still disagree about the answers.[12]

The most frequent charge laid against him is this: that Hancock used his wealth to buy his way to power and status. He certainly did that, with the help of his aunt Lydia. Together they spun a web of patronage by lending money to fellow Bostonians and making lavish gifts to Harvard College. They even paid for a new fire engine for the town. But from a British perspective, the career of John Hancock seems far easier to understand. He behaved as any gentleman would in England in the eighteenth century. Far from being vain or conceited, Hancock simply tried to fulfill the obligations of his rank. In the words of one biographer, "Hancock loved being the public man," which was perfectly normal in the age in which he lived.

In Great Britain, when a man made a fortune in trade—or, better still, if his uncle acquired it for him—first of all he would buy as much real estate as he could afford. Having done so, he went into politics, because only there, in the House of Commons, could he command the full respect of his contemporaries. If he had to spend money to succeed in public life that was not only his right but also his duty if he believed he had something to offer the nation.

John Hancock simply wanted to do the same. Of all the Boston patriots, he had the closest ties with Britain, not only via his London partner George Hayley, but also through his connections in the port of Bristol, where his agent, Henry Cruger, served on the town council. Both Hayley and Cruger would in due course enter the British Parliament themselves. From day to day, Hancock gave the running of his business to his confidential clerk, William Palfrey, who lived on the Boston waterfront but pored over all the latest news from England. Twice Hancock sent him to London, where he dined with John Wilkes. Palfrey kept a portrait of Wilkes on his parlor wall, a present from Mrs. Hayley, and described its value as "inestimable."[13]

For Hancock and the people around him, the politics of the mother country were as compelling as those of Massachusetts. Far from thinking of himself as a provincial, Hancock fashioned his own identity as an enlightened citizen of the world, the equal of any man of rank in England. The books he presented to Harvard told the same story of good taste and generosity. Devoted to the college, his beloved alma mater, he gave it the very latest literature, some of it bordering on the scandalous. The books included not only twenty-seven volumes by Voltaire but also the works of the philosopher David Hume, a guidebook to London in six parts, and even Robert Adam's studies of Roman architecture. The Hancock donation filled an alcove in the college library.[14]

By rights, a gentleman so progressive should have taken his seat alongside Edmund Burke in the House of Commons, where Hancock would have enjoyed the public career he longed for. But this could never happen. Ever since the seizure of the *Liberty*, Hancock had been a marked man in London, which meant that he had no chance of high office in Massachusetts either. By the end of 1772, it was clear that however much he tried, he could never achieve within the colonial system the success that he felt was rightfully his. In business the outlook seemed equally grim.

His uncle had possessed a genius for commerce, which the nephew did not share. Thomas Hancock had begun by selling books. He went on to create an empire of property, including Beacon Hill, fed by the money that flowed from maritime trade. Like the Browns of Providence, he had to overcome the old New England problem, the scarcity of goods to export and hence a shortage of hard currency. His solution was a form of arbitrage. If Boston and its hinterland needed tea and hardware, they could be found in London, where the English merchants would also give him credit. To settle his account, Hancock dealt in a host of different items— molasses and rum, but also flour and whale oil—and swapped them back and forth, between Boston, Newfoundland, the West Indies, and Spain. Bills of exchange, otherwise known as IOUs, passed to and fro between the parties, and Hancock used them to pay his debts in England.

He dealt on the black market as well; in colonial America, as we saw, often there was really no alternative to smuggling, even if only as a temporary expedient. And then, in the 1740s, his lucky break arrived: a war between the British Empire and the French. During that conflict, and then the next, Thomas Hancock became a defense contractor and one of the largest bankers to the British army. When he died in 1764, all of this passed to his nephew, but by now the world was changing. The contracts from the army disappeared, the navy made a smuggler's life far harder, and the economics of Boston remained fragile. During the next ten years, the Hancock fortune became a wasting asset, as the young man tried and failed to emulate his uncle.

He changed the family's business model by creating a new and larger fleet to specialize in sending potash and whale oil to Great Britain. In theory his instincts were sound, given the greedy appetite of England for commodities like these, but in practice John Hancock had little chance of success. The British had their own whaling ships, they could buy potash elsewhere, and Hancock could not hope to corner either market. Worse still, the town of Boston was often flooded by a glut of imports from the mother country.

By 1772, Hancock's business had fallen into terminal decline. With each year that went by, his debts in England increased. The financial crisis came close to ruining his firm. And so we find him close to despair, even as the new church on Brattle Square is rising to the heavens. John Hancock cannot meet his liabilities in England, because the price of whale oil has collapsed. Nobody in Boston can afford to buy the things he has to sell. "I am extremely sorry," he tells his agents in the mother country. The times are "precarious," he writes in November. "Goods are at present sold here so excessively low."[15]

In politics as well, the sky was darkening. Ever since the autumn of 1770, when the British appointed Thomas Hutchinson as governor, a cold war had existed between him and the colony's elected assembly. It was a conflict that Hutchinson seemed to be winning. With the army gone from the streets, the popular party led by Samuel Adams lost the political initiative. For nearly two years, an uneasy calm fell over Massachusetts, during which Hancock distanced himself from Samuel Adams, seeking to play the peacemaker between the governor and the General Court. And then, in the autumn of 1772, as the economy began to deteriorate again, suddenly politics flared into life once more. Alarming news arrived from London and reawakened old anxieties. Although at first John Hancock hesitated, soon enough he threw his weight behind the movement led by Adams.

The Revolution of Ideas

Despite the fiasco of the Stamp Act, Lord North and his colleagues had never abandoned the idea of using taxes levied in the colonies to pay the cost of imperial administration. The threepenny Townshend duty on tea still survived, and while the revenue was only small, it should cover the salaries of the royal officials in Massachusetts. And so, when Hutchinson became governor, his stipend was quietly paid by the Crown. Rumors to this effect began to circulate in Boston, but only in the middle of 1772 did Hutchinson confirm that they were true. Far from being a technicality, the issue might have grave implications for liberty. The charter of 1691 had been a little vague on the subject, but the usual practice was to finance official salaries with the local taxes voted each year by the House of Representatives.

If that system were changed, it was argued, the principles embodied in the charter would be undermined. A governor paid directly by the British could choose to ignore the will of the people. Worse still, a precedent would be established. Soon *all* the officials in the colony would become little better than hirelings of the king or, as Samuel Adams put it with his gift for understatement, "pimps, parasites, panders, prostitutes and whores." Even judicial salaries might be funded in the same way. Once on the imperial payroll, the judges would be answerable only to the authorities in London. Did Lord North intend to pay the justices directly, making them hirelings too? At the end of September 1772, news arrived in Boston that the British meant to do just that.[16]

A month or so before Lord Hillsborough resigned, he had asked the Treasury's permission to pay the five most senior judges in Massachusetts from the proceeds of the tea tax. During the meeting in July at which he heard the report about the *Gaspée*, North signed the relevant order. It is hard to say whether he knew just how provocative this was. He certainly wished to curb the power of the colonial assembly. But, as so often, Lord North might have been acting from short-term political motives. At this moment, he was embroiled in the cabinet crisis. In a vain effort to hold his team together, he might simply have chosen to placate a colleague, Lord Hillsborough, whom he did not wish to lose.

Whatever North's intentions were, the news caused an uproar in Boston, leading to the tirades in the press of early October. A few weeks later another ship arrived with the reports about the *Gaspée* commission of inquiry. It seemed that Rhode Island and Massachusetts had been targeted for persecution by the Crown. Trial by jury and the independence of the judiciary: these were two sacred principles, closely linked to each other, both of which the British seemed determined to subvert. On October 24, the story about the *Gaspée* commission ran in the Boston press. Four days after that, a town meeting assembled at Faneuil Hall, chaired by Hancock, to prepare a response to this impending crisis. It took three weeks to write, but the document that emerged came close to being a revolutionary manifesto.

Drafted by a committee including Samuel Adams and Joseph Warren, it is usually known as the Boston pamphlet. It was formally adopted on November 20 by another town meeting with about three hundred people in attendance: a good turnout for a place the size of Boston. Although the pamphlet ran to little more than forty pages, in large print with wide margins, it would be hard to exaggerate its importance. Not because it contained anything new by way of theory: it leaned very heavily on the work of John Locke, dating from the 1680s, and even quoted him verbatim. The pamphlet's originality lay elsewhere: in its daring and in the use to which it was put. Because the pamphlet was short, clearly written, and carefully divided into numbered sections, nobody could fail to understand it. The opening section begins with an uncompromising statement of what the authors call "the Natural Rights of the Colonists as Men." In a single paragraph of fewer than sixty words, the pamphlet sets them out precisely.[17]

The first law of nature is self-preservation: that is to say, human beings have a *duty* to seek their own welfare. But if that is so, then it follows that men and women must also have *rights*, because, if they did not, they would be unable to preserve themselves as the law of nature dictates. Human beings have a right to all those things without which self-preservation is impossible. They have a right not only to life, to liberty, and to property, the pamphlet says, but also to defend those rights when they are under threat. From these simple principles, the pamphlet developed a point-by-point critique of the defects inherent in the British regime. In all, it listed twelve grievances against the colonial system: twelve ways in which the empire had put property, life, and liberty in danger.

They included not only taxation without consent but also General Gage's standing army, the judges' salaries, the *Gaspée* inquiry, and the rules of trade that handicapped the American economy. Right at the top we find the most fundamental grievance of all, and here the pamphlet bordered on sedition. The authors entirely rejected the Declaratory Act. "The British Parliament have assumed the powers of legislation for the colonies in all cases whatsoever, without obtaining the consent of the inhabitants," they said, and this, according to them, was intolerable and wrong.

It would also be hard to exaggerate how hazardous the situation in Boston was becoming for the British. Far from having a coherent policy for bringing America to heel, Lord North and his colleagues had very little policy at all. Small, tired, and demoralized, the Colonial Office had just acquired in Lord Dartmouth a new and perhaps a naive secretary. The western wilderness was on the way to being lost, and so was the battle with the smugglers. In any event, the king and his ministers were preoccupied elsewhere. However dearly they wished to tighten their grip on America, their approach was patchy and piecemeal.

And yet Lord North had managed to convince the people of Boston that he was bent on their subjugation. The pamphlet said exactly that. Written to appeal to the widest possible readership, it was swiftly disseminated. While it was in preparation, Samuel Adams and his colleagues organized the new Boston Committee of Correspondence. The committee sent the pamphlet to like-minded friends and allies throughout the colony. As many as fifty other towns in Massachusetts joined the network, exchanging ideas with Boston: towns such as Pownalborough, which was about to issue its own outspoken denial of British authority. Six months before the Tea Party, the people of Pownalborough were already dropping hints about resistance to the Crown by force of arms.

It seems likely that the pamphlet was intended to push Thomas Hutchinson into some extreme response. If so, it was entirely successful. In the wake of the *Gaspée* affair, the governor believed that London wished him to stand firm against sedition. For this Lord Dartmouth was largely to blame. Uncertain what line to take, he tended to reply to Hutchinson's letters with vague statements of principle that led the governor to believe that the British would support whatever steps he took. And so, in the first week of 1773, he braced himself for action of the kind he thought Dartmouth wished to see.

Fatally, Hutchinson made the error of attacking Samuel Adams and his allies on the philosophical battlefield where they were strongest. A wiser man would have fudged the issue, offered some bland reassurance, and waited for the fuss about the judges to die down. Instead, the governor did what came naturally to a Harvard graduate. On January 6, when he opened a new session of the colonial assembly, Hutchinson delivered his own long speech about fundamentals. The town meetings in Boston were illegal, he told them, and the publication of the pamphlet was a crime. Worst of all, its authors understood nothing about the empire. So the governor gave the assembly a lecture on the constitution. No line could be drawn, said Hutchinson, between the supremacy of Parliament and the complete independence of America.[18]

While his logic might have been impeccable, his timing was appalling. In politics, many words are better left unsaid. By speaking so plainly, the governor wrecked any hope of reconciliation. On January 26, the House of Representatives gave its reply: a dogged reiteration of the Boston pamphlet. Most outrageously, they denied that Parliament could make laws for the colonies without their free consent. They began to draw up a petition to George III calling for an end to the plan to pay the judges from the tea tax. Much later, speaking privately in 1775, Lord North identified this as the moment when, in effect, the people of Massachusetts declared their independence. It was also the point at which John Hancock aligned himself forever with Boston's most outspoken radicals.

In order for the American Revolution to begin, a broad coalition had to be created across the province, united in hostility toward Great Britain. The alliance would need to include not only the people who attended the church at Brattle Square but also storekeepers, mechanics, laborers, and the unemployed. In addition, it would have to encompass the farmers from the interior. The farmers, not the people of Boston, had to supply the military vanguard of the revolution, because the town was simply too small to be decisive. Boston accounted for less than 6 percent of the colony's population.

By the spring of 1773, this alliance was close to completion, with John Hancock the man most likely to lead it. No one had shown more firmness than Hancock in the defense of liberty, wrote Samuel Adams in April. He said that in a letter to his friend Arthur Lee in London, which he asked Lee to give to John Wilkes. And it was there, in London, that the next step was taken down the road to war.[19]

At last, Lord North was ready to show his hand with regard to Bengal. He was about to announce his plan to rescue the East India Company in exchange for a package of reforms. He secured its passage through Parliament at a time when, suddenly, he found himself basking in glory. Without firing a shot, the cabinet ministers achieved something in which every Briton could take pride: they put the French to shame. In a triumphant mood that lasted until the end of the year, the king and his ministers blundered into their clash with the colonies.

Chapter Nine

THE BOSTON TEA PARTY: PRELUDE

Your conduct has given the greatest satisfaction.

—GEORGE III TO LORD NORTH, 1773[1]

It took only an hour or so on April 26, 1773, for the House of Commons to agree that the East India Company could send its surplus tea to America. No vote was taken. The members of the opposition were far too few to have any hope of defeating the measure.

Briefly and with little energy, the Rockingham Whigs pointed out that if the tea sailed to the colonies with the threepenny tax still in force, the Americans would resist its importation. "If he doesn't take off the duty, they won't take the tea," said their leader in the Commons, William Dowdeswell, a man already dying of either cancer or tuberculosis. His most vocal supporters in the debate were the agitated Scotsmen George Johnstone and his brother Pulteney, who wanted to end the tax on tea entirely and gave the same warning of potential unrest.

Old Jacobites they might be, but the Johnstones counted Adam Smith among their closest friends. As the free-market economist might have done, they denounced the tea duty as an affront to what they called "the plain principles of commerce." If it were abolished, consumption in the colonies would soar, and the smugglers would be eliminated. But Lord North gave that argument short shrift. Yes, he wanted to end the illegal trade in tea from Holland, but for the good of the empire he had to think of politics as well as money. "I am unwilling to give up that duty upon America upon which the colonial salaries are charged," he told the Commons. Americans could not expect any more concessions while "the temper of the people there is so little deserving." At that point the man keeping shorthand notes broke off. What else Lord North said is not recorded.[2]

After an even easier passage through the House of Lords, the Tea Act became law on May 10. With that, the issue faded from the stage of British politics. Only sketchy reports appeared in the press, and Benjamin Franklin hardly noticed them. In his next letter to America he did not mention the episode at all. Nor did Edmund Burke when he wrote to the colonial assembly in New York in July. Neither man recognized the significance of what had taken place.

Meanwhile, Lord North seemed to be invincible again. After such a gloomy winter, the political climate had steadily improved. True, the economy remained fragile, with credit still almost impossible to obtain. In the textile trades and in London, the slump continued, while bread remained expensive, leading to strikes and more riots by the hungry and the unemployed. Even as North announced the Tea Act, a few miles to the east the weavers and the men who shoveled coal were gathering in their hundreds to protest against the price of a loaf. But the panic in the markets had subsided, and gold had begun to flow back into the Bank of England. In the spring, North's budget speech went wonderfully well, with another healthy surplus to report. The stock market rose to a peak not seen since 1768.

Lord North had also made excellent progress with his plan to rectify the corrupt administration of Bengal. At last the egregious Colebrooke had followed so many other bankers into insolvency, white waistcoat and all, and lost his seat on the East India Company's board. The company found a new chairman, a loyal supporter of the cabinet called Henry Crabb Boulton. Even so, it took seven difficult weeks, beginning in late April, for North to pass his Regulating Act for India. But with Boulton's help he eventually won every debate: in the Commons, in the Lords, and in the stockholders' meetings at East India House. Henceforth, Bengal would have a governor-general and judges chosen by the cabinet and the king. In return, the Treasury would lend the company the money it needed. The deal to save it from collapse was finally done in the last week of June, and at last the financial crisis was resolved.

Against this background, it was only too tempting to see New England as a little local difficulty of scarcely more consequence than the interminable wrangling in South Carolina. During the whole of 1773, America was never mentioned once in any of the scores of letters that passed to and fro between Lord North and George III. Their gaze was turned elsewhere, toward the Baltic and the Mediterranean. They were about to win a famous victory that warmed the nation's heart.

During the spring and early summer, while the plan for the tea drew ever closer to fruition, once again Great Britain stood on the brink of hostilities with France. War scares were frequent, but this one ranked as by far the most serious since the Falklands affair three years earlier. Although it ended well for Lord North, success had ambiguous consequences. It made the British overconfident, leaving them temporarily strong but even more isolated diplomatically. In due course, this would have grave implications for their strategic position in the North Atlantic and the Caribbean.[3]

The war scare arose indirectly from the Swedish revolution of 1772. In Stockholm the young king Gustav III had led a military coup against his Parliament, with the open support of Louis XV. At that the Russians began to rattle their sabers, warning of preemptive action if France attempted to make Sweden a vehicle for its own ambitions in the Baltic. Soon enough, reports reached the British that the French were arming their fleet, not on their country's Atlantic coast, but in the southern harbor of Toulon. It appeared that they meant to attack a Russian squadron that Catherine the Great had sent to the Aegean as part of her grand design to dismantle the Ottoman Empire.

Were France and Russia about to go to war? If so, then a general European conflict seemed the likely outcome, something that would place the interests of Great Britain in grave danger. The British wanted neither France nor Russia to emerge as the dominant power on the Continent, but while the Russians might still be won over with diplomacy or gold, the French could never be trusted. And so it was against them that British efforts were directed.

On April 24, two days before the Commons debate on the Tea Act, Lord Sandwich ordered a frigate out of Gibraltar to follow every move the French might make. Fireships were prepared to enter Toulon if necessary and burn their fleet at its moorings. At home the Royal Navy began to make ready for sea, either to scare the French into retreat or to sink them if need be.

At the outbreak of any war in the period, a race for mobilization occurred, a race that the British always had to win. Their foreign policy depended on the navy as an instrument of deterrence. This could only be credible if they could deploy it swiftly in a situation such as this. But for reasons of economy, in peacetime the bulk of the fleet was laid up in dock with masts and sails stowed onshore and with only skeleton crews.

The French, it was estimated, had 74 ships in their line of battle, while the British had nearly 130. But many of these were under repair, only 80 or so were fit for action, and in theory even these might need four weeks to be ready to sail.

All eyes were on Lord Sandwich, who had worked so tirelessly to prepare for a crisis of precisely such a kind. For their part, his officers were spoiling for a fight. To lead his task force to the Mediterranean, Sandwich made an excellent choice: Charles Saunders, the sailor who had landed General James Wolfe at Quebec in 1759. "If I sail, there will be a war," said the admiral, and for once the seamen of the Channel ports flocked to the colors without a press gang to round them up. Two days after receiving his orders, Admiral Saunders had ten ships at sea.[4]

For three weeks the nation remained in suspense, while the newspapers beat the patriotic drum. And then a dispatch arrived from Paris saying that the French had thought again and ordered their fleet to stand down. Only six months earlier, Frederick the Great had been calling the British feeble and irresolute. Now even the skeptical Prussian had to admit that they had stood their ground. And then, far from offering an olive branch, the British chose to teach the French another lesson. Lord Sandwich had a taste for spectacle—in Handel's *Messiah*, he liked to play the timpani—and so in his moment of glory he invented something new: an immense

George III reviewing the fleet at Spithead, June 22, 1773, with the royal yacht in the center, by John Cleveley the Younger. © *National Maritime Museum, Greenwich, London*

display of naval might. With the diplomatic corps invited to attend, the king would review the fleet at Spithead, with a front seat reserved for the ambassador from France.

In the early hours of June 22, George III left his palace at Kew with an escort of cavalry. Over the heaths of Surrey they galloped down to Portsmouth, where they were greeted by a salute of guns heard sixty miles away across the hills. Behind the king, Lord North and the rest of the government came hurrying down as well, with Lord Dartmouth bringing his son, whose term at Oxford had recently ended. To feed the royal entourage, the finest chef in London joined the procession to the coast, carrying with him His Majesty's silver plate, acres of white linen, and a cellar full of wine and brandy: six thousand bottles, more or less, to lubricate the banquets on the flagship. In brilliant sunshine, George III toured the dockyard, the forts, and the fleet, drawn up in two lines abreast. The sailors rowed him up and down in a gilded barge, past twenty battleships fully rigged and newly painted. Onshore he watched the blacksmiths repair a huge anchor, and he doubled their ration of beer. A choir of shipwrights sang "God Save the King," and the king was duly gratified.[5]

Nothing like this had been seen in England before. The roar of the cannon brought spectators to the waterfront in their thousands. And when after three days the king left for home, the crowds lined the streets of every town along the route. In Guildford and Godalming they struck up the national anthem, "expressing, in the warmest manner, their Duty and Affection," said the official report in the *London Gazette*. Later that year, David Garrick turned the review into a play to entertain the audience at Drury Lane. Eager to surpass his rivals in the theater, Garrick hired the finest set designer from Paris and put on a reenactment of the great event, complete with rolling waves and model ships and choruses of "Rule, Britannia."

The cabinet was equally delighted. Lord Rochford kept the French envoy at his side and gleefully reported his grudging admiration. The fleet had saved the peace, said his poetical friend Lord Suffolk. "How must our royal master exult in the proud pre-eminence it gives!" he wrote. "How must this display of national strength, these floating bulwarks of his kingdom, strike his maiden view!"[6]

And yet, in every capital in Europe, old hands at diplomacy knew that for all its ships and artillery, Great Britain was powerless to determine the course of international affairs. The British still had not a single ally overseas. Unable to intervene, the cabinet had watched the cruel partition of Poland come and go. And while Corsica had fallen to the French, in the east the Turks were soon to lose the Crimea to Catherine the Great. Nothing could be done to prevent either development, despite the strategic importance of both pieces of territory.

To all of this, the British were merely bystanders, entering their period of not-so-splendid isolation. Their lack of allies would cost them dearly during the war for America, when they had to fight on many fronts without an ally. But nobody in London expected anything so extraordinary to occur. For the time being, the mood in Whitehall remained confident and calm.[7]

On July 1, Parliament rose for an unusually long recess. With India dealt with, the budget passed, and the French put back on the leash, no business remained outstanding. Lord North had even pacified the London weavers with a new law to regulate their wages. Not for another six months would Parliament reassemble, and by then it would be too late to prevent the calamity in Massachusetts.

The Veil of Error

It might have helped if in Virginia the royal governor, Lord Dunmore, had noticed the signs of increasing disaffection. Of all the businesspeople in America, the tobacco farmers had probably suffered the most from the financial crash. After borrowing heavily from British merchants to expand their acreage, suddenly they faced demands for swift repayment, and for a while new loans were almost impossible to find.

Already uneasy about the empire, the planters read the news from the northern colonies with all the more dismay. Their sympathies lay with John Hancock and his comrades. When Virginia's House of Burgesses met in March 1773 for its annual session, the members had before them press reports about the *Gaspée* commission and the British plan to pay the judges' salaries with the tea tax. They had also seen the Boston pamphlet and Hutchinson's foolish reply. On March 12, the assembly chose its own committee, eleven strong, to correspond with Boston and watch for more signs that American freedom was in peril. Its members included not only Richard Henry Lee, brother of Samuel Adams's friends in London, but also Patrick Henry and Thomas Jefferson, who was in his first outing as an activist against the Crown. Again, it would be hard to overstate how dangerous this situation was for the British. Via the network of correspondence, created by Adams, Joseph Warren, and their allies, the sense of grievance felt in New England came to be shared across the continent.

And yet barely a word of this reached Whitehall from the governor in Williamsburg.[8]

A proud, flamboyant man, Lord Dunmore once had himself painted in full Highland dress by Sir Joshua Reynolds. In later life, in retirement in Scotland, he erected a giant stone pineapple on top of a summerhouse to commemorate his years of service in the colonies. But while he was there, it did not occur to him to listen to public opinion or to relay it back to London. In the first half of 1773, he sent only six official letters home, and none of them mentioned the new committee. Then, at the end of July, he fell silent. Nine months passed before he wrote his next dispatch in the spring of 1774. With so little information to go on, it was all too easy for the British to imagine that Massachusetts and Rhode Island were alone in their discontent.

Sometimes Lord Dartmouth would receive private letters from English travelers who knew America well and wanted to alert him to trouble ahead. Occasionally, their observations were very accurate indeed, but they appear to have been ignored. One such letter arrived on his desk in March 1773 from the pen of a merchant named Charles Smith. A shrewd, observant man, every few years Smith crossed the Atlantic and rode from New England to Pennsylvania, collecting debts as he went, reading newspapers, and listening to the people whom he met.

That year, he came home alarmed by what he had heard. Along the coast and even three hundred miles inland he encountered a spirit of rebellion, forming what he called "a regular connected chain, from New England to Georgia." Everywhere Americans were talking about John Wilkes, whom they took for a hero. Everywhere the press ran incendiary attacks on the British. On the frontier, Smith found "an uncultivated banditti," villains given to theft and murder, many of them recent arrivals from Ireland with a record of insurgency in their native land. As for Massachusetts, that was very nearly lost, according to Smith. In a few years, he said, the people there would "throw off their dependence on England—be assured it will be the case." How should the British respond? Coercion would fail, Smith argued: "rough threatening measures" would never work, but only "those of a more lenient mild nature." Every colony needed better governors, he said, Massachusetts should be closely watched, and most of all "the wisest heads in ministry" should devise a comprehensive plan to reconcile the colonies to the empire.[9]

We have no idea what Dartmouth made of Smith's comments, because no reply has survived. In any event, nothing was done. The system did not allow the Colonial Office to intervene directly. They had to work through the governors they had appointed. If the men in question neglected their duties like Lord Dunmore, or if they were as self-seeking and corrupt as William Tryon in New York, they might *eventually* be recalled, but only when it was too late. No comprehensive plan of the kind proposed by Smith was ever formulated. And then, on March 26, word arrived in London that the *Gaspée* commission had failed to break the wall of silence in Newport. Not a single reliable witness would come forward to testify against John Brown of Providence.

Three days later, after eight weeks at sea—an unusually long passage—a dispatch came in from Thomas Hutchinson describing his verbal fracas with the House of Representatives. An earlier report about the governor's speech had already raised eyebrows in London, and now, when the Baltic crisis was growing ever more serious, Lord Dartmouth discovered that Hutchinson had provoked the assembly to adopt the Boston pamphlet as its own. Massachusetts seemed to be going the same way as Rhode Island. His lordship replied, telling Hutchinson to keep quiet. If the assembly made any more gestures of disobedience, he should simply dissolve it and call new elections. Other than that, Hutchinson should do nothing. The colonial secretary was even more forthright about the governor early in May, when he saw Franklin again.

"What difficulties that gentleman has brought us all into by his imprudence!" Dartmouth said. As far back as December, the colonial secretary had warned Hutchinson not to indulge in what he called "nice distinctions of civil rights and legal constitutions," which would simply arouse more controversy. For reasons not only of political expediency but also of faith, Dartmouth hoped to avoid unnecessary strife. When he wrote to the governors in America, his language carried religious connotations drawn from his Calvinist reading of the Gospel. In his eyes, every human being was a soul in danger, inclined to sin, but he also believed that Christ had the power to save them. Dartmouth was convinced that the unrest in Massachusetts arose not from any genuine grievance but from a defect of the spirit.*

---

* Under Lord Dartmouth, the Colonial Office became a bastion of the new evangelical Christianity that was gaining ground inside the Anglican Church. For example, when early in his tenure a vacancy arose on his staff, he appointed a young man named Ambrose Serle, a disciple of Dartmouth's friend the Reverend William Romaine. In 1775, Serle published an antirevolutionary pamphlet titled *Americans Against Liberty; or, An Essay on the Nature and Principles of True Freedom, Shewing That the Designs and Conduct of the Americans Tend Only to Tyranny and Slavery*. It included a description of American patriots as "noisy restless animals." He

Like sinners everywhere, the people of Boston saw the world, he wrote, through "a veil of error," cast over them by atheists and fanatics. Far from patriots defending liberty, they were merely men and women imprisoned by their carnal passions. And yet, if they would only pause and listen patiently to a government that cared only for their welfare, perhaps the Bostonians might be won over, like the London prostitutes who filled the hospital wards at the Lock. "The seat of the disorder is rather in the head than in the heart," Dartmouth told Thomas Hutchinson. "A time may come when men will see that they have been cutting up the root of their own felicity, under the false notion of resisting injuries that never existed." The last thing he wanted was to bully them into submission.[10]

By now, however, a moment was rapidly approaching when the hawks in the cabinet could argue that coercion was the only option. Although the Tea Party was still six months away, by the end of June it had already become practically inevitable. In theory, it was still possible for Lord North to delay the implementation of the Tea Act, and the precise manner in which the tea would be sent to America was still open for discussion. But in practice, the flow of news from the northern colonies gave His Majesty's Treasury no reason to alter course. On the contrary, New England seemed to become more annoying with every month that passed.

In Massachusetts, the House of Representatives had at last drawn up its petition to the king. Badly timed, badly written, and addressed to the wrong party, it took far too long to draft and even longer to arrive. Dated March 6, it reached Whitehall only on May 12, when Franklin gave it to Lord Dartmouth, just as the Anglo-French crisis reached its peak. Tactless or even insulting, the petition began by lecturing George III about the history of England. Under the charter of 1691, it said, the colony made its own laws and voted its own taxes. Parliament in London had no right to interfere. As for the plan to pay the salaries from the tea duty, it was a clear infringement of their rights as loyal but self-governing citizens. They appealed to the king to save them from what they called "the perversion of law and justice" by judges in thrall to Lord North.

For any number of reasons, this document could do nothing but harm. A month earlier, the king had received an equally rude petition from the liverymen of the city of London, demanding the reinstatement of John Wilkes as member of Parliament for Middlesex. If that was a flagrant

---

went to America in 1776 as private secretary to the new British commander in chief, Admiral Lord Howe. In later life Serle wrote a series of Calvinist tracts, the most popular of which—*The Christian Remembrancer*—was still being reprinted as late as the 1850s.

piece of impertinence, the same was true of the lecture from the colonists. In addressing their petition to the monarch, Samuel Adams and his
allies had displayed their own misunderstanding of the British system of
government. The king ruled not by fiat or decree but only by the consent
of Parliament. Even if George III had wanted to, the constitution did not
permit him to interfere. A matter concerned with taxation and finance, the
scheme to pay the salaries out of the tea duty arose from a law passed by
the House of Commons. Only the Commons could repeal a statute it had
approved but by now the parliamentary session was very nearly over. On
June 2, Lord Dartmouth wrote to Benjamin Franklin conveying the king's
response: he refused to intervene, and condemned the petition as the work
of what he called "the artifices of a few who seek to create groundless
jealousy and distrust."[11]

Even so, Dartmouth tried to salvage something from the wreckage.
Along with the petition, Franklin had given him a covering letter filled
with more grievances from the assembly in Massachusetts. The list was
long. Besides the judges' salaries, the assembly members complained about
the customs service, the navy, the *Gaspée* commission, and the troops at
Castle William. Dartmouth took it all in his stride and did the best he
could.

On June 19, shortly before he left for the Spithead review, he went
behind Thomas Hutchinson's back. Against protocol, and apparently
without consulting his staff, Dartmouth wrote privately to Franklin's closest contact in Boston, Thomas Cushing, the Speaker of the House, a man
believed to be a moderate. Dartmouth tried to offer him a deal. As he
explained, Parliament could never surrender its authority over the colonies. It was a matter of principle, without which the empire could not
function. But it might agree to suspend its right to levy taxes in America
provided Massachusetts, in its turn, agreed to be reasonable. The assembly
would have to disown the Boston pamphlet and withdraw the motion it
had passed on January 26. If it did, he would go to Parliament in the next
session and attempt to have the grievances removed.

In writing this, Dartmouth went beyond anything that hawks like
Sandwich and Suffolk could endorse. But it would have made no difference even if his colleagues had undergone a conversion of their own. The
minister's letter took two months to cross the ocean, arriving only in the
middle of August. By that time, the Massachusetts assembly was also in
recess. Cushing shared the letter with Samuel Adams and other members
of the Boston Committee of Correspondence, who flatly rejected the deal.

By now, the situation had passed beyond the control of any politician, however wise, in either nation. Since the Virginians met in March, five other colonies, from New Hampshire to South Carolina, had created their own Committees of Correspondence. "The alarm is universal," Cushing wrote to Franklin late in August. "The eyes of the whole continent are turned upon this province."[12]

In fact he was exaggerating—New York and Pennsylvania were still hanging back—but Cushing made an important point: that after spreading the word so widely about its plight, Massachusetts could no longer act unilaterally. Even if it wished to—which it did not—the House of Representatives would have to consult its counterparts in the other colonies before it could comply with Dartmouth's suggestion. Cushing replied to the colonial secretary, telling him that the British would have to redress American grievances before Massachusetts could back down.

Although Cushing wrote that on August 22, his letter did not reach Lord Dartmouth until November. By then the ships with the East India Company's tea were already halfway across the Atlantic and beyond recall. And here we come to what might seem, at first sight, a bizarre turn of events. While Lord Dartmouth was aware of the Tea Act, he apparently knew nothing about the way it was put into practice. Neither he nor John Pownall took part in the final decision to ship the tea to America in enormous quantities and in a manner bound to end disastrously. This was less remarkable than it might appear, and it goes to the heart of the misunderstandings between Great Britain and the colonies.

Many Americans had come to view the British government as an evil machine, single-mindedly doing the bidding of a clique of men obsessed with power. While some blamed Lord North, and others blamed King George III, they believed they were dealing with a ruthless autocracy out to do them down. And this was exactly what John Wilkes and his supporters in the London press had been telling them for nearly a decade. But in fact it was a travesty of the truth. In reality, North led a cabinet and not a tyranny. His government consisted of rival departments, each one with its own agenda. Power lay scattered among them. So did information, and they answered to a Parliament often uncertain and divided. Apart from Lord Dartmouth, who was above this kind of thing, ministers briefed the press against each other, off the record. Each one fought to enlarge his share of public spending, just as their successors do today.

Only a very gifted British prime minister can make the cogs and wheels of government mesh smoothly together. Although in his own era nobody surpassed Lord North as a manager of Parliament, he rarely thought through the implications of official policy. Even when he did, he could not ensure that everyone cooperated to fulfil it. In terms of power and prestige his own department, the Treasury, stood head and shoulders above the rest, as it still does, but this only added to the confusion. North and the Treasury Board had devised and passed the Tea Act without consulting their colleagues about its practicalities. As a result, the policy was hijacked from outside by self-interested sharks from the business community keen to make it serve their own purposes.

The Tea Ships Sail

The Tea Act of 1773 allowed the East India Company to apply to the Treasury for a license to ship tea to the colonies without any duties paid in the United Kingdom. That was all. The text of the legislation said nothing about the methods by which the shipment should be made or the tea distributed in North America.

The simplest option would have been to put the tea up for auction in London in the usual way but with each wooden chest stamped "only for export." Any merchant could have placed a bid for however much he chose, subject to a written undertaking that it would be sent only to the colonies, where the threepenny Townshend tax would have to be paid. If so, the tea might have traveled in small consignments on many different ships, denying the people of Boston their opportunity to produce a political motion picture by torchlight in December. It seems that Lord North's aide Charles Jenkinson initially intended the tea to sail to America in just such a piecemeal fashion.

But then William Palmer intervened with a more sophisticated plan. The ink was scarcely dry on the Tea Act before Palmer and his competitors laid siege to the company with schemes of their own. At last, merchants who sent tea legally to America could hope to outwit the smugglers by matching the price at which it was sold on a colonial street. Palmer had a head start: his friend Governor Thomas Hutchinson had written to him at the end of February, giving him discretion to order as much tea that year as he thought fit.

With the wholesale price in London still very low, Palmer urged the company to send all its surplus tea to the colonies, but in bulk and not in dribs and drabs. Armed with data supplied by the Hutchinsons, he reckoned that the American market could easily take about ten thousand chests, enough to generate nearly £300,000 in cash. A contest began between Palmer and his rivals to win mandates to handle the business. Palmer moved first, on May 19, but by the end of June at least eight London firms were bidding for contracts from East India House.

They all agreed on one thing: instead of putting the tea up for auction, the company itself should ship it out to agents whom each firm would appoint in the leading American ports from Charleston up to Halifax. Although the company would have to share its profits with the dealers in London and the consignees in the colonies, its margin would still be very attractive.

Best of all, the tea would hit America in such a huge quantity that it would saturate the retail market and forestall the smugglers, whose own supplies would not arrive until after the Amsterdam sales in September. William Palmer volunteered the Hutchinsons to act as the consignees in Boston.[13]

Speed was of the essence, but first the East India Company's chairman had to fight off another shareholder revolt. For months the Johnstones, William Crichton, and a few Rockingham Whigs had sought to derail Lord North's proposals to reform the company. It took until the middle of July for Crabb Boulton to win a vote in favor of the tea scheme. As later events would show, this delay was more than inconvenient, but at last, on July 30, ten of the leading tea traders in London gathered at India House to finalize the details.

Five days later, the company's directors gave their blessing. By August 10 the size and composition of the cargoes had been agreed. Nine days after that, and without informing the Colonial Office, Lord North and the Treasury Board issued the license for the tea to sail.* The lion's share would go to New York and Philadelphia, the largest markets, with the rest headed for Boston and Charleston. Cautiously, just in case their agents in America failed to find buyers, they chose to send only 600,000 pounds of tea. That was only a tenth of the amount the colonies drank each year, but even so the volume was enormous, coming to more than two thousand chests. More than three-quarters were filled with the cheapest variety, Bohea. But then the plan began to go awry.

A cargo so large took weeks to load, and so it was September 27 before

---

* Ironically enough, by this time the East India Company no longer needed to export the stuff to America at all, because its future had been secured by its deal with the government embodied in the Regulating Act. But the tea scheme went ahead all the same.

all the tea ships had left the Thames. With the wind against them, it was the middle of October before they could leave the English Channel and enter the Atlantic. Four were bound for Boston: two brigs, the *Beaver* and the *William*, and two larger ships, the *Eleanor* and one called the *Dartmouth*. The earliest they could expect to arrive would be late November. By that time word of their mission had circulated all over the colonies, with awful results.

In London, however, the voyage of the tea ships still aroused little interest, partly because so few people actually knew that they had left. At the Colonial Office, John Pownall seems to have learned of their departure only in December. Meanwhile, during the autumn, with North away and Parliament in recess, politics remained in its season of suspended animation. And when the capital began to fill again in late October the chief talking point was not America but Ireland.[14]

To the dismay of the Whigs, the parliament in Dublin proposed to put a tax on the Irish income that accrued to absentee landlords. The scheme had originated with the government as a means to pay off the debts that Ireland had run up to pay for its military garrison. Time and again in the century that followed, issues to do with Irish land and Irish finance would rear their heads to baffle English politicians. So it was on this occasion. Among the Rockingham Whigs two men—not only the marquess, but also the Duke of Devonshire—extracted huge rents from a reluctant Irish tenantry. And so, oblivious to what was happening in the colonies, the Whigs mobilized to defend their rights as people of property. Until January 1774, Edmund Burke and the Rockinghams filled their correspondence with huffs and puffs about the absentee land tax. They ignored the rising tide of resistance in America, obvious though it should have been from the colonial newspapers available in London's coffee houses.

Meanwhile, Benjamin Franklin was growing ever more uneasy. As always he spent the summer in the country, but when he returned to the capital in September, he wrote to Speaker Cushing to give him a belated warning about the tea ships. The tone of his letter betrayed his mounting frustration with Dartmouth and Lord North. During the second half of 1773, Franklin began to lose his last vestige of loyalty to Great Britain. Never popular with the hawks in Whitehall, he was about to incur their outright hatred. In England, the game of politics had certain rules by which gentlemen were expected to abide. In the government's opinion, Franklin broke them in a manner close to criminal. In due course they would take their revenge by seeking to humiliate him, with more dire consequences for the empire.[15]

SATIRE AND SUBVERSION

By midsummer, anyone who knew Franklin well could tell just how irritated he had become. Tired by what seemed to be endless muddle—about the Ohio country, about colonial boundary disputes, and most of all about Massachusetts—he felt he could do nothing more in London. He began to make plans to leave for America in the autumn.

In July, Franklin wrote to Samuel Cooper in Boston to congratulate him on his new church at Brattle Square, suggesting that the building be heated with the latest kind of iron stove. As for the differences between the mother country and the colonies, the British would never act, he predicted, "till the breach becomes greater, and the Difficulty of repairing it greater in a tenfold proportion." Pleased to hear that Virginia was aligning itself with Massachusetts, Franklin hoped that the anger aroused by Hutchinson's speech in January would lead to a continental congress to defend American liberty. "Nothing would more alarm our Ministers," he wrote. Only a shock would bring them to their senses. And as it happened, the previous year Franklin had already taken steps to bring about a shock of such a kind at the expense of Thomas Hutchinson, whom he regarded as a pedant and a fool.[16]

Over the years, so many indiscreet letters had flowed from Hutchinson's pen that sooner or later some were bound to see the light of day. In particular, the governor had exchanged some embarrassing correspondence with a British politician, Thomas Whately. In six of these letters, Hutchinson had chosen to grumble about the freedoms that Massachusetts enjoyed under its charter from King William. In one of them, the governor had hinted that the charter ought to be amended or revoked. The empire could not endure, he wrote, without "an abridgement of what is called English liberty." This was, at the very least, a very unfortunate turn of phrase. In the summer of 1773, the letters were published in America after Franklin sent them to Thomas Cushing. When they appeared, they aroused another furor, just before the news of the Tea Act arrived.

To be fair to Thomas Hutchinson, he had some valid reasons for writing letters so unguarded. A gifted and wide-ranging intellectual, an expert on landscape gardening and Shakespeare, Thomas Whately was immensely well connected. Among his closest friends he counted the former prime minister George Grenville, whom he helped to draft the Stamp Act, and in due course he became a senior aide to Grenville's protégé Lord Suffolk. The son of a banker but trained as a lawyer, Whately had a special aptitude for finance, on which he wrote with elegance and learning. He also took a special interest in New England, where his family had been early settlers. By making contact with him, Hutchinson gained access to the innermost circles of Lord North's administration. This was not unreasonable. Sooner or later there *had* to be a new deal of some kind between the colonies and the mother country, and the governor's voice needed to be heard in whatever negotiations might occur.[17]

And then, in 1772, Whately died suddenly, at forty-five, without leaving a will. In the confusion that followed, somebody took the governor's letters and gave them to Benjamin Franklin for reasons that remain obscure. Franklin would never reveal his source, except to say that he was "a gentleman of character and distinction." But the fact was that Hutchinson had few admirers in England. An awkward, prickly fellow, apt to ask for favors, he worked hard: but was he *really* quite up to his job?[18]

Clearly the man who passed on the letters thought not, and neither did Franklin. By now, Franklin had come to see Hutchinson as a primary source of division between Massachusetts and Great Britain. And so, in December 1772, he sent the offending letters to Cushing. He wanted the Speaker to share them with the Boston Committee of Correspondence, but confidentially, without letting them reach the columns of the press.

In doing this, Franklin took an enormous risk. He clearly intended to undermine the governor. Given his dim view of Hutchinson, which was honestly held, that was his duty, but it was a rash course of action even so: indeed, perhaps one of Franklin's most endearing features is just this, his unusual tendency as he grew older to become more radical and more daring. Once Cushing showed the letters to Samuel Adams, it was only a matter of time before they were published. And so they were, in June 1773, when Adams read them aloud to the House of Representatives. A printed version duly followed. Every newspaper in New England ran the story, and the House sent another petition to George III, calling for Hutchinson's immediate dismissal for gross misconduct.

The petition arrived in England in August, but again the Americans were asking the impossible. Perhaps it would have suited Whitehall to be rid of the governor, who had outlived his usefulness. Even so, the law had to run its course: an office such as Hutchinson's was regarded as a form of personal property, protected by due process of law. No British monarch could recall a governor on grounds of misconduct without a full inquiry by the Privy Council. But it would not meet until January, when Parliament reassembled after its extended break.

In the meantime, the Hutchinson letters ran in the British press as well, serialized in August in the paper read by the king, the *Public Advertiser*. As yet, Franklin's involvement remained a secret, and so he chose to raise the stakes again. Detached though he was from the political mainstream, he kept in close touch with a few journalists, especially at the *Advertiser*, where he found a willing helper. With a blend of serious news, humor, and acid commentary on public affairs, it was the finest newspaper of its day. The *Advertiser* also prided itself on its independence from the Wilkesites and the government alike. One of its proprietors, Caleb Whitefoord, summed up its editorial stance. "What first engaged me in political controversy was a desire of undeceiving the Publick," he wrote. "Whenever any change of Ministry happen'd, I have always endeavoured to make such changes a matter of laughter."[19]

In 1773 the *Advertiser* was fighting hard for circulation against an upstart rival, the *Morning Post*, recently created to serve a growing taste in the West End for gossip, scandal, and tales from backstage in the theater. With the *Advertiser* in need of good copy, Whitefoord instantly agreed when his friend Benjamin Franklin—they lived in the same street—offered him a series of columns defending American freedom. Hoping to capitalize on the impact made by the governor's letters and weary of Dartmouth's well-meaning inertia, Franklin took up the weapon of ridicule. By means of satire he would try to jolt public opinion in England into a new, more enlightened attitude toward the empire. Written with verve and wit, and with irony and passion, his columns ran nose to tail for two weeks.

However little he knew about North and the cabinet, Franklin perfectly understood the English sense of fun. In a few thousand words, he conveyed every grievance felt by the colonies in a style that appealed to men and women raised on Jonathan Swift and *Tristram Shandy*. His articles reached their brilliant climax on September 22, with a satire cast in the form of an edict from the king of Prussia. An elaborate hoax, the article poured scorn on the official British view, so dear to men like Thomas Whately, that the colonies should pay taxes to help meet the empire's running costs. It purported to contain a proclamation from Frederick the Great, dated from his palace at Potsdam a few weeks earlier. Its premise was this: since the Anglo-Saxons came from Germany, they owed allegiance to the Prussian king, and, being his colonists, they owed him money too, for the cost of defending them in the Seven Years' War. "Those who are descendants of our ancient subjects should contribute to the replenishing of our royal coffers," said the edict. The readers clearly enjoyed the joke, because the edition sold out within hours.[20]

Clever though they were, Franklin's articles might also be described as rash and counterproductive. His thinking apparently ran as follows.

With a general election due to occur by the summer of 1775 at the latest, Franklin expected America to be one of the issues on which it was fought. North was weak, he believed, like the nation he led, and frightened of gains by the Wilkesites at the polls. So North *might* be prepared to offer new concessions to the colonies, but only if the newspapers kept him under pressure.

Franklin's strategy sprang from a misreading of the British system. In fact, eighteen months was a very long time in politics; for the time being, the American question remained a relatively minor issue; and the articles appeared when Parliament was on holiday and the London social season had yet to begin. And so the articles merely came and went without raising more than a laugh. The publication of the Hutchinson letters was quite another matter. This *did* excite genuine anger in the government and convinced it that Franklin had become an enemy in league with the worst elements in New England.

The early death of a colleague as competent as Thomas Whately had left his friends distraught, and they were powerful men with sharp tongues of their own. They also had ready access to the law. Had the letters been stolen? It certainly seemed that they had. If it emerged that Franklin had sent them to Boston, at best he would find himself pursued through the courts for civil damages; at worst, he might face a criminal charge of theft.

Of all Whately's closest friends, one man posed by far the greatest threat to the American. This was a Scotsman, Alexander Wedderburn, a barrister renowned for his intellect, the size of his fees, and his vindictive nature. Under Lord North, he served as solicitor general, advising the cabinet on points of law. In that capacity, he helped the attorney general, Edward Thurlow, to compose the opinion that the *Gaspée* raid was treason. On the Treasury bench in the Commons, one observer recalled, Thurlow and Wedderburn sat "like two brazen pillars" on either side of the prime minister. Both men fiercely rejected any concessions to the colonies. If Franklin were named in connection with the letters, Wedderburn would seek to destroy him: partly in revenge for the affront to Whately's memory, and partly as a warning to other outspoken colonials.[21]

At first, suspicion pointed at a former customs official in Boston, John Temple, who nursed an old grudge against Hutchinson. Accused of having taken the letters, Temple protested his innocence to the point of fighting a duel against Whately's brother William. It appears that neither man had any experience of affairs of honor. Even so, they met in Hyde Park at dawn on December 11. Whately fired first and missed, Temple discharged his pistol into the air, and then they drew their swords. Whately was wounded nine times, it was said, but he survived, and the duel became another sensation in the press.

With lives at stake, Franklin could no longer hold his tongue. Even now it took him two weeks to come forward, but on Christmas Day the *London Chronicle* ran a brief statement in which he cleared John Temple's name. Franklin said that he had obtained the letters elsewhere, from the gentleman of character whom he would never identify. In his defense, he argued that far from being truly private, they were written by a man in public office. "Their tendency was to incense the Mother Country against her colonies," Franklin went on. That being so, it was his duty to give them to the Massachusetts assembly for which he acted. Although it contained elements of comedy, the affair had also become a political matter of the utmost seriousness. Even if the Boston Tea Party had never taken place, Franklin would have faced at the very least a sharp rebuke when the Privy Council met. As it was, something much worse lay in wait at the hands of Alexander Wedderburn.

For many years since the repeal of the stamp tax in 1766, other matters that seemed to be more pressing had pushed colonial affairs into the background of British politics. This would only change when the first reports of the Tea Party arrived in London. The news would fall like a sword on Lord North, whose education and career had left him entirely unprepared for such a turn of events. In America, meanwhile, the army and the navy looked on with emasculated fury as acts of rebellion unfolded before their eyes.

Chapter Ten

THE BOSTON TEA PARTY: CLIMAX

Nothing but severity will do now.

—LIEUTENANT COLONEL ALEXANDER LESLIE, WRITING
FROM BOSTON, TEN DAYS BEFORE THE TEA PARTY[1]

I t was a crime, pure and simple, carried out with the threat of blood-shed. That was how the British officers in Boston saw the Tea Party. Even before the first chest of Bohea fell into the harbor, they began to call for retribution of the harshest kind. General Gage was away on leave in England, but his opposite number in the Royal Navy witnessed every disloyal move the Americans made.

On November 17, 1773, a sloop came in from England, the *Hayley*, owned by John Hancock, carrying word that the tea ships were approaching. Although they would not arrive for another two weeks, already Admiral Montagu expected a violent insurgency. From his flagship, HMS *Captain*, moored near the Long Wharf, he could plainly see the waterfront mob in ferment.

His contacts in the town had passed the word to Montagu that plans were being laid to attack the fleet and the tea ships, with rafts set ablaze and pushed into the harbor. "I ordered a strict watch to be kept, night and day," the admiral wrote in his journal on the evening of the eighteenth. With the *Gaspée* affair still fresh in his memory, he could take no chances. His officers prepared grappling hooks, placed in the bows of longboats, to tow away the burning rafts if the need arose. The fleet's small force of Royal Marines stood to arms, their pouches filled with cartridges.

From an American point of view, the Boston Tea Party is usually seen as a peaceful incident: defiant or even disorderly, but nothing remotely resembling an act of war. It took a very different shape in the eyes of the admiral and his opposite number in the army, the officer in command at Castle William. What the British saw was another *Gaspée* raid, undertaken with the same contempt for life, property, and the rule of law. The blame lay entirely, they believed, with what Montagu called the "evil disposed," the radicals led by John Hancock and Samuel Adams, the only men from Boston they named in their letters home. And neither the redcoats nor the navy could lift a finger to stop them.[2]

On board the *Captain*, an elderly ship of the line, the admiral could run out sixty-four guns, but in the circumstances his artillery was useless. Even a direct request from Governor Hutchinson would not have permitted the navy to open fire on a port full of civilians under British rule, an action for which there would have been no precedent. For its part the army lay confined to its squalid barracks on the island in the harbor. Since the wells at Castle William had run dry, their water had to come from the town, leaving them at Boston's mercy. At the fort the British had ten companies of soldiers, from the Sixty-Fourth Regiment of Foot, but all of them were under strength. Low on gunpowder—the nearest arsenal was in New York—the redcoats numbered little more than three hundred. It seems that their morale was weak, as well it might be, given the state of the sheds in which they lived. Six privates had deserted since July.

Castle William fell under the command of yet another Scotsman, a lieutenant colonel aged forty-two, a keen golfer by the name of Alexander Leslie, a scion of a military dynasty in Fifeshire that had always supported the Crown against the Jacobites. After the war an old comrade remembered Leslie as a popular officer, correct and polite, but a soldier of only moderate abilities. Ten days before the Tea Party, the Bostonians had already goaded him almost beyond endurance. His half brother, the Earl of Leven, had recently sent him a set of clubs; and when the lieutenant colonel sent a letter of thanks on December 6, he filled it with a tirade against the town's unruly citizens and his own political masters.

"The East India Company's tea has made a fine dust," he wrote. "The people are in actual rebellion, and where it will end none can say." In Whitehall, the politicians had acted feebly, the weakest being Lord Dartmouth, who, said Leslie, had "not enough of the devil to manage the ungrateful Americans." Things had been allowed to drift until, like children spared the rod, the colonists had been spoiled: treat them leniently, and they would always ask for more. The time was long overdue for the use of force. All the lieutenant colonel needed was an invitation from

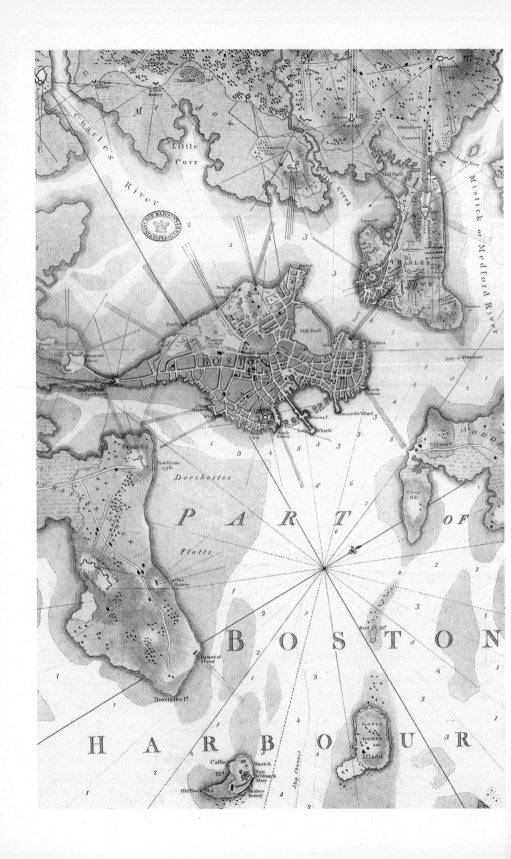

Governor Hutchinson, and he would happily restore order at the point of the bayonet.[3]

That request would never come. Instead, the army and the navy had to stand by while the Bostonians did as they pleased. When they reached America, the tea ships sailed into the most outrageous episode of treason since the '45, and one that left, like the *Gaspée* incident, a legacy of bitterness and resentment in the British officer corps. The Tea Party persuaded them to seek military answers to political questions; and within another eighteen months, this would lead to the disastrous march to Lexington and Concord.

THE MOHAWKS PREPARE

As so often, it had all begun with an item in the press. During the summer, the American papers carried a few lines about the Tea Act, with sketchy reports about the company's plans for its tea, but nothing substantial until the end of September. On the twenty-ninth, the *Pennsylvania Journal* printed a letter from Samuel Wharton, a merchant from the colony based in London, where he had been involved with Franklin in the scheme for settling the Ohio country. In the summer, Wharton had been at India House for the decisive meeting about the sending of the tea. His letter in the *Journal* gave the gist of the scheme: six hundred chests to come to the Delaware, and the same to the Hudson River and to Boston, for auction on the company's behalf. Within the week, the news reached New York. At first, doubts arose about the terms on which the tea was traveling. Would it carry the loathsome threepenny tax, or had it been abolished as Americans had hoped? Soon enough, it emerged that the duty remained in place, and within days the first protests began.[4]

On October 6, a paper called *The Alarm* appeared on the streets of Manhattan. As usual it was anonymous, but New York had a large contingent of Liberty Boys, led by an immigrant Scotsman, Alexander McDougall, known to his friends as the Wilkes of America. Working in partnership with his friend Isaac Sears—both men had been fierce opponents of the

Left: Drawn up during the siege of Boston in 1775, with north at the right-hand side and Castle William at the bottom, this British military map shows the town as it was in the early stages of the revolution. The Long Wharf is clearly visible poking out into the harbor, while to its left are the mudflats and Griffin's Wharf, just above the two fathom mark, where the Tea Party took place. *Detail, from the British National Archives, Kew*

Stamp Act—McDougall might have been *The Alarm*'s principal author, or at any rate its publisher. However, the speed with which it appeared and the nature of its contents support another hypothesis: that it was at least partially written in London, perhaps by Arthur Lee. The author seems to have read the exposés of the East India Company published by the House of Commons. Crime and extortion in Bengal and fraud and corruption in England: such were the company's stock-in-trade, said the writer, soon to be exported to America with the tea, whose arrival would be fatal to the cause of freedom. By cornering the market and driving other traders to the wall, the company would create a monopoly and then extend it from tea to other goods as well. Worse still, if Americans bought the tea and paid the tax, they would sacrifice the doctrine of no taxation without consent. Other taxes would follow until Lord North had the colonies at his feet.

The Alarm ran for three issues, striking a chord not only in New York but also in Philadelphia. Both towns had thriving communities of smugglers who stood to lose heavily if the company's tea flooded their markets. But while this helped arouse resistance to the scheme, the smuggling fraternity could not dictate the course of events. On October 16, as many as seven hundred people came to a town meeting in Philadelphia to pass ten resolutions against the Tea Act, branding anyone who handled the tea "an Enemy to his Country." Doubtless the gathering included many men who dealt in contraband, but they cannot have formed the majority of an assembly so large. The sense of patriotic outrage was authentic, and all the more deeply felt because of the way the tea scheme had been organized.

By now the East India Company had appointed local merchants to act as its consignees in each American port. They swiftly became targets of derision, easily portrayed as villains in league with avaricious financiers and the tyrannical Lord North. In New York, for example, the consignee Abraham Lott doubled as the colony's tax collector; a colleague, Henry White, sat on the council that advised Governor Tryon; and a third man, Frederick Pigou, a Londoner, came from an Anglo-Dutch stockbroking family. His father spent nearly thirty years as a supercargo in China, and in 1773 he sat on the company's board. Pigou's partner Benjamin Booth had run a dry goods store in New York for years, but he was English too.[5]

In Philadelphia some of the four consignees were equally easy to depict as tools of the British establishment. One firm, James & Drinker, owed its contract to Pigou's influence. Another consignee was Gilbert Barkley, who was en route to the town from England, on the tea ship *Polly*, after lobbying hard for a role in the tea scheme. That left Jonathan Browne, of whom little is known, and Samuel Wharton's brothers Isaac and Thomas. Merchants of Quaker stock, the Whartons had sound American credentials—Franklin counted them as friends—but this only left them all the more open to intimidation.

Here and in Manhattan, resistance to the tea took the form of dogged campaigns—in the press, at public meetings, and on the streets—to compel the consignees to step down. In both towns threats of violence were made, especially in New York, where, despite or because of the presence of the army, the atmosphere was particularly volatile. During the Stamp Act riots, New York had come the closest of any seaport in America to a firefight with the redcoats. As recently as 1770, British soldiers had clashed in the streets with the Liberty Boys in the bloody incident known as the Battle of Golden Hill. And so on November 5, Guy Fawkes's Day, when a crowd made an effigy of one of the consignees and hanged it from a gibbet, he and his colleagues were in genuine fear for their lives.

In Pennsylvania and New York these tactics achieved complete success. By the end of November, all the consignees had either resigned or quietly gone to ground. In New York on November 27, we find the first mention of patriots arrayed as Indians like their counterparts on Martha's Vineyard in 1772. Another anonymous handbill appeared, coming from a party who called themselves "the Mohawks." Under the noses of the British military, they warned that anyone who tried to land or store the tea would receive "an unwelcome visit." On the same day in Philadelphia, which had no garrison of redcoats, another menacing handbill hit the streets issuing dire threats against the master of the *Polly*. "What think you, captain, of a Halter around your neck?" the handbill inquired. "Then gallons of liquid tar decanted on your pate—with the feathers of a dozen live geese?" Soon the Whartons and their colleagues decided that discretion was the better part of valor. They stood down. In both New York and Pennsylvania, nobody could say what might happen when at last the tea cargoes arrived, but one thing was perfectly clear. Although Governor Tryon hoped to bring his ashore at the Battery under armed guard, the British plan had already failed in its essentials. No orderly public sales could take place.

But as always, Massachusetts was another story. In that emotional province, so full of idealism and resentment, it would never be possible to end the affair simply by bullying the consignees until they stepped aside. William Palmer had done his work far too well by having the governor's own sons named as recipients of the tea. It became a matter of honor and family money for Thomas Hutchinson that the tea must enter harbor regardless of the risk. But even if the East India Company had selected different consignees in Boston, the outcome would probably have been identical.

Months before the tea ships left the Thames, the politics of Massachusetts had already entered a deadlock that could be broken in only two ways: either by Hutchinson's removal or by a revolutionary act, even if it was unplanned and spontaneous. The situation in the province had become an angrier version of the standoff in South Carolina, where the wheels of government had already ground to a halt. The same thing was happening here as well but far more dangerously. Under the terms of the Massachusetts charter, each arm of the government—the assembly, the law courts, and the executive—had to work together, or the system could not function. By the summer of 1773, it was close to breaking down entirely.

Because of the Boston pamphlet, his inflammatory speech, and the publication of his letters to Thomas Whately, Hutchinson had lost what personal authority he possessed. The same was true of the judges, their position undermined by the British decision to pay their salaries from the tea tax. By now both chambers of the General Court—the Governor's Council and the House of Representatives—had risen in what was, in effect, a *coup* against the royal authorities: that was certainly how it seemed to Lord North. And while Hutchinson's prestige evaporated, his antagonist John Hancock gained in popularity, emerging as a kind of alternative governor, ready to assume the role *de facto* when the appropriate moment arrived. By autumn, the members of the House of Representatives knew that George III had rejected their petition against the judges' salaries; and they also knew that when Parliament sat again in 1774, their complaints were unlikely to be listened to.

They had reached a stalemate; and early in October, apparently before he heard of the tea ships, Samuel Adams said as much in a brilliant piece of political analysis. It was contained in two private letters to a member of his network, Joseph Hawley, another old agitator against the Stamp Act, based deep in rural Massachusetts at the town of Northampton.[6]

According to Adams, two problems lay uppermost in the mind of Lord North: the impending general election in Great Britain, and the likelihood of war with France. From his friends the Lees, Adams also knew that the Wilkesites were making solid progress in the capital. Thanks to hard work at the grass roots, John Wilkes stood an excellent chance of at last becoming lord mayor of London. The Wilkesites could also hope to make gains in the parliamentary poll; but from this, Adams drew the opposite conclusion to Benjamin Franklin's. Although Adams still held some odd views about the British constitution's finer points—he never really understood the relationship between the Crown and Parliament—he did not fall into Franklin's trap of underestimating the prime minister. Adams believed that the politics of Great Britain made it all the *less* likely that the cabinet would address American grievances. Instead, Lord North would shelve any colonial reforms until the war with France and the election were both over and done.

The British, Adams wrote, would simply offer "cakes and sugar plums" in an effort to "sooth America into a state of quietness, if they can do it, without conceding to our rights." It was all the more essential to stand firm until one day the king and his ministers saw the light: when, perhaps, they found themselves losing another confrontation with the French. Five years before Louis XVI came to America's aid, Adams already knew that the fate of freedom in the colonies might hinge on the French navy. In the meantime, they had to remain united and resist any compromise. So Adams argued, and the files of his Committee of Correspondence make it plain that many towns in Massachusetts agreed. In a mood of deep intransigence, they heard the news that the tea was on its way and that McDougall, Sears, and their other friends in New York intended to turn it back.

As historians have often pointed out, Boston was slow off the mark in joining the campaign against the tea, but the delay amounted only to a week or two, and probably arose merely because incoming ships had hit rough weather. By itself it tells us little. When the town learned the names of its consignees on October 18, a furor began there as well. The choice could not have been worse. Besides the younger Hutchinsons, the consignees included their kinsman Richard Clarke. Another importer of legal tea, Clarke had given his daughter in marriage to Thomas Hutchinson Jr. The other two were Benjamin Faneuil, brother of the builder of the hall, and Joshua Winslow, from an old *Mayflower* family: famous names and conspicuously pro-British. During the war both men would support the Crown.

Within three days, Adams's committee had written to the other colonies, denouncing the Tea Act's iniquities. Two days after that, on the twenty-third, at the Green Dragon Tavern, the members of the political caucus from the North End met and pledged to stop the sale of the tea, if necessary with "their lives and fortunes." Among them were Joseph Warren and Paul Revere, and of course Samuel Adams, but also two less familiar characters, William Molineux and Thomas Young. Seven weeks later, all except Revere would play prominent roles in the town meetings that led to the destruction of the tea. Only Molineux came from a mercantile background; and although he might have been a smuggler, the evidence

remains inconclusive.* For Molineux and his friends, politics had come
to be a mission to which they were passionately committed: it was neither
a game nor a front for contraband. Perhaps the most radical was Young,
another admirer of John Wilkes, with whom he exchanged letters. And
since Young was apparently the first Bostonian to propose in public that
the tea should be destroyed, his case may be the most interesting.[7]

Like his close friend Joseph Warren, Young practiced as a physician, but
he made his name in Massachusetts not as a doctor but as a philosopher,
expounding avant-garde views about theology: atheistic, it was said. In
Boston, where he lived close to poverty, his enemies called him "a flaming
zealot" or "a bawling New England man," but his origins lay far away, not
in a town, but in rural New York, where high rents and the hunger for land
had led to popular uprisings long before the Tea Party. The son of Irish
immigrants but raised in the Hudson valley, Young became a fierce critic
of privilege, counting Ethan Allen among his closest acquaintances. They
even co-wrote a book, *Reason the Only Oracle of Man*, attacking orthodox religion, and Young lent his support to Allen's campaign against New York's
attempt to annex the valley of Vermont.

Here was an intellectual in politics, the Robespierre of Boston; but
unlike the Frenchman Thomas Young had a common touch. Of all the
radical leaders of 1773, with the exception of Revere, Young enjoyed the
closest ties to the working people of the North End, whom he would
come to see as the stormy petrels of the revolution. An activist like Young
did not oppose the tea from narrow self-interest. Whatever might be true
elsewhere, in Boston resistance to the tea arose from principle or from
ideology, call it what you will. In the background, of course, there lay an
economic grievance, a sense of frustration at the town's relative decline
that could not be halted inside the empire; and certainly no one wished to
pay more than they needed for a cup of tea. But even more than the raid
on the *Gaspée*, the Tea Party would be driven by ideas.

When he burned the sloop, John Brown had simply taken to its logi-
cal conclusion the Rhode Island theory of local independence developed
by Stephen Hopkins. In Boston, the ideas behind the Tea Party mostly

---

* So is the evidence that John Hancock smuggled tea. Governor Hutchinson said that he
did, a claim often repeated, but documentation is lacking. Certainly his uncle Thomas
dealt in illegal Dutch tea, and John Hancock smuggled wine in the 1760s. But his surviving
business papers from the 1770s show no trace of smuggling of any kind. On the contrary,
a document preserved in London shows that in the spring of 1773 one of Hancock's ships
carried thirty chests of legal, duty-paid tea from the Thames to Boston.

came from the pamphlet of 1772, but they had equally lethal consequences for loyalty to Great Britain. It was this that made the popular campaign against the tea so fatal for the British: an ideological content whose appeal the authorities could not grasp.

While a smuggler would retreat when the risks of protest outweighed the financial reward he hoped to make, an intellectual like Young would never stand down at all. And within weeks of the news that the tea ships were heading for Boston, we find a similar mood of principled defiance in corners of Massachusetts very different from the waterfront. At Harvard College on November 10, a professor's wife writes to a friend, mocking the governor as "the First Personage," afraid to stir out of his house without an armed guard. Hardly a firebrand, Hannah Winthrop tells Mercy Otis Warren about the commotion in New York. She calls the threepenny duty "the unconstitutional revenue," and she uses language similar to Adams's. She describes the consignees as "pusillanimous sons of avarice and ambition" and looks forward to their defeat.[8]

If a faculty spouse at Harvard was saying such things, the British had already lost the battle for hearts and minds without even realizing that it was taking place. With barely a source of information other than Thomas Hutchinson, the British had no means for gauging the depth of feeling in the colony. They did not know how wide the radical movement was or what close ties the patriots in Boston had with rural activists as far from the scene as Joseph Hawley and Ethan Allen. When the reports of the Tea Party finally reached Whitehall, all the ministers beheld was felony, driven by a rising tide of insolence and hatred. That was the dark side of Boston's campaign against the tea; and soon it made itself brutally visible.

THE FIRST CONFRONTATION

By the end of October, some observers already feared that when the tea arrived, a mob would board the ships and either burn their cargo or throw it into the water. On the evening of November 2, another meeting at the Green Dragon called for the consignees to step down. The following day the first riot took place.[9]

At the southern end of Boston, there stood a great elm tree, as ancient as the colony itself. According to some, the elm was already mature when the first Puritan settlers came ashore in 1630; others said that it dated from 1646; but either way, the Liberty Tree served as a proud symbol of the town's integrity. From its branches the people would hang mocking effigies of popes and British politicians, and here they met to jeer at the Stamp

Act. As the church bells struck eleven on the morning of November 3, a crowd at least five hundred strong began to gather beneath a flag tied to the elm. A rabble, said Hutchinson, including "boys and negroes," but it was a rabble with leaders: John Hancock, Samuel Adams, and William Molineux.

Thirty-six hours earlier, under cover of darkness, the consignees had received a summons to come to the tree at noon—"Fail not upon your Peril," they were told—to resign their commissions to receive the tea. That morning, placards posted up around the town had urged every man in Boston to attend the meeting to witness their humiliation. Ominously, the bills were signed "OC"—for Oliver Cromwell—an allusion to Puritan rebels from the past.

For an hour, the crowd waited until the appointed time. But twelve o'clock came and went, and the consignees failed to appear. Another half hour passed, and then the meeting voted to pursue the guilty men. From the Liberty Tree it was little more than fifteen minutes' walk to King Street, where the consignees had gone to ground in the warehouse occupied by Richard Clarke. It seems that Adams and Hancock had other duties to perform, because Molineux led the procession. A learned man as well as a merchant—he frequently quoted the Greek and Roman classics— Molineux cast himself in the role of Brutus, the republican tyrannicide, defending liberty and virtue against unjust authority.

Actually, the authorities were absent: the streets already belonged to the people. Boston had no professional police force, and the town's selectmen—the elected committee that managed its affairs—were mostly allies of Samuel Adams. There was a militia, known as the Corps of Cadets, but who was its colonel? None other than John Hancock. Meanwhile, the army remained at Castle William, unable to move without a request for help from the governor, which Hutchinson could not make for fear of a repetition of the massacre of 1770. Only one brave magistrate dared to intervene, and he came from out of town. Mr. Hatch from Dorchester, a justice of the peace, chanced to be in Boston that day and saw what happened at one o'clock, when the crowd reached King Street. He sent a deposition back to England, where the lawyers pored over it, searching for evidence of treason.

Leading a small delegation, including Joseph Warren, Molineux climbed the steps to Clarke's office. "The people are greatly affronted," he told the consignees, and asked them to sign a paper agreeing to send the tea straight back to England. When Clarke refused, Molineux gave him a warning: "they must feel the full weight of the resentment of the people, or words to that import," a witness recalled. Like Brutus after Caesar's assassination, Molineux added a theatrical rider. "I have done my duty, and I am afraid of no man," he said as he retreated down the stairs. For a moment or two, that seemed to be the end of the affair. Molineux said something, and the crowd moved off up the street. They stopped, moved on, and stopped twice again, and then suddenly Molineux lost control of the demonstration.

Back in a rush they came, with clubs in their hands, while Clarke issued frantic orders to lock the doors. Mr. Hatch stepped forward. At the top of his voice he ordered the crowd to disperse. In reply he received a whack on the arm. Twenty young men burst into the warehouse and made for the glass door that barred their way to the office upstairs. With sticks of their own, Clarke's men fought their way back to safety. For ninety minutes the crowd laid siege to the consignees, smashing the glass, yelling, and beating on the ceiling. At last, some kind of truce was patched together, and Clarke, the Hutchinson boys, Faneuil, and Winslow were allowed to leave, but only after threading a noisy cordon of protesters.

In effect, the rule of law had been suspended, with the authorities rendered powerless. Just around the corner in the town house, the governor tried to rally his council to take action against the mob. Led by Hancock's fellow worshipper at Brattle Square, James Bowdoin, the council was supposed to form the executive branch of the colony's government, but since it was elected by the House of Representatives, in practice Hutchinson had already lost his fragile grip on its loyalty. So few of its members turned up that the governor could not assemble the quorum he required. When at last a full council convened the following morning, including Hancock, of course, they all agreed that a riot had occurred, and that evidence should be gathered and the culprits prosecuted. But who would take the witness statements or make the arrests? Nothing could be done, and the situation deteriorated still further as the government of Massachusetts more or less ceased to function. On November 5, at Faneuil Hall, the voters of Boston gathered for a town meeting, convened by the selectmen. They began by adopting the ten resolutions from Philadelphia. Then they chose a committee, led by Hancock and including Adams and Warren, to demand the resignation of the consignees. Gradually, the patriots were closing a net around them and the governor, forcing them into a corner where only two options would be left to Thomas Hutchinson: either abject surrender, or a desperate resort to military force. Meanwhile the radical papers, the *Gazette* and the *Massachusetts Spy*, ran a stream of stories about the unrest in New York and Pennsylvania, and the threat of more violence hung in the air.

So the consignees played for time. At this point, no one knew precisely how many tea ships were coming or when they might arrive. So they wrote Hancock's committee an evasive letter, pointing out that they had not yet received official word of their appointment by the East India Company. Technically, this was correct—the paperwork was coming with the tea—but their opponents would not be fobbed off so lightly. On the sixth the town meeting assembled again and dismissed the letter as an insult. An uneasy calm descended on Boston and lasted eleven days until the *Hayley* tied up in the harbor on the seventeenth. As well as more detail about the tea ships, she carried Richard Clarke's son Jonathan, fresh from London. And that night, as the selectmen hurriedly arranged another town meeting, the people took direct action a second time.

The Clarkes lived in School Street, one of the town's most affluent neighborhoods, a few doors away from King's Chapel. As the family gathered to celebrate Jonathan's arrival, they heard the familiar sound of horns, whistles, and shouts. After failing to track down Thomas Hutchinson Jr., a crowd of about 150 had come in search of the Clarkes, hoping to catch them unawares. Richard Clarke managed to bolt the door, but while the women fled upstairs, the crowd began to break it down. A shout was heard—"You rascals! Be gone, or I'll blow your brains out!"—and a pistol shot rang out from one of the Clarkes.

For a moment, the crowd backed off. But when they realized that no one had been hit, they returned to the door and the windows, smashing the glass and shattering the frames. They laid siege to the house for an hour or two, until at last another truce was agreed. The following morning another town meeting appointed a new committee to tell the consignees to resign. They refused again, but this time they supplied an explanation. Their agents in London had signed undertakings on their behalf—"penal engagements of a commercial nature"—that prevented them from sending the tea back to London.

This was probably untrue. Their opposite numbers in New York and Philadelphia said nothing of the sort. In principle, the consignees were liable to pay the cost of shipping the tea and the threepenny tax, which—because it was an import duty and not an excise—fell due for collection within 20 days of its entry to Boston Harbor, even if it remained unsold. But in fact it seems that neither the East India Company nor the Treasury ever pursued the consignees for the money they were owed. When at last the dust settled in 1774, the company demanded compensation from the government, not from its agents in America. So the response from the consignees seems to have been just a ploy, as well it might be. From HMS *Captain* the admiral could already see that Boston was beyond redemption. It was at this point that he armed his marines and equipped his boats with grappling hooks. As for the governor, he felt entirely isolated. Three times his council met between the nineteenth and the twenty-seventh, but each time it refused to come to his aid. Since they opposed the landing of the tea, Bowdoin and his colleagues would not intervene to protect the stuff when it came ashore.

"I am in a helpless state," Hutchinson wrote to Governor Tryon on the twenty-first. From this moment forward, his letters become almost painful to read. Filled with excuses, regret, and recrimination, they show us a lonely man, adrift amid the wreckage of a sinking empire. Proud, obstinate, but also courageous in his own way, Hutchinson looked for a means to resolve the crisis, but as each day went by his position became more hopeless.

A political compromise seemed impossible. At first, the governor had assumed that the disorders would resemble the riots against the Stamp Act eight years earlier. There would be trouble, but it would blow over when the better sort of people—wealthy men like Hancock—decided that the Boston mob had gone too far. But as Hutchinson's own council deserted him, and as it became ever more obvious that Samuel Adams had captured Hancock for the rebel cause, so the governor's mood switched from complacency to alarm. By the end of November, he was obliged to consider the military option, only to rule it out. Under English law, the governor had not only a right but a *duty* to call in the army to protect life and property; but he would have to do so on his own authority. Other laws would punish Thomas Hutchinson if Lieutenant Colonel Leslie committed atrocities for which the governor could be held responsible. Nor could he take the risk of a civil war in which his sons would be the first casualties.

And there were other things that preyed on his mind. As the governor knew, his letters to William Palmer had helped instigate the scheme to send the tea. Although nobody could blame him for the plan eventually concocted by Palmer and the Treasury, at best his role in the affair would be deeply embarrassing if its full extent were made public. It was an error of judgment Hutchinson tried to keep quiet, and with some success, since historians rarely allude to the subject. The governor also knew that soon he would be in England himself. Whitehall had agreed to give him leave of absence for a trip to London, where he was bound to face probing questions about his stewardship of Massachusetts. Desperate not to make more mistakes, or to appear weak or disloyal, Hutchinson fell into a kind of seizure, unable to advance or to withdraw.

In this tortured frame of mind the governor waited for the tea. If he were lucky, the first ships would dock in New York, where the army was far stronger and Tryon could forcibly land their cargoes. That might break the colonial will to resist. But if the tea ships reached Boston first, Hutchinson would have to take the lead. In an emergency he could flee to Castle William and rely on the navy to protect the tea from destruction. Other than that he felt there was nothing he could do.

At last, on November 27, the waiting came to an end. That evening the first tea ship, the *Dartmouth*, entered the outer reaches of Boston Harbor, carrying eighty chests of Bohea, twenty of Singlo, and another fourteen of varieties more refined and costly. It was Saturday night, too late for a pilot, but early the following morning she passed Castle William and made her way to a mooring close to HMS *Captain*. By noon on Sunday the town was in ferment again. The selectmen met, and so did Adams's Committee of Correspondence, to discuss their plan of action. Once inside the harbor, the *Dartmouth* and its cargo fell under the jurisdiction of the customs officers and a clock began to tick toward a deadline on December 17. At that moment, if the import duty remained unpaid, the customs service and the Royal Navy would be obliged to seize the ship, confiscate the cargo, and sell the tea themselves.

For everything that follows, we face on a grander scale the same problem of conflicting sources that arose with the *Gaspée* incident. Because they knew they were breaking the law, only a few of the raiders who dumped the tea in the harbor ever revealed their names. Neither Samuel Adams nor John Hancock left memoirs, and by the end of 1777 Thomas Young, William Molineux, and Joseph Warren had all passed away, long before the time for writing reminiscences. The British collected sworn depositions from every witness they could find, which were probably reliable as far as they went but omitted many essential details. Hutchinson wrote copiously about the affair, but mainly in the hope of showing that Samuel Adams planned the Tea Party many weeks in advance. This may well be true—conceivably, Arthur Lee in London might have given Adams the idea—but for lack of evidence no historian can make that charge stick in front of a jury, any more than the British or the governor could at the time.

Although George III would retain control of Canada and the British

West Indies, the rest of his colonial system in America was starting to disintegrate. As the economist Adam Smith would point out in 1776, the old empire on the mainland had always been a kind of illusion, too expensive to rule and sustainable only by the consent of those whom it claimed to govern. As the deadline approached, Boston called the empire's bluff.

A State of Nature

On Monday, November 29, another great public meeting took place. It began at Faneuil Hall, but when several thousand people arrived to take part, not only from Boston, but from other towns nearby, they had to adjourn to a larger venue. The only space large enough was the Old South Meeting House. And there, for two whole days, they held what amounted to a preliminary convention for the rebellion that would follow.[10]

This was no ordinary town meeting. In fact, it was not really a town meeting at all, because anyone could attend, and not merely those adult males who held the right to vote. From a British point of view, the assembly was unlawful, because it deviated from procedures laid down in the colony's legal code. Like the *Gaspée* raid, it broke new ground in the history of the empire. Eleven years earlier, in 1762, the philosopher Jean-Jacques Rousseau had described the general will of the people as the only legitimate source of authority. When he wrote *The Social Contract*, it was hard to see exactly what Rousseau meant, for lack of concrete examples in Europe at the time. But over these two days in late November the Bostonians gave a vivid demonstration of what he had in mind. They displayed the general will in action, which means that they rejected any authority but their own.[11]

Amid all the detail, it is all too easy to lose sight of that essential point. Long before the tea ships dropped anchor, the colonial system had already reached a dead end in Massachusetts. In order to break the impasse, the British would have had to appoint a new, visionary governor, capable of shaping some new political settlement; but this was inconceivable. And so, as we watch the meetings unfold, we find that while the fate of the tea ships came first on the agenda, the debate soon extended to other, more fundamental questions about Boston's place within the empire.

The meeting swiftly decided that the tea could not come ashore. It was up to the owners to take the cargo home to England. But this was far more easily said than done. The ship belonged to a whaling family called Rotch, Quakers from Nantucket and rivals of John Hancock in the oil trade, who took little interest in politics. That afternoon their representative in

Boston, Francis Rotch, came to the meeting with the *Dartmouth*'s skipper, James Hall, and told the gathering that they were asking the impossible.

Captain Hall pointed out that he could not leave harbor without a permit from the governor, which Hutchinson could not give. Once the ship was officially logged as an arrival—which it had been—the tax became due, and somebody had to pay it or the vessel would be impounded. At this, Samuel Adams took the floor. The people had spoken, he said—"they had now the Power"—and Rotch would simply have to tell the truth: that a mob had forced his hand and left him no option but to send the *Dartmouth* back out to sea.

When Adams finished, a vote was taken, and the meeting appointed a watch of twenty-five men to board the *Dartmouth* each evening and prevent the tea from being unloaded in the dark. At that point the session might have ended, except for the arrival of John Hancock, fresh from another uneasy standoff with Hutchinson. The fate of Hall's cargo was one thing, but more was at stake: nothing less than the fate of the colony and all the liberties it held so dear. That morning, Hancock had sat among the Governor's Council, as again it refused to help land the tea in safety. Soon afterward, he learned that Hutchinson planned to call in the town's magistrates to order any rioters to disperse, as a prelude perhaps to bringing in the army.

Using the language of Shakespeare—his words echoed lines from *Coriolanus*—Hancock denounced the governor as nothing better than "a tool of power and enemy of his country." He called on the people to pass a vote of censure, which they did. The *Dartmouth* had still to be dealt with—the consignees had yet to be heard from, with the artist John Singleton Copley acting as a go-between—but as the sessions went on, that day and the next, they ceased to be merely concerned with James Hall and his ship. This is perfectly clear from the language used by Hancock, by Adams, and most of all by Thomas Young. Ever since the middle of 1772 and the news about the judges' salaries, Boston had been drawing closer to a point of no return; and whatever happened to the tea, that moment had arrived.

In the Boston pamphlet the town had already denied Parliament's claim to sovereignty, with the support not only of both chambers of the General Court but also, the Bostonians believed, of as many as fifty other towns in the province.* With so much radical momentum behind them, the people

---

* The General Court had not yet voted to resist the Tea Act, but there was little doubt about the stance both chambers would take if the opportunity arose.

of Boston could not retreat. On the contrary, on November 30 the meeting went further and committed an act of rebellion. Later, the British government paid especially close attention to reports of its proceedings, which the Crown's lawyers saw as clear evidence of treachery.

Tuesday morning's session began with the reading of a letter from the consignees. It was out of their power, they said, to refuse to take the tea, but since they had already fled to Castle William to take shelter with Lieutenant Colonel Leslie, it did not really matter what answer they gave. Only the governor could decide the fate of the tea and whether it should stay or leave. Although the law required the collection of the tea duty, Hutchinson might have taken it upon himself to allow the *Dartmouth* to leave with the tax still unpaid, on the grounds that this was the only way to avoid bloodshed. It seems unlikely that he would have faced any official censure if he had done so—the British would have blamed the Boston mob—but in any event the governor had already decided to stand firm. While the people were mulling over the letter from the consignees, a sheriff entered the Old South, sent by Hutchinson to break up the gathering on the grounds of its legality. He was hissed and booed, and the meeting voted unanimously to throw him out. His arrival provoked a twenty-minute speech from Samuel Adams, who rose to the occasion as few other people would have dared to do.

Like Hancock, Adams has aroused endless debate about his motives and his tactics. Was he a man of principle, speaking for a broad consensus, or merely a scheming rabble-rouser, devious and manipulative? The latter view is simply naive. Of course his tactics were sometimes underhand: he was a politician, and by the standards of eighteenth-century public life his Machiavellian cunning was scarcely unusual. On November 30, Samuel Adams said nothing new—he merely repeated the doctrines of the Boston pamphlet—but he displayed to the full two talents that a successful politician had to possess. First, a sense of timing: Adams saw that *this* was the moment that he had to seize, or spend his life regretting it. And second, he knew how to take abstract ideas about democracy and convert them into a call for action that everyone could understand.

In what an eyewitness called "the most abusive, virulent and vilifying manner," Adams attacked the governor directly. In the message carried by the sheriff, Hutchinson called himself His Majesty's representative, so Adams took that as an excuse for mockery. The governor was tall and thin—a "shadow of a man," said Adams, "scarce able to support his withered carcase or his hoary head! Is he a representation of majesty?"

And then he went on to reiterate the pamphlet's ideas. The people were supreme, and in extremity they could ignore the law. "A free and sensible people," he said, "when they felt themselves injured always had a right to meet together to consult for their own safety."

When Adams finished, amid an ovation from the floor, it fell to Thomas Young to bring the meeting to a climax. At some point during those two days—exactly when, we cannot say, or what precise words he used—Young called for the tea to be destroyed. In London the following January, four witnesses testified to that, and a note taken by a member of the audience confirms it. But when he rose to follow Adams, Young spoke not about tea but about principles, citing as his authority the greatest legal scholar of the period, the English judge William Blackstone. When the government would not listen, the people had no alternative, said Young: they were in "a state of nature," where, according to Blackstone, they had no other option but to disobey. For Thomas Young, the meeting at the Old South resembled the gathering of the barons at Runnymede, with the people of Boston poised to draw up their own Magna Carta, like their forebears in protest against Plantagenet tyranny.

After that, what else was left to say? That afternoon a merchant, John Rowe, made what he seems to have intended as a joke, suggesting that the tea could be destroyed. Part owner of another of the tea ships, the *Eleanor*, whose arrival was expected imminently, Rowe was apparently trying to defuse the situation with some good-natured banter. One man recalled that Rowe asked "whether a little salt water would not do it good, or make as good tea as fresh," and again the meeting shouted its applause. Then Copley the painter arrived from Castle William to give the final response from the consignees. The most they would offer was a pledge to warehouse the tea onshore. They could not send it back across the ocean. At that, the meeting finally passed the resolution that the British authorities regarded as outright rebellion. The Tea Act, they said, was "accursed and unrighteous," and they voted to stop the cargoes coming ashore "at the risks of their lives and fortunes."

The town's most radical element had prevailed. As a way to prevent any second thoughts, the meeting voted to send the resolution to every other colony. Then John Hancock gave a closing address. A man with a great deal to lose, he knew how far they had traveled in the space of two days. "My fellow countrymen, we have now put our hands to the plough," said Boston's wealthiest citizen. "And woe be to him that shrinks or looks back."

The Destruction of the Tea

For the next two weeks the town fell quiet, but the lull was wary and uncertain. Both sides waited nervously for news from New York and Philadelphia, where more tea ships were thought to be due at any moment. Men began to arm themselves, clearing the shops of firearms and ammunition. Out at Salem, the *Essex Gazette* ran a story suggesting that Boston intended to fight—it was "hazarding a brush," the writer said—if the army or the navy intervened. Meanwhile, at Hutchinson's request the British sealed the entrance to the harbor to prevent the *Dartmouth* from leaving without official clearance.

Besides his flagship, too large and unwieldy to operate close inshore, Admiral Montagu had a frigate with twenty-eight guns, the *Active*, and a lightly armed sloop called the *Kingfisher*. He sent them to patrol the channels into the port, while from Castle William the army kept watch with its cannons and its small supply of gunpowder. But when Hutchinson insisted that no redcoat be seen with his weapons on the streets of Boston, Lieutenant Colonel Leslie refused to comply. Expecting his men to go ashore unarmed was out of the question. Indeed, almost every morning Leslie came to town himself to test the atmosphere and buy a leg of ham with which to feed his guests.

Samuel Adams was simply biding his time, Leslie believed, until the other colonies gave a clear signal that they would also bar the tea from landing. If they did not, he wrote in a postscript to his earlier letter home, the movement would die away. But even as he tried to keep spirits high over dinner at the fort, Leslie acknowledged that the situation had become alarming. "They never were so unguarded before," he added, not even at the time of the Stamp Act.[12]

By now Captain Hall had brought the *Dartmouth* right up to the waterfront, mooring her at Griffin's Wharf, located at the southern end of Boston beneath a low eminence called Fort Hill. Every night, with muskets and fixed bayonets, a posse from the town watched over the vessel, with John Hancock making at least one personal tour of inspection. On December 2, the *Eleanor* entered the harbor and tied up alongside, with 114 chests identical to Hall's. Five days later the *Beaver* sailed in with another 112, but she also carried smallpox and had to wait a week in quarantine, before joining her sister ships at Griffin's Wharf on the fifteenth.

Meanwhile, Hutchinson still wrote compulsively, as though the mere flow of words could resolve the crisis. In the two weeks before the Tea

Party, he composed no fewer than seventeen long letters, most of them addressed to men in England, each one filled with excuses, anxiety, and indiscretion. "I am at a loss where it will end," he confessed to William Palmer on the ninth. In this, the most candid letter of all—"I desire no copies may be made," he told his friend—the governor admitted his crucial mistake. For years, the people of Boston had bought legal, duty-paid tea as well as the smuggled variety; and because of that, he had expected only token resistance when the Tea Act and its implications became known.

Even now Hutchinson failed to predict what would happen. "There certainly is danger of some violent explosion," he wrote on the fourteenth, but he expected something wild, a sudden, incendiary riot by a mob, and not the smooth operation that eventually occurred. Two days earlier more rumors had reached the governor that the people were threatening to burn a tea ship. But until almost the last moment, he preferred to plan for another outcome. The owners of the ships, he believed, would try to take them out to sea without a permit, in which case HMS *Active* would detain them. For Hutchinson, this would have been the best result. No one could accuse him of disloyalty; and when it heard the news, the British cabinet would have to end the unrest in New England with the rigorous measures that had been postponed too long.

All the time the deadline drew closer. The next move had to come from Francis Rotch, because his ship, the *Dartmouth*, was the first to which it would apply. On the fourteenth, another mass meeting assembled at the Old South, with Rotch compelled to attend. Faced with the loss of his ship and her cargo, whether she stayed at the wharf or was seized by the navy, at last he gave in. Reluctantly, Rotch agreed to ask for the permit he needed. It took two days for him to find all the relevant customs officers, but their hands were tied by the same laws and regulations that required the payment of the tax. They refused: until they received the duties, they could not permit the ships to leave. Only Governor Hutchinson could waive the rules and issue the pass the *Dartmouth* required.

And so we come to the morning of Thursday, December 16. By now less than twenty-four hours remained before the first cargo of tea was due to be impounded. Out at Castle William, keeping in touch with the shore via a relay of couriers, the redcoats were waiting, ready to fire a warning shot if the tea ships tried to leave. Leslie was quietly confident, believing that Samuel Adams had overreached himself. "They have run themselves aground & find they have gone lengths they can't support," he wrote to headquarters in New York.[13]

All that week the weather had been cold, damp, and dull, with heavy clouds hanging over the coast. It was raining at ten o'clock as the crowds began to gather at the Old South for the last time. Two thousand people attended the meeting, said John Rowe, while other sources say five thousand, arriving not only from Boston but from towns up to twenty-five miles inland. Even with all its seats and partitions folded away, the Old South would have struggled to hold so many, but the exact number is beside the point. For what was taking place, Adams and the North End Caucus needed a broad coalition against the British, and now they knew it stood behind them.[14]

Here again, Hutchinson had been mistaken, believing that while Adams and his colleagues had tried to raise the rest of the province, their calls for action had gone unheeded. In fact, in the twelve months since the Boston pamphlet, the Committee of Correspondence had won the backing of four-fifths of the towns in nearby Essex County, including Marblehead and Salem. To the west, in Middlesex County, the figure was still higher. And by the sixteenth, the town of Boston also knew that in New York and Philadelphia the tea consignees had been compelled to stand down.

The morning session had only one item to discuss. Told that Francis Rotch had failed to obtain his pass, they sent him on one last errand. He would have to ride ten miles to the governor's country house at Milton. If Hutchinson would grant the permit, the tea could go to sea again. But if he refused? "Let us take our axes and chisels and split the boxes," somebody cried out from the gallery, "and throw their contents into the harbour." We know that someone shouted such a thing, but amid all the competing testimony it is impossible to know precisely when it was said, or by whom, and whether or not he was speaking about a plan that had been laid in advance.

Soon after it began, the meeting adjourned, to reconvene at three o'clock that afternoon. In the meantime, Francis Rotch set out for Milton, a round-trip of close to six hours. He found Thomas Hutchinson, who made one last suggestion. The *Dartmouth* could leave without a pass and then hand itself over to Admiral Montagu for safety until the uproar died down and the tea could be safely unloaded. This idea left the young man in despair. Not only would Rotch lose his ship, confiscated by the navy. He would also become a marked man in Boston. His own life would be in danger, as well as those of Captain Hall and any sailor rash enough to help him. Rotch said no, and the governor sent him away without the pass. Back he rode through the wet, reaching the Old South just as darkness was falling.

Inside the people were excited and impatient. For nearly three hours they had waited, while Adams and Young kept up the flow of oratory. At one point, a young lawyer leaped to his feet to give a fiery warning of what lay in store. This was Josiah Quincy Jr., closely related to Hancock by marriage, brilliant but erratic, sometimes a moderate, sometimes a hothead, but never a man lost for words. Like his kinsman, he used the language of extremity. The crisis was upon them, and it was one they could not resolve, he cried, merely with "shouts and hosannas." They should pause and think carefully before they took steps that would incur the wrath of England and bring on "the most trying and terrific struggle this country has ever seen."

His intentions remain unclear. Perhaps Quincy hoped to calm the people down, or perhaps he was trying to arouse them to some new peak of emotion. Again the truth remains elusive, and perhaps even Quincy himself did not know what he was seeking to achieve. For a while, it looked as though the meeting might disperse, as Rotch failed to return. Were they bored and tired and eager to go home? Or were they restless because the tea was so close and begging for destruction?

Even an eyewitness might have found it hard to assess their mood, but then suddenly no room was left for doubt. Shortly before six o'clock, a commotion began near the door. The noise in the hall became deafeningly loud. At last Francis Rotch had come in from the street. When the shouting died away, he told them what the governor had said. No pass could be issued, and so the tea must stay at Griffin's Wharf. Only one man could follow that. Samuel Adams stepped forward. They had done all they could, he said, for the salvation of America, and they could do no more. Rotch should go home to rest, free from blame. Amid applause, the meeting voted its agreement, and while they did so, the party was already beginning.

As Rotch was speaking, part of the crowd near the exit had begun to slip away into the night. When Adams had finished, the meeting paused for an interval that may have been as long as fifteen minutes. Then suddenly yells and whistles were heard from outside, and the war cries of Indian braves, audible three blocks away. Inside the hall, the same yells rang out. In the porch a band of young men appeared, about twenty strong, their faces blackened with burned cork and soot, with feathers on their heads and blankets slung around their shoulders.

There was a dash for the exit. Two or three hundred people had already left before Hancock, Adams, and Young could call the meeting to order once again. Thomas Young gave a speech, consisting of jokes and badinage about "the ill-effects of tea on the constitution." He drew to a close, the applause died down, and the Old South emptied swiftly. It was less than half a mile to the wharf and the ships. Off went the crowd down Milk Street and Hutchinson Street, turning left at Belcher's Lane to reach the waterfront. The rain had stopped, the night was clear, and in the distance they could hear the sound of splitting wood.

With thousands of spectators gazing down on what they did, the raiders at the wharf apparently numbered between 100 and 150. At least that many men were needed to shift such a large consignment of tea. Armed with clubs and sticks and cutlasses, while others with firearms stood guard on the shore, they divided into three teams, one assigned to each ship. They swarmed aboard, some in their Indian costumes, and brushed aside the customs officers, warning them to leave or face a beating. Only one skipper was aboard his ship, Hezekiah Coffin on the *Beaver*, and the next day he gave a sworn statement describing the scene.

Forty men had filled his deck, broken open the hatches, and dropped down into the hold. They set up a hoist and hauled the tea chests aloft with blocks and tackle. Each one had come unopened from China, with those of Bohea weighing at least 335 pounds. The finer teas came in smaller boxes, but even those weighed 70 or 80 pounds each. It would take nearly three hours of hard labor to empty each ship, smashing holes in every chest and dumping the leaves into Boston Harbor. The tide was low and the water was shallow, but even so the tea spread outward in long plumes, drifting away to the south. Out from the shore came a few men in rowing boats, perhaps intending to scoop it up and take it home. They were swiftly warned off by the squad with muskets on the wharf.

By nine o'clock the deed was done. It was another *Gaspée* raid, without the gunshots and the violence, but inspired by similar motives and ideas and with the same enemy in sight. Far from being just a protest against an irksome tax, the Tea Party meant rejection of British rule in its entirety. That was what Hancock and Quincy and Young had said, by the very clearest implication.

The Tea Party also resembled the *Gaspée* affair in another way. In Rhode Island eighteen months earlier, John Brown had led not an unruly crowd but an alliance of shipowners, sea captains, artisans, and students, with the blessing of Judge Hopkins and the leaders of the province. At Griffin's Wharf, we find another wide coalition among the men who took part. Again, they could never be called a mob, any more than we can use that term to describe the crew who burned the *Gaspée*.

The first list of the Tea Party raiders did not appear until the 1830s. Even then it was incomplete, with fewer than sixty names. Nonetheless, the data it contains show us a movement with roots as broad as they were deep.[15]

The job needed muscle. So among those who took part we find young working men, in their twenties, living in the poorer parts of Boston but not from the worst slums of the far North End. At least five worked in construction as carpenters, or masons. Another was a blacksmith. Seven came from the shipyards or the ropewalks, with careers as shipwrights or makers of oars, barrels, and rigging. During the Revolutionary War, at least five of the raiders served as artificers, building forts or repairing cannon.

But alongside the laborers, we also find Paul Revere, from the luxury trades, another side of Boston represented at the wharf. While he worked in silver, four of his comrades that night did other kinds of skilled manual work, building or painting coaches, dressing leather, or making upholstery. Others earned their living in commerce: William Molineux, for one. There was an insurance broker, an importer of lemons, and a young merchant, Thomas Melvill, whose grandson would write *Moby-Dick*. No lawyers appear on the list and no clergymen, though John Adams and Samuel Cooper gave the Tea Party their enthusiastic support. Apparently, only one old college boy took part: Melvill had been to Princeton. Even so, their backgrounds were diverse.

The same was true of their leadership. For lack of entirely firm evidence, historians have often hesitated to name Samuel Adams, Hancock, and Young as the Tea Party's organizers. But their actions and every word they uttered—especially those of Dr. Young—point to that conclusion. And yet these three men were also a coalition of a kind. There was Adams, the old campaigner, from a dynasty of Boston politicians; Hancock, rich but frustrated, his business in decline, while his ambition grew; and finally Young, the volatile outsider, a heretic driven by philosophy and by a conviction that injustice was inscribed within the very fabric of the empire. Each radical came from different roots and a different milieu, and each one had his own different motives for resistance to the British.

By sending the tea, Lord North had given them a cause against which they could unite, with most of Massachusetts falling in alongside them. In the form of the Boston pamphlet, the movement already had a manifesto to which it could turn for an expression of its beliefs. A popular front, embracing farmers, artisans, lawyers, preachers, and professors' wives, it was not a movement that Lord North could comprehend.

The Tea Party's Origins

However theatrical it might appear, and however accidental or contingent the events that led to it may seem, the Tea Party came about neither by chance nor simply as a plot by smugglers to protect their trade. Its roots can be found in deep flaws within the system that the British had brought into being. From the time of the *Gaspée* raid, the empire had begun to crack apart, along hidden lines of weakness that North and his colleagues only dimly recognized.

The British Empire in America had no plan, and it had no center of command. It had no guiding vision, and it had no high ideals. From a British point of view, the American colonies existed to serve one purpose alone, which was crudely economic. For that very reason the old regime could not endure. More than eighty years ago, this point was forcefully made by the British historian Sir Lewis Namier, whose analysis of the American Revolution's origins still remains one of the most useful.*

By birth a member of the Polish landed gentry, Namier belonged to that brilliant generation of central European Jews who settled in England in the first half of the twentieth century and immensely enriched Great Britain's cultural life. In the light of his background—he spent his boyhood in Austrian Galicia, where he acquired a deep dislike of the Habsburg monarchy—Namier achieved some especially penetrating insights into the fall of empires. Although in detail his arguments were subtle and complex, he clearly identified the defects in the British system in North America that led to its collapse.

By the 1770s, Great Britain had long since come to view itself as a thoroughly commercial country. Even people who owed their rank to the ownership of land agreed that business was the lifeblood of the nation. "Every country and every age has dominant terms, which seem to obsess men's thoughts," Namier wrote. "Those of eighteenth century England were property, contract, trade and profits." Indeed the British took this as a badge of pride. Their achievements in commerce marked them out as a free and liberal race very different from the French, whom they regarded as merely lackeys of Versailles.[16]

Genius though he was, Namier never developed his ideas into a full-length account of the crisis in America and the Revolutionary War; but the logic of his argument ran as follows. While the British ideology of

---

* It can be found in the opening chapter of Namier's *England in the Age of the American Revolution* (1930).

commerce had its merits—it helped to produce a relatively open, flexible society—it also had its grave defects. Their devotion to trade often descended into a narrow materialism that impaired the vision of the nation's leaders. As a result, the British came to see their overseas dominions as no more than a means for making profits for the mother country. On those rare occasions when Parliament discussed colonial affairs, the speakers would say just that, rarely feeling the need to embellish their case for empire with moral rhetoric of any kind.

This was true even of a man as friendly to America as Edmund Burke, whose finest speeches on the subject dwelled chiefly on the benefits of peaceful commerce beneath the British flag, which he saw as the imperial system's raison d'être. Of course Burke had grave doubts about the East India Company, that entity so vile, which cruelly exploited the people of the Ganges: but the king and his ministers agreed with him. All of them shared his deep misgivings about the company's regime in India. Even so, they dared not think of abandoning it to the French. Like the West Indies and Virginia, the nation's possessions in Bengal were simply far too profitable to surrender. Together they formed a system of global trade that could not be allowed to slip away from Britain's grasp.

It would be facile to suggest that the British were wrong to wish to make money. But some kinds of profits are better than others, less destructive, less venal, and more permanent. The problem was simply this: while the British were determined, for commercial reasons, to keep their empire, they did not really understand the way it had come to work. By the early 1770s, the system as a whole had become too large, too diverse, and too volatile for the British to administer. This was obviously true in India, but the point applies to America as well. Ironically enough, most sections of its economy were actually thriving, like that of the West Indies, as the trade in sugar, molasses, tobacco, rice, indigo, fish, and grain continued to expand. But too much of this arose from a boom in credit that could not be sustained: the same boom that caused the East India Company's brush with disaster.

Starting with the banking crash, one crisis erupted after another with no logic that Lord North and the cabinet could discern. How could they end the epidemic of smuggling in the colonies or in the British Isles? In fact the prevalence of smuggling was simply another side effect of a speculative empire, and of a fiscal system that relied too heavily on the taxation of commodities that lent themselves to illegal traffic. But the only solution they offered was the Royal Navy and officers like Lieutenant Dudingston.

And what could the British do when the tea trade collapsed and the company came so close to ruin? Ship the stuff to America, of course, and hope that it would sell. The Treasury did not anticipate the effects the tea might have upon arrival.

That was how the tea came to be sent. It was a short-term expedient, intended to prop up the company, undercut the smugglers, and reassert the doctrine that Britain had the right to levy taxes in America. It did not occur to North and his colleagues that while for them tea was just an object of trade, in the colonies it would acquire a new meaning. In Boston, tea became a symbol against which men and women would mobilize on that chilly evening in December; and this Lord North could never understand.

In fact the British scarcely saw the colonies at all as anything more than a bundle of economic resources or a destination for convicts. Often the American people themselves remained almost invisible, mere accessories dotted about in a landscape where, in British eyes, the objects in the foreground were fields of tobacco, sacks of rice, and barrels of molasses. Even writers of genius like Edward Gibbon never thought of crossing the Atlantic. Neither did Burke or David Hume, James Boswell or Adam Smith, despite the relative ease of the voyage—a ticket to New York and back cost only £20—and their own wide interests.

"In America there is little to be observed except natural curiosities," wrote Samuel Johnson in 1762. In his opinion, the western continent had nobody worth talking to. Perhaps Benjamin Franklin was an exception, but he had removed the necessity of going there by coming to England himself. And if the colonies appeared to be bereft of civilization, their politics struck the British as provincial, misguided, and dishonest. To North and his colleagues, American demands for liberty seemed to be nothing more than a fraud, a masquerade behind which the colonists were intent on tax evasion.

In many different places—in Charleston, in Virginia, and most of all in Boston—the British encountered new societies with their own agenda. An empire built on maritime trade required customers and clients, but as the century went on, the Americans who played those roles developed their own distinctive ambitions, as they were bound to do; and they also developed their own reinterpretation of political principles and ideas first acquired from Great Britain and then modified to suit colonial circumstances. If British statesmen had visited the colonies, they *might* gradually have come to accept that these Americans' aspirations were valid. But they might also have come away even more appalled by what they found: a political culture that, by the 1770s, had evolved until it was radically different from their own.

Besides their obsession with trade, another fetish enjoyed the devotion of Britain's elite. They were utterly loyal to a political system built on the ownership of property. A gentleman's rank and status depended on his assets, and in England the best, most prestigious asset of all was real estate. When merchants strove to succeed, they did so in the hope of acquiring land and becoming the equals of men above them who already owned many acres. The national obsessions with commerce and with landed property were merely two sides of the same coin, but they threw up another barrier between Britain and America.

It was very rare for Lord North to set out his own political philosophy. He had no need, since everybody knew precisely what it was. But when occasionally he did so, he staunchly upheld a system in which English landowners occupied the commanding heights of power, not only in the British Isles, but also, by virtue of Parliament's sovereignty, in the dominions overseas. In 1785, when the House of Commons debated some modest proposals by William Pitt the Younger for parliamentary reform, North stood up to defend the old arrangements. According to him, the country gentlemen should *always* form the majority in the nation's legislature. The British constitution, he believed, was "the work of infinite wisdom—the most beautiful fabric that, perhaps, had existed from the beginning of time." It rested, he proclaimed, on the landed gentry, whom he called "the best and most respectable objects of the confidence of the people."[17]

Holding views such as these, Lord North could hardly fail to antagonize Americans for whom this kind of thinking was already antiquated and absurd. From North's perspective, a planter from Virginia might just qualify as the equal of an English landlord. But even there he had his doubts, and the artisans and laborers of Massachusetts did not count at all. In November and December 1773, when the people of Boston threw open their meetings to everyone, including the landless and the unemployed, they not only broke the law. They violated every principle of government to which North and his colleagues adhered.

When the news of the Tea Party reached Whitehall, it came as an appalling surprise to the governing elite. Unable to see New England as it was, instead the British cabinet beheld a mirage, in which the mobs of Boston or Rhode Island stood for forces of sin and disorder. They were nothing but criminals led by fanatics, or so they seemed to be from London. The cabinet reacted in two equally misguided ways. First it opted for punishment. Then it tried to put in place in Massachusetts a new regime based on empty and abstract ideas having to do with sovereignty and the will of Parliament. The British government's obsession with the rule of law would lead it into a war it had never expected to fight.

Part Three

DOWN THE SLOPE

Chapter Eleven

THE CABINET IN WINTER

It was yesterday reported . . . that at one of the North American sea coast towns, the inhabitants had sunk near 500 packages of tea.

—*The Morning Chronicle*, JANUARY 21, 1774[1]

London in January: ice in the river, weeks of frost and then of heavy rain, but a city looking forward to the pleasures of the season. Back they came from the country, the landed gentry and the lords, for the theater and the gaming and a session of Parliament expected to be brief and tranquil. The French were quiet, at last the markets were stable, and the royal family gave everyone cause to rejoice. Queen Charlotte was about to reach the age of thirty, and although she had been born in May, the official celebrations would take place on Tuesday, January 18. Because she was with child and near her term, the occasion was especially superb. Guns fired at noon to salute her, and in the evening there were displays of fireworks. At St. James's Palace, with her husband at her side, she held a levee to receive the praise of doting bishops, peers, and politicians. After that they went to her birthday ball, where minuets were danced by young ladies making their debut at court, each with a ticket from the Lord Chamberlain.

On the nineteenth a ship came in from New England. After four stormy weeks on the ocean, the *Hayley* arrived at Dover filled with barrels of tar sent over by John Hancock which, perhaps as some kind of omen, had leaked all over the hold. The day after she dropped anchor, the price of the East India Company's stock suddenly began to fall, as traders with inside knowledge rushed to sell. The following day the press had the gist of what had taken place in Boston. By the weekend they had the whole story, complete with the Mohawks, the meetings at the Old South, and even the number of tea chests tossed into the harbor. They also knew that a similar fate was likely to befall any tea that reached Charleston, New York, and Philadelphia, whose resolutions against it they printed at length.

None of this should have come as a surprise, and yet it did. Two weeks before Christmas, Lord Dartmouth had received another bundle of papers from Thomas Hutchinson, reporting the first of the riots against the consignees. But it was holiday time: the minister sat on the letter for nearly a month before merely telling the governor to keep his nerve. In the new year, the company alerted Dartmouth to warnings it had received from its agents in America, but again he did not share them with his colleagues. Parliament knew nothing when it met in the middle of January.

And then, suddenly, the news was out, and the press instantly saw how serious it was. In a city where the papers fought each other so hard for readers, the Tea Party became the biggest story after years of indifference when few people cared about the colonies. By the end of the month, parts of the press were claiming that six regiments were already on the way to Massachusetts. This was false—it took several more weeks before the cabinet decided to send military reinforcements to Boston—but it set a pattern that would endure throughout the crisis.

Usually ahead of the politicians, with the facts as well as with speculation, Fleet Street began to whip up something close to war fever. As the editorials soon pointed out, the Tea Party had amounted to a repudiation of Parliament's right to rule the colonies. The press swiftly divided between papers of a Wilkesite tendency, which supported America, others that bayed for revenge, and some chiefly concerned with the implications for politics at home.

They posed an obvious question: Would Lord North survive a crisis for which he appeared at least partly responsible? After four years as chief minister, he had already served a longer term than anyone else since the Seven Years' War. His cabinet contained rivals who would not hesitate to oust him if he showed signs of weakness. As the weeks went by, this became a constant theme. "A correspondent is of the opinion," said the *Morning Chronicle,* as early as January 22, "that if some vigorous measures are not immediately resolved upon respecting the rioters at Boston, that the men in power will be held in almost equal detestation with the wretched gang who repealed the stamp act." Perhaps the columnist had been speaking to Gower or Sandwich, the cabinet's most hawkish members. The journalists were often so well-informed that they must have been receiving tip-offs from men in high places. In an atmosphere suddenly electric, and with Parliament standing by impatiently, Lord North had to be seen to act with speed and firmness.

At first, however, the cabinet floundered for lack of an official account of the Tea Party from Hutchinson or Admiral Montagu. Caught off guard, Dartmouth hesitated until, on the twenty-fourth, it occurred to him or his officials to invite James Scott, the skipper of the *Hayley*, to tell them what had happened at Griffin's Wharf. The next day Scott gave them the details, trying not to implicate John Hancock. But even while Dartmouth listened, another individual far less Christian was preparing his own form of revenge. Before the cabinet met for a full discussion of the issues, the hawks struck first against the American target closest to hand.

In the wake of the duel between John Temple and William Whately, the Privy Council had summoned Benjamin Franklin to explain his role in the disclosure of Hutchinson's private letters. One hearing had already taken place, and another was due at the end of the month. The proceedings would be led by the Crown's lawyer Alexander Wedderburn. With an eye to the press, he launched an attack on Franklin so personal and scathing that Englishmen who were present remembered it vividly thirty years later. When reports of the encounter reached the colonies at the end of March, they would cause justifiable outrage at the insult meted out to America's most famous son. This could only deepen the rift with Great Britain, even before the colonists knew the details of the hard line that Lord North was bound to take.

Wedderburn's Tirade

Arrogant by nature, Alexander Wedderburn plied a trade where in the eighteenth century conceit was almost mandatory. In his early years as a barrister, he displayed a courtroom manner so sarcastic that he had to quit his home city of Edinburgh as a result. In 1757, when he was twenty-four, a judge dismissed him as a presumptuous boy, and Wedderburn replied by calling him a cuckold to his face. Told to apologize, he took off his gown, bowed, strode out of court, and rode for London that night.

Once there, he hoped to conquer the English bar, where the pickings were far richer than at home. Likely to face resentment as a Scotsman, he erased his accent by taking lessons in elocution from an actor, Charles Macklin, the greatest Shylock of his age. Small in stature, with a thin but handsome face and a long, aquiline nose, Wedderburn spoke in a deep bass voice, with perfect timing and dramatic gestures. It was said that he practiced his lines in front of a mirror.

Alexander Wedderburn
as lord chancellor in
1785, by Sir Joshua
Reynolds. *Bridgeman Art
Library*

At first he did only averagely well south of the border. A fine scholar
of Greek in his youth, as he grew older Wedderburn lost his taste for hard
work with legal precedents culled from the books in his library. Nor did
he master the art of cross-examination that a barrister needed to win a
case in the criminal courts. "That damned Scotchman has the gift of the
gab—but he is no lawyer," said his colleague Edward Thurlow, an advocate
of a very different sort.[2]

Instead, Wedderburn made his name in chancery practice, dealing with
wills and trusts, the field British barristers choose when they seek an affluent career unencumbered by the scrutiny of jurors. There he earned a
fortune from clients who included Clive of India. It was also the custom
for a rising barrister to enter politics, which he did, attaching himself to
Lord Bute, the premier in 1763, and then to George Grenville, his succes-
sor. Entering Parliament for a distant Scottish borough that Bute and his
friends controlled, Wedderburn acquired a reputation not only for the
brilliance of his speeches but also for his cunning and duplicity. Even the
king used those words about him.

For several years, Wedderburn championed John Wilkes in the Commons, but when Lord North took office, he chose to leave the opposition
and accept the post of solicitor general. Members who crossed the floor

were never popular, especially when they came from Scotland. His enemies liked to repeat some lines of verse that summed him up to perfection: "a pert prim lawyer of the northern race—guilt in his heart, and famine in his face." But jeer as they might, Wedderburn inspired fear as well as mockery. Nobody knew better how to crush an opponent with cold but cruel invective. And that was the stance he took toward Franklin on January 29, when at last the Privy Council met, with Lord Gower in the chair.

In those days, a slightly shabby range of old brick buildings stood on the western side of Whitehall, left over from the palace of the Tudors. Known as the Cockpit, because they had once included a space for fighting birds, they contained offices for the government and an audience chamber for Gower and his colleagues.* The room was hot, lit by a blazing fire. Arriving late, Edmund Burke had to elbow his way in and found thirty-five members of the council already in session. With Sandwich, Suffolk, and Rochford among them, it was the largest assembly of the kind that Burke had ever seen. By now, the official dispatches had arrived, with a full account of the destruction of the tea. It was also known that in Philadelphia the tea ship *Polly* had been forced to sail back to England with her cargo after the townspeople refused to let it land.[3]

With spectators filling every spare inch of space, Gower sat at the center of the council table with the archbishop of Canterbury pondering nearby. They made Franklin stand in a recess behind them and to one side. Throughout the meeting, the American remained as still as a rock, said one eyewitness, his chin resting on his left hand.

According to its official agenda, the meeting was merely due to hear the petition from the General Court of Massachusetts, dating from the previous June, for the removal of Governor Hutchinson. In fact, Alexander Wedderburn launched a fierce attack on Franklin, sending out a clear signal that Boston could expect stern retribution for the destruction of the tea. Franklin had brought along his own barrister, John Dunning, a man with pro-American views, a fine lawyer who at his best would have been more than a match for any opponent. But that winter, Dunning was suffering from a lung infection. His voice was almost too hoarse to be heard.

So the meeting belonged to the Scotsman. Each sentence Wedderburn spoke was carefully shaped for rhythm and clarity. From time to time he would pause to allow the full weight of his irony to take effect. He spoke for an hour, with what one newspaper called "all the licensed scurrility of the bar," drawing gales of laughter from Gower and the rest. He began by

---

* The site of the Cockpit is occupied today by the Cabinet Office.

tearing to shreds the case against the governor. With the private letters to Whately as its only evidence, the General Court had called Hutchinson an evil man, conspiring to deceive the government. It was Hutchinson's purpose, the assembly said, to drive a wedge between Westminster and the colony in the hope that Great Britain would revoke its charter and install a new, authoritarian regime. But according to Wedderburn, the facts told a very different story. Ever since the Stamp Act, Hutchinson had behaved with calm moderation, and even the General Court had admitted as much in the past. "The governor's character stands fair and unimpeached," he said, and then he turned to Franklin.[4]

The letters were stolen, Franklin was to blame, and if anyone led a conspiracy of evil, it was he. "I hope, my lords, you will mark and brand the man," Wedderburn continued. "Men will watch him with a jealous eye; they will hide their papers from him, and lock up the escritoires." Devious, malign, and utterly vindictive, Franklin had acted in league with the very worst elements in New England: a secret cabal, bent on independence. "They wish to erect themselves into a tyranny greater than the Roman," he said, "and get even a virtuous governor dragged from his seat, and made the sport of a Boston mob."

The solicitor general had carefully studied the papers from Massachusetts and found sedition everywhere. One place troubled Wedderburn most of all: the little town of Petersham, out in Worcester County. In response to the Boston pamphlet, the people there had openly spoken of using force to resist the new arrangements for the judges' salaries. The evidence was plain: Franklin and his allies hoped to raise a storm of disobedience, there and in the other colonies, and only Hutchinson had tried to stop them. As he drew to a close, Wedderburn dwelled briefly on the Tea Party and the *Gaspée* incident, warning the people of New England that they had set foot on a path to self-destruction. Wedderburn finished, and Dunning replied in a feeble voice. All the while, Franklin stood motionless, "with all the unchangeable features of philosophy," one journalist said. "The fire seemed to have been extracted from his frame."[5]

At last the Privy Council retired to consider its verdict. Some accounts say that the spectators cheered and clapped Wedderburn and tossed their hats in the air. Outside in the anteroom, he lingered for a while amid an admiring circle of friends. Franklin hurried away arm in arm with a supporter, having said barely a word. A few days later, he was fired from his position as deputy postmaster in the colonies. In the meantime, the Privy Council had issued its opinion, rejecting the petition and calling it false and vexatious.

During Wedderburn's speech, one privy councillor had remained aloof, unable to share in the laughter. Another latecomer, Lord North stood quietly at the back, as well he might. His role in the weeks ahead would require statesmanship of a sort for which his training had been irrelevant. It was all very well to heap insults on Benjamin Franklin, but rhetoric alone could not resolve the imperial crisis that the Tea Party had crystallized. At last Great Britain would have to be decisive, but first it had to define the problem with which it was confronted.

The reports from America still left some scope for doubt. Conceivably, the events in Boston might have been primarily a local affair, arising from a feud between rival factions, with the arrival of the tea used simply as a pretext for a riot. That was possible, but the protests in the other colonies made it seem unlikely. Had disobedience become endemic in the colonies? If so, it would be futile to take reprisals against Massachusetts alone. Sooner or later, another *Gaspée* would be sunk, for some other reason in some other place, and one by one every colony would become ungovernable.

In the winter of 1774, the British badly needed a new and grander strategy, one that could strike at the root of sedition wherever it might be found. But what sort of strategy might it be? The hawks would call for far tighter control, a larger army, and a stronger fleet. That might have been a way to save the empire, though as we know it failed. Alternatively, the British might have made more concessions to address the specific grievances of which the colonies complained, having to do with paper money, the customs service, boundary disputes, and the western wilderness. The wisest strategy would have combined the two approaches, offering carrots and sticks in the hope of detaching American moderates from their radical brethren. Given time, an approach of that kind might have been successful.

In the best of all possible worlds, the British cabinet would have paused for breath, making up for years of failure with a careful reappraisal of the empire and its future. But the political climate did not permit it to do so. Time was a luxury that Lord North did not possess.

THE WHOLE TALK OF THE TOWN

As so often in British politics, the prime minister had more to fear from his friends than from his enemies. His opponents, the Whigs, found themselves in utter disarray. Again the Marquess of Rockingham dallied up in Yorkshire with his hounds, while those of his friends who had come to

London offered no ideas of their own. "The American business engrosses the whole talk of the town," wrote one of them, Lord John Cavendish, to whom the news of the Tea Party had come as something worse than a surprise. Eight years earlier, the Rockinghams had repealed the Stamp Act, and now they found themselves vilified as men guilty of a policy of appeasement that had failed.

Clearly, the destruction of the tea had been a crime: "indefensible," Cavendish told the marquess. But they dare not offer excuses for Boston, for fear of being castigated as weaklings. Nor could they support Lord North if he pursued a hard line that, in their opinion, was likely to end disastrously. In the circumstances, Cavendish felt obliged to hold his tongue. For his part, Edmund Burke lacked the rank and authority needed to make policy for his party while the marquess was away. In any event, he was equally flabbergasted by the news from Massachusetts. And so, in these crucial early days of the crisis, the Rockingham Whigs said next to nothing.[6]

In the newspapers, the Wilkesites rallied in defense of Dr. Franklin, calling Wedderburn "a witling, a punster and a prig" and accusing him of trying to stir up a civil war; but these were merely words. In the city of London, the radicals now reigned supreme, with a Wilkesite as lord mayor, not Wilkes himself, but a close friend, a tea merchant called Frederick Bull. In Parliament, however, where the real battle would be waged, they were too few to make a difference. In fact Lord North came under much heavier pressure from his right. By the time of the session at the Cockpit, the hawks against America had already seized the initiative.[7]

They included Lord Buckinghamshire, an old comrade of Gower and the Bloomsbury gang. "Are we to be free, or slaves to our colonies?" he asked his colleagues in the House of Lords. With the aim of pushing the government into action, he put down a motion calling for the release of all the official files relating to Boston. Lord Dartmouth could hardly refuse, but the request was highly embarrassing. The papers would show just how weak and complacent the government had been in the face of so many warnings of unrest in Massachusetts dating back to the autumn of 1772.[8]

With this threat hanging over it, the cabinet met on the evening of January 29 at Lord Suffolk's home in Duke Street, Piccadilly. It was the first of many sessions about America held discreetly, away from the eyes of the press, in private houses in London's West End. It would take three weeks to contrive a new colonial policy, and then another two before it could be put to Parliament, but by midnight they already knew what they wanted to achieve. First they approved the release of the documents. Then they signed a resolution pledging to take "effectual steps . . . to secure the dependence of the colonies on the mother country."

They had only the barest outline of a plan for doing so, drawn up by the weary officials in the Colonial Department. It contained nothing remotely resembling an olive branch. Instead, they began with a scheme to punish Boston in two ways: by moving the government of Massachusetts to another town, and by shutting down the port where the tea had been spilled. In the past, Thomas Hutchinson had already tried the first of these measures, with little success. Closing the port was a much bolder move, but it raised questions of its own. It might require an act of Parliament, and that would entail delay. The cabinet met again on February 4 and decided that it needed nothing more than an executive order from the king. But as all the ministers agreed, punishing the town was not sufficient. They chose to target the ringleaders as well.

Although this approach had failed in Rhode Island, they decided to try again, even if this meant hanging William Molineux, John Hancock, and the others. This was next to impossible, as the cabinet ministers would soon discover, and yet, for the next few weeks, the idea dominated their discussions. Like the attack on the *Gaspée*, the Tea Party cried out for retribution. Everyone in the cabinet knew that, including Lord Dartmouth, despite his attempts the previous year to avoid a confrontation in New England. Meanwhile, George III had made his own feelings very plain.

Before the cabinet assembled on the fourth, the king received a visit from General Gage, still on leave from his post as commander in chief in America. It might have been better for all concerned if the interview had never taken place, because Gage persuaded the king to opt for severity. Nine years earlier, during the Stamp Act crisis, Gage had seen the mob run riot in New York. Like Lieutenant Colonel Leslie in Boston at the time of the Tea Party, the general had come away angry and frustrated. Ever since, he had tried to persuade London to take a tougher line with the colonies. As far back as 1770, he had wanted to do away with the Massachusetts charter, abolish town meetings, and give the Crown direct control of every branch of government.[9]

And that is what he urged the king to do. A sedentary officer, Gage had spent most of the previous decade in Manhattan. Rarely if ever did he venture south to Virginia or up into New England. Knowing little about the region firsthand, the general gave an absurd assessment of the mood in Massachusetts, telling George III that the rebels would never dare to fight. Be firm, and they would back down and show themselves "very meek":

those were the words he used. Gage volunteered to return to his post at twenty-four hours' notice, without a single extra soldier. As it happened, four regiments were already under orders to sail from England, but only to replace existing units in America. Divert them to Boston, said Gage, and the unrest would soon die away.

All of this was nonsense. The general merely revealed his ignorance about the size of the colonial militia and their willingness to take up arms. Even Fleet Street knew that Massachusetts had part-time soldiers, and a few days later they printed a guess that they might number as many as eighty thousand. This was a wild overestimate, by a factor of four or five, but the story was far less ridiculous than what Gage had to say. The London press, or some of it at least, fully expected the people to take up arms if they had to. As for the charter, it should have been obvious—not least from Hutchinson's letters—that any attempt to revoke or amend it might cause a violent insurrection.[10]

And yet the king chose to believe the plausible general Gage. Years had passed since the last time George III had voiced an opinion about the administration of America, a matter he had left entirely to his ministers. Although the king had never liked the repeal of the Stamp Act, he accepted the decision made by Parliament in 1766. Now the situation was entirely different. Parliament had yet to vote, and so the king felt free to intervene in the cabinet's discussions. That evening he wrote to North, urging him to listen to the general, whom he called "an honest determined man." And like Gower and Sandwich, the king traced the Tea Party's roots back to the Stamp Act's abolition.

While George III made his voice heard, so did another constituency that Lord North had to please. On his own backbenches in the House of Commons the rank and file were growing restless, eager for measures to bring the colonies to heel. One obscure politician decided to lead the charge. In due course, he would incur almost as much hatred in America as Alexander Wedderburn.

Deep in the backwoods of conservatism, there lurked a member of Parliament called Charles Van, a country squire from Monmouthshire. It took him four attempts, but at last Van managed to win a by-election, entering the Commons in 1772 for the distant Welsh borough of Brecon. He soon became a regular speaker in defense of law and order and Lord North. He loathed John Wilkes, and he did not care for Boston either, and on January 26 he became the first MP to stand up in the chamber and call the Tea Party a rebellion. It appears that he also sought out the editor of the *Morning Post*. Five days later it printed a story saying that Van had drawn

Edward Thurlow as lord chancellor in the early 1780s, by George Romney. *The Honourable Society of the Inner Temple*

up a scheme "to quell the riotous behaviour of the Bostonians," which he intended to put before the Commons.[11]

If Van had been an isolated case, an extremist with few supporters, he might have been ignored. But he spoke for a great battalion of like-minded gentry in the shires, each with a thousand acres or so, squires and magistrates with brothers and cousins in the army or the church. Far less plutocratic than the Rockinghams, they did not subscribe to the notion that Great Britain was corrupt. By habit and by choice, they upheld authority from the pulpit or the bench of justice: How else could the country be run? These were the kinds of people who surrounded Lord North in Somerset, where he found a wife from exactly this social stratum. He saw them as the core of his support.

With the army, the navy, the king, and its own backbenchers so hot for retribution, the cabinet began to move forward. On February 5, Dartmouth wrote to the governors in every colony where the tea had been resisted, telling them to stand by for orders intended to restore authority. That same day, he asked Thurlow and Wedderburn to say whether or not the Tea Party was treason. Nearly a week passed before the attorney general replied. The delay upset even the amiable Lord Dartmouth, but Edward Thurlow was not a lawyer who could be hurried into making errors.

A fierce and forthright barrister who enjoyed his wine, Thurlow played a pivotal role in the decisions that led to war. Aged forty-two, he lived in sin in suburban Dulwich with the daughter of a caterer who kept a coffee-house. People called Thurlow the Tiger because of his temper—he once fought a duel with pistols after insulting another lawyer—and because of his appearance. During a trial, he would scowl at the defendant from beneath great bushy eyebrows. Some people might call him a thug. Later in life, when Thurlow was on holiday in Brighton, a servant brought him a dish of peaches that he did not like, and so Thurlow had everyone's dessert hurled out of the window into the street. But despite his irascible nature, Thurlow possessed some qualities that commanded respect and admiration.

Like the colonial secretary, Thurlow had befriended the gentle, deeply troubled poet William Cowper, who thought of him with deep affection. Most of all, Thurlow had a reputation for being invincible in argument. Another of his friends, Samuel Johnson, regarded him as the one opponent he could never verbally defeat. "I would prepare myself for no man in England but Thurlow," he told James Boswell. "When I am to meet with him I should wish to know a day before." Like Dr. Johnson, Thurlow had no time for Americans, whom he detested, but he did not trust his colleagues either.[12]

Wary of taking the blame if anything went wrong with the scheme to prosecute the culprits, Thurlow told Lord Dartmouth to go and find more evidence about the Tea Party. In London only one witness had given personal testimony, Captain Scott of the *Hayley*, whose story was far too thin. And so, with time hurrying by, the Colonial Office had to look for more arrivals from Boston. Altogether it found twelve witnesses, including two who should have been stars: none other than Francis Rotch and his skipper, James Hall.

For two days, beginning on February 16, Lord Dartmouth interviewed them all, passing the results to the cabinet each evening. Soon they had a complete account of the chain of events, from the riots against the Clarkes until the last tea chest fell into the water, and a long list of names of men who could be charged with treason.* They were ready to take the next step by calling the witnesses before the Privy Council to repeat their words under oath.

By now, nearly a month had passed since the *Hayley* dropped anchor,

---

* The names on the list included not only Samuel Adams, John Hancock, Joseph Warren, and Thomas Young but also Edward Proctor, who is known to have been one of the Mohawks who actually destroyed the tea.

and the first flood of excitement had subsided. The press had temporarily lost interest in America, and Edmund Burke complained of a kind of torpor in the capital. But for Benjamin Franklin, who had been caught equally unawares by the news from Boston, it was a worrying time in which—and this was rare for him—he fell into something close to despair. Three days after the meeting at the Cockpit, he wrote to Cushing, Adams, and Hancock, pleading with them to avert disaster by offering to pay compensation for the tea. As he must have suspected, this was entirely out of the question. From the press, Franklin could see how much enthusiasm the Tea Party had aroused in America. Even a patrician as restrained as George Washington shared Boston's hostility toward the Tea Act, much as he disliked the violent methods that the Mohawks had adopted.

In Massachusetts the patriots had no intention of turning back. Indeed they planned to go further and impeach the royal judges for accepting the salaries paid by the Crown. Franklin had no inkling of that yet, but he could sense that events were slipping out of control. As the unofficial leader of London's American community, he soon heard about Dartmouth's interrogation of the witnesses. On February 18, he wrote a series of gloomy letters home, telling his friends about that and describing the abuse that he had suffered. "It seems that I am too much of an American," he wrote to one. "The treatment of the tea has excited great wrath," he said to another. And in a letter to the *Pennsylvania Gazette*, which printed it anonymously, he precisely captured the mood of the moment. "Fleets and troops are talked of, to be sent to America," he wrote, "but what they are to do when they come there, I am at a loss to know . . . God give us all a little more wisdom."[13]

In private Lord Dartmouth experienced similar emotions. Although he kept his distance from Franklin—it seems that after the Tea Party, they never again met face-to-face—he desperately wanted peace. Via a friend, a merchant and evangelical Christian named John Thornton, Dartmouth tried to reach out to New England, pleading for a change of heart. Thornton had a contact in Massachusetts, William Gordon, a nonconformist clergyman from England who had become the pastor at Roxbury, near Boston, and a confidant of the radicals. On February 12, his lordship wrote to Thornton, urging him to forward his comments to America. If only Gordon could speak to Hancock and the others and persuade them of the need for moderation. He could not promise to repeal the tea tax—he would be thought insane if he even hinted at it—but if the Americans backed down, one day it might be done. If they did not? Then, said Lord Dartmouth, "there is an end to all reconciliation."[14]

Taken in the 1930s, this rare photograph shows the London home of
Lord Dartmouth in St. James's Square. His was the house at the center,
with awnings on the windows and a car outside. It was here that the
cabinet met in February 1774 and drew up its coercive measures against
Massachusetts. The house was demolished in the 1950s, and on the site
today is the corporate headquarters of the oil company BP. *Canada Life
Assurance Company*

In fact, by the time he wrote those words, it was already too late for anything of the kind. The parliamentary clock was ticking fast. Lord North
would soon be obliged to release the papers that Buckinghamshire had
demanded. At that point, he would have to be ready with a package of
measures that would satisfy the Lords and the Commons alike. It would
have to be announced by early March at the latest if the legislation were
to pass both houses before the end of the parliamentary session in June.

The issues came to a head on the evening of Saturday, February 19,
when the cabinet assembled at Dartmouth's house in St. James's Square.
By now, two warships were already under orders for Boston to reinforce
Montagu's squadron, General Gage had been told to go back to America
with the four regiments, and the cabinet also believed it had the evidence
required to justify the arrests of the guilty men. Armed with the sworn

statements, the Privy Council could issue the necessary warrants and have them hauled back to Westminster for trial. But this left two matters still on the table: the closure of the port of Boston and the problem of the old Massachusetts charter, which had given the colony so much freedom to defy the empire.

Shutting the port proved to be far more difficult than expected. When the officials examined the legalities, they found that George III could not close the harbor simply with an order issued under the royal prerogative. Although it was arcane and medieval, the law of havens had to be observed. The king could open a port for business, but once granted, the right to sail in and out and handle cargoes could not be removed. In order for this to happen, Parliament would have to pass a special law, the Boston Port Act, which was bound to arouse even deeper outrage than the sending of the tea.[15]

This sort of snag kept recurring throughout the crisis. Far from acting arbitrarily, the British agonized about procedure even when it threw new hurdles in their path, causing delays and leading to awkward side effects that only made New England more intractable. The charter raised a similar problem. In Britain in the eighteenth century, the government often did away with local privileges and charters that seemed to be obsolete. Each time, however, it had to take the measure through Parliament first, because the king could not revoke them purely by decree. And each time the risk arose of a noisy, protracted debate, such as occurred in 1772 with Lord North's Regulating Act for India. But the government had no choice. At the meeting on the nineteenth, the cabinet girded its loins and decided to produce a regulating act for Massachusetts too, along the hazardous lines that General Gage had urged on the king.*

It would take many weeks for the officials to write the legislation, but the concept behind it was all too clear. After more than a century in which the colony had enjoyed something close to democracy, the cabinet decided to impose what amounted to direct rule from England. In the future the governor would be supreme, at the head of a council consisting of royal appointees known as the mandamus councillors. The judges would answer directly to the Crown, unlicensed town meetings would become a crime, and juries would cease to be elected. In addition, a law would be passed to protect the military from prosecution in America for homicide if they shot rioters dead without due cause. This would prevent a repetition

---

* Usually referred to as the Massachusetts Government Act.

of the trial of soldiers for murder that followed the Boston Massacre. Instead, any redcoat who acted illegally would be returned to England for prosecution.

For years, the hawks in the cabinet had argued for just such a package, and for years the likes of Samuel Adams in America had predicted that they would eventually have their way. At the Colonial Office, John Pownall had misgivings about the proposals, but he was obliged to draft the new laws nonetheless. When the news reached New England, it would give the radicals in Boston a huge propaganda victory, and all the more so because of collateral damage caused by the angry words that irresponsible men would speak in Parliament.* The worst offender would be Charles Van.

And then, as the deadline drew near for Lord North to unveil the package, suddenly Edward Thurlow cut the ground from beneath one vital element of the plan. The attorney general had served his legal apprenticeship at the assize courts in the western counties of England, acting in cases of larceny and murder. For a criminal lawyer of his caliber, the rules of evidence were sacrosanct. Thurlow looked again at the sworn statements taken by the Privy Council and decided that they would not do. While he agreed that the Tea Party was treason, too much of the testimony was hearsay, insufficient to prove the charge against named individuals. On February 28, he told his colleagues that he could not write out the warrants for the Privy Council to sign.

Nor could the attorney general conceal his doubts about North and Dartmouth. He regarded them as second-rate compared with the late George Grenville, whom he had revered. A few days later, waiting outside the cabinet room, Tiger Thurlow exploded in front of poor John Pownall. "Don't you see that they want to throw the whole responsibility upon the solicitor-general and me?" he said. "Who would be such damned fools as to risk themselves for such fellows as these?"[16]

This was very revealing. While Dartmouth had his detractors who saw him as a timid *ingénu*, North also had his critics, frustrated by his obsession with the minutiae of politics and his lack of strategic vision. While their older colleagues were veterans of two great wars with France, their own careers had been either brief, in Dartmouth's case, or devoted almost exclusively to domestic affairs and finance, in that of Lord North. When Americans gazed across the Atlantic, they saw powerful foes, arrayed against them like a Spartan phalanx, out to crush their liberties by every

---

* Collectively, the package came to be known as either the Coercive Acts or the Intolerable Acts, depending on the writer's political stance.

means at their disposal. This was an illusion. Although the cabinet ministers wished to be resolute, often their spears were blunt and their quivers only half-full of arrows. Beset by internal rivalries, they pushed each other into a program of coercion in New England without appreciating that they lacked the means to enforce it.

Without an ally in Europe, and now at odds with America too, the cabinet advanced into the mist with Lord North at their head. At this very moment, he almost succumbed to another bout of depression. Toward the end of February, he suffered one of his rare defeats in the Commons. It arose from a merely technical debate about electoral law, but he found himself on the losing side, with 250 votes against him, including even the ultra-loyal Charles Van. Once more North spoke about resignation. The king tried to calm him down, Suffolk hurried round to see him before breakfast, and he regained his composure. Even so, the omens were inauspicious.[17]

Little more than a week later, North would have to face the house with his new American policy. With the plan for treason trials in London now abandoned, it was all the more urgent to press on with what remained. The date of the first debate was fixed: March 7. It would mark the opening of a parliamentary battle that, in its drama and importance, can claim a status alongside others far better known: the debates in the Commons on the reform bill of 1831–32, the repeal of the Corn Laws in 1846, and those much later on the eve of the Second World War. In the spring of 1774, the Rockingham Whigs finally rose from their trenches in a long overdue rearguard action against the government.

The campaign of resistance would be led by two politicians who were both, in their own ways, idealists very different from Lord North. Not the marquess himself, who found the task beyond him, but Edmund Burke, at the height of his powers as an orator, and somebody else less famous but often far more effective. At last an unlikely hero appeared, to make the case for colonial liberty: Charles Lennox, the third Duke of Richmond, one of the most original characters of his age.

Chapter Twelve

"Boston Must Be Destroyed"

And when the Day shall come, the Fate of all,
That Britain's Glory, Wealth and Pow'r must fall,
Then shall her Sons, for such is Heavn's decree
In other Worlds another Britain see:
For what she is, America shall be.

—LINES IN A LONDON NEWSPAPER, MARCH 1774[1]

It was a theatrical era, when lawyers behaved like actors and politicians wrote for the stage. For better or worse, the House of Commons provided the greatest auditorium in the kingdom. On the Treasury bench and on the opposition side, its leading members played the roles of tragedians and comics with a repertoire of jokes and soliloquies. Outside in the country the house had a vast audience, following its debates through the pages of the press. Inside the debating chamber, the stalls and circle were occupied by backbench members of Parliament like Edward Gibbon who were there to listen and to vote, though rarely in silence.

Nine feet shorter than a cricket pitch, the chamber was small, occupying St. Stephen's Chapel, erected by the Tudors to serve the old Westminster Palace. It was approached by way of an elegant corridor, built of white Portland stone and only recently completed. The Commons had a coffee-house, called Alice's, as well as barbershops nearby, because Parliament had to offer the facilities of a club. A member would come up the corridor, pass through the lobby, and enter a space that still resembled a church. On either side it had four rows of benches, covered with green cloth, upon which the members would sprawl, eating nuts and oranges. Above their heads, elegant pillars carried long wooden galleries, added by Sir Christopher Wren to give more room for members and spectators. Even so, the chamber could only hold three hundred, little more than half the number of MPs. It was so cramped and crowded that on one famous occasion, as the myopic Lord North struggled to reach his seat he stuck the point of his scabbard through another member's wig.

When they were bored or disliked what a speaker had to say, the members would jeer or "chatter like magpies," said one reporter, or vanish off to Alice's, only returning when a vote was called. Some came back the worse for drink. Others would fall asleep, including Lord North, who could doze through anything: he kept a colleague close by to make notes of what he missed.[2]

At three o'clock in the afternoon of Monday, March 7, North rose to deliver an address from the king about America. The clerks had put on the table a thick sheaf of papers, 109 in all, copied from Lord Dartmouth's files, including the witness statements for any curious member to read. For the time being, North spoke only briefly, to condemn the Tea Party and the resistance elsewhere, but he used the crucial form of words the cabinet ministers had agreed. They would take steps "to secure the dependency of the colonies," a vague but menacing phrase that left his exact intentions unclear.

Over the weekend the cabinet ministers had met again with some second thoughts and decided to postpone the port bill by seven days. It needed to be legally secure, and they also had yet to draft the bills they needed to reform the charter and the courts in Massachusetts. And so this first debate was just a skirmish, thinly attended, mainly a verbal tussle between Wedderburn and Burke. Even so, it set the tone for what would follow, and it placed the fundamental issues squarely before the house.

It would be hard to imagine two men more unlike each other: the Scotsman who had turned his back on his origins facing a Dubliner who, far from losing his accent, still spoke in a brogue as broad as Phoenix Park. No one could call Burke a careerist. An aesthete and a journalist, invariably wearing spectacles and sometimes smelling of alcohol, he had sat in Parliament for eight years, with an ever decreasing prospect of holding high office. By now Burke had reached his mid-forties. Each year the Whigs saw their numbers dwindle a little more as their friends deserted them, tired of the languid marquess and hoping for favor from North or the king, until by 1774 fewer than fifty were left in the Commons. And yet Burke remained loyal to the Rockingham flag, always fighting hardest for causes that were already lost. Funny, mercurial, and often short of money,

The House of Commons as it was in 1774, with on the left its recently
constructed entrance and corridor in white Portland stone, leading to
the debating chamber, with the House of Lords in the foreground on
the right.

he inspired some verses of his own, written by his friend and fellow Irishman the poet Oliver Goldsmith: "In short, 'twas his fate, unemploy'd or in
place, sir—To eat mutton cold, and cut blocks with a razor."

Of course Burke had his faults, including sycophancy. He was apt to
bend the knee at the altar of privilege, treating Rockingham, Devonshire,
and the other aristocratic leaders of his party as beings of a lofty, super-
human kind. His devotion to their cause sometimes led him astray: in the
second half of 1773, he worried so much about the proposed new tax on
their Irish estates that he failed to spot the developing crisis in America.
Shortly before the Tea Party, the colonial assembly in New York had to
write to Burke to complain about his neglect of its affairs. Worst of all,
Burke suffered from a lack of focus in his life and his political creed alike.
"He's very friendly, warm, and cheerful," said a Frenchman who met Burke
in Paris at about this time. "But his philosophy is vague, as well as his
principles—neither fixed, nor properly connected, one to the other." But
when Burke was on top form, nobody could surpass him for eloquence
or visionary grandeur. His speeches on America were some of the finest
ever heard in Parliament, with barely an equal until the 1840s and those of
Benjamin Disraeli on the Corn Laws and the Irish question.[3]

On that first day, Wedderburn left no room for doubting the govern-

The chamber of the old House of Commons, with the government benches on the left. *Crown Copyright: U.K. Government Art Collection*

ment's resolve. "An event has occurred in one of the colonies," he said, "which if it had occurred in a hostile place must have been the immediate cause of war." As yet the cabinet had made no public charge of treason, but it was obvious that it intended to do so. Burke replied in the same ominous language.

"If the colonies are in a state of resistance, they are in rebellion, and rebellion is war," he said. "War can only be quelled by war; but take special care that you do not mistake the case. Discover if they have not been driven into measures unjustifiable, by mischievous measures of your own: by relaxation when you should have been firm, by fury when you should have been relaxed." The debate lasted less than three hours; there was a "dead, dull, stagnant feeling" in the chamber, according to Burke; and most newspapers gave only brief accounts of what was said. Even so, a shrewd observer would have seen a pattern starting to appear.[4]

On purpose, Wedderburn had been evasive, avoiding detail about the legislation due to be announced. The government used this tactic repeatedly, with Lord North choosing to let his coercive laws emerge only gradually, leaving his opponents with little time to prepare a response. He often asked the Commons for a vote to close the gallery and exclude the public, to prevent the press from passing the word to the colonies before General Gage could arrive with a fait accompli.

On the other side, Burke also set the tone for what was to come. Caught in the old dilemma of his party, he was obliged to fight a campaign of maneuver. Because the Rockingham Whigs had passed the Declaratory Act, they could not deny that the colonies had to obey the will of Parliament. Nor could the Whigs condone an offense so heinous as the Tea Party. Despite all that, they had to find a way to oppose Lord North and defend America as best they could. So Burke tried to make his way around the government's flanks and rear. He would harry Lord North about his history of errors and delay, he would issue dire warnings about the bloodshed the cabinet might provoke, and he would eventually set out his own vision of a different kind of empire. Edmund Burke would fail, but he would fail in style.

The Touchstone of Lord North

With the cabinet poised to unveil the bill to close the port of Boston, suddenly North scored a propaganda victory of his own. On March 8, news arrived of another despicable crime committed in Massachusetts. In late January, a Boston mob had seized a customs officer, John Malcolm, stripped him naked, and tortured him for hours with whips, tar, and feathers. At the Treasury Board in 1772, Lord North had been told about violent attacks on the customs service in America and had allowed them to go unpunished. On this occasion he had to act far more decisively.

Two days later, the cabinet told General Gage that he would replace Thomas Hutchinson as governor of Massachusetts, combining the role with that of commander in chief. It was a fateful step because, in effect, Gage would become the virtual military dictator of New England. Nothing quite like this had been seen in the colonies since the days of Governor Andros, ninety years earlier. The news was bound to cause consternation in America, and so, for the time being, the cabinet kept this quiet as well, waiting until early April to make it known officially, just before the general set sail.

Even without the assault on John Malcolm, Gage would have been chosen as the new governor, but the feathers and tar caused justified revulsion in London and served to stiffen the cabinet's resolve. The outrage also gave Lord North some powerful ammunition when at last, on March 14, he placed the Boston port bill before the Commons. Outside the heavy rains of winter had continued, filling the Thames until it burst its banks, reaching the highest level anyone could recall. Inside the chamber North rose to speak with the galleries emptied of visitors and the press. It was said that he spoke in a lackluster way, without his usual humor and high spirits. He was clearly very tired. Malcolm had suffered, he said, "greater cruelty than any that went before," in an incident that set the seal on Boston's history of wickedness.

Despite his fatigue North spoke for an hour or so, carrying all before him as he described the penalty that Boston would receive. The customs officers would be withdrawn to Salem; from the beginning of June the port of Boston would be closed to all but the most essential supplies, with the navy standing by to ensure that the order was obeyed; and the town would have to make financial restitution to the East India Company. The port would reopen only when the king was satisfied that this had been done.*

Wrong-footed again, the Rockinghams tried to respond with help from the Wilkesites and from a young man, Charles James Fox, making the first of many speeches against the government's American policy. But again they advanced no alternative strategy of their own. All they could do was state the obvious: that while Boston had to be brought to book, closure of the port was a drastic step without a precedent that anyone could recall. Not only would it be hard to enforce; it would also be unfair, because three other towns had resisted the tea and shared the responsibility for what had occurred. The speeches by Fox and the Rockinghams made little impact. The debate was "one of the coldest proceedings I ever was at," one MP wrote in his diary. Two weeks of argument still lay ahead before the king could sign the bill into law, but the cabinet already seemed to be close to success.[5]

Beyond the confines of Parliament, New England had some vocal allies in the business community, but politically they were weak. On the seventeenth, the merchants who traded with the northern colonies sent a deputation to Downing Street to meet Lord North and plead for Boston to be given a second chance. Like Franklin, whom they knew well, they hoped that the Massachusetts assembly might volunteer to make amends. But for a host of reasons, they had little chance of changing the government's mind. In the first place, the colonial lobby was simply far too small. Half of all the trade between England and North America passed through the hands of just ten firms in London, most of which dealt mainly with Charleston and Virginia. Nor did it help that the merchants who domi-

---

* The tea had a sterling value of £9,659, according to an invoice from the company. Divided among the taxpayers of Boston, this would have come to nearly £5 each: a heavy bill to pay, equivalent to more than a month's wages for a craftsman.

nated the colonial trade included Wilkesites open to accusations of disloyalty. At least three of the London firms were run by Wilkes's friends and political supporters, including George Hayley, John Hancock's agent, who hoped soon to enter Parliament himself.[6]

By way of religion, Hayley and his allies tended to be nonconformists, Presbyterian or Baptist, which rendered them all the more suspect in the eyes of politicians like North who still saw the Anglican Church as the moral center of the nation. And it was all the harder to listen to their complaints on behalf of America when everyone knew how deeply the colonies, on the mainland and in the Caribbean alike, relied on human bondage. Immensely valuable though the West Indies were, the wealth they produced tended, once again, to flow into a relatively small number of pockets. Among the aristocracy, it was hard to find a peer who invested in Jamaica or the other sugar islands. In fact, the elite in London were already beginning to turn against slavery as a sin that had no place in a Christian country. The king disliked it, as did the greatest judge in the land, Lord Mansfield, who called it "odious," and Dartmouth moved in religious circles where the antislavery movement had begun to gain ground.

So it was difficult to take Americans seriously when they spoke about freedom in peril. On the streets of Boston, Negroes were bought and sold, while in London it was common knowledge that the Wilkesites included investors who had invested aggressively to buy slave plantations on the Windward Islands. This became another propaganda weapon the government could use to cast the friends of liberty as hypocrites. Ninety years before Gettysburg, it did not seem obvious that America stood for justice and emancipation. On the contrary, the attacks on the *Gaspée*, on John Malcolm, and on the tea displayed the exact opposite: mob rule. As the days went by, the tide of public opinion appeared to flow ever more strongly in favor of coercion.

Carefully, North had avoided any mention of the scheme to change the Massachusetts charter. But somebody—most likely Lord Gower and the Bloomsburyites—leaked the story to the *Morning Post*, presumably with the aim of forcing the premier's hand. Printed on the day the merchants' deputation went to see him, the item was prophetic too. The writer warned that a war might have to be fought, but if so it was a price worth paying.[7]

According to the *Morning Post*, the time for appeasement had long since passed. Some men in the government did not realize, the writer said, that New England was already in rebellion. With his plan to change the charter, to make the members of the Governor's Council servants of the Crown—

which was "certainly right," said the *Post*—North would only arouse even more resistance, but if he did, the sooner the better. "His success in this affair will be the touchstone of his power," the piece went on. "If he stands it, he will stand everything. If he brings in proposals full of indecision, experimental and unmeaning, he will only make bad worse; and on the contrary, if he is firm, vigorous and decisive, America resists him, and the sword must be drawn." So be it, said the *Morning Post*, which reminded its readers that New England could be done without. From an economic point of view, tobacco and rice from the South mattered far more to the mother country.

By now, few days were left for legislation before Parliament rose at the end of March for its Easter recess. And another deadline was looming up ahead in the middle of April, the latest date for General Gage to sail from England if he had to be sure of reaching Boston in time to shut the harbor on June 1. And so, on March 23, Lord North appeared in the Commons again for the first of a series of debates that marked a new high point in his career but caused no end of trouble in America. When he passed the Tea Act the previous year, North had overplayed his hand; and now he did so once again.

Before the port bill could become law, he had to fight off a last-ditch attempt to defeat the measure, led by a member of Parliament called Rose Fuller, a sugar planter from Jamaica. Always inclined to speak up for New England, for the sake of the business the northern colonies did with the Caribbean, Fuller proposed that instead of closing the port, the government should simply fine the town some £25,000. Although this would have been a heavy penalty, Fuller found few supporters: the West Indian lobby spoke for no more than a handful of seats in Parliament. It took only four hours on the twenty-third for North to crush Fuller's effort at compromise. Even Edmund Burke held his tongue. That evening, George III sent Lord North a note, timed at exactly 8:35 p.m.—he liked to be precise in every way—offering his congratulations. Once again, the opposition had been languid, he wrote, further proof that the government was acting wisely. It seems that the king knew nothing about some unhelpful remarks uttered in the debate by the honorable member for Brecon.

For nearly two months, Charles Van had been waiting for his chance to call for reprisals against Boston even harsher than those North had announced. Toward the end of the debate, he rose to his feet to denounce colonial treason and dishonesty. In his constituency in South Wales, the foundry masters made iron and shipped it to the colonies, but often they received not a penny in return. Americans *never* honored their obligations, said Mr. Van. The annual bill for General Gage's army and the naval squadron came to half a million pounds, all of which fell on the British taxpayer. The worst offenders were the people of Boston, a hateful place. Shut up the port forever, he said: "Demolish it, that is my opinion: *delenda est Carthago.*"*

It would be hard to conceive of a more foolish and more inflammatory speech. At the time, Parliament kept only a journal of its decisions, not verbatim minutes of what each member said. So we have three different versions of Van's comments, two of them from notes hastily scribbled down by fellow MPs. All of them agree that he quoted the Latin tag from the Roman orator Cato the Elder, but when Van's words appeared in the press, they took a still more appalling form.

Without a seat in Parliament himself, John Wilkes could do little directly for the American cause; but ever since news of the Tea Party arrived, he had kept a close watch on the situation, dining regularly with Arthur and William Lee and even meeting some of the witnesses from Boston. For Wilkes and the Lees, Van's speech came as a gift from heaven, an opportunity to show Lord North's supporters in the worst possible light. Of all the papers that leaned toward the Wilkesites, the *London Evening Post* commanded perhaps the largest following, and its editor, John Miller, had recently lost a cripplingly expensive libel action brought by Lord Sandwich. And so, on March 26, the *Evening Post* wrote up the debate in full, elaborating on Van's remarks and awarding him rather more verbal fluency than he actually possessed. According to Miller, the MP had said this: "The town of Boston ought to be knocked about their ears . . . you will never meet with due obedience to the laws of this country, until you have destroyed that nest of locusts."[8]

The *Evening Post*'s article would not reach Massachusetts until the middle of May; but the timing was disastrous, because the story came hard on the heels of reports of Wedderburn's tirade against Franklin and then the news of the closure of the port. While in London some of Van's fellow politicians and the press dismissed him as a buffoon, in the colonies his words were widely reprinted. Americans took them as a serious threat, issued with the government's approval. This was a calamitous piece of public relations, but one that the cabinet ministers had brought upon themselves, by using language sometimes almost as extreme. And while Van was an

---

* Carthage must be destroyed.

oaf, he only expressed in public the hard line that other backbenchers were probably taking in private, at Alice's and elsewhere. In any event, with the hawkish Gower and Sandwich snapping at his heels, Lord North had no option but to press ahead, regardless of what Americans might think.

He reached the Easter break in what seemed to be splendid shape. After so much rain and even a few late snowstorms, the winter had given way to a warm and sunny spring, during which the port bill swiftly passed into law. Again, the opposition did not even call a vote, because they dared not defend the Tea Party and Lord North's majority seemed sure to be overwhelming. And then, on March 28, as Sandwich sent orders to the navy to arrest any ship that tried to enter Boston, at last the government confirmed the details of its regulating bill for Massachusetts.

Meanwhile, the Rockingham Whigs remained below the parapet, still reluctant to risk their political lives for criminals in the colonies. Unwilling to be seen as troublemakers, they held their fire, hoping that North might offer the Americans at least one concession—the abolition of the Tea Act—unlikely though that was. Their disarray was all the more complete because their leader in the Commons, William Dowdeswell, had reached almost the point of death. A gifted politician, one of the few who could match Lord North in a debate about taxes and spending, Dowdeswell would leave for the Côte d'Azur that summer and pass away early in 1775. But as the weeks went by and the government showed not the least sign of softening its stance, it became apparent that the Whigs could wait no longer.

Although Edmund Burke had already made one excellent speech, his best were yet to come. And soon enough, he would be able to count on powerful reinforcements. Among them was Lord Chatham, elderly, frail, and eternally unpredictable. Another friend of the *London Evening Post's*, the old war hero stood ready to intervene on behalf of New England, whether out of vanity or for love of country. It was impossible to say precisely what William Pitt's motives were—even in his years of greatness, Chatham had always been a loner and an egotist—but he would not allow Lord North, whom he despised, to win more victories unchallenged. And elsewhere in the House of Lords the Rockinghams could deploy a maverick peer of their own who was equally determined to fight. As the port bill passed through the upper chamber, the Duke of Richmond had attacked it with far more energy than even Burke had displayed in the Commons. As the war approached, the Americans found their best and most outspoken British friend in the topmost tier of the aristocracy.

Charles Lennox, third
Duke of Richmond,
by James Watson after
George Romney. ©
The Fitzwilliam Museum,
Cambridge

A Noble Duke

Clever, rich, handsome, and rather eccentric, Charles Lennox had lived
thirty-nine years in the world with a great deal to vex him. He belonged
to an echelon of dukes who regarded themselves, not George III, as the
rightful leaders of the nation. When he surveyed the political horizon, the
Duke of Richmond saw nothing but corruption everywhere: a vast but
tawdry scheme by the king and his friends, led by Lord North, to gather
all the reins of power into their hands.

In his opinion, Lennox had every right to question the monarch's
authority, and not least because he outranked the upstart dynasty from
Hanover. A bastard member of the Stuart royal family, he owed his rank
to his great-grandmother Louise de Kérouaille and her skill at fornica-
tion in the expert arms of Charles II. The king had said thank you to his
mistress with the dukedom and a handsome gift of money. In the future,
her family would have the right to collect a tax on all the coal shipped
out of Newcastle. By 1774, this yielded £15,000 a year, an income that
gave Charles Lennox the freedom to be difficult. "I pass in the world for
very obstinate, wrong-headed and tenacious of my opinions," he once told
Edmund Burke.

Shy, abrasive, and prone to depression, the Duke of Richmond knew precisely how to upset the orthodox. Perhaps it would be hard to dislike a man who put central heating in his kennels to keep his foxhounds warm, as he did, but many people hated him, including George III. "His whole conduct is dictated by malevolence," fumed the king, when Richmond opposed the Regulating Act for India. In return, Lennox called the king a liar.

An enlightened politician far ahead of his time, the duke had studied biology in Paris, met Frederick the Great, and read Rousseau and Voltaire. A soldier in his youth, he served in combat in the German theater of the Seven Years' War with a military record arguably rather better than General Gage's in America. At home in England, Richmond joined the Rockinghams, but he showed himself to be far broader in his sympathies. Long before his contemporaries, he called for a fair deal for Ireland and for religious dissenters, eventually becoming a Unitarian himself. In France he befriended John Wilkes, whom he supported in his bid to enter Parliament. As early as 1780 the duke called for sweeping constitutional reform: a vote for every male over eighteen, a secret ballot, fair and equal constituencies, and elections every year, all as a means to curb the overweening power of the executive.[9]

On ten separate occasions between the Tea Party and Lexington, Lennox rose in the House of Lords to try to stop the drift to war. Because debates in the upper chamber were only sketchily reported, often we do not know exactly what he said, but he left a deep impression. "The Duke of Richmond spoke warmly for Boston," wrote Horace Walpole, who admired him immensely, about one debate in 1774. "Said they would be in the right to resist . . . and if they did resist, he should wish them success."[10]

Nobody else in Parliament dared to voice such unpopular opinions, but when they reassembled in the middle of April, the duke had little choice. While some of the Rockinghams still dragged their heels, the duke understood how desperate the situation had become. General Gage was just about to leave England—on HMS *Lively* from Plymouth, on April 16—and so far the opposition had scored not a single point. The government rode the crest of a wave, with the king quietly confident that the package of new laws for Massachusetts could be completed swiftly.

Twenty-four hours before the general set sail, Lord Dartmouth produced yet another tranche of documents, twenty-eight papers in all, to show just how little support Governor Hutchinson had received from his council of advisers. Lord North struck again the same day, April 15, with the text of his bill to sweep away democracy in the province by making the councillors and the judges royal appointees and by curbing the power of town meetings.

That evening he went still further and announced a third measure: the Impartial Administration of Justice Bill, a clumsy name for another coercive law. Like the others, it would come into force on June 1. From that day forward, if Gage believed that a jury in Massachusetts could not be trusted, then he could move the site of a trial to another province or to England. This could already be done with a writ from a judge in the Court of King's Bench, but Gage needed the power to act quickly to protect his soldiers or himself if and when they spilled American blood. When word reached the colonies, people called it "the murder act," and although it seems that it was never used, it gave the Boston patriots another stick with which to beat the British.

Yet again the cabinet had failed to understand an essential feature of American life: in this case, the deep attachment the colonists felt to their own local laws and legal culture, not only in Boston and Rhode Island, but in every other province. And again, the new law aroused all the more anger because of a threat made by Charles Van. After Lord North sat down, it fell to Alexander Wedderburn to give a long speech of justification. "If you go with the olive branch without a sword, you drop the sword for this moment you give up the authority," the solicitor general said, according to the shorthand notes, and then, just before the house adjourned, Van made another atrocious comment. "Set the woods on fire!" he suggested. The following day the *London Evening Post* quoted him again, like this: "If they oppose the measures of government that are now sent out, I would do as was done of old, in the time of ancient Britons, I would burn and set fire to all their woods, and leave their country open; and if we are likely to lose that country, I think it better lost by our own troops, than wrested from us by our rebellious children."[11]

Although Van probably never uttered a sentence quite so eloquent, the story traveled to Boston, where the threat to burn the forests of New England entered into revolutionary folklore. In the colonies, the reports about the justice bill hardened attitudes still further, partly because the proceedings in Parliament seemed to be so one-sided. If the opposition in the mother country lacked the stomach for a fight at Westminster, what course lay open to Massachusetts but all-out resistance? By the time General Gage arrived, the colony's distrust of the British political system had become almost terminal. But ironically enough, by the end of April, at last the Rockingham Whigs had begun a sustained counterattack against Lord North.

This had always been a possibility, if only the Whigs could agree to work with the Wilkesites, the followers of Lord Chatham, and a few other mavericks in a last stand against the Coercive Acts. Although they could not stop the government in its tracks—North's majority was far too large—a united opposition might at least delay the implementation of his policies. They also had to think about the future: a situation where, perhaps, America resisted the new laws so fiercely that they became a dead letter. If the kingdom came to the brink of war, then conceivably the government might weaken or even collapse. At that point, the opposition had to be ready to step forward and form a new administration, perhaps in the wake of the general election due in 1775. And so the Whigs and their allies had to use the debates in the spring of 1774 to put down a marker, positioning themselves as the statesmen who had warned that coercion would fail.

And this they began to do. Of all the Rockingham Whigs, Richmond had always been the most open-minded and the most willing to reach out to members of Parliament of whom the marquess disapproved. Behind the scenes, and working with Burke, Lennox began to organize a new campaign against the government. For this, he could count on old comrades with whom he had tried to save the East India Company from control by North and the cabinet. Foremost among them was George Johnstone, the angry Scotsman, with his years in Florida to give him some authority on colonial affairs. He enjoyed the rare distinction of having spoken out against the sending of the tea.

There was also Franklin's lawyer John Dunning, gradually regaining his health, and an old soldier, Isaac Barré, who had served with General Wolfe at Quebec. Both were close to Lord Chatham, sharing his hostility toward the Declaratory Act, and both men had a history of opposing foolish schemes to tax America. With them came another fine lawyer, Charles Pratt, Lord Camden, a former lord chancellor who held the same opinions. And last but not least they had the assistance of Benjamin Franklin, who had at last emerged reenergized after his mauling by Wedderburn. "The torrent is still violent against America," Franklin wrote to his Boston friend Speaker Cushing on April 16, but he was doing what he could, briefing the opposition with the facts it needed.

Three days later, the Whigs were ready. Richmond would have to wait until May for the next debate in the Lords, but in the meantime Burke seized an opportunity in the Commons. Unable to make a credible case against the port bill, the Whigs had been looking for a chance to appeal to independent members of the house. The moment arrived on April 19.

At three o'clock that afternoon, Rose Fuller, the Jamaican, called for a vote to review the threepenny tea tax, the source of all the trouble. Here the opposition found an easier target: the tax was clearly an absurdity that the smugglers had already defeated. With the Americans united against it, any attempt to enforce the law would only end in violence. Take the path of reconciliation, said Fuller. North had already abolished the other Townshend duties: if he did away with this one as well, Britain would offer the colonies the olive branch that was so obviously necessary. A few other MPs said the same thing, and Wedderburn replied—"if you give up this duty, you give up the whole of your authority," he said—and then, at 5:15, Edmund Burke rose to give his great speech on American taxation.[12]

He spoke for two hours. According to the *London Evening Post*, the Commons hung on his every word, but the *Post* could never be trusted to report debates objectively. Other accounts of his speeches that year suggest that Burke was always jeered at by the Northites. He tended to speak too quickly, and sometimes his Irish accent left his audience puzzled and confused. Even so, Burke lifted the debate to a new peak of intelligence.

"I know the map of England," he said. "And I know that the way I take is not the road to preferment." Burke struck that note throughout: bold and unrepentant. Refusing to apologize for the repeal of the Stamp Act, he gloried in it, as a magnanimous gesture that had simply restored the colonial status quo before Grenville. After repeal, America had fallen quiet, and so it would again if Parliament removed the tea tax. "Nobody will be argued into slavery," said Burke in a speech full of brilliant lines. "Reflect how you are to govern a people, who think they ought to be free. Your scheme yields nothing but discontent, disorder and disobedience; and such is the state of America, that after wading up to your eyes in blood, you could only end just where you began: that is, to tax where no revenue is to be found."

The core of the problem, he said, was simple: that the government had never risen to what he called "large, liberal ideas" about the colonies. Without a plan or a vision for the empire, it had dealt in "bits and scraps... full of meanness and full of mischief," until at last it was close to causing a war for the sake of a trivial tax: "a tax of sophistry, a tax of pedantry, a tax of disputation." Abolish it, and peace would follow, based on mutual respect and justice. And when again the time came to fight the French, the Americans would freely volunteer to help with soldiers and money.

These were fine words, but they came too late. The general had already boarded his ship for Boston, with news about the revocation of the charter soon to follow. And however hard Burke tried, he could not escape his party's old predicament. For all his eloquence, his speech contained a fatal weakness, which he could not conceal: logic was never really Edmund Burke's strong point. His difficulty was this: taxation had ceased to be the principal issue at stake. As the weeks went by, in both London and America the political debate had shifted its focus, moving on to more urgent questions about the very nature of imperial authority. "The disturbances in America proceed from deeper causes," said Lord North. "Mere tax is not their objection."

In theory, the Rockinghams upheld the Declaratory Act and the doctrine that Parliament was supreme. In practice, said Lord North, they were calling for retreat in the face of violence and mayhem, despite the evidence that retreat would arouse even more resistance. Every newspaper in London had printed angry words from the colonies, denying that Parliament had any say in their affairs. If Parliament scrapped the tea duty, it would reveal itself to be powerless against Americans already pursuing independence. It had come to that: a choice, which the British had to make, between a cowardly surrender, which would spell the end of empire, and a firm resolve to force America into line. Both North and Wedderburn made that very clear. After eight hours of debate, the opposition called a vote and lost. The Whigs and their allies went down to defeat by 182 votes to 49. At that moment, all the technicalities of tea and tax fell away into the shadows in Britain and the colonies alike. As the war approached, they would briefly return to the stage, but only to play a relatively minor role in the drama of events. Instead, the spotlight shifted elsewhere, to the matters of fundamental principle that the town of Boston had already been discussing for so long.

In Parliament, a fortnight passed before the next great encounter. When it came early in May, at last it filled the Commons to overflowing. The measure before them was the most controversial of all: the bill to change the government of Massachusetts, which was reaching its final stage. Once again, the cabinet seemed to hold the upper hand. Since the news about John Malcolm, little more had been heard from the colonies, but silence had done nothing to reduce British animosity toward New England.* On the contrary, in Parliament the independent members were swinging all the more firmly behind Lord North.

---

* On April 18, after a long delay caused by bad weather, the tea ship *Nancy* finally reached New York, only to turn back without unloading her cargo when her captain saw how much opposition he would face. News of this did not reach London until June 7.

There seem to have been three reasons why this occurred, the first of which was commercial. Since the crash of 1772, the nation had slowly pulled itself out of the economic mire. In response to the recession, the factory masters looked to continental Europe as a market, with Josiah Wedgwood in the lead, launching an export drive that carried his pots all the way to Siberia. As British sales to Europe grew, America diminished in importance, and a trade boycott by the colonies ceased to be as worrying as in the past. The industrial lobby felt no need to agitate again on America's behalf, as it had done at the time of the Stamp Act.

Meanwhile, the press hammered on with stories that the colonists intended to resort to bloodshed. The newspapers carried reports of gunpowder shipments on the way to rebels in New England, and although they were premature—the Americans did not begin to arm seriously until August—they served to raise the political temperature. Even the king was rumored to have cracked a tasteless joke at one of his levees, saying that he would as happily fight the Bostonians as the French.[13]

Last but most important, the prospect of a general election concentrated the mind. Long before the polls were held, candidates began to look for safe seats, especially those that Lord North and the Treasury could help them win. What better way to catch his eye than to stand up and support him on the colonial question? On the other side, in those open boroughs where the election was likely to be hard fought, radicals and Whigs did the opposite: they put themselves forward as friends of America and liberty.

Against this background, the Commons met on May 2 for the final debate on the Massachusetts government bill. Four hundred MPs had arrived at the house by four o'clock for a session packed with business for which time was running out. As a preliminary, they were told about yet another measure, a fourth coercive law, allowing General Gage to requisition buildings in Boston as billets for his men. And then the real battle began, with the opposition in full flood. Out of his tent came John Dunning, stung by the memory of the humiliating session at the Cockpit; later, Colonel Barré rose to his aid, and so did Charles James Fox, and finally Edmund Burke. On both sides of the house, MPs spoke in the bluntest terms, trading insults and blaming each other for causing an imperial crisis so grave.

Since January, Charles Van had found allies ready to use language as intemperate as his own. Up stood Richard Rigby, fifty-two years old, a heavy drinker with a purple face, a fighter of duels, and a loyal supporter of Lord North. "I say: stand and deliver to the Americans," he bellowed.

"America, at this instant, is a downright anarchy—let us give it a government!" He might have been misquoted—a surviving shorthand note suggests that Rigby used slightly more delicate language—but these were his words as they appeared in the *London Evening Post,* to be read in the colonies later that year.[14]

It was a noisy debate, in which Burke received the roughest handling from the benches opposite. "You will lose America," he said, but time and again they drowned him out as he spoke from midnight until one o'clock, an effort so exhausting that he took two days to recover. Feeling free at last to attack the government head-on, the opposition denounced the coercive laws on the most basic constitutional grounds. Taken together, they amounted to an infringement of freedom of a kind that Britons would never tolerate at home. The opposition united around the principles for which the Rockinghams had always claimed to stand: the defense of civil liberty against the arbitrary power of the king and his minions.

According to Colonel Barré, the Americans would rise in rebellion with consequences almost too appalling to contemplate. There would be war with the colonies, he said, a war that would require more than thirty battalions, half the fighting strength of the British army, and all the while the French would be watching, biding their time to intervene. "The voice of humanity, law and justice is against you in this wicked proceeding," the colonel said as he sat down, "and I fear the hand of heaven will take the same direction." At two o'clock, the vote was called. For the government, 239; for the opposition, 64. At Downing Street, before he went to bed, North scribbled a note to George III, who replied later that day. "I am infinitely pleased," he wrote.[15]

With that, the campaign in the House of Commons began to wind down. There were still more bills to pass and more debates to be had, but after losing on May 3 by such a large majority the opposition could not hope to inflict any serious wounds on Lord North. Gradually the Whigs fell back, leaving it up to the Duke of Richmond to lead a last stand in the upper chamber. There Charles Lennox could muster at least twenty votes, enough to make it very clear that the ruling elite was divided. Again, he was thinking about the future, preparing for the *next* phase in the crisis. It was no use trying to compromise. The Rockinghams had to be outspoken so that one day the political classes would look back and see that the Whigs had entirely opposed a policy that led to catastrophe.

So the duke sought out the young bishop of Lichfield, Brownlow North, to warn him that he intended to be outrageous, knowing that the bishop would pass this on to his half brother. It was a tactic presumably intended to provoke the government into a showdown where Richmond could speak as plainly as Barré. Indeed, because they were unelected, the duke and his friends in the upper house could make the same case against the government even more vigorously.

As usual, the debates in the Lords were not reported in great detail. On May 11, the peers voted on the regulating bill; on the eighteenth, the justice bill to protect the army; and on the twenty-sixth, the quartering bill to give the troops billets in Boston. Even the Marquess of Rockingham found time to attend between the end of foxhunting and the best of the flat racing season. And for that last debate, the duke had another eccentric ally, in the person of Lord Chatham, finally appearing from the wings for a performance that reeked of anticlimax. The old Agamemnon was sixty-five, theatrically ill, leaning on a crutch, and wearing black velvet boots to ease the pains of gout. He gave "a feeble harangue," said a cruel observer, Horace Walpole, in which Chatham condemned everything—the tea tax, the Stamp Act, and the rioters in Boston—but without a hint of what course he might follow if he were Lord North. Then Chatham took his exit, leaving his audience little the wiser.

Of course the government won every vote, but that was not quite the end of the story. The procedural rules in the Lords gave Richmond a weapon of a kind that Edmund Burke could not deploy in the Commons. In the Lords, a peer could propose a motion of dissent, a gesture of protest whose text was entered in the record for everyone to see. Seizing an opportunity, Charles Lennox put down two motions of the kind, each one long and strongly worded, carefully drawn up in numbered paragraphs to condemn every single component of the Coercive Acts. They included words of warning as strident as Barré's. To enforce the new laws, the British would need to use military force: a force so large and so expensive that it would bring about "the inevitable ruin of the nation."[16]

And that was the final scene in the rearguard campaign by the Rockinghams and their allies. The curtain fell on a performance that had occupied three months of political time. What had the opposition achieved? On the face of it, very little, since Lord North had accomplished his mission, and Gage was on his way. In the closing days of May, the king signed the remaining bills for Lord Dartmouth to send to Gage on June 3 with a secret letter of instructions sealed inside the messenger's pouch.

If Great Britain had been the despotic tyranny that Americans liked to think it was, the politics would have ended there; but in fact, the parliamentary campaign had taxed Lord North to the limit, leaving him even more uneasy and fatigued than he usually was by midsummer. With the general election looming up ahead, North also had to contemplate what might prove to be a still deeper crisis if Barré's predictions were fulfilled.

And at this moment North made another serious mistake. Until now, none of his new laws had affected any colony other than Massachusetts, but before Parliament rose, the cabinet chose to look further afield. For years the future of the western wilderness had gone unresolved, despite constant worries about a general Indian war. At last the time seemed right to deal with this matter too; but in doing so, Lord North would unite the colonies in resistance to Great Britain.

THE QUEBEC ACT

Two years earlier, when Lord Hillsborough resigned, his departure had seemed like a triumph for the bankers and visionaries, including Benjamin Franklin, who sought to open the Ohio country to new settlers. But among the officials in Whitehall, this still aroused deep anxiety for the usual reasons. It would provoke the Indians and weaken the mother country's control over the colonies on the seaboard. The law officers, Thurlow and Wedderburn, dug in their heels and prevented the Grand Ohio Company from obtaining the land grants for which it had applied.

The British government, however, could not prevaricate forever about the wilderness. In Canada and the Illinois country the old French pioneers, all of whom were Roman Catholic, had made a convincing case to be given their own civil government, with a French system of law and a promise of freedom for their faith. If arrangements such as these would guarantee the settlers' loyalty, so be it, thought the ministers in London; and they found nothing alarming about Catholicism three thousand miles away. Loyal Anglicans though they were, North and his colleagues had shaken off the crude old English hatred of the Vatican. In the upper ranks of society, that sort of prejudice had lost its appeal at a time when the last Jacobites were dying out and every young British nobleman went to Rome to look at statues and to catch the pox.[17]

On May 2, Lord Dartmouth announced a new Quebec bill, drafted mainly by Wedderburn, intended to answer the western question forever. Despite some fierce criticism, especially from John Dunning, it passed swiftly through the Commons, often with very few members taking the trouble to attend debates about what seemed to be a tedious, provincial matter. In the Lords, Chatham reappeared to denounce the measure, on a variety of grounds that included an appeal to anti-Popery, but Richmond opposed it only halfheartedly. Like Edmund Burke, who favored Catholic emancipation in Ireland, the duke held liberal views about religion and did not stoop to bigotry.

In some ways the bill was a farsighted, even progressive piece of legislation, but the ministers were playing with fire. It would have been far wiser politically to leave the Canadian question on one side, for perhaps another year or two, in the hope that in the meantime New England would fall quiet. As it was, the bill contained elements that were bound to antagonize the colonies, the Wilkesites, and the people on the streets of London. The new law said that in Quebec the French would be entirely free to worship as they chose; they would join a new legislative council to help the British governor rule the province; and its boundaries would be pushed a long way southward and westward all the way to the Ohio and Mississippi rivers. In other words, Quebec would encompass the western wilderness in its entirety, blocking the path of settlers from Pennsylvania, Virginia, and New York. The Indians would be protected and their reservations guaranteed.

When news of the Quebec Act reached the colonies, it did indeed cause a furor; and because, far from being trivial or technical, its scope was so wide, it offended men and women in every single province. It was a plot, some would say, not only to bring Catholicism into America by the back door but also to confine Americans to the East, where they would lie at Britain's mercy. Indeed Wedderburn freely admitted that this was so. The Ohio would set a limit that settlers must not cross. "We ought to confine the inhabitants," the solicitor general told the Commons on May 26, "to keep them according to the ancient policy of this country, along the line of the sea and rivers."[18]

Meanwhile, in London, the Quebec Act's religious dimension aroused the fiercest opposition. Here as well as in the colonies the bulk of the population lagged far behind the cabinet in its tolerance of Roman Catholics. Even the bishops of the Church of England grew uneasy about a measure that might lead in time to a Catholic revival on both sides of the Atlantic. Up to this point, the Wilkesites in the capital had done little to help their cousins in New England, other than in the columns of the press. But now, with the old Roman enemy in full view, they finally began to stir. At the very last moment, when the act was just about to become law, they organized a protest against it, but one that owed as much to sectarian hatred as it did to the love of freedom.

The campaign against the Quebec Act found its leader in Frederick Bull, the lord mayor of London, who also sat in the Commons as an MP for the city. A successful tea merchant and an associate of John Hancock's friend

George Hayley, Bull cut a curious figure, becoming an object of ridicule in parts of the press. While the *London Evening Post* called him "the patriotic chief magistrate," others dismissed him as "a weak and silly character," a toady manipulated by John Wilkes, to whom he was very close: they would dine together several times a week. A religious dissenter, probably a Baptist, Bull had run for mayor on a platform that included "the restoration of the liberties of our American brethren." Among his allies were two genuine colonials: Stephen Sayre from New York, an adventurer who ran a rather suspect banking house, and William Lee, Arthur's brother. Lee and Sayre had both taken large bets on the West Indies, buying slave plantations on the island of Dominica at the peak of the boom in real estate.

Together with Bull, they belonged to a small London caucus that had built the radical, Wilkesite majority in the capital. As a means to qualify their friends to vote and hold office, the caucus had quietly taken over a small livery company, the Framework Knitters, an empty shell run from the New England Coffee House with Sayre and Arthur Lee among its members. Thanks to deft organization, as well as the appeal of their ideas, the caucus gradually gathered support among the other livery companies until it had the backing of nearly 60 percent of the city's voters.[19]

The previous year, they had engineered the choice of Sayre and William Lee as the two sheriffs of London, while also keeping in close touch with Samuel Adams in Boston. With the general election approaching, they were hoping to win seats in Parliament not only in the London area but also in Bristol, Hull, Newcastle, and Worcester, where radicalism still ran deep. While they advocated parliamentary reform, they also appealed to anti-Catholicism, the blind emotion that formed the Wilkesite movement's dark side. In Parliament that spring, Bull never once rose to his feet to speak against the new coercive laws for Massachusetts. Instead, he waited until the Quebec Act had already passed both houses before he rallied the city against Lord North.*

On the evening of June 18, the day after the last vote was taken and close to the end of their terms of office as sheriffs, Sayre and Lee paid a visit to Downing Street, where North turned them away. He knew precisely what the two Americans wanted: to make an appointment for Bull to present a petition against the act before George III gave it the royal assent. "I think it scarcely decent to receive them," North told the king, but sooner or later

---

* In 1778, Bull vehemently opposed a modest measure of reform that restored some civil rights to English Catholics. Two years later he helped to foment the anti-Catholic Gordon Riots, which left nearly five hundred people dead.

First published in London in May 1774, and later reprinted in Boston
by Paul Revere, this cartoon depicts the Quebec Act as a plot by
English bishops to foist Roman Catholicism on America, while Lord
North looks on with a Jacobite in Highland dress. *Library of Congress*

they would have to be heard because, by ancient precedent, the lord mayor
always had the right to address the monarch directly. On the morning of
the twenty-second, the petition arrived at last, signed by the Corporation
of London, only moments before the king was due to go to Parliament to
close that year's session. The city accused him of breaking his coronation
oath to defend the Protestant faith.

For weeks, the press had been full of agitation against the act, and now
a crowd gathered in St. James's Park and outside the House of Lords to
shout, "No Popery! No French government!" According to one report,
John Wilkes appeared at a window to greet them as they passed. First
as the royal coach arrived, and then again when it left, the crowd jostled
around it, shaking their fists at the king with cries of "Remember Charles I!
Remember James II!" It was all very different from the applause that had
greeted His Majesty a year earlier at the naval review. George III was left
visibly shaken, unable to give his speech without stumbling over his lines.[20]

This was the only recorded case of Londoners taking to the streets to
protest on behalf of America. The demonstration did nothing but harm,
and it helped to make war more likely. The king and Lord North swiftly
recovered, all the more convinced that they stood for reason and enlight-
enment, while their opponents were bigoted and seditious. From the riot
against the Quebec Act, they also drew the lesson that the Wilkesites

would make the colonies an election issue; and, in due course, this persuaded the cabinet to deliver a preemptive strike of its own, to be launched at the end of September.

On the far side of the Atlantic the riot left another dangerous legacy. The press reports about it arrived in Boston in August and were reprinted by newspapers all over the continent, giving a false impression of the breadth of support the colonies commanded in the mother country. For this, Lord Chatham must also bear much of the blame. With his futile and xenophobic speech against the Quebec Act, Chatham encouraged Americans to believe that with him at their head the ordinary people of England stood shoulder to shoulder with their colonial cousins. In London and a few other cities a great many did, but not in the shires of middle England, where so much political power still lay. However much the English disliked Catholicism, it seems that no demonstrations occurred outside the capital.[21]

Meanwhile, as the summer wore on and General Gage's orders crossed the ocean, Lord Dartmouth had little to do but wait anxiously to see how Massachusetts would respond. Shy and tongue-tied, always worrying about his son at Oxford and the godless morals of the kingdom, he had mostly sat through the parliamentary debates in silence. In reply to Richmond, he made only one substantial speech in the Lords at the end of March. Horace Walpole the diarist heard it and came away thinking he hoped for reconciliation. The colonial secretary had been "conscientious and mild," Walpole thought, but Dartmouth's secret letter of instructions to Gage told a different story. Whatever his private feelings, he did not have the power to waver from the hard line taken by his colleagues.

As yet, no one had explicitly laid down the doctrine, so central to British politics today, that the cabinet must take collective responsibility for every decision it reaches. But even so, the convention was usually observed, despite the personal rivalries that drove Lord North to distraction. Neither he nor Dartmouth could make policy in isolation. Once the new coercive laws were passed, they had to be enforced to the letter whatever private reservations Dartmouth might have.

When he wrote to Gage on June 3, he gave the general the clearest instructions: ensure that the port remained closed until such time as the town of Boston had made amends for the destruction of the tea; convene the new mandamus councillors; find the Tea Party's ringleaders of December, and bring them to justice; and if anyone stood in his way, Gage should use the full rigor of the law. Of course, Dartmouth hoped that in Massachusetts people of goodwill—"the thinking part," he called them—would see sense. He still believed that the Tea Party had arisen merely from a cynical plot by a handful of fanatics. But if disobedience continued, then the general's orders were unambiguous. "Whatever violences are committed must be resisted with firmness," Dartmouth wrote. "The authority of this kingdom . . . must be vindicated, and its laws obeyed."[22]

It would take until the autumn, but at last the colonial secretary would discover that the general's mission was impossible. When Gage set off for New England in April, neither he nor his political masters could see just how volatile the colonies had already become. Shocked though they would be by the news of the Coercive Acts, the Americans soon regained the initiative. For the rest of 1774, they would always be two or three steps ahead of the British.

Chapter Thirteen

THE REVOLUTION BEGINS

Soon very soon expect to hear the thirsty earth drinking in the blood of American sons.

—NATHANAEL GREENE OF RHODE ISLAND, JULY 1774[1]

In the eighteenth century, treason could take many forms, with the sword or with the pen. Long before the general arrived in Boston, and even with the war a year away, we find young patriots in America already committing lines to paper that might have sent them to the gallows if any British spy had read them.

For the British, the crisis had blown up suddenly, a storm coming out of a sky that was cloudy but not yet tempestuous. But for a rising generation of radicals in New England the events of 1774 were something for which they had been preparing ever since their childhood. William Molineux in Boston was only one of many people who had grown up with the Greek and Roman classics, reading accounts of civil war and tyrannicide. It is often said that Americans were reluctant to rebel—"revolutionaries despite themselves," in the words of a recent scholar*—but this tells us only part of the story. While it is certainly true of Washington, Franklin, and John Adams, men who had rebellion thrust on them, it is equally clear that some Americans were only too willing to fight. As early as the spring of 1774 they began to prepare, at first with words only, but soon enough with deeds as well.

This was the last thing Lord North expected. Time and again, during

---

* Jack Rakove, in his book *Revolutionaries* (Boston, 2010).

the debates in Parliament, speakers had risen on both sides of the chamber to argue that America would not shrink from war. In the press in London, many writers had said the same thing, but commentary such as this was easily dismissed if it came only from journalists or from oddballs in the Commons like Colonel Barré. With General Gage briefing them, the cabinet ministers remained convinced that Massachusetts would back away from bloodshed. If they had thought any differently, they would have increased the budget for the army when it came before Parliament late in January. In fact, the War Office left the numbers unchanged and even cut by two battalions the forces allocated to America and the West Indies. As for the navy, Lord North believed that only four frigates would be needed to seal the port of Boston. So the budget for the fleet was also frozen.

They had no reason to increase it because, for the first nine months of 1774, the British envisaged no military threat from this or any other colony. From the papers sent over by Governor Hutchinson—whose letters became all the more grim as the time for his departure approached—they had a thick dossier about the patriot leadership in Boston. They knew that government was breaking down, but what they saw was merely agitation, not a tight and disciplined insurgency. In time, the British infiltrated Samuel Adams's Committee of Correspondence, but not at this early stage before General Gage arrived in Massachusetts. They had no idea how avidly some of Adams's allies were already discussing the possibility of war or how widely the talk had spread.

For years, some radicals had been hinting at an armed struggle with the mother country. In 1771, for example, a columnist calling himself Centinel—this might have been Josiah Quincy Jr.—had begun to write for Boston's new, radical paper, the *Massachusetts Spy*, branding Hutchinson a tyrant and calling the colonies "the asylum of freedom." Attack their liberties, he wrote, and Americans would make "the appeal to the sword," words that would later become a revolutionary mantra, repeated all along the eastern seaboard. But did a phrase like this really mean what it seemed? It might have been mere rhetoric, spoken figuratively, by orators with no intention of picking up a musket. In order for the crisis to spin entirely out of control and become a revolution, men and women in New England had to move beyond words and begin to make active preparations.

For the first hard evidence in 1774 of people in the region smuggling in arms and gunpowder, we will have to wait until the fourth week of August. It will be found in Rhode Island, where the plot apparently involved veterans of the *Gaspée* affair. But months earlier, in March and April, we can already hear serious talk about military action, not only in Boston, but also

Elbridge Gerry in 1798,
by John Vanderlyn.
*Harvard Art Museums/Fogg
Museum*

sixteen miles away in the harbor town of Marblehead. Already a bustling
little place, it would become all the more important on June 1, when the
port act came into force, because ships from England would arrive first
either here or nearby at Salem. If small towns on the coast and in the hinterland aligned themselves with the radicals in Boston, Gage's task would
be hopeless. He would face a wide and diverse movement of resistance,
rural as well as urban, with little warning of where the next Tea Party or
the next *Gaspée* raid might occur.

In fact, the towns of Essex County were quite as anti-British as their
bigger neighbor to the south and already thinking about the practicalities
of armed resistance, as well as the principles on which it might be based.
In Marblehead there lived a future vice president of the United States,
Elbridge Gerry. A Harvard graduate from the class of 1762, the son of a
leading merchant in the town, he was wiry and intense, filled with nervous
energy. Elected to the House of Representatives, he spoke with a stam-
mer, but he outdid even his mentor Samuel Adams in the passion of his
rhetoric.

On April 4, Gerry denounced the British in a letter addressed to
Adams's committee. North and his colleagues were evil men and tyrants,
enemies of liberty with whom no compromise was possible. "They have

taxed the colonies, and with unremitted ardor tried every measure which wicked policy could suggest," he wrote. The British could never be trusted. He called the king's ministers "persons of the most sordid principles, possessed of neither honour, honesty or knowledge . . . from whom no accommodation can be expected, and none ought to be looked for."

These were fighting words from Mr. Gerry, and all the more significant because he wrote them before hearing a whisper about the Boston Port Act or any of the cabinet's other measures. For many weeks, bad weather had kept ships in their harbors or blown them off course so that only a trickle of news crossed the Atlantic. Since the Tea Party, New England had received nothing from London except a few lines carried in the local press on March 28. Even then, the story gave no clue about the official response except a rumor—false, as it happened—that more battleships were on their way from England.

And yet, even with so little evidence to go on, Gerry assumed the worst about Great Britain and went on to issue something close to a call to arms. His letter had an urgent, practical purpose: he wanted the committee to form a new colonial militia to supersede the one that already existed. He argued that the empire kept the colonies in thrall by projecting an image of military might. "They have artfully taught Americans," said Gerry, "the most exalted idea of British troops, and the most diminutive opinion of their own." Just across the water in Salem, another Harvard graduate, Timothy Pickering, from the class of 1763, had been campaigning for years for a new, improved militia, drilling according to the latest methods, known as the Norfolk system and taken from a manual published in Britain during the Seven Years' War. Gerry adopted the same idea. It was time, he said, for every town in Massachusetts to form a new force, with a salaried captain to train them in each county, paid for by the colonial assembly and using the Norfolk method.[2]

Whether Elbridge Gerry was aware of it or not, this was treason. As the law stood, both in England and in the colonies, it was a felony punishable by death to raise and finance an independent army or even to advocate this in a letter. Legally, an officer of a militia could hold his commission only from the governor, and only the governor could call the militia out to fight. As yet, the young assemblyman from Essex County had not incited anyone to actual rebellion. But he was clearly on the brink of doing so, even before word arrived about the closure of the port or the changing of the charter. If Gerry had been an isolated case, his comments might be dismissed as merely idle talk, but in fact a far more influential figure was saying exactly the same thing.

This was John Hancock, a keen part-time soldier in his role as Boston's colonel of cadets. On March 5, displaying a new confidence and energy, he gave the annual address in memory of the Boston Massacre. Mounting a passionate defense of the Tea Party, he came close to accusing George III of waging war against his people. And toward the end, Hancock made his own impassioned plea for the creation of a new and improved militia.

If it were well trained and well regulated, Massachusetts would have nothing to fear from "the well known Grenadiers of Britain," he said. "We want not courage; it is discipline alone in which we are exceeded by the most formidable troops that ever trod the earth." If the colony were invaded, the militia would turn to fight "for their houses, their lands, their children . . . for their liberty, for themselves and for their God."[3]

It was stirring stuff, but again the question arises: were these merely words, designed to frighten the governor, rather than a serious plan of action? But either way, Hancock and his comrades had already gone too far to turn back. Unless the British cabinet surrendered and simply ignored the Tea Party—which it could not do—some kind of armed conflict was all but inevitable.

Ever since December, the colony had been waiting to see how the British would react. If the colonial assembly had done nothing more in the meantime, perhaps the tension would have eased and tempers would have cooled. If Thomas Hutchinson had been able to send word to England that all was quiet, perhaps the destruction of the tea would have gradually faded in importance. Although it would always be seen as a crime, requiring some form of retribution, the British might have ceased to regard it as an act of outright treachery which proved that the colony's government needed to be reformed entirely.

In fact, the situation went from bad to worse, with Hutchinson once again reduced to paralysis as his opponents became ever more aggressive and outspoken. The attack on John Malcolm was bad enough, but then, in March, two days after Hancock's speech, Boston staged a repeat performance of the events at Griffin's Wharf. A brig called the *Fortune* arrived, with a brave or foolhardy skipper who tried to land a load of tea. Sixty men in Indian costume came on board and dumped it in the water. And if these were only incidents of riot, hardly worthy to be deemed a threat to the empire as a whole, the same could not be said about another step taken by the House of Representatives. From a British point of view, the assembly had already declared de facto independence long ago, with its impudent petitions to the king, and now it committed an even more serious offense.

On February 24, the House had voted to impeach the chief justice, Hutchinson's kinsman Peter Oliver. He was charged with accepting the salary paid by the Crown from the customs duties. Accompanied by threats of violence, the vote was more than just a gesture about a technicality. It meant that long before the Coercive Acts came into force, the colony was already headed for another collision with royal authority. Sooner or later, a judge would try to take his seat in a Massachusetts courtroom, and a crowd of patriots would have to prevent him from doing so. A week before the vote was taken, Hutchinson could already see which way the wind was blowing.

On February 17, he wrote a long, despairing private letter to Lord Dartmouth—private, so that it need never be disclosed to Parliament—in which he painted a portrait of disorder. "I see no prospect of the government of this province being restored to its former state," he wrote. "Anarchy will continually increase, until the whole province is in confusion." Everywhere, people denied the authority of Parliament; far to the west, in the Berkshire Hills, armed gangs were defying the rule of law, and in Boston every servant of the Crown found himself exposed "to the resentment and rage of the people." The letter would arrive on Dartmouth's desk at Easter, just in time for the second round of the parliamentary debates.[4]

Like Elbridge Gerry with his call for a new militia, Hutchinson was writing *before* the news arrived about the closure of the port of Boston. The anarchy that he described had arisen even though nothing had been heard from the mother country. This state of suspense continued into April, when, with the mood of the province already so inflamed, the ships began to arrive from England. They brought a stream of reports from London, each of which was more distressing than its predecessor. The first—describing Benjamin Franklin's humiliation at the Cockpit—was received on about April 10. Within the week, in every port town from New Hampshire to the Delaware, the press ran the story of Wedderburn's tirade, picked up from the *Public Advertiser*, where the coverage had been relentless.

Initially, the reports were brief; but as the weeks passed, they sprawled over many pages, with some newspapers even printing special supplements. Everywhere they caused outrage, and most of all in Philadelphia, which claimed Dr. Franklin as its own. His old neighbors took to the streets. They made a stuffed effigy of the Scottish lawyer, with a placard around its neck—"The Infamous Wedderburn"—and, for good measure, one of Thomas Hutchinson as well. They were carted through the town, kicked around for a couple of hours, and hanged from a scaffold. Somebody with a sense of humor brought along one of the doctor's electrical machines. A spark was struck, and the effigies were burned to ashes, amid the cries of "a vast concourse of people." The protest took place on the evening of May 3, by which time another ship had reached Massachusetts.

All the way over the North Atlantic the weather was splendid that spring. On May 1 the *Minerva* tied up in Boston, forty-two days out from England, a swift passage, two weeks shorter than the average. Her voyage was so fast, in fact, that she had carried a report of Lord North's speech of March 14, in which he revealed the bill to shut the harbor. The *Minerva* also brought the leak from the cabinet about the plan to change the Massachusetts charter, something North had tried to avoid disclosing too early. In Virginia, the newspapers printed the story just two weeks later.[5]

At first, the Bostonians seem to have been reluctant to believe that the British would go quite so far. For a while, Wedderburn remained the chief talking point, arousing fury in Boston as well and pushing other matters to an inside page until the stories about the port bill and the changing of the charter were official. And then nine days later, on May 10, another ship entered the harbor—ironically, a brig named *Harmony*—with mail from London up to April 2: the very day when Van had said that like Carthage, Boston must be destroyed.

With General Gage still three days away from his own landfall, the *Harmony* brought not only the intemperate words of Mr. Van but also the text of the Boston Port Act. In three weeks' time the harbor would be sealed. The letters and papers on board the brig confirmed that the law would be changed to make the governor entirely supreme, with the seat of government transferred to Salem. The news found the radical party in excellent shape to respond. In the words of Thomas Young, "the perfect crisis" had arrived.

Falling ill again, John Hancock had taken to his bed, but only after receiving another great vote of confidence. Spring was election time, and the voters of Boston had recently met to choose their four members of the House of Representatives. Hancock topped the poll with Samuel Adams and Thomas Cushing close behind. With their positions secure, their friend the town clerk William Cooper called a town meeting, again at Faneuil Hall, on the morning of Friday, May 13, to debate their reply to the news that came with the *Harmony*. Samuel Cooper led a prayer, and his brother read the port act aloud. By the end of the session, the town had voted—unanimously, it was said—to use an old weapon against the British, but in a form far stronger than before. They called for a sweeping prohibition, by Massachusetts and every other colony, of any trade with

Great Britain or the West Indies, import and export alike, until the port
act was repealed. They sent Paul Revere to carry their words to Hartford,
New York, and Philadelphia.[6]

In fact, the town was far from unanimous, with more than a hundred of
its leading citizens openly willing to strike a deal with Great Britain and
pay compensation for the destruction of the tea. Nor could Revere be sure
of a friendly reception from merchants and farmers in colonies where that
year's crop of rice, wheat, and tobacco was already rising in the fields and
the harbors remained open. But in Boston, the crisis was about to deepen
still further. That same Friday afternoon, the townspeople heard a salvo
of gunfire from across the harbor. The cannon were fired at the order of
Lieutenant Colonel Leslie, welcoming HMS *Lively* with the new governor
on board. From the town, Hutchinson hurried out to Castle William to
join the welcoming party and hear directly from General Gage the details
of Lord North's package of reprisals.

THE PERFECT CRISIS

Thomas Gage set foot in Boston filled with preconceptions about its citizens. "America is a mere bully, from one end to the other," the general had
said in 1770. "And the Bostonians are by far the greatest bullies." Four years
later, at the age of fifty-five or so—his exact date of birth is unknown—
finally the new dictator of Massachusetts found his opportunity to teach
them the error of their ways. In his official correspondence, which runs
to many hundreds of pages, Gage often struck a note of exasperation, like
the headmaster of some unruly private school where the pupils seemed
impervious to discipline. In his eyes, Americans behaved like irritating
juveniles, always devising new forms of disobedience with which to tor-
ment their tutors.

More than two centuries after his death it serves little purpose to heap
personal blame on the general for the poor decisions he made as the war
approached. At the time, some of his own officers did so all too readily.
According to one veteran of Bunker Hill, a Scottish major named James
Wemyss, the general was unfit for his command: he described Gage as an
officer "of moderate abilities, altogether deficient in military knowledge."
But Wemyss wrote those words with hindsight, after the war was lost. And
while Gage was certainly a failure, it is hard to see how in the spring of
1774 any British officer available to take his place would have acted differently. In Boston, Gage was obliged to play two different roles—as a soldier

Major General
Thomas Gage in
about 1768, by John
Singleton Copley.
Bridgeman Art Library

and as a politician—which in reality were incompatible. His mission was hopeless from the moment it began.

Of course, Gage had brought this plight upon himself, with his misguided briefing of George III in January. But his colleagues and political masters at Westminster were equally responsible for the fiasco that occurred in New England. His dismissive views about Americans were widely held in London; when his colleagues in the army criticized him, they usually accused him of being too cautious, rather than too hotheaded; and the navy, in the person of Lord Sandwich, remained bitterly angry about the *Gaspée* as well as the Tea Party. In the spring and summer of that year, no one in authority in Great Britain had any doubts that retribution was required or that Thomas Gage was the right party to deliver it.

Gage's career had been as busy as any to which a soldier could aspire. A veteran of Culloden, where he stood beside the Duke of Albemarle, a butcher of the Highland clans almost as bloody as the Duke of Cumberland, Gage had seen rebels before. Nor did he lack experience in combat in America, against the French and the Ohio tribes. In theory, he knew its people and its problems. Since 1755, Gage had made the continent his vocation, marrying a charming beauty from New Jersey, Margaret Kemble, and building a circle of friends in New York. His affection for the country extended to the ownership of land, eighteen thousand acres up toward Lake Erie, as well as a slave plantation on the West Indian island of Montserrat. In military science, Gage had even been an innovator for a while, raising a regiment of light infantry suitable for warfare in the wilderness, made up of soldiers trained to spy out the land and fight on the run.

Only one incident tarnished his record. In 1759, when the British were advancing into Canada against the French, Gage had been in command of a column based at Niagara. The town of Quebec had already fallen to General Wolfe, and Gage was supposed to sail up Lake Ontario, take the French fort at La Galette, and then head for Montreal to trap the enemy in the jaws of a pincer. But the winter drew near, and Gage worried about his supplies and his line of retreat. To the dismay of his superiors, he stayed where he was, and the chance was missed to end the war that year. But although the affair was embarrassing, by the time of the Tea Party it had largely been forgotten. In due course, his critics revived the charge that General Gage was a ditherer—according to Wemyss, he was "timid and undecided in every path of duty"—but again this was said with hindsight, and Wemyss might have had some personal ax to grind.

In 1774, Gage certainly vacillated, occasionally losing his nerve, but his mistakes arose not from character defects but from the same cultural handicaps and prejudices that beset the cabinet in Whitehall. Despite his long career in the colonies, Gage still knew far too little about America, and what he did know was shaped by ideology. Like Alexander Leslie, Gage had come to view the old New England charters as anachronistic and dangerous, a relic from a distant, alien period when dark Puritans ran wild. He did not really care for New York either, where the mob was just as bad and the local politicians tiresome and self-serving. Even so, he might have gathered information and laid plans for forestalling any insurrection. But in the British army at this period, no one expected a peacetime commander to demonstrate that degree of forethought.

A bureaucrat in scarlet, happy in his office or the salon of his wife, Gage worked hard at what crossed his desk, but he felt no need to put his ear close to the ground. He rarely left New York, and he did not study maps with the care a general needs. Gage had a poor eye for terrain, he collected no statistics, and he gave no time to the study of colonial trade and finance. As a result, he lacked the information required to assess the resources his enemy might muster if it ever came to rebellion or to war. His ignorance about the South was especially damaging. He scarcely mentioned Virginia in his letters home. He left its military affairs entirely to the ludicrous Lord Dunmore. As a result, in 1774–75 it came as a complete surprise to General Gage when Virginia joined the insurgency.

During his long, sedate years in command in Manhattan, Gage also lost his taste for military science. While light infantry were essential in America, with its vast distances and its forests, a general really needed light cavalry as well. In any future conflict, hussars or light dragoons would be invaluable, as scouts for reconnaissance or to form a mobile reserve, which could move swiftly across country and fight dismounted on arrival. During the Seven Years' War, the British had created regiments of light dragoons to serve these purposes in Germany. But in his letters to London during the decade before the revolution, Gage never once referred to cavalry. It did not occur to him to ask for light horse until it was already too late, even though they might have saved the day at Concord.

However, again it would be unfair to lay all the blame upon General Gage for the military failures that occurred. When he was appointed governor of Massachusetts, he found himself in an impossible situation, obliged to take decisions of a kind for which his training had not prepared him. In the later history of the British Empire, especially in Asia in the twentieth century, other professional soldiers far more competent than Gage would experience a similar predicament when they were compelled to double as statesmen. Their reputations rarely survived intact. In Gage's case, the dilemmas he faced were especially acute. Even before he left England, he allowed political considerations to undermine a strategic principle that he had laid down himself many years earlier.

As far back as 1766, Gage had realized that if New England rose in revolt, the key to its defeat would lie along the Hudson valley. This was obvious even to him, despite his lack of interest in mapmaking and topography. The valley created a formidable barrier between the northern colonies and their potential allies to the south. At all costs, the British had to hold the river crossings between the Bronx and the high ground near West Point. It was also essential to control the trails that led north to Canada. With the Hudson valley secure, and the navy safely based in New York Harbor and at Halifax, the British could isolate New England, placing a line of denial between it and the rest of the continent.[7]

In a letter to the War Office written soon after the Stamp Act riots, Gage had put the case for such a strategy. Crucially, it would have required the bulk of his forces to remain in Manhattan. If this course of action had been pursued in 1774, the American Revolution would still have occurred, but its opening phase would have taken a very different shape. Worn down by blockade and unable to obtain arms and ammunition, the rebels in

New England might have been forced to back down. But once it had been decided that Gage would go to Massachusetts as governor, he had little choice but to ignore his earlier advice and occupy its principal seaport. This was a dreadful mistake.

After the war was lost, the general's chief engineer, Colonel John Montresor, drew up a list of reasons for the debacle. Right at the top, he placed what he called the "blunder in sending General Gage with four regiments to Boston." Located a long way from the principal lines of communication, the town had no military value. Its site on a peninsula overlooked by high ground rendered it indefensible, and so it became nothing but a trap for the British army. Before he boarded HMS *Lively*, Gage should have pointed this out to the politicians, but even if he had, it is unlikely that they would have listened. In view of the anti-American fervor among Lord North's supporters, the soldiers had to be sent to Boston to uphold the empire's authority. But once the redcoats were ashore, it would be very hard to get them out again.[8]

As the spring and summer unfolded, Gage permitted Boston to become an obsession. Betrayed by the promise he had made to the king, he let his political mission dictate the way he distributed his forces. He began to make a series of mistakes, starting in April. With only the Sixty-Fourth Regiment of Foot available at Castle William, he ordered his deputy in New York, Major General Frederick Haldimand, to send sixty men and eight field guns up to join them. While this might have seemed a sensible thing to do, the general's rationale was very dubious. Although Lieutenant Colonel Leslie needed more artillery at the fort, Gage planned merely to park the cannon on Boston Common, along with the extra regiments of infantry due in from the British Isles.

In other words, he intended to make a show of strength. He would overawe the town in the hope that moderates would take heart and recover the initiative from John Hancock and Samuel Adams. It was a queer sort of plan, given its previous failure during the occupation that led to the massacre of 1770. It seems all the more strange when we think about the winding streets of Boston, along which a cannon could not shoot without destroying loyal property as well as rioters.

Clearly, Gage never expected that his guns would be fired at all. Since he made no attempt to find quarters other than tents for his troops, he seems to have believed that the port act would put a stop to Boston's insolence long before winter set in. Indeed, at first he met with something less than outright hostility. At noon on May 17, a cold and windy day with heavy rain, he landed at the Long Wharf, inspected the militia, and took the oath as governor. He even received a few cheers.[9]

Dinner followed at Faneuil Hall, with a loyal toast, and within the week Gage was writing to Lord Dartmouth with quiet confidence. Hutchinson was just about to leave, heading for England at last, while the port was due to close in two weeks' time. Although the newly elected assembly was ready to meet, he proposed to make them wait until June, when Salem became the capital. At about the same time two more regiments, the Fourth Foot and the Forty-Third, were due to arrive from England. The port act had already taught the radicals a lesson, Gage told His Lordship, "but minds so inflamed cannot cool at once, so it may be better to give the shock time to operate, and I may find the assembly in a better temper."[10]

He intended to play a waiting game until the Massachusetts assembly and the town of Boston came cap in hand to apologize for destroying the tea. To be fair to the general, at first he had little choice. He had not yet received the text of all the Coercive Acts or Dartmouth's final orders for their implementation. Nor was he supposed to provoke a confrontation that might end in violence. Gage soon discovered that nobody would testify in court against the Tea Party's organizers, and so he chose not to haul Hancock and Adams in for questioning, however obvious such a step might have seemed in London. But he failed to understand that a waiting game played directly into the hands of his opponents. Confined to Boston, days or even weeks away from larger cities to the south, he did not realize that time was on the American side, as it would remain for the rest of that year.

A trade boycott was the strongest weapon the Boston radicals could deploy; but if it were to be effective, it would have to be intercolonial. At the very least, they needed New York, Philadelphia, and Charleston to join, but ideally they also required the cooperation of Virginia and Maryland. Only a stoppage of tobacco and naval stores—tar from the Carolinas—would hurt the British enough to make them think again about their plans for Massachusetts.* All of this would take time to organize, because each of the colonies had its own sectional reasons for objecting to a sweeping ban on exports to the mother country. But the longer the port of Boston remained shut to traffic, the more resentful the other American seaports would become, and the more opportunity Samuel Adams and his allies

---

* A point made very clearly by a writer, who might have been Benjamin Franklin, in the newspapers in Boston and Pennsylvania that autumn.

Published in London just before Parliament reassembled in November 1774, a cartoon showing the Royal Navy surrounding Boston and redcoats laying siege to the Liberty Tree while supplies of cod arrive to feed the town. *Library of Congress*

would have to put the case for a boycott. Although the closure of the port had seemed to be a clever strategy, it had a fatal flaw. It was open-ended, which meant that it gave the radicals all the time they needed.

By the end of May, Josiah Quincy Jr. had already produced a pamphlet making this very point. As befits a Bostonian, Quincy had a lawyer's eye for detail. He focused on one especially sensitive clause in the Boston Port Act. Instead of setting a limit on the closure of the port or giving the governor the discretion to end it, Parliament had said that the port would remain shut "until it shall sufficiently appear to his Majesty" that Boston had made amends to everybody it had harmed, not only the East India Company for the loss of the tea, but anyone else with a claim for damages, including the consignees, the customs officers, the shipowners, and the sea captains they employed. Whatever Boston offered by way of restitution, only the king could say if it was full and fair. Months might go by—or even years—while the town waited for an answer from His Majesty. All the while the harbor would stay closed by what amounted to an arbitrary royal decree that also tied the hands of General Gage.[11]

In a later era, Quincy would have excelled as a constitutional lawyer. His analysis was irrefutable. But even before his pamphlet appeared, the port act had antagonized the other colonies, where political activists had reached similar conclusions. By the end of May, the Chesapeake was rallying to Boston's aid. At the tobacco harbor of Annapolis, a town meeting on the twenty-fifth urged Maryland to join the boycott, calling for reprisals against any colony that failed to follow suit. And in Virginia, the British suffered another stroke of bad luck when news of the port act reached Williamsburg just as the House of Burgesses was meeting in its yearly session.

"We cooked up a resolution," Thomas Jefferson remembered, opposing the act and calling for a day of prayer and fasting in support of Boston. Soon afterward, Governor Dunmore dissolved the assembly, and then, on May 27, at the Raleigh Tavern, eighty-nine burgesses called for a continental congress to organize an anti-British movement. But as late as the last week of June, a month after the meetings at Annapolis and Williamsburg, Gage still had no idea of their significance. His negligent counterpart Lord Dunmore did little to help. After sending a brief letter to England about the meeting at the Raleigh Tavern, the governor of Virginia took off for the frontier on a punitive expedition against the Shawnee, an affair that kept him out of touch until the winter.

The general was almost as ignorant about the discontent abroad in Pennsylvania and New York. As always, in both these provinces the politics were complex, with the people split into factions, and their response to the Coercive Acts was hard to call. The merchants were divided, but mostly afraid of the damage a trade boycott might cause. Even so, any British officer who took a walk on the Manhattan waterfront would have encountered intense hostility. On June 15, a crowd running into thousands built a gallows and burned more effigies of Wedderburn, Hutchinson, and Lord North. And this demonstration took place long before anyone in America had an inkling of the legislation for Quebec, which would arouse so much more resentment.

Gage must have known what the Quebec Act contained, at least in outline, since it had been through two drafts even before he left England. And if he did, he should have foreseen the hostility that it would arouse far beyond the borders of Massachusetts. But instead he focused all his attention narrowly on Boston and the towns nearby. For Gage, so ignorant about so much, it was all too easy to believe that Boston's call for help from the other colonies would go unheeded. In his opinion, New York and Philadelphia would never join the boycott, and the Continental Congress might never even happen. "Boston may get little more than fair words," the general wrote to Lord Dartmouth on June 26, with an almost breathtaking degree of complacency.

And so Gage simply went on waiting, with scarcely a trace of a strategic plan. Long before the end of the month he gave up on the House of Representatives, which had met in Salem on the seventh in an uncompromising mood. With Elbridge Gerry to the fore, the assembly did nothing but agitate, voting behind closed doors to send delegates to the Continental Congress that Virginia proposed. Ten days later, Gage dissolved the house and set no date to reconvene, but even this was a mistake, serving as an open invitation to the delegates to reconvene illegally whenever they saw fit. He also read too much into a tactical setback suffered by Samuel Adams. For weeks, Adams's Committee of Correspondence had been trying to build support for a document called the Solemn League and Covenant, which called on every town and county to ban the consumption of British goods. Fiercely opposed by the mercantile community, it failed to win widespread support, but from this Gage leaped to the conclusion that public opinion was turning in his favor. Privately, the general was already tired and frustrated, worn down by the constant slander of Great Britain in the press, but his letters home to Dartmouth in midsummer still struck a note of self-assurance. It would take time, but the people would gradually see reason. If he remained calm and waited for the closure of the port to take effect, the agitators would slowly lose their grip, people of goodwill would reemerge to take the lead, and the likes of Hancock would be brought to justice.

If the Quebec Act had never been passed, perhaps Gage would have been proved right; but as it was, the waiting game was doomed to end in failure. Behind his back, Alexander Leslie was already accusing him of something close to cowardice. Writing home in early July to his family, the lieutenant colonel boiled over with anger and frustration at Gage's inactivity. Several times—"for fear he forgets, or does not know them as well as I"—he had dropped hints to the general about the need for harsher measures, especially against "that most artful clever fellow Adams, who has nothing to lose." Leslie remembered a Spanish commander who could teach the British how to deal with traitors. In 1769, General Alejandro O'Reilly—otherwise known as Bloody O'Reilly—had crushed an uprising in New Orleans by executing five rebels by firing squad. It was, according to Leslie, the only language Americans could understand. "If half-a-dozen that I could name were sent home to garnish Tyburn Tree, it would be better than shutting up the port," he wrote. "Nothing but hanging or shooting will do now, the child is already spoilt, gentle correction is of no use."[12]

If Gage had followed this wise counsel, he would merely have started the war nine months early, but the lieutenant colonel made a fair point about the closure of the port. Although the measure was far too severe, for the reasons given by Josiah Quincy, it might have been worth the risk of arousing a backlash across America if Boston had been isolated entirely. But the navy had grave doubts about its capacity to do so. By now, John Montagu had ended his tour of duty, to be replaced by the sixty-one-year-old admiral Samuel Graves. The new commander remembered the arduous blockade against the coast of France in 1758 and 1759, which had stretched the fleet close to its breaking point. While the waters off New England were less hazardous and the enemy less awesome, Graves knew how hard it was to seal the approaches to a port tightly week after week.

When he reached America on June 30, Graves found that his squadron consisted of just nineteen ships, of which only nine—mostly frigates or schooners of the *Gaspée* class—were on station in Cape Cod Bay. Soon he was writing home for more, not only to deal with Boston, but also to police the smuggling coast from Nantucket to New York, which otherwise would lie unguarded. But Lord Sandwich had few resources to spare. In May, the old king of France had succumbed to smallpox, Louis XVI had come to the throne, and again reports arrived of naval rearmament at Brest and Toulon. Until the new monarch's intentions were clear, Graves would have to wait for reinforcements. Only three more frigates were sent before year's end, while Sandwich kept a close watch on the English Channel.

Meanwhile, General Gage had entirely lost his way. Hearing vague rumors about armed resistance, which he passed on to London in early

July, he could think of only one course of action. He decided to cram as many battalions as he could into his camp on Boston Common. Late in June, the first detachments had arrived from another regiment of foot, the Fifth. Two weeks later, Gage began to strip his military resources from New York and Nova Scotia, sending for more infantry, the Forty-Third and the Fifty-Ninth, and another three companies of field guns. On their arrival, they had no clear mission to fulfill. An urban uprising was highly unlikely—in the recent past, the few outright insurrections in America had been rural, in North Carolina or in up-country New York—but if that was Gage's greatest fear, he should have begun to fortify the high ground around the peninsula, from Dorchester Heights to Charlestown. The general did no such thing, and his army merely idled away the summer.

Once his regiments were all in Boston, two thousand men in tents with their wives and children, surrounded by unfriendly neighbors, they became a problem of their own. Supplies had to be found; sooner or later despite his earlier optimism, winter quarters and clothing would have to be provided; and in the meantime his officers had to keep the camp safe and hygienic. They fought a constant battle with squalor and indiscipline. There were no latrines other than holes in the ground or straw in the tents. While the Common had few wells for drinking water, liquor was everywhere, on sale at stalls set up by people from the town. Close at hand the whores of Boston, "infamous and obnoxious," lay in wait for any redcoat on a spree.[13]

As the temperature rose, the general saw no reason to sweat it out alongside his troops in a town that was sullen but outwardly peaceful. On July 20, just before he left for what amounted to a vacation at Danvers, near Salem, Gage wrote another letter to Lord Dartmouth, urging him not to worry. While Massachusetts remained its surly, uncooperative self, everywhere else the colonies were quiet. "The virulent party at New York is routed, and Philadelphia is moderate," the general said. Six weeks after the port act came into force, Boston was starting to suffer as traders ran short of stock and prices rose for rum and molasses. Otherwise all was quiet, here and in New York. Gage still saw little sign of a continental congress. It was "talk and noise only," he told the colonial secretary.[14]

In fact, the Congress was already scheduled to meet early in September in Philadelphia, and in the meantime the southern colonies were moving ever closer to rebellion. Widely reprinted, Quincy's brilliant dissection of the port act had left no room for doubt that the measure was tyrannical. His pamphlet was soon followed by a more famous work by Thomas Jefferson that plainly contradicted Gage's complacent appraisal of the situation. Jefferson's essay—*A Summary View of the Rights of British America*—took a line more radical than any other writer before him. For years, it had been commonplace for Americans to deny Parliament's right to make laws for the colonies, but the southerner went further and questioned the entire apparatus of the empire and the very concept of loyalty to the Crown.

Like the rioters who mobbed the royal carriage at Westminster, Jefferson displayed a new personal animosity toward the king. "His majesty has no right to land a single armed man on our shores," he wrote; George III was merely a "chief magistrate," with only those powers in America that Americans saw fit to give him; and if the empire were to survive, the empire had to become a free and equal union with the mother country, designed according to some new plan agreed by both sides. During the debates in Parliament, this idea had been alluded to, but only briefly and in passing. Given the prevailing views within the British cabinet, it had no realistic prospect of coming to fruition. Jefferson was being very radical indeed, but leaving aside political philosophy, his tract was significant for something else. The *Summary View* showed just how swiftly attitudes were hardening in the South, that old Achilles' heel, a region about which Whitehall knew even less than it did about New England.

By early July, the essential points of all the Coercive Acts were widely known in the South, and even some vague reports of the measure for Quebec had reached Maryland and Virginia. Far from being merely talk and noise, the Continental Congress was already having a profound effect, as the southern colonies began to debate the line they wished it to take when it assembled. By July 8, South Carolina had held a three-day convention, uniting all the elements within the province: backcountry farmers, artisans from Charleston, and the richest planters from the coast. They chose their delegates for Philadelphia and set up a committee to run the colony's affairs, creating a provisional government in all but name. Three weeks later, the lieutenant governor was speaking of "a universal spirit of jealousy against Great Britain." It was "catching like wildfire," he said, not only there, but throughout America. His dispatch reached London only in September, when the Continental Congress had already assembled. In the meantime, some thirty counties in Virginia had already voted for a total boycott of trade with Great Britain.[15]

Unseen by the authorities, Jefferson's *Summary View* circulated privately in the tobacco country; it appeared in print in America in late August; and suddenly it hit the streets of London on November 5, at a price of one and sixpence, with a fanfare of publicity in the *London Evening Post*. No one in Whitehall seems to have read it, but even if they had, it was too late to prevent the revolution. By that time, the people of Massachusetts had been in open rebellion for two months.

The Powder Alarm

"A throne cannot be established on unrighteousness," wrote the Marblehead Committee of Correspondence on July 28, with the same new antipathy toward the king. With the heat so extreme that the army could not exercise, only a few days remained before Gage would receive the text of the Massachusetts Government Act. Everywhere around him the language of resistance was reaching a new peak of truculence.

From his summer home at Danvers, Gage began to grow uneasy, scanning the press for clues about the nature of the opposition the act might arouse. Early in August, a story surfaced in the local paper, the *Essex Gazette*, about a letter sent out from Boston that the general took to be a coded signal intended to incite an insurrection across New England as a whole. It began to dawn on him that perhaps Alexander Leslie had been correct, and at last the tone of the general's dispatches began to change.[16]

Until now, Gage had clung to the idea that Hancock and Adams led only a faction, but all the time it seemed to grow more numerous and powerful. Supplies of rice, grain, and fish were flowing in to feed the people of Boston from as far afield as Charleston. From the pulpit, even at Harvard, the clergy were spouting sedition, decrying the British as agents of the Roman Catholic Antichrist. As for the Continental Congress, it had left the realm of the merely possible to become a certainty. Samuel Adams and his fellow delegates were due to leave for Philadelphia within the week.

"I hope the acts may soon arrive, which will be a kind of test of people's conduct," Gage wrote home to Lord Dartmouth. As though to raise the stakes, he dismissed John Hancock from his post as colonel of cadets, a step long overdue, and then, on August 6, the general's wish was granted. In sailed a frigate, the *Scarborough*, carrying £10,000 in silver—by now, the army was very short of cash—and a bundle of dispatches, including the official text of the regulating act. With it came his final orders from Whitehall, drawn up nine weeks previously.

The waiting was over. The general summoned the king's chosen councillors to Salem to be sworn in. Out of thirty-six Massachusetts worthies named in his orders, only twenty-four turned up, and their arrival heightened his anxieties about the colony's mood. Traveling in from all corners of the province, they brought word of what Gage called "a frenzy . . . of

Popular rage" running wild in every county, leaving them in fear for their lives and property.[17]

Months earlier, Thomas Hutchinson had warned that the Berkshires were restless, but now the general heard of trouble not only there but in Springfield, in Worcester, and spilling over the border into Connecticut. It was what he had feared might happen after he read the *Essex Gazette:* Boston had rallied the countryside against him. And so the general returned to the town with three purposes in mind. On August 13 he convened the Boston selectmen to read them the law, to prohibit town meetings without his approval, and to warn them against any more opposition. Then, in the cool of the evening, he went to the Common to meet his deputy, Hugh Percy, recently given the rank of brigadier. An old Etonian of thirty-two, the sort of officer the British call hard but fair, kind to his troops but severe with any who stepped out of line, Percy had sealed the camp more tightly, banning outsiders and cracking down hard on shirkers and privates absent without leave.

He and Gage toured the camp together, closely inspecting the corporals and sergeants who would form the backbone of the army in the field. Seven months before the war began, it was already clear that they might have to take the offensive and march out of Boston to quell disorder in the interior. That night, they ordered each unit to set up a baggage store to hold equipment too heavy to be carried. As the week went on, at last the weather broke, showers of rain began to fall, and the exercises could resume but with far more vigor than before.

With the prospect now before them of a battle in the open, Percy hurried to prepare the artillery for action. By now, two more infantry regiments had arrived, giving the British seven altogether, one in Salem and six in Boston, mostly on the Common but also in a makeshift camp beside the harbor. On the seventeenth, Percy took twenty men from each one to be trained as extra gunners. Every morning they turned out to practice, firing at a mark on the slopes above Back Bay.

During the ten days after the *Scarborough* arrived, the general held the initiative, and he had the firepower to retain it, but then it began to slip away in the face of opposition from every part of the colony. Like the Boston Port Act, a measure too broad and too draconian to be effective, the regulating act for Massachusetts was simply too ambitious. Far too widely drawn and too intrusive, it created a kind of rolling insurgency throughout the province, a movement so extensive that the general could not hope to stand in its way.

"We are indeed in a most critical situation, and what the grand event may be, heaven only knows," Samuel Cooper wrote to Benjamin Franklin from Boston on August 15, but even before he posted the letter, the revolution was already near at hand. Because of the way the officials in Whitehall had drafted the regulating act, the British had given the colony an obvious weapon of resistance. It would be used the first time the following day in the depths of Berkshire County, nearly 100 miles inland.[18]

Yet again, the British had failed to understand the internal dynamics of New England. If the cabinet had confined the new regulating act to the central offices of state in Massachusetts, merely giving additional powers to the governor, his council, and the most senior judges, the new law might have stood a fighting chance of success. Instead, the regulating act reached down to the very lowest levels of local administration, threatening to end democracy across the board. In the future, all the jurors in every court, even the most junior, would be appointed by the county sheriff rather than chosen by the people. With town meetings virtually banned as well, the act struck a blow at every adult male, depriving him of rights of self-government dating back more than a century. Every county had an Inferior Court of Common Pleas, which met each month to settle minor disputes, license taverns, enforce debts, and issue writs against delinquents who failed to pay their taxes. If the people simply closed the courts when next they met, then the governor would lose the means to enforce the law. The new regime would be stillborn.

On August 16, the farmers of the Berkshire Hills struck first. It was harvesttime, the busiest period of the year, but they turned out in their hundreds to fill the streets around the courthouse at Great Barrington, barring the way of the judges as they tried to take their seats. Led by a blacksmith, Timothy Bigelow, the patriots to the east in Worcester County met and made plans to do the same, writing to Boston to call for a conference to ensure that every other county followed suit. The meeting would convene in the town on the twenty-sixth and last for two days. By the time it ended, the American Revolution had begun.

In the meantime, more news arrived from England and threw more fuel on the fire of protest. One of Marblehead's sea captains, Benjamin Calley, sailed back and forth between America and Spain and often called at Falmouth, in the far west of England, a haven used by fast packet boats that carried official mail. As a result, Calley and his ship the *Molly* had a knack of being first with any sensational story from Europe.

On Saturday, August 20, the *Molly* docked in Marblehead with newspapers as recent as early July, running stories about the riot against the king at Westminster. According to Calley, Lord North was about to fall from power, swept away by a rising tide of popular anger against the Quebec Act. In London, public opinion had swung behind the American cause, and with a general election just around the corner gamblers were laying bets at five to one that the government would be gone by Christmas. That evening, Elbridge Gerry sent these stories to Boston, where they appeared in the press on Monday. On the twenty-first another ship reached New York with the same reports from London. A week after that they arrived in Charleston, where they filled the columns of the *South Carolina Gazette*.[19]

It was all wild exaggeration; but the stories tallied with what Samuel Adams had been telling his friends for months. Fed with misinformation from the Lees, Adams had come to believe that the British were too weak, too disunited, and too scared of the French to stand and fight against a solid front of colonial disobedience. Actually, Lord North had never been stronger, the French had not the slightest intention of sending their navy to sea, and the press reports that sailed with Calley came only from the Wilkesite papers in the capital. They gave an entirely false impression of the prevailing mood in the mother country. But as it was, the news brought on the *Molly* screwed up the tension in New England to such a degree that it could only end in outright insurrection.

On the morning of Monday, the twenty-second, with the British still firing their guns on the Common, the *Boston Gazette* printed two full pages of reports from the heart of the empire. Opening with a diatribe from the Duke of Richmond, in which he condemned the Coercive Acts, and then going on to report Lord Chatham's unsuccessful speech as though it had been a matter of great significance, they painted a picture of a ruling class in turmoil. The *Gazette* also ran a letter from William Lee, which left no doubt about the path the Bostonians should follow.

According to Lee, who had recently finished his term as sheriff of London, the Coercive Acts had amounted to what he called "the most open and explicit DECLARATION OF WAR . . . against your province." Hitherto, Lord Dartmouth had largely escaped the insults and abuse the colonial press hurled at every other minister, but now Lee branded him a villain too. "You have not a friend in the whole administration," he wrote. "Lord Dartmouth, notwithstanding his fawning and deceitful expressions to the Americans, is in the cabinet as determined and violent an enemy to you as any in this country."

Again, this was highly misleading—that very week, Dartmouth was privately telling friends that he might open talks with the Continental Congress—but in Massachusetts the time for negotiation and compromise had already passed. In the interior, a campaign of intimidation had begun against the mandamus councillors, with a few shots fired and many demonstrations in the streets. On the coast, the next move came from the Committee of Correspondence at Salem, with Gerry's old college mate Timothy Pickering foremost among them. Apart from closing a courthouse, the most obvious way to annoy the British and subvert royal authority was to hold a town meeting in defiance of the law. Salem called such a meeting on the morning of August 24.

At eight o'clock, an hour before it was due to convene, General Gage summoned Pickering and his comrades, told them the meeting was seditious, and ordered them to make the people disperse the moment they arrived. They refused. The general had redcoats standing by from the Fifty-Ninth Foot, and he sent them into town. With the soldiers on their way, the meeting assembled, swiftly did its business, and then adjourned. The troops marched back to camp, but twenty-four hours later Gage put the committee under arrest. That evening, armed men began to gather in the towns nearby, determined to free them by force if necessary.[20]

All this time the weather had been foul, with heavy rain and thunderstorms. On the morning of Friday, August 26, at last the sun rose in a cloudless sky, shining down on farmers gathering in the last of the harvest, threshing their crops, or turning out their sheep to graze on the stubble. But to General Gage, hearing reports of unrest from all sides, the colony seemed to be collapsing into chaos, and he expected an imminent attack on his headquarters. At Danvers, Gage had two companies from Leslie's regiment, the Sixty-Fourth; at Salem, the Fifty-Ninth was still in readiness; and a small detachment had gone to Marblehead. The general stood them all to arms. "If the attacks should be serious, that is made with firearms," he wrote, "the 59th will march & disperse the rebels; and they will remark that the Committee of Correspondence are the sole authors ... of every mischief that shall happen."[21]

It was the moment Alexander Leslie had been longing for. For the first time, the general had given his officers written permission to open fire. Not since the riots against the Stamp Act had Gage seen America so close to rebellion, but the general was looking for treason in the wrong place. While the redcoats waited in vain for trouble in Salem, remaining on the alert until night fell, the revolution was about to occur behind closed doors in Boston. Ten days after Worcester first proposed a conference, delegates assembled from the Committees of Correspondence of four counties—Timothy Bigelow from Worcester, Elbridge Gerry from Essex, and representatives from Middlesex and Suffolk—to plan a coordinated campaign of resistance.

With Joseph Warren in the chair, they had only one item to discuss. If, as they all agreed, the courts of law had been transformed into vehicles of tyranny, then the conference had to create new institutions of government to take their place. They chose five men to form a subcommittee, including Gerry, Bigelow, and Dr. Young, the Tea Party veteran, and sent them off to produce a blueprint. At eleven in the morning on Saturday, August 27, the conference met again, heard their report, and then adjourned until the afternoon. At three o'clock they signed a declaration, carefully drafted and checked to ensure that their position was absolutely clear.

At that moment the revolution began. "Every officer belonging to the courts aforesaid who shall attempt to exercise authority will be a traitor, cloaked with the pretext of law," ran the declaration's central paragraph, "and so are all others to be considered, whether officers or private persons, who shall attempt to execute the late acts of parliament for violating the constitution of this province."

To replace the courts, they called for a provincial congress, composed of members chosen by each county, which would meet in October to act as a provisional government. The document ended with an ominous clause in which the hand of Elbridge Gerry was plainly visible: "The Military Art according to the Norfolk Plan ought attentively to be prosecuted by the People of this Province, as a necessary means to secure their liberties."[22]

Although none of this would appear in the press—if it had, all those who attended the meeting could have been indicted for treason—the declaration went to every county to be put to a vote in the weeks that followed. Even before the conference ended, Worcester had already risen, with perhaps as many as three thousand men flocking to the town to compel one of the mandamus councillors to resign. By the evening of the twenty-seventh, Gage had written a long dispatch to Dartmouth, warning him that he would have to march on Worcester to protect the judges when they met in session in the town ten days later.

"Popular fury was never greater," he told the colonial secretary before hurrying down to Boston, where the situation was deteriorating by the hour. In the camp, he found four of his councillors taking shelter with the troops, two more were on their way, and from all across the province word arrived that town meetings were gathering illegally. Gage doubled the guard and gave orders for the army's timber yard to be protected against incendiaries.

The Sabbath passed quietly enough, but Monday, the twenty-ninth, brought another alarming development. A letter arrived from the elderly William Brattle, who practiced law and medicine in Cambridge. An old ally of Thomas Hutchinson, Brattle held the rank of major general in the colony's militia, a post that gave him the keys to the province's gunpowder store. Six miles north of Boston, it was housed in an old stone mill on a grassy knoll called Quarry Hill, amid the cornfields that sloped up from the Mystic River. It had not occurred to Gage to move the store to a place of safety or to put it under guard, using his legal powers as Brattle's commander in chief. For weeks, said Brattle, towns had been quietly removing the quota of powder that each one was supposed to keep in the mill, until all that was left was a reserve supply of 250 half barrels. From all sides he was hearing rumors of local militia companies telling their men to be ready "at a minute's notice."[23]

Indeed, by now the leaders of the rising were clearly preparing for bloodshed. Again, the Marblehead committee was one of the most outspoken when it wrote that week to its counterparts in Boston. The committee members hoped an armed struggle would be unnecessary; they urged their comrades to hold the people back, at least for a month or two, in case the government fell in London; but if it did not, and the shooting started, the colony had to be ready to fight. "When once the sword is drawn, we must expect a long and bloody war," the letter continued. All of this was treason, and although Gage never saw that letter, and knew nothing about the Boston conference on August 26 and 27, he was hearing reports from Worcester that rebels were buying guns and making bullets. But even now he hesitated. After receiving Brattle's letter, he waited some forty-eight hours before issuing his next set of orders at seven in the evening of August 31.[24]

Clearly, he had to rescue the gunpowder together with two small cannon parked nearby at Cambridge. To undertake the mission, he took two hundred soldiers from the infantry, each one equipped with a day's rations, and twenty gunners from his artillery. Instead of the fire-eating Alexander Leslie, he chose another lieutenant colonel to command the force, George Maddison, an older man recently arrived from England. At dawn the next morning, Maddison led them down from Boston Common to the longboats that would ferry them up the Mystic. They landed at a spot less than a mile from the magazine and marched up the slope to Quarry Hill to meet the county sheriff. He handed over the keys and gave the gunners a train of horses borrowed from a local tavern keeper. While the gunners headed over to Cambridge for the cannon, the redcoats emptied the mill, loading the powder into wagons arranged by the sheriff. That afternoon they were back in Boston, with their mission a complete success.*

But in the meantime Gage had done nothing else, failing to anticipate the uproar that would follow his seizure of the powder. In the next twenty-four hours, he found himself thrown off balance by the pace at which intelligence could circulate in New England. By the morning of September 2, word of Maddison's expedition had sped around the eastern half of the colony, setting off a chain reaction of rumor and alarm. It was said that the redcoats were on the rampage after shooting six Americans dead, a falsehood that brought insurgents flocking into Cambridge in their thousands. "A vast concourse of people assembled," the general wrote, as he struggled to make sense of what happened that day.[25]

Somehow the text of Brattle's letter had been made public. The people mobbed his house, a few hundred yards from the Harvard campus, only to find that he had vanished. Because this was a popular rising, without a structure or a guiding hand, the precise sequence of events remains as confusing and obscure today as it was to General Gage at the time. Filled with people loyal to the British—even then, Cambridge served as a dormitory for Boston's more affluent citizens—the town supplied a host of targets for attack by men and women convinced that the British were bent on imposing their authority by force.

No servant of the empire was secure. It so happened that three of Gage's most senior officials were in Cambridge on the second, and although they escaped unharmed, they were forced to flee to the protection of the army. The general's lieutenant governor, Thomas Oliver, was a Cambridge resident, and so was Jonathan Sewall, the colony's attorney general. By nightfall both of them were sheltering in the tents on Boston Common. The third man was Benjamin Hallowell, the commissioner of customs, who was en route from Salem armed with a pistol. Nine months earlier, Hallowell had refused to allow the tea to be sent back to England. As he passed through Cambridge, his carriage was spotted, and a crowd gave chase. With rebels on horseback close behind him, Hallowell narrowly escaped the fate that had befallen his junior officer John Malcolm.

At six o'clock that evening, General Gage tried to assess the situation. After so many weeks of denial, he began to draft an abject letter to Lord Dartmouth that amounted to a confession of defeat. "Civil government is near its end, the courts of justice expiring one after the other," he wrote.

---

* Gage never gave Lord Dartmouth a full account of the mission to rescue the gunpowder. Doubtless he did not wish to raise questions about his failure to secure it in the first place.

One by one, the new mandamus councillors were resigning, even the senior judges were too frightened to sit on the bench, and the flames of protest had spread to Connecticut and Rhode Island, where Nathanael Greene was among the officers leading a new independent militia pledged to come to Boston's aid. And the following day, the position deteriorated still further. It was rumored that the navy had bombarded Boston. By noon on the third, militiamen running into tens of thousands were converging from all over the region to save the town from destruction.[26]

When they saw that the alarm was false, they stood down, but again the speed and the scale of their mobilization took Gage entirely by surprise. In angry words that echoed those of Alexander Leslie, the general spoke of a "bloody crisis" looming up ahead, for which he would need a far larger army than the one he had so far assembled. "Conciliation, moderation, reasoning is over, nothing can be done but by forcible means," he told the colonial secretary. By the time his dispatch to Lord Dartmouth was at sea, the people of Worcester County had risen again, six thousand strong, and forced the closure of their courthouse.

This was the point at which the general lost his nerve, descending into a state of near panic in which his intellect deserted him even though his plight was far from desperate. While Graves's naval squadron was still far too small to blockade the entire northeastern seaboard, it could sail where it pleased, and it gave the army mobility. The bases at Halifax and New York remained entirely safe, and more troops were on their way from home. Although Massachusetts had become ungovernable, this was hardly new: the riots of September merely set the seal on a history of disobedience that went back two years, to the Boston pamphlet of November 1772. It was clear that the British cabinet's strategy had failed—except for the port act, the coercive laws could not be enforced—but that being so, it needed to be rethought and not pursued blindly until another catastrophe occurred.

At this moment, Gage might have saved the day by temporarily letting Massachusetts go and withdrawing to New York and the Hudson valley. New England could have been recovered later, like Scotland after the rebellion of 1745, at a time when Gage had assembled a larger army and the Admiralty had sent a far stronger fleet. In order to change course so radically, first he would have had to convince the cabinet that it was necessary. This would have been difficult but not impossible, provided Gage mustered his evidence and set out a persuasive plan for the reestablishment of royal authority. But in fact the general made no serious attempt to devise an alternative strategy.

Instead, Gage chose to remain all too preoccupied with Boston, a town that was more a symbol of the empire than a strategic asset. For the sake of preserving a semblance of authority, he felt that he had to remain to protect citizens loyal to Great Britain and to fly the flag. Again, he allowed his political mission to dictate his thinking even when it had already proved to be incapable of fulfillment. Forgetting about the rest of the continent, Gage chose to make Boston an American Singapore, a fortress supplied by sea but surrounded by a hinterland that he could neither defend nor control. In doing so, he more or less ensured that 1775 would be a year of calamity.

On the evening of September 2, Gage told his engineers to fortify the Neck, the narrow strip of ground that connected Boston to the mainland. Redcoats would patrol the streets by night, while the fleet kept watch on the harbor. Counting all the soldiers in his seven regiments of foot, his artillery, and his headquarters staff, the general had about three thousand troops at his disposal. With that small force, outnumbered at least five to one by those the rebels could call out, Gage settled down to wait again. As he did so, Lord North was about to make yet another error of his own. His victory in Parliament had left him all too confident about the future.[27]

Chapter Fourteen

AN ELECTION IN ARCADIA

It was yesterday reported that General Gage was killed and two regiments of his revolted.

—*London Evening Post*, OCTOBER 1, 1774

In England the summer had begun with glamour and festivity. Even while Parliament was still in session, its members took a brief vacation for a party so exquisite that it filled the columns of the press. On the ninth of June, little more than a week after the British closed the port of Boston, Lord North hurried through a debate about Quebec and let his colleagues have an evening in the country south of London to celebrate the finest betrothal of the year. They were invited to the Oaks, a mansion in Surrey, for a masque, a banquet, and a ball.

The event was a *fête champêtre* arranged in honor of a noble couple, the young Edward, Lord Stanley, and his bride-to-be, Lady Betty Hamilton, who came from the richest family in Scotland. Alas, in 1779 the match would end in tears, when Lady Betty ran off with a duke; but her engagement party at the Oaks was wonderful. Lord and Lady North attended, as did the rest of the cabinet; and the event had a choreographer, another soldier-cum-politician, Lord Stanley's uncle John Burgoyne, the general who would lose at Saratoga, almost the worst defeat the British would suffer in the war that was to come.

To help him stage the party, Burgoyne enlisted the support of the ubiquitous Robert Adam, who designed the pavilion where the ball took place. Between them, Adam and Burgoyne created an occasion that caught Britain's imagination and supplied a talking point for months. The event even

The supper room from Robert Adam's pavilion for Lord Stanley's
party at the Oaks in June 1774, engraved from a painting by Antonio
Zucchi. *The Master and Fellows of St. John's College, Cambridge*

made the papers in America, which reported sneering words from the
opposition in the Commons. Later that year, while New England was in
ferment, David Garrick turned the masque into a musical comedy, putting
it on the London stage, where the king could enjoy it too. Like one of
those parties that adorn the pages of Marcel Proust, the *fête* at the Oaks
captured the mood of a ruling elite at a dangerous moment in its history.

To their way of thinking, the British ruling class embodied all the virtues of which the human race was capable. They were elegant, they were
erudite, but they were funny too; they lived in the best society that men
and women could devise, where liberty and discipline existed side by side;
and while they loved tradition and the past, they took delight as well in
modern ingenuity. In the words of Burgoyne, in the script he wrote for
the party at the Oaks, England was "a new Arcadia." In the *fête* in Surrey
he gave the kingdom a looking glass in which its rulers could admire the
nation's features and their own.

Among the guests was Lord North's sister-in-law Henrietta, the lady
prone to losing money playing cards, married to Bishop Brownlow. The
bishop was away doing something ecclesiastical, and so he missed the
party, but she gave him a full account of the event. It was, the bishop

told his father, "the finest and prettiest entertainment that ever they were at." The party cost £4,000, enough to keep a regiment of redcoats for six months. The largest single item was the grand pavilion, for supper and for dancing, built from painted canvas, wood, and papier-mâché and taken down at once the morning after.[1]

Three hundred guests arrived in fancy dress and were greeted on the lawn by dancers, miming scenes of rustic frivolity, while music floated around them from the shrubbery. The evening was warm, the trees were hung with flowers, and songbirds sang from cages hidden in the branches. On one side of the house, Adam had put up a portico to serve as the Temple of Venus. The guests passed through an arch and corridor to reach the temporary ballroom, lined with colonnades and hung with silk in white and gold. There they danced cotillions until a moment came when Burgoyne gave a signal and a curtain rose, revealing tables spread with food and drink.

While they ate, the curtain fell, to rise again at midnight. They watched the masque that Burgoyne had composed, performed by nymphs and fauns in tiger skins. In came an actor playing a Druid, the Spirit of the Oaks, to wave a wand of mistletoe and bless the happy couple. Lord Stanley danced a minuet with Lady Betty, and the actors sang a patriotic anthem in praise of the oaks that built the Royal Navy:

> *Grace and strength of Britain's isle,*
> *Mayst thou long thy glories keep,*
> *Make her hills with verdure smile,*
> *Bear her triumphs o'er the deep.*

After that there came more minuets, and then the country dancing, while outside the gardens shone with lanterns in the shape of pyramids. Not until dawn did the guests depart. In Parliament the day before, the prime minister had faced sarcastic jeers from Edmund Burke—he would be "smothered in roses, and crowned with never-fading laurels," said the Irishman—but North left the Oaks in the highest of spirits. At eleven o'clock the following night, the government won the last vote in the Commons on the new law for Quebec.[2]

In a host of different ways, the party had epitomized the culture of the period: or at least the taste and attitudes of the aristocracy. Like the review of the fleet at Spithead, it appealed to an ardent love of spectacle, intended to be dazzling and to make observers envious. Just before the war, this appetite for glamour reached a new peak of extravagance in the shows produced by Garrick and even in the dresses worn by women. Necklines were plunging; hair was combed up high above the forehead in a beehive crowned with feathers; and the very latest gowns were cascades of drapery, sweeping freely round the body to emphasize its curves, as though the woman were a figure from a mural at Pompeii.*

Like the Adelphi or the party at the Oaks, the fashions of the time harked back to ancient Rome. The elite even had a Pantheon of their own, opened in London's Oxford Street in 1772, to provide a pillared rendezvous for peers and courtesans. In each case the message conveyed was much the same: that the British could outdo the achievements of antiquity. Not only did they enjoy the benefits of science. As Edward Gibbon never tired of pointing out, the British had given themselves a free constitution, and in that respect as well they surpassed the Roman Empire. Best of all the British had the navy, with its wooden walls protecting the liberty they prized.

It would not occur to the guests at the *fête champêtre* that America, so far away and so provincial, might represent the future, or that the colonies might prefer a different kind of progress and prosperity to their own. With all its talk of covenants and charters, in British eyes Boston seemed to be a throwback to the obsessive age of Oliver Cromwell. For Lord North and his friends, New England was a vast, unruly sink of prejudice and hatred, where no one would appreciate the masque of Venus.

An Audience with the King

And so the summer holidays drew near, with the king and his cabinet apparently in control of events. After such a warm and sunny spring, they even had the prospect, for the first time in many years, of an abundant harvest. By now the economy had begun to thrive again, and all Great Britain required was a bumper crop of wheat and barley to complete the recovery in its fortunes. At the end of June, a week after Parliament rose, a ship arrived at last from Massachusetts carrying, like some specter from the west, the tall cadaverous figure of Thomas Hutchinson. He landed at Dover on the twenty-ninth and hurried up to London, where he found the government relaxed and optimistic.

In the weeks that followed, the man from Boston met every member of the cabinet. They were grateful and sympathetic about the seasickness that

* The fashions of 1774–75 can be seen in contemporary paintings by Sir Joshua Reynolds: for example, his portrait of Mrs. Elizabeth Carnac in the Wallace Collection in London.

made his journey wretched, about the abuse he had endured, and most of all about the theft of his private letters. Six months after the affair at the Cockpit, the cabinet still seethed with anger at Benjamin Franklin. Hutchinson found Lord Suffolk especially charming, between attacks of gout; he talked to Wedderburn about the law of treason and whether General Gage could shoot at rioters, and of course he met Lord North. He also went to hear the preachers whom Dartmouth recommended. He even dined with Robert Adam at Kenwood, the house above Hampstead Heath that the architect had beautified for Lord Mansfield, the lord chief justice. For three months, in fact, Hutchinson toured the south of England, visiting the landed gentry and encountering strong support for the stance the cabinet had taken. But something was strangely absent: in all his conversations with the government, he heard nothing about an alternative plan in case Boston failed to give in.

During the whole of this period, lasting until the end of September, North and his colleagues did nothing more about the colonies, but merely left the Coercive Acts to take effect. Although Dartmouth sometimes felt uneasy, the cabinet as a whole clung firmly to decisions it had already made. No military plans were laid; no one, least of all Lord Dartmouth, thought of trying to bribe or seduce the Continental Congress; and the cabinet ministers remained obsessed with Massachusetts. Like General Gage, they scarcely gave a thought to discontent elsewhere.

Early in July, word arrived from Virginia about the meeting at the Raleigh Tavern, but Dartmouth merely promised to consult his colleagues. The session at the tavern had been "extraordinary," he said, "it has given me the greatest concern," but he took no further action. Once again, the British displayed their old, familiar inattention to the tobacco planters of the South, at the very time when they were thinking hard about rebellion.[3]

In order to make New England submit, the British needed to isolate the northern colonies from Virginia and Maryland. This might have been achieved by reaching out to the planters of the Chesapeake with an array of commercial concessions intended to blunt their appetite for disobedience of their own. Lord North might have granted them complete control of their own currency; he might have cut the import duty on tobacco, if only temporarily; or he might have given farmers like George Washington entirely free access to Great Britain to sell their wheat. Nothing of the kind was proposed until it was too late. The South was allowed to fall away with scarcely an effort to keep it within the fold.

That summer, in all the discussions in which Hutchinson took part, the gaps and the omissions were as revealing as the words men spoke. At the heart of British policy there lay nothing but a void. It was born of ignorance, and of a failure to take a broader view of America as a whole. With their eyes so firmly fixed on the wickedness of Boston, the cabinet ministers missed the point that seemed so obvious to Jefferson. If the empire were to last, it would have to be reformed entirely, with some grand, overarching scheme for all the colonies, not merely Massachusetts. There would have to be some great new plan of union to satisfy the needs of every section of the continent, all the way down from Maine to Savannah, and those of the mother country as well.

That was what Jefferson said in his *Summary View*. But although Dartmouth had begun to muse about something of the kind, in practice nobody in power in London could meet the Virginian even halfway. Preoccupied with Boston, a problem that they saw as merely one of law and order, they could not find a point of vantage from which they could survey the colonies in their entirety. They simply wanted to bring New England to heel, as though it were another tiresome pack of hounds. Of all the meetings that Hutchinson had, the most significant were those with the king and with Lord North. Again, the discussions showed no trace of a wider plan, either to pacify the rest of the colonies or to impose a harsher regime upon them.[4]

Twice a week at noon it was the custom for the king to hold a royal levee, open to any adult male who could afford the uniform of a courtier. It was always held at St. James's Palace. On the morning of July 1, Hutchinson received a card from the colonial secretary, who had welcomed him to England with his usual good grace. Dartmouth asked him to attend that day's levee but took so long to dress that they missed the formal part of the proceedings. Instead, the former governor enjoyed a rare privilege: a private audience with the king for whom Hutchinson had done so much.

They ushered him into His Majesty's closet, the room in which he conferred with his ministers. George III held out his hand for the governor to kiss, and then for two hours they talked about America. It was a friendly but eccentric encounter. Given the nature of the British constitution, the king could not talk in detail about the policy his ministers had chosen. That was something he had to leave to Lord North, whom he had to trust as his executive. Even so, the king's remarks were very revealing. Although they betrayed no sign of ill will toward America, they also showed just how deeply attached he was to the status quo. Apart from the coercive laws for Massachusetts, he saw not the least necessity for reform, whether at home or in the colonies.

Fourteen years had yet to pass before King George would suffer his first episode of madness. When he met Thomas Hutchinson, he was thirty-six and in his prime, a man at peace with himself and with the God in whom he fervently believed. Every morning at eight o'clock he would kneel in worship in the royal chapel with Queen Charlotte at his side. By now, they had ten children, making the succession entirely secure. The king was tall and lively and alert, with the ruddy cheeks and muscular strength of a keen equestrian. His mind was sharp, and his manners were gracious, if sometimes a little strange.

Although inclined to shyness—in childhood, he was lonely, cut off from other boys—he did his best to calm the nerves of anxious visitors. At any royal reception, George III would try to speak to every guest, stooping down to peer at him or her with eyes almost as shortsighted as Lord North's. In public, the king could be nervous himself, with a tendency to walk too fast and talk too quickly. In private, and especially when the queen was with him, people found him "cheerful, affable and easy," according to a visitor who met the couple in 1773. He was also well-informed. Hutchinson faced a stream of detailed questions, which showed that up to a point the king had been carefully prepared.[5]

He knew the names of many men in Boston: John Hancock and Samuel Adams, of course, but also Cooper, Cushing, and Bowdoin. He even knew that Hancock's business was in difficulties. How had Adams come to be so influential? asked the king. "A great pretended zeal for liberty," Hutchinson replied. Would Virginia support its northern cousins? Probably not, thought the former governor. What about those awkward people in Rhode Island? They were a problem, Hutchinson agreed, but he saw no signs of trouble in Connecticut. New York was quiet as well.

And so it went on, with nods and smiles from George III and every so often a deferential comment from Lord Dartmouth. But soon enough the conversation wandered away from politics and toward the topics that the king preferred. Throughout his years of sanity, he liked to talk about two subjects above all: agriculture and the Almighty.

So George III asked about religion in New England, the different sects, their liturgy, their prayers, and the unruly sermons preached by Dr. Cooper and the rest. "I have heard, Mr. H.," the king inquired, "that your ministers preach that for the sake of liberty, any immorality may be tolerated?" The governor admitted that they did. "That's a strange doctrine," said the king, who did not care for anything unorthodox. After God, he turned to farming, where Hutchinson had to struggle under close interrogation. What did they eat? What crops did they grow? Did they *really* make bread with maize? It was all very odd, said the king, before he turned to population, climate, and the Indians, who would soon die out entirely, Hutchinson replied, due to the loss of their land and their own taste for liquor.

At last the audience came to an end with Dartmouth, kind as ever, worried that their guest was tired. In the presence of their sovereign, both visitors had to stand throughout the meeting, as did the king himself. Not once had George III shown any anger with the colonies. The king said nothing about revenge or retribution. He never made a threat or mentioned the use of force. Just as he had from his meeting with Gage, the king came away persuaded that it would not be necessary. Massachusetts was "a scene of anarchy," he told Lord North that evening, in another brief note, dated at exactly 9:02; but after listening to Hutchinson, he felt entirely satisfied with everything the government had done. "I am now well convinced that they will soon submit," he wrote.[6]

Never a tyrant and never a bully, though often he condoned acts of cruelty performed in his name, the king had no desire to fight a war. Although he loved his navy and his army—he liked to be painted in uniform, and he carefully vetted the choice of generals and colonels—he shared with North a deep reluctance to embark on costly military adventures. His principal flaw was simply this: a narrowness of vision, as revealed by his session with Hutchinson. He could see the details but not a larger picture.

This flaw arose not from a lack of intellect—the king read all the latest books, by Gibbon, Burke, or Dr. Johnson—but from his firm attachment to tradition. From his mother, Princess Augusta, and from the tutors she appointed, the king had acquired a painful sense of duty. It helps to explain his addiction to routine, his early rising, and his love of punctuality. His life was a mission with two purposes: to uphold the highest standards of morality, and to maintain what he once called "the beauty, excellence and perfection of the British constitution." And that included the preservation of the empire. Time and again by wide majorities, the Lords and the Commons had voted to assert their sovereignty in America. Even if the king had disagreed, his respect for Parliament would have compelled him to adopt the same hard line.[7]

When Hutchinson met Lord North a few days after the levee, he found him equally relaxed and intransigent. For the first time, Hutchinson let it be known that he had doubts about the plan to change the constitution of his province. Why had no one thought to tell the colony first and allow its assembly a chance to have its say? Because, North replied, time was up for Massachusetts. Long before the Tea Party the colony had already declared its independence, when the assembly voted to endorse the Boston pamphlet. Parliament had waited far too long, hoping that the colony would mend its ways. Now that its behavior was "so gross and so notorious," the government could not flinch from measures to make it toe the line. And by the way, North added, do not think that British industry will rally to support Americans. Trade was healthy once again, at home and abroad. In Lancashire, the merchants who made woolen textiles were tired of bad debts from the colonies, and they could easily sell their goods elsewhere. After they parted, Hutchinson wrote a letter home to New England. "There is no going back," he told a friend.

That was on July 8. Briefly, in early August, there was a minor panic in Whitehall, when word arrived from General Gage about the Solemn League and Covenant, the defiant manifesto promoted by Samuel Adams, and about the general's failure to arrest the culprits. In a state of high anxiety, Dartmouth hurried round to see Hutchinson. "He was not one who thirsted for blood," he told the governor; he simply wanted to see just punishment for Hancock and Adams. But the mood soon passed away, the king remained relaxed—"matters go on well in America, they are coming right," he said—and at last, in the middle of that month, Lord North could leave the capital for Somerset. Far away in the colonies, the delegates were leaving home to gather for the Continental Congress, but in England the holidays were beginning, with North convinced that the Congress would produce nothing more than idle chatter.[8]

Everything seemed to be quiet, but the summer was not as uneventful as it would appear. Unknown to Hutchinson, whom the British trusted rather less than they led him to believe, the cabinet ministers were making other plans. Catching their opponents off guard, they decided to call an early general election. It would end with an overwhelming victory for Lord North. But as sometimes happens in British politics, too large a success at the polls can lead to a crushing defeat of a different kind.

THE GENERAL ELECTION

It was not supposed to happen, the election, until the spring of 1775, seven years after the last time Britain chose a new House of Commons. Already many candidates were out campaigning in the field, making speeches, looking for friends in the press, or greasing the palms of the voters. Suddenly they found that they had only a few days in which to make their final preparations.

When the announcement appeared, it caught everyone by surprise, not least the Marquess of Rockingham. "I am not a little perplexed," he wrote, which was exactly the effect the cabinet intended to achieve. The idea for an early poll apparently came from Lord Suffolk. The Americans, he believed, would try to influence the result by stirring up what he called "jealousies, fears and prejudices" among the voters, especially those from the business community, worried by the prospect that the colonies might boycott British trade. Best to go early, said Suffolk, to catch the Whigs and the Wilkesites unawares and forestall the arrival of any more news of unrest in America.[9]

He seems to have spoken to George III because, on August 24, the king wrote to North in the country, making the case for a snap election. With the Congress now assembling in Philadelphia and with a war in Europe still a possibility—he had his eye on both the Russians and the French—the king agreed with Suffolk. Once the election was out of the way, Lord North could ride out any storm with a secure majority, safe in office for another seven years. The polls might even produce a better quality of member, with fewer radicals or men enriched by African slavery or the plunder of Bengal. "I trust it will fill the House with more gentlemen of landed property," wrote the king, "as the Nabobs, planters and other volunteers are not ready for the battle."[10]

Since this was the eighteenth century, only ninety-five constituencies would actually witness a contest. The rest were either counties where the local gentry struck deals between themselves to choose the successful candidates, or boroughs with a small electorate controlled by a local patron or the government itself. Even so, an election was a great event. In the previous decade, the press, John Wilkes, and men like Edmund Burke had brought excitement into politics, even for the vast majority who had no right to vote. For the British, an election represented another entertaining spectacle, full of beer and controversy. That in itself was one more reason to make the campaign as brief as possible, and especially in the capital, where the Wilkesites had high hopes for their political machine.[11]

"It will shorten that period of drunkenness and riot that always attends elections," said Lady Mary Coke, a close friend of the royal family's, when she heard the announcement.* But even before the news was official, it seemed that the gods were angry. In the middle of September, with the harvest yet to be complete, suddenly the rain began to fall. The bad weather went on for weeks, with London often waking to a cold and heavy fog. On the twenty-ninth, with the Thames in flood again, North gathered his

---

* Born in 1727, the daughter of the second Duke of Argyll, Lady Mary Coke kept a private journal that amounts to an intimate portrait of the aristocracy at the time, informal but very revealing about the political climate.

colleagues in Downing Street to make the formal request for Parliament to be dissolved. That evening the news rushed around the court, arousing mixed feelings of enthusiasm and dismay. "It puts everything in a bustle," wrote Lady Mary, "and displeasures some." As Lord North warned the king, he would probably lose some seats himself for lack of time to organize, and among the disappointed men there might be members of the royal entourage.[12]

His Majesty brushed these worries aside, but the following day their plans were interrupted by a dreadful item of news. A dispatch arrived from Boston on HMS *Scarborough*, bringing word of the powder alarm and the uproar that followed. This was the letter, written in a panic, in which General Gage reported his failure to make the colony see sense and told Whitehall that the province would have to be subdued by force. At noon on Friday, September 30, the general election was proclaimed, a few hours later the *Scarborough* dropped anchor, and that evening London was full of rumors that Massachusetts had risen in an armed rebellion.

"The town was all joy on Friday night, at the dissolution of parliament," said one paper close to John Wilkes. But his friends at the *London Evening Post* carried a far more sensational story. Alongside a few garbled lines about the powder alarm, it claimed that the army had been attacked, that two regiments of redcoats had mutinied, and that General Gage was dead. It was the first in a series of false alarms of war, recurring every few weeks until the following spring, which led many Britons to believe that fighting had already begun months before the actual moment came. These reports made the war all the more likely, not least because they ran alongside genuine scoops that the press received before the same information reached Whitehall officially. The same thing had happened after the Tea Party, but the autumn was a season much busier with traffic from the colonies. With scores of tobacco ships arriving, mostly via Liverpool or Glasgow, which heard American news a week ahead of the capital, the flow of news across the Atlantic sometimes became overwhelming.*

A mixture of fact and fiction, the stories in the press embarrassed the government; they accustomed people to thinking that bloodshed was inevitable, even when it might still be avoided; and they undermined official confidence in General Gage. Soon even John Pownall, who sincerely wanted

---

* Thanks to the prevailing winds and currents, the fastest sailing route between America and Britain passed around the north of Ireland. Despite this, the navy ignored the Mersey and the Clyde and persisted in using the ports of the English Channel. This increased the average journey time for official mail by up to 20 percent.

peace, was privately sharing his doubts about him with Thomas Hutchin-son. Pownall spoke "but lightly of his powers," Hutchinson recalled, and reminded the governor of the poor advice that Gage had given the king.[13]

For the government, the timing of the *Scarborough*'s arrival could not have been more inconvenient. Lord Dartmouth had begun to think about calling his own congress in America, with delegates chosen by each colony and a chairman appointed by George III, to design a new government for the continent as a whole. But this was no more than a vague idea, suddenly overtaken by the bad tidings from Boston. The reports reached England to find the cabinet in disarray. Again, Lord Suffolk had fallen ill, while his colleagues were mostly away in the shires, fixing their local elections, and their opinions differed widely. Rochford was calm and confident—"I do not yet despair"—but Gower was fretful and alarmed by news that he called "big with mischief."[14]

Should they try to placate the colonies by giving a firm undertaking never to impose any more taxes? Or should they go even further and abol-ish the hateful duty on tea? In private conversations in Whitehall, both ideas were gaining ground, with even hawks like Edward Thurlow seeking a formula for compromise. But proposals such as these kept running up against familiar obstacles. How could they convince the Americans that they were serious without doing away with the Declaratory Act as well? And if they did that, or abolished the tea tax, how could they still claim that Parliament was supreme? "In what way or in what manner this could be done without giving up all, he was utterly at a loss," the attorney general told Thomas Hutchinson.[15]

All North could do was convene a small emergency meeting on Octo-ber 3, at which Lord Dartmouth made the case for a cautious response. He persuaded his colleagues not to order more troops to Boston, at least for the time being. While the king suggested the dispatch of two more regi-ments from Ireland, the cabinet chose only to send three more warships and as many marines as Lord Sandwich could spare. There was little other action they could take. Although the general had shut the port of Boston, the rest of the Coercive Acts had already failed: that much was obvious. But by calling the election—a decision he could not revoke—in effect Lord North had paralyzed the work of government for perhaps three months or more.

The new Parliament could not assemble until the second half of November at the earliest. Even then, another four or five weeks might pass before they could vote on any new initiative against New England. At that time, the electoral system was so complex, with so many different rules about who could vote, who could stand, and how a poll should be conducted, that the outcome of the poll would take many weeks to settle entirely. When Parliament met, it would have to resolve disputes about dozens of individual elections. That, and the annual debates about the budgets for the army and the navy, would consume all the time available before the Christmas break.

But meanwhile the general election still had to be fought. For all his lack of foresight and his tendency to worry, Lord North resembled his American opponents in his will to win the game of politics. As every politician must, North had a very thick skin; when he tripped and fell, he picked himself up and went on fighting; and he kept at his desk or on his feet in the Commons until the job was done.

In the autumn of 1774 ministers had no bodyguards, despite a recent spate of armed robberies around the capital. On the night of October 4, in a country lane at Gunnersbury, two highwaymen held up his coach and relieved Lord North of his wallet after shooting his postilion in the thigh. His instincts were those of a gentleman, and so Lord North made light of the affair. "I lost a very few guineas," he said, showing more concern for the postilion than for himself. Next morning he was back at work, writing letters and pulling levers to secure every winnable constituency.[16]

In his constituency at Banbury, where only eighteen citizens could vote, his position was impregnable. His agent, the vicar, assembled them for supper, with wine and cheese and a bowl of punch, and they duly elected Lord North. A few weeks later, the Norths said thank you with a handsome gift of venison. "I never remember to have seen the people better pleased," said the vicar, regretting only the fact that His Lordship would have to be carried around the town in a chair to celebrate his victory. Elsewhere, however, Lord North had to work much harder for success. To help him, the Treasury supplied a slush fund of £50,000, but this would buy only twenty-five seats in Parliament from patrons happy to sell to the highest bidder. He could not afford to be complacent. All the time North worried more about the Wilkesites than he did about the Rockinghams.[17]

As always the latter were badly led, and their morale was weak. "I confess indeed," said the marquess, "all politics are now in such a low state, and so little likely to revive, that I should feel a hesitation . . . to drudge on in such a laborious occupation." Rockingham was feeling out of sorts and found the election simply too vexatious. Among his friends in the aristocracy, only the radical Duke of Richmond showed any eagerness to fight, but he spoke for no more than a few seats in Sussex. At Bristol, with little money behind him and no help from the marquess, Edmund Burke came only second in the vote. That was enough to get him reelected, because the borough had two seats, but at the top of the poll was the American radical Henry Cruger, the business client of John Hancock's, a man with his own close ties to Wilkes.[18]

The voting was mostly done by October 20. When the dust settled, it emerged that Lord North had kept his solid majority in the Commons, with about 320 members likely to support him. But while the Wilkesites had taken only a handful of seats, they performed far more strongly than mere numbers would suggest. Their appeal was broad and genuine. Wherever the electorate was large and free and urban, they did well, with a manifesto that could not have been more outspoken. At its heart lay the old Wilkesite program—shorter Parliaments and a wider franchise—but it also called for justice for America in the most uncompromising terms. "No Popery Members—No Unrepealers of the Quebec and Boston Acts," cried the *London Evening Post* the day after the election was called. With the press still full of Massachusetts, the Wilkesites swept the capital, taking six seats in the London area, with Hancock's friend George Hayley among the victorious candidates. Better still, John Wilkes won the election to follow Frederick Bull as lord mayor, by a margin so wide that this time it could not be vetoed.

Up to a point, they owed their success to the bigotry so crudely visible in the riot outside Parliament in June. The unpleasant Mr. Bull was baiting Roman Catholics again, using the powers of his office to close two chapels where priests said Mass. But the evidence from elsewhere in the country suggests that the Wilkesites were building a wider radical movement that, over time and under different leadership, might have evolved into a popular party of a modern kind. If only it had been far larger, it might have prevented the war.[19]

A case in point was Worcester, the English cathedral city, whose politics looked a little like those of its namesake in Massachusetts. A place that earned its keep by manufacturing—gloves, carpets, and the chinaware for which it was already famous—it was lively, educated, and alert to every modern trend. With six meetinghouses for Presbyterians, Baptists, and the like, the English Worcester had a reputation for dissenting views about religion and much else. For discussion of the issues of the day it had a coffeehouse called Tom's, where in the pages of the local newspaper its citizens could read all the American news and even an extract from Jefferson's *Summary View*. As for the women, a small but gallant band showed their support for Boston by refusing to drink tea.

And so, when the election came, the Wilkesites saw this constituency as one that they might win. By a fluke of history, the city charter had created an unusually large electorate, with two thousand names on the roll, more than half the adult males. At Worcester the polls were always riotous, and bribery was rife, but in 1774 no fewer than seven hundred voters backed a London radical, Sir Watkin Lewes, another member of Wilkes's inner circle in the capital. Although he lost, the result was revealing. In the dynamic, progressive parts of the country, if the people were given a choice as many as a third of them would favor a pro-American candidate.[20]

Much later, when the war for the colonies was nearly lost, Lord North would claim that it had been a people's war, urged upon him by public opinion and supported by the vast majority of Britons. This was certainly true in 1775, after the news arrived of the casualties at Concord and Bunker Hill. At that point the British public began to cry out for vengeance. But nine months earlier, at the time of the election, their views about the crisis in America had yet to crystallize, and a case for reconciliation could still be made. Perhaps James Boswell captured the mood of the moment most accurately in a letter to Samuel Johnson filled with doubts about coercion in America. "Imperfect hints ... float in my mind," he told his friend, but he feared that the government had been, as he put it, "precipitant and severe" toward the Bostonians. "Well do you know that I have no kindness for that race," Boswell went on. "But nations or bodies of men should ... have a fair trial, and not be condemned on character alone."[21]

These might have been the views of a minority of Britons, but the results from London, Bristol, and Worcester suggest that the minority was actually quite large, with a strong groundswell of sympathy for Boston. But sadly the nation had only a handful of open boroughs where it could influence the ballot. In practice the electoral system ensured that places such as these were merely scattered islands of liberty, surrounded by a sea of dogma and reaction. The drift toward war continued, and in four different ways the general election helped to make it all but irreversible.

In the first place it tied the hands of the government until the new year of 1775. Second, the outcome strengthened the position of the hawks—Suffolk, Gower, and Sandwich—who had urged Lord North to call an early poll. Third, Lord North's victory in the country had been so large that it left him unable to deviate from the hard line he had already chosen. Behind him in the Commons he would have a loyal army of conservatives, eager to give him a mandate for military action in New England. If North were to flinch or to waver, his supporters would be horrified. At worst he might face a leadership challenge from a rival determined to use force.

The fourth and final point concerns the king and his response to the election. As the weeks went by, he became ever more hawkish himself. "The die is now cast, the colonies must now submit or triumph," he wrote in September, even before the voting began. "I do not wish to come to severer measures but we must not retreat." As the election unwound, the king closely followed each result. While he loathed the idea of John Wilkes as mayor of London, in the country as a whole the outcome was excellent. With Lord North safely returned to Downing Street, George III saw all the less reason to appease America. It would take only one more item of news to convince him that General Gage had to take the field.

Soon enough it came. In the middle of October a secret dispatch arrived from the Netherlands, bringing word of yet another act of treason by the people of Rhode Island.[22]

Chapter Fifteen

THE ARMING OF AMERICA

This country is now in as open a state of rebellion as Scotland was in the '45.

—BRIGADIER GENERAL PERCY, BOSTON, SEPTEMBER 1774[1]

Some thirteen years earlier, the British had appointed as their ambassador to The Hague an abrasive old military man named Sir Joseph Yorke. An envoy with an odd approach to diplomacy—for him, it involved berating the Dutch until they did as he wished—Yorke was another veteran of Culloden Moor, where at the age of only twenty-one he had helped defeat the Jacobites. His political views boiled down to little more than a hatred of the French. Everywhere the ambassador saw their evil hand at work. With the help of Britain's ring of naval spies, Yorke kept a close watch for any signs that they or the Russians were on the move; and early in October 1774, his agents in Amsterdam sent him word of something quite extraordinary.

A small ship called the *Smack* had sailed into the port from Rhode Island under a skipper called Benjamin Page. In itself, this was unusual—it was rare and generally illegal for colonial ships to visit Dutch or German harbors without clearing British customs first—but the voyage of the *Smack* looked like something far worse than a simple case of smuggling. Dealing with a Mr. Hodson, an Amsterdam merchant with long-standing connections in New York, Page was said to be loading his vessel with firearms, gunpowder, and forty small pieces of cannon.

On October 11, Sir Joseph sent the report to Lord Suffolk, who sprang into action at once, alerting the navy. Lord Sandwich sent a cutter, HMS

Wells, to patrol the Dutch coast and seize the *Smack* if she tried to cross the North Sea. At home a few weeks earlier, the War Office had already stopped a cargo of gunpowder leaving for America, and now the news from Holland made it essential for the cabinet to act decisively. Within the week, the king signed an order forbidding any shipments of powder or weapons to the colonies. Published in the London press on October 20, news of the decree instantly revived the talk of war, running close to long stories from Boston about the army's fortification of the town. [2]

Meanwhile, Yorke's agents had obtained more intelligence. It was said that Page had purchased swivel guns for use at sea and hid them beneath coils of rope in the bow of his ship. A dispatch arrived from Hamburg about a craft from New York loading ammunition, and then new reports came in from Amsterdam about more sloops from Rhode Island doing the same thing. Sir Joseph asked the Dutch authorities to search the *Smack*, which they refused to do. The evidence collected by the spies amounted to hearsay and nothing more. So the cutter *Wells* remained on watch while Yorke tried to persuade the Dutch to cooperate.

The affair was very murky. It took another four months for the British to obtain the proof they needed that Rhode Islanders were running guns from Holland, and the records that survive remain open to more than one interpretation. But of one thing there can be no doubt. By the end of October the king and his ministers believed that Americans were arming themselves for war. The intelligence from Sir Joseph Yorke convinced them that this was so. It hardened British attitudes and made the outbreak of hostilities all the more likely. But if that is the case, then the affair raises important questions about colonial responsibility for the bloodshed that occurred.

Were these American ships acting on behalf of the patriot movement in New England? Were the arms they bought intended to supply the militia in Massachusetts or Rhode Island? If they were, what did that imply? A spring campaign against General Gage—or merely a defensive action if the redcoats tried to march out of Boston and subdue the interior? Or had Benjamin Page and the other skippers sailed to Europe freelance, purely in the hope of making money? Whatever lay in store in 1775, the price of gunpowder was hardly likely to fall, and any guns they bought would find ready takers in America on one side or the other of the political divide.

These questions cannot be answered conclusively, for the obvious reason: gun runners try not to leave a paper trail. But their significance is more than merely academic. If the *Smack* and the other ships sailed with the knowledge and the blessing of John Hancock, Samuel Adams, and their allies, then Hancock and the New England patriots were clearly committing an act of provocation. While the Americans had every right to defend themselves, they must also have known how furious the British would be if and when they discovered what was going on. The king and his ministers would have to take preemptive action to forestall the arming of America, and if they did so—by arresting colonial ships or searching for hidden caches of weapons in the Boston area—then lives were bound to be lost as a result.

From the fragmentary evidence available, it would appear that Benjamin Page did indeed belong to an organized conspiracy to arm and equip a force to fight the Crown. Ostensibly, the American ships planned to sail from Amsterdam to the Caribbean island of St. Eustatius, which was Dutch, or to the Danish colony at St. Croix. This would have been perfectly legal, even though everyone knew that both were used by American traders in smuggled tea and molasses. But it seems more likely that Page actually intended to take the guns straight to New England.

Significantly, the *Smack* had left Rhode Island on August 22, at a moment when the papers in Boston and Providence were full of stories about the Quebec Act and the protests it had aroused in Great Britain. The press was claiming that the British had, in effect, declared war on the colonies, and already volunteers were drilling with their arms in Worcester, Massachusetts, and other towns, including Providence. As for Benjamin Page, a young Rhode Islander of that name took part in the attack on the *Gaspée* and went on to fight at sea against the British during the Revolutionary War. In 1818, at the age of sixty-five, Page applied for a pension from the United States, setting out his record in detail. He had served under the command of Captain Abraham Whipple, the man from Providence who led the *Gaspée* raid.[3]

Conceivably, the skipper of the *Smack* might have been another Benjamin Page—the name is hardly unusual—and the date of the *Smack's* departure for Europe might have been coincidental. But while the evidence might not be enough to convince a jury, it looks very much as though the men who burned the *Gaspée* took the decision to arm a navy of their own, complete with swivel guns, at a time—August 1774—when the British had no plans for war of any kind. Of course this raises another question: were the Rhode Islanders acting alone, or did they share their plans with their comrades in Massachusetts? All one can say is this: that for years Samuel Adams had been exchanging letters with like-minded friends in Providence, including Darius Sessions, who was Rhode Island's deputy governor and the officer commanding its militia.

Wherever the truth might lie, the dispatches from Sir Joseph Yorke changed the atmosphere in London. The cabinet ministers began to think seriously about the use of force. In the final week of October, with the reports from The Hague still fresh in their minds, they received another shocking piece of news from America that pushed them further in the same direction. The news came not from Boston—nothing more had arrived from General Gage—but from the Congress assembled in Philadelphia.

Until now the British had remained almost entirely in the dark about its discussions, and what little they did know suggested that it might opt for compromise. Lord Dartmouth had read some letters from a friendly delegate, Joseph Galloway of Pennsylvania, who struck a note of cautious optimism. According to him, writing just before the proceedings began early in September, the Continental Congress would behave with "temper and moderation." While he expected angry words from Boston and Virginia, calling for a sweeping boycott of trade, he hoped the majority would see sense. They might even agree to send envoys to England, said Galloway, in an attempt to settle their differences with the empire.

Although he knew it would be hard to reach a deal of any kind, Lord Dartmouth was certainly willing to talk. But on October 28 a report arrived that seemed to dash all his hopes for peace.

To its horror, the cabinet learned that far from being moderate, the Congress had thrown its weight behind the worst extremists in New England. Again the London newspapers had the story first, from a cargo ship that docked in the Mersey, while the ministers were left to flounder with no sources of their own.

Six weeks earlier, with not one voice raised in dissent, the Congress had approved a startling document known as the Suffolk Resolves. Coming from Suffolk County, Massachusetts, which included Boston, it blazed with outrage at the British seizure of the powder store. Like every other county in the province, Suffolk had received the revolutionary manifesto drawn up in Boston on August 27 by Joseph Warren, Elbridge Gerry, and their comrades. After inserting some furious invective of its own, the Suffolk County meeting endorsed all their proposals, including a new militia and a provisional government to be created by the Provincial Congress due to meet in Concord.

When it voted for the Suffolk Resolves, it seems that the Continental Congress merely intended to make a gesture of solidarity with Massachusetts. The vote came at an early stage of its proceedings, when it had not yet decided what form a national movement of resistance should take. But when it appeared in London in late October, the story left the cabinet "thunderstruck," said Thomas Hutchinson. "Why, if these resolves are to be depended on, they have already declared war against us," Dartmouth told the former governor. In the days that followed, the cabinet found itself in disarray once more, stricken with fear that America was being lost but unable to conceive of any strategy to save it. Its confidence in General Gage began to disappear entirely.[4]

A week or so later Jefferson's *Summary View* became available in London, followed in the middle of November by Quincy's pamphlet about the port act. But still the cabinet had no word from the general. Unable to spare a sloop from Admiral Graves's naval squadron, Gage had sent his most recent dispatch on a merchant ship so slow that the letter took seven weeks to reach Whitehall, a fortnight longer than it should have. And when at last it arrived on November 18, it damaged his reputation almost beyond repair. Even George III lost patience with the soldier who had been so certain of success.

It was a brief and fatuous dispatch, devoid of hard facts and equally lacking in analysis. Dated three weeks after the powder alarm, Gage's letter failed to give an estimate of the military resources of Massachusetts, something the cabinet urgently required. General Gage said next to nothing about the rest of the region, about New York, or about the busy goings-on in Philadelphia. What little he did say was deeply worrying. He could hold Boston and Salem, but that was all: the remainder of the province was beyond his control. To enforce the Coercive Acts, the army would have to recapture New England, an enterprise for which he would need far more troops than he had. In a separate, private letter Gage suggested suspending the new laws, but he could not say when they might be restored or what alternative might take their place.

The very idea was absurd, said the king: to do as Gage proposed would make a mockery of Parliament, exposing its claim to sovereignty as nothing but a hollow sham. Lord North agreed entirely. By the third week of November, the king and his premier had decided that a rebellion had begun, leaving them little option but the use of force. From that moment, the scales began to tilt in the direction of war: a limited war against the rebels in New England, but a war nonetheless. "Blows must decide whether they are to be subject to this country or independent," wrote the king on November 19, with the full agreement of a clear majority in the cabinet. Reluctantly, Lord Dartmouth had reached the same conclusion: the army must suppress the insurgency.

This was easily said but far from easily done. It would take nearly three more months for the government to issue the decisive orders telling Gage to take the offensive. For a host of reasons, most of them aired at great length in the press and then in Parliament, it had to act slowly and with deliberation. The government would need to talk to its lawyers, it would have to make one last, futile effort at diplomacy, and, as we shall see, it would even have to wait for the weather to change in the Atlantic.

Above all, the cabinet feared that if it acted too hastily, it might drive the other colonies into the arms of Massachusetts. As yet the British did not know the final outcome of the Continental Congress. Despite the vote in favor of the Suffolk Resolves, perhaps Joseph Galloway might still be proved right. What if the delegates backed away from confrontation and left some room for a peaceful compromise? However pessimistic he might be about the rebel towns of New England, Lord Dartmouth remained open to negotiation with moderates elsewhere. It was always possible—or so he thought—that a silent majority of loyalists would emerge, from the Hudson valley, rural Connecticut, or the backcountry of the South. If so, then they needed encouragement from London, but it was hard to say what form it ought to take.

Despite their strategic importance, the tobacco colonies remained the region the British found hardest to call. Lord Dunmore had still failed to report from Virginia, while in Maryland the empire now had no representative at all. In theory, the province fell under the supervision of a British governor, a young man of thirty-two named Robert Eden, married to a lady from the Calvert family, the colony's ancient proprietors. In practice, Eden had already chosen the path of abdication. When the colony's assembly finished its annual session at the end of May, he promptly sailed for England with his wife for a long holiday, pausing only to pay his wine bill and enter a horse for the local races. On arrival he failed to visit the ministers in Whitehall, and he wrote them not a line. The Maryland file remained empty.[5]

With Eden acting on its behalf, it was scarcely surprising that the empire lost touch with the tobacco country. To the extent that he thought about anything at all, Eden's reasoning seems to have been as follows: however unhappy the South might be, the landowning class of the region would never renounce its allegiance to the Crown. An economy based on slavery produced its own local elite, composed of wealthy planters very different from the northern radicals. Like those of the West Indies, they relied on the British for a market for their produce and for protection if the slaves rose in revolt. This idea—that Maryland and Virginia were inherently loyal—cast its spell in London too, where John Pownall said as much to Lord Dartmouth. And yet, as the autumn wore on, it became apparent that the opposite was true. The planters were veering away toward a rebellion of their own.

Along with the alarming news about the *Smack*, the letters from The Hague had revealed that tobacco farmers from Virginia were planning to sell their next year's crop in Holland. This was illegal, but what did it signify? It might be a sign that the planters were falling in alongside the rebels in Massachusetts. Or perhaps they were simply trying to forestall a British ban on colonial tobacco, a measure that North might impose as a means to pressure the Continental Congress. Here was another riddle that the cabinet could not solve, though a glance at Jefferson's *Summary View* might have helped it make up its mind.

And while they pondered that conundrum, Lord North and his colleagues also had to think about the law of treason. It was one thing to form a private opinion that John Hancock, Samuel Adams, Joseph Warren, and the rest were rebels. It was quite another to arrest them, hang them, or shoot them dead without firm evidence of specific acts of treachery. Unwilling to cede the moral high ground, especially with the powers of Europe looking on, the cabinet needed more proof before it could act against them.

As a way to overcome this obstacle, the king and his ministers began to consider another option: a formal declaration, issued by Parliament, proclaiming that a state of rebellion existed in Massachusetts. This would legally justify the use of force. As November drew to a close, this idea began to circulate in Whitehall, but it posed problems of its own that led to further delays. The last great rebellion had been the 1745 uprising, when Charles Edward Stuart branded himself a traitor by raising his banner beside the loch at Glenfinnan. Before Parliament could vote, the rebels led by Hancock and Adams would have to produce their own Glenfinnan moment: they would have to attach their names to an act of treason so visible and blatant that no one could doubt their guilt or the need for military action.

All the time, the critics of General Gage became more strident, as it became ever clearer that he lay beleaguered in Boston, unable or unwilling to venture beyond a tight perimeter. Doubts were cast on his courage as well as his powers of analysis. Why had he done so little? Why had he failed to quell the insurgency at Worcester? As early as November 22, Lord Suffolk called for his dismissal. "It is idle to do things by halves," Suffolk said. Although North and the king did not go so far, they agreed that Gage needed help from new major generals sent from England to bolster his resolve. And meanwhile, even his closest friend at the War Office was questioning the wisdom of occupying Boston.

For many years, Gage had shared his private thoughts with the secretary at war, Lord Barrington. Loyal and efficient, with nearly two decades behind him in his post, Barrington could see how pointless it was to wedge the army so tightly into the town, where it would be condemned to what he called "a disgraceful inaction." Aware of the general's earlier view that the Hudson held the key to North America, Barrington urged his colleagues to remove the redcoats from Massachusetts, leaving only a small garrison to hold Castle William and sweep the harbor with its artillery.[6]

Barrington wrote those words on November 12, but his advice came too late, with not a chance of being listened to. Despite his title, his high intelligence, and his years of service, Barrington did not rank as a member of the cabinet. His influence was limited, and if accepted his proposal would throw a still heavier burden on his opposite number at the Admiralty. The task of ending the rebellion would fall primarily to the navy, at a time when Lord Sandwich still wanted to keep the vast bulk of the fleet in the British Isles to deter the French from any act of aggression.

And so the weeks passed, with still no word from Philadelphia about the outcome of the Continental Congress. War seemed ever more likely, but the cabinet could form no definite plan of action until it knew what the Congress had decided. Even the weather changed for the worse again, with gales in the Channel and weeks of bitter cold and rain turning to early snow. All around the capital the crime wave continued, with burglary rife in the suburbs and robbers stalking the lanes that led across the fields to Piccadilly. With more than its usual panache the London season began, with at its heart a great new beauty, Lady Mary Somerset, eighteen years old and outrageously chic in clothes and a hairstyle fresh from Paris. At Drury Lane, Garrick put on *The Maid of the Oaks*, with as a companion piece a satire, *The Lottery*, making fun of the gambling craze. But when Parliament reassembled, its mood was anxious and subdued.

On November 30, George III opened the session with a grim assessment of the situation. In Massachusetts he beheld "a most daring spirit of resistance to the law." His speech promised firm measures to reassert British authority, but the king gave not a shred of detail about the form that they might take. The following day, in private the cabinet formally decided to seek a declaration of rebellion. As a preliminary, it asked Attorney General Thurlow to study the dispatches from General Gage and give a legal opinion: Could he see clear evidence of acts of treason? Apart from that, the government's paralysis continued.

As always, the Commons had to discuss the king's speech, but although Lord North won the debate by nearly two hundred votes, his eloquence had deserted him. Embarrassed by his own inaction, he could offer only lame excuses when he rose to speak on December 5. Of course he wanted reconciliation with America, but the Congress had yet to offer any terms. Until it did, matters remained in what he called "a state of suspense." In the House of Lords the Duke of Richmond rebelled again, leading thirteen peers in a motion of dissent from what the king had said, but this was only a skirmish. The next great battle in Parliament was still eight weeks away. With its timetable choked by election disputes, it would be late January before it could vote on the declaration the cabinet required.

But as the suspense continued, men and women grew ever more accustomed to the thought of violence. This process can be seen in the diary of Lady Mary Coke. Several evenings a week, she would lose forty guineas at a time playing cards with Princess Amelia, the aunt of George III, and so her developing attitudes reflect those of the royal family and the people clustered around it. It was hard for Lady Mary to say which was the worst: the Somerset girl's décolletage, the disorders in New England, or the wicked agitation by Charles Lennox. But on December 7, with her garden frozen solid and the papers full of blood, she resigned herself to what she feared was coming. "'Tis believed that there has actually been an engagement in America," she told her diary. "I pity those who have relations in that part of the world, where there is beginning a civil war."[7]

These were dangerous words, the kind that can become a self-fulfilling prophecy, but her intuition was correct. Since early summer, the colonies had captured the initiative, forging ahead while the British lay mired in hesitation. Even their divisions proved to be a source of strength, as debate between the different sections of American society helped to sharpen their thinking about the future. Six weeks before Lady Mary spoke of civil war, the Glenfinnan moment had already occurred.

The October Days

It took place in Cambridge, Massachusetts, on October 26. Six days earlier, after many weeks of debate, the Continental Congress had reached its own point of no return when it issued a document—the "Association"—that rejected compromise and called for unified resistance. Without waiting for the final text, Paul Revere had already ridden north with the news of what the Congress planned to do. He found John Hancock chairing a meeting of his colony's provisional assembly, whose reaction was decisive. It passed

a series of resolutions that amounted, in British eyes, to acts of unequivo-
cal rebellion. With an audacity that appalled the cabinet in London, the
rebels published their treachery in the press. With that, Massachusetts put
itself beyond the pale, and war became inevitable.

By the autumn of 1774, across much of North America the empire had
come close to collapse. Everywhere we can find sedition: on the streets, in
the pulpits, in the newspapers, and on the frontier. From the outset, the
British had failed to understand the chemistry of protest and the speed
with which it could spread and diversify. Although it began in August and
in Boston, the revolution soon acquired many centers and a host of leaders. It might have different causes in each different place, and sometimes
the sedition amounted to nothing but rhetoric. But in the aggregate its
meaning was quite clear. By the middle of October, there were few counties in America where the British could speak and confidently expect a
majority of the inhabitants to obey.

With so few royal officials, no police, and a small army widely scattered, the British had always relied on local habits of deference to keep the
empire in some semblance of submission. In Massachusetts, this customary loyalty to the Crown had been in decay for many years, and now it collapsed across the rest of the colonies as well. In Vermont, Ethan Allen was
already up in arms, staging his own rebellion and making the Bennington
area independent by the end of the year. In South Carolina and Maryland,
the empire had ceased to exist in anything but name; at Annapolis, a crowd
went all the way and forced the burning of a tea ship and its cargo, rather
than merely dumping the stuff in the water; and on the streets of New
York, the king became an object of open derision. "You now hear the very
lowest orders call him a knave or a fool," said one young citizen.[8]

That was in early September, a week or so after the news arrived of the
protests in London against the Quebec Act. Of all the new laws that Lord
North had introduced, this was the one that caused the deepest anger in
America, because it appeared to demonstrate a callous disregard for faith
as well as freedom. The Quebec Act seemed to endanger the Protestant
religion, and in the words of a man from Maryland it "raised a universal
flame." And then there came the reports from Boston, false though they
were, of townspeople killed by the redcoats and the waterfront on fire.
Spreading outward from New England, the stories reached all corners of
the colonies and found an echo among men and women with other grievances of their own.[9]

Before the *Gaspée* raid and the Tea Party, we saw how anger gave birth
not only to protest but also to new and radical ideas with a philosophical

cast. From a British point of view, this feature of the revolution seems all the more striking and original. In England, when the Wilkesites made their play for votes at an election, they tended to deal either in slogans—"No Popery" being the most frequent—or in a list of specifics. They called for annual Parliaments, or they demanded the exclusion of paid royal officials from the House of Commons. They rarely theorized about fundamentals or questioned the very basis of the British constitution. In America, men and women did exactly that.

In the weeks that followed the powder alarm, the political debate in the colonies entered new, uncharted waters far deeper than those with which the British were familiar. Jefferson's pamphlet had shown the way, but many other people went as far or even further. Take, for example, an anonymous writer in the *Pennsylvania Packet* who went to the very origins of law and government, which he found in the will of the people alone. "The history of kings," he wrote, "is nothing but the history of folly and depravity." The time was coming, and coming soon, when America would sever its connection with Great Britain. It would throw off the monarchy and strike out for its own independent future. The writer looked forward a hundred years and imagined how the nation would recall the events he

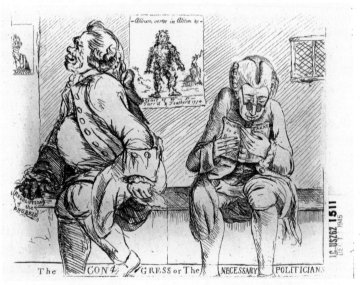

Two members of the Continental Congress in a privy (or a "necessary"), with on the wall pictures of John Wilkes as lord mayor and Lord Chatham tarred and feathered, from a cartoon printed in London in 1775. One of the congressmen is reading Samuel Johnson's anti-American pamphlet, *Taxation No Tyranny*. *Library of Congress*

saw unfolding all around him. "I almost wish to hear the triumphs of the jubilee in the year 1874," he wrote. "To see the medals, pictures and fragments of writings that shall be displayed." They would revere the memory of the Continental Congress, an assembly whose authority came from the highest source of all. "The American congress," he went on, "derives all its power, wisdom and justice, not from scrolls of parchment signed by kings, but from the people."

In saying this, the writer preempted Thomas Paine, who was just about to arrive from London and make the same point far more famously in his pamphlet *Common Sense*. In this excited atmosphere, filled with talk of revolution, the Continental Congress followed Massachusetts down the path of disobedience.

Everything Joseph Galloway had told the British proved to be false. The Congress in Philadelphia sat for seven weeks, starting on September 5, and although its early sessions were confused and hesitant, the tone soon changed to one of staunch defiance of the king and Parliament. Samuel Adams won a crucial victory when, on the sixteenth, the delegates voted to endorse the Suffolk Resolves. Twelve days after that, Galloway went down to defeat when he made his own attempt to save the empire.

Speaking of peace and moderation, he proposed a new Anglo-American deal that, he believed, would resolve the differences between the two nations. He called for a formal union of the colonies, with a parliament of their own, and a British lord lieutenant to represent the Crown. An interesting idea, it came a century too early. It would have made America resemble Australia and Canada as they were in 1914: self-governing dominions, managing their own affairs but united in allegiance to Great Britain and committed to supporting it in time of war. The Galloway plan has appealed to many modern scholars, who argue that it might have worked, but it did nothing for his colleagues at the time. The Congress let his motion die without debate.

Among the delegates there were differences of emphasis and strategy, there were rivalries and squabbles, but we also see a high degree of unanimity. They held a common view about the king and his cabinet. With the Coercive Acts and with the new law for Quebec, the British had shown themselves in their true colors. Lord North and his friends had laid siege to American freedom, or so the Continental Congress believed. By revoking the charter of Massachusetts, the British had done away with popular government in that colony, and the rest might soon suffer the same fate. They had attacked the right to trial by jury, they wanted to close the wilderness to settlers, and they undermined the Christian faith. Parliament would tax the colonies, whenever it saw fit, and if Americans objected, the army would march in to make them pay.[10]

In effect the Congress drew up a long indictment of the empire, clearly and carefully itemized. If there had been some international court of law, willing to hear both sides and rule impartially, Lord North could have offered a credible defense to many of the charges. He could certainly deny that the British intended to foist the Catholic faith on the colonies against their will. That accusation was entirely baseless. With regard to the western frontier, he could claim that the government did not wish to ban new settlements entirely, but simply to prevent headlong expansion that might cause an Indian war. Yes, Great Britain wished to change the charters in New England, but only because Massachusetts and Rhode Island had failed to propose reforms of their own. For evidence that reform was long overdue, the British could point to the Boston Tea Party, the *Gaspée* raid, and the tactics of intimidation the colonies had employed to prevent the culprits from being brought to trial.

Before a fair-minded judge, the British government could have made a case along these lines to justify most of the steps that it had taken, however unconvincing Americans might find it. But no such tribunal existed; and even if it had, there remained one great, divisive question that even the wisest lawyers could not arbitrate. Above all the debates in Philadelphia, there loomed the British claim that Parliament was sovereign over every corner of the empire. For as long as the Declaratory Act remained in force, with its assertion that the British could make what laws for America they chose, their conflict with the colonies could not be resolved. But time and again during the debates at Westminster earlier that year, Lord North and his colleagues had insisted that the act would never be repealed. The delegates in Philadelphia knew that this was so, and it left them with only one option.

On October 20 the Continental Congress issued a formal statement of its conclusions. Fifty-one men, coming from twelve colonies—only Georgia failed to sign—put their names to the Association. They demanded the abolition of all the Coercive Acts, the new law for Quebec, and every other statute for America that Great Britain had passed since the end of the last war with France, including the Declaratory Act. They amounted, said the Congress, to "a ruinous system," created with the clear intention "of enslaving these colonies, and with them the British empire." The system had to go, and if it did not, the colonies would force its demolition with a complete ban on trade with the mother country. Imports of British goods would end on December 1, 1774. From the following September the ban would extend to exports as well. Not a single cargo would sail from the colonies to the mother country.

The export ban was utterly new, it went far beyond the trade boycotts used against the Stamp Act or the Townshend duties, and perhaps it might not stick. Even so, it was enough to scandalize Lord North and the cabinet when the news reached London two weeks before Christmas. The reaction it evoked from Massachusetts was equally outrageous. When Revere reached Cambridge on about October 17, without the Association but knowing what it would contain, the Provincial Congress had been in session for a week with Hancock as president. The assembly was unlawful, and to begin with it was also divided. While fifty-six men had come from Worcester County to call for the creation of an army, and their comrades from the Berkshires said the same, others held back, waiting for official word from Philadelphia. But soon enough the radicals gained the upper hand.

The debates were held behind closed doors, and only the decisions were recorded. But they were quite enough to constitute acts of rebellion. A committee drew up a list of the weapons that Massachusetts would need to defend itself. On the twenty-fifth, the Provincial Congress voted to buy enough material to equip an army: twenty-two field guns, four wide-barreled mortars of the kind used to besiege a town, thirty-five tons of grapeshot, round shot, and bombshells, a thousand barrels of powder, five thousand muskets and rifles each with a bayonet, and seventy-five thousand flints. The following day, the members passed the crucial resolution creating the new militia that men like Elbridge Gerry had advocated for so long. The old colonial militia would cease to exist and be replaced by a new force consisting of local companies, each of which would elect its own officers.

This was definitely treason, as any English judge would understand the word. Two days later, the Provincial Congress repeated the offense when, on October 28, it voted to withhold the local taxes due to the colonial treasurer, a staunch supporter of Great Britain who had held the post for twenty years. In the future, the money would go to a new fund created by the congress, with a treasurer of their own to oversee it. This was rebellion, too, and committed openly. A few days later the *Boston Gazette* printed the text of both resolutions, signed by the secretary who kept the minutes: an important detail. In an English court of law signed minutes would suffice to hang John Hancock and every other man at the meeting.[11]

Meanwhile, the rest of the region was also preparing for war. In October the assembly in Rhode Island authorized each town to set up its own

independent militia company and promised to march to the aid of Massachusetts, while Connecticut drilled in arms and doubled its own stocks of
ammunition. But news of what was going on reached England unusually
slowly, as the elements conspired to create still more delay.

The bad weather that brought an early winter to Great Britain encompassed the whole of its western approaches. There were tales of shipwreck
everywhere, with voyages across the Atlantic suddenly doubling in dura-
tion. The first reports about the Association and the votes in Cambridge
did not arrive in London until about December 9, carried by a cargo ship
from New York; but shocking though they were, these were only stories
in the press that might be inaccurate. A few days later Attorney General
Thurlow delivered his opinion that the insurgency at Worcester, Massachusetts, in late August had been an act of rebellion, but even this was not
enough. The men he named as rebels, led by Joshua Bigelow, were small-
fry, and perhaps they did not speak for the colony as a whole.

For better or worse, the cabinet needed to hear officially from General
Gage before it could take any new decisions. Immediately after the votes at
Cambridge he assembled a bundle of incriminating papers, including the
relevant issue of the *Boston Gazette*. To go with them, Gage wrote a dispatch
saying that the rebels planned to put an army in the field against him. The
packet traveled on a naval schooner, the *St. Lawrence*, which left Boston early
in November but did not reach England until the new year. In the meantime, the newspapers jeered at the king's chief minister for what seemed to
be irresolution or even cowardice.

Lord North had behaved like an amateur, said the *Public Advertiser* in
a brief, dismissive profile of the premier: "He has achieved a degree of
importance in politics, to which from his talents he is certainly not entitled." The mood in Whitehall became brittle and fractious. With North
still enjoying the support of George III, if not the press, his colleagues
placed the blame for the debacle with Gage and Dartmouth. The colonial
secretary was proposing a commission of inquiry to be sent to America
to meet with people of goodwill, in the hope of finding some formula
for reconciliation, but the idea had ceased to be feasible. A fact-finding
mission might have served a useful purpose *before* the Coercive Acts were
passed. Now the suggestion merely angered the rest of the cabinet, whose
trust in Dartmouth and Gage reached an even lower ebb.

And yet, ironically enough, in New England the British commander
was at last adopting a hard line of his own. Despite his lack of communication, Gage had shaken off his spell of low morale. Even before the
congress met in Cambridge, he had come to terms with the knowledge

that his initial advice to the king had been deeply flawed. Gradually, his mood had changed. The general ceased to be a politician, acting primarily as governor, and during the autumn he regained his nerve as a soldier.

At the beginning of October, Gage had written at last to his friend Lord Barrington, telling him exactly what he required for New England's reconquest. Faced with a rebellion in a region with close to half a million inhabitants, he would need twenty thousand troops and far more artillery. Belatedly, he mentioned cavalry—"three or four regiments of light horse"—to throw a screen of scouts around the front of a marching column. His demands were entirely unrealistic—with the army still at peacetime strength and with twenty battalions tied down in Ireland, the British had nothing like so many troops and horses available—but at least General Gage had begun to recognize the dimensions of the challenge he faced.

He also began to listen to the hawks in his own ranks, such as Brigadier General Percy and Alexander Leslie. Less than a year had passed since Colonel Leslie had to stand by impotently while the tea was thrown into the harbor. By the late autumn of 1774, Gage had come to share his opinion that the colony must be subdued by force of arms. Scholars have read the general's mind that winter in different ways, but only three sources of evidence survive: his letters to England; the government's own papers, showing what it understood him to be saying; and—most revealing of all—Gage's daily journals of his orders to his officers, preserved today in the Boston Public Library and the New York Historical Society. Taken together, the evidence shows that far from hoping for a truce or a deal, General Gage wished to be told to take the offensive against the Provincial Congress.

"I hope you will be firm, and send me a sufficient force to command the country, by marching into it . . . to secure obedience through every part," Gage wrote to Barrington on December 14. "Affairs are at a crisis, and if you give way it is forever." For weeks his every move, even when he seemed to be appeasing the Bostonians, had been directed toward one end. A rebellion had occurred, and it would have to be suppressed. The general knew that he would have to take the field the following spring, even if the reinforcements he required had not yet arrived.

His order book shows how his thinking was developing. His chief concern was this: to delay any fighting until he had what he wanted; firm instructions from London telling him to pursue the rebels. In the meantime, Gage wished to avoid provoking the other colonies to come to the aid of Massachusetts before he was ready to move. For the same reason, he needed to prevent random incidents of violence between his troops and the citizens of Boston that might lead to a premature encounter.[12]

And so from the end of October the army's discipline became especially severe. Three men were flogged as deserters, with a thousand lashes apiece, the sentries were ordered not to bandy words with passersby, and Gage told his officers to liaise with Boston's magistrates to ensure that they arrested any soldiers caught brawling in the streets. From November 14 he imposed a strict curfew on his camp, with no redcoat allowed outside it after eight at night.

With work nearly finished to fortify the Boston Neck, and temporary barracks rising on the Common, despite a campaign of obstruction by the citizens, the general stepped up the training of his battalions. On every fine day, they practiced firing independently or by platoon. The infantry had to learn to turn and wheel "with the utmost rapidity," said their commander in chief. They were drilled in loading their muskets quickly, with the hammers hardened to prevent misfire.[13]

At the end of November, General Gage drew up an order of battle for the engagement that he knew was bound to come. Ten regiments—more had arrived, as well as ammunition from New York—divided into three brigades, amounting to nearly four thousand men: that was all he had at his disposal. Their winter would be hard, soldiers and their families living in huts short of firewood, with dysentery and smallpox taking many victims. Around them the town of Boston was as hostile as ever. But on the other side of the ocean the months of delay and hesitation were at last about to end.

While the Americans had begun the revolution, the British were ready to start the war. In the first week of January, Lord North received the necessary confirmation that John Hancock and his comrades had set up an illegal government. It left the British with no choice. Like the Scottish Jacobites of old, the rebels in New England could expect no mercy and no quarter.

Chapter Sixteen

THE FATAL DISPATCH

An account is come of the Bostonians having voted an army of 16,000 men, who are to be called minute men, as they are to be ready at a minute's warning.

—HORACE WALPOLE, JANUARY 15, 1775

In London, the old year drew toward its close in a mist of rumor and confusion. With Parliament in recess, the army stuck fast in Boston, and no sign of a new plan from Lord North, speculation filled the vacuum of policy. By the middle of December everyone knew the outcome of the Continental Congress, with the text of the Association reprinted many times in Fleet Street. What would the cabinet do in response? Did the ministers view the boycott as another act of treason, or did they see it merely as a gesture or a bluff? As yet it was impossible to say. The government gave mixed signals and left the public to guess whether it intended to fight or to negotiate.

As always the British took refuge in laughter, in the worst possible taste. With the party at the Oaks still so fresh a memory, mistletoe and fauns were all the rage that winter. At Covent Garden, in the presence of the king, the company staged a pantomime, *The Druids*, with dances, masques, "elegant transparencies," and a famous comic in the role of Harlequin. At the climax of the show, he tormented Pantaloon with what the newspapers called "an American suit of tar and feathers." George III, the critics said, "seemed much disconcerted." Elsewhere the rumor mill ground on with its usual combination of the true and the false.[1]

For this we can partly blame Lord North, who did something so apparently bizarre that it was bound to make men and women scratch their heads. On December 16, a few days before the vacation, the ministers came to the Commons with the budget for the forces. Despite the turmoil in America, they proposed to increase the army in the colonies by only four hundred men. The navy would actually shrink, with four thousand fewer sailors in home waters.

This was hardly the sign of a cabinet bent on war, and yet its language and the king's had seemed to point in that direction. Up stood the prickly Scotsman George Johnstone, the old assailant against the Tea Act, to expand upon the paradox that seemed to be so obvious. Opposed to any measures to coerce the colonies, Governor Johnstone had voted against them the previous spring. Given the stance the cabinet had taken toward America, "nothing but the sword can now decide the contest," he said. And yet, he went on, the navy was about to be depleted, leaving Great Britain exposed if the French picked this awkward moment to attack.[2]

In fact this was highly unlikely, since Louis XVI had his own afflictions to endure. It was because of this that Lord North had felt able to save money. In the hope of repairing his weak finances, the new king had appointed a *philosophe*, Anne-Robert-Jacques Turgot, to act as controller general. An ardent free marketeer, Turgot hoped to revitalize the French economy by doing away with old regulations that controlled the price of grain. Here was another bold idea whose timing was inept. In France, the series of bad harvests had already caused hardship even more severe than in England, and the reforms came into force in September 1774 at just the moment when the heavy rains made another poor crop inevitable. As the price of a loaf soared again, riots spread across the north of France and reached the very gates of Versailles.

The *guerre des farines*—the "flour war"—continued for nine months, closely watched from London by Lord Rochford. Seeing France in turmoil, the British could relax about the threat to India, and they saw no danger that their old enemy would intervene to help the Americans. And so the cabinet cut the military budget. Its spending plans easily passed through the Commons, thanks to Lord North's huge majority, but the decision was damaging strategically. With the fleet reduced in size, it would now become impossible for the government to change its mind and do what Lord Barrington had proposed: withdraw the army from New England and rely on the navy to make the colonies see sense.

As Christmas drew near with the mind of the cabinet still so hard to read, many different stories flowed around the capital. Was General Gage about to be recalled? Would he be replaced by some new soldier more skillful and more brave? By the fourth week in December, this was what many thought likely. Just before Parliament rose, Edmund Burke joined the chorus against him: Gage, he said, was "both besieger and besieged" and his strategy absurd. His dismissal was imminent, the papers claimed, in sly little articles following reports about the efforts Boston had made to frustrate his fortification of the Neck.

It was even said that North himself was about to fall from office. He would be superseded by a ministry led by Gower and Hillsborough, who would take the steps required to end the crisis. Since the king still seemed so loyal to Lord North, this idea was surely absurd. And yet during the Christmas break this story went the rounds as well, from sources so apparently reliable that Arthur Lee sent it home to Virginia. And what about that old friend of America's, Lord Chatham? It was rumored that he would soon rise from his sickbed to act as the broker of some new settlement with the colonies. Because Chatham's parliamentary following was small and erratic, nothing of the kind was even remotely likely, but somehow—doubtless from the noble lord—talk of such a great event leaked into the public domain, with the newspapers awaiting a decisive speech when the lawmakers gathered again in January. Indeed, Benjamin Franklin for one believed that only Chatham, as the sole British statesman whose word Americans would trust, could prevent catastrophe. The previous August the two men had met to share ideas. As the months went by, they kept in touch, while in deep midwinter Chatham also spoke to Arthur Lee.[3]

Most probably, Lord Chatham was simply maneuvering. It seems likely that he merely wished to stake out his ground again as a critic of Lord North so that much later, if disaster struck and a war went badly wrong, he could step forward as the only person who could either bring the Americans to the table or crush them militarily. If this is what he hoped for, it was equally ridiculous. However well he had led the nation to victory during the Seven Years' War, Chatham's arrogance and selfishness in peacetime had alienated almost every mainstream politician in Great Britain. But he had many friends in the press, and he carried weight across the ocean. If he rose to the occasion, his eloquence might gravely undermine the government, even if he could not topple it from power. Lord Chatham was one of two political opponents whom the cabinet could not ignore. The other was Benjamin Franklin.

If Great Britain were ever to negotiate with the Continental Congress, the ministers would have to begin with the American. Despite the loathing he aroused in Whitehall, they had no one else to speak to. And indeed on December 23 the stock market rose sharply on a story that Franklin and

Lord North had reached a deal to keep the peace. The story was another wild exaggeration, but the market has a way of sniffing out things politicians prefer to keep secret. In fact, at the end of November, Franklin had received two separate approaches from well-connected people who suggested that the government might be willing to talk about a compromise. In response, he opened a new dialogue with Lord Dartmouth that continued fitfully for three months. The talks had not the slightest chance of success.

The more serious of the two approaches came from a pair of Quakers, David Barclay and John Fothergill, whose motives were clearly sincere: they wanted to prevent a war. A prosperous merchant, Barclay came from the family that gave the modern bank its name. Friendly with the Wilkesites and with businessmen who dealt with the West Indies, he worked hand in hand with Fothergill, a physician who acted as family doctor not only to the Dartmouths but also to Franklin. At the end of November, Fothergill and Barclay contacted Franklin with a hint that the colonial secretary might be open to discussion.

For the obvious reason—the American remained persona non grata for the cabinet—any exchanges, however tentative, would have to be kept secret and undertaken at arm's length. With that understood, Franklin overcame his skepticism, and talks began. To this day their significance remains obscure. The British kept no official record that any discussions had taken place, leaving Franklin's papers and a few rough notes by Lord Dartmouth as almost the only source of information about them. It may be that Barclay and Fothergill acted on their own initiative, reaching out to both sides in the hope that they might find some common ground. Another possibility is this: that Lord Dartmouth, dreading the thought of bloodshed, saw this as one last avenue that he must explore, and so the two Quakers acted at his instigation. This seems just as likely. Given his Christian beliefs, Dartmouth could never forget Saint Matthew and the duty placed on him to make peace. But neither could he waive his other obligation: to uphold the law that kept the sinner from committing evil in the fields of Massachusetts or the alleyways of Covent Garden.

And so in early December he entered the talks with Franklin, perhaps unsure of what he wanted to achieve. A divided soul, lost between charity and rigor, Lord Dartmouth could only try to do his best. One great question had to be answered first. What *did* the Americans want? How little, or how much, would they require to satisfy their urge for liberty? Fothergill and Barclay asked Franklin to put the colonial case. By December 6, the American had drawn up a paper setting out some terms. Cogent and detailed, it carried the title "Hints for Conversation." In seventeen numbered paragraphs, Franklin outlined a plan to preserve "a durable union" between the mother country and America. Boston would pay for what it had destroyed, and Britain would repeal the tax on tea: a fair exchange, he thought.

Indeed, his paper contained many sensible ideas, but as so often with Benjamin Franklin they were also too far ahead of their time. For example, he suggested a modest tax to help finance the army and the navy, to be levied in America in time of war with France or Spain. The amount would be linked to the land tax the British paid themselves, adjusted to allow for America's smaller population. In principle, this might have done the trick; indeed, in 1800 when they negotiated the terms of their union with Ireland, the British devised a similar arrangement, apportioning each nation's taxes according to a formula based on their population and economic resources.[4]

But in the 1770s Franklin's ideas still seemed far too extreme. In particular, he proposed three conditions to which Lord Dartmouth could never agree. No redcoats in the colonies, unless each colony gave permission? The British could never say yes to that. Franklin also demanded the repeal of the Quebec Act and the new laws for the government of Massachusetts. This was unacceptable as well. Most provocatively, Franklin wound up his paper with a bald rejection of the empire's right to rule. His seventeenth item was this: "All powers of internal legislation in the colonies to be disclaimed by parliament."

Perhaps this merely represented an opening gambit in a process of give-and-take, but Franklin's paper offered Dartmouth very little to work with. He could never sell these ideas to his colleagues or to George III, who had already set his mind against any concessions. Even so, the talks continued into the new year of 1775, with Dartmouth still listening. And while Franklin went on meeting Fothergill and Barclay, the American held separate conversations with an admiral in the Royal Navy who also believed that war could be avoided. These meetings began in the following way.

At about the same time that the two Quakers approached him, Franklin received an invitation to play chess with an attractive widow of fifty or so called Mrs. Caroline Howe, whose younger brothers had both served courageously in the armed forces. A clever, stylish woman, with a flair for mathematics and intrigue, Mrs. Howe met Franklin twice across the chessboard. During their second encounter, which took place on December 4, she steered the conversation toward Great Britain's quarrel with the colonies. "I hope we are not to have a civil war," the lady remarked. "They should kiss and be friends, says I." Expert in flattery as well as algebra, she suggested that Franklin was the ideal diplomat to settle the dispute. He thanked her kindly and went on his way for another session that evening with Fothergill and Barclay.

Three weeks later, on Christmas Day, Franklin called on Mrs. Howe. By now the press had run the story that he had struck a deal with Lord North. It was ridiculous of course—both Franklin and Mrs. Howe knew that—but seizing the moment, she suggested that he speak to her brother Rear Admiral Richard Howe, who might have his own useful contacts in the government. A brilliant commander who had led daring raids on the coast of France during the Seven Years' War, he was still only forty-eight, and likely to achieve the highest rank in any future conflict. Warily, Franklin agreed to a meeting: whereupon the admiral appeared through the door, and another intermittent round of talks began. Under cover of more games of chess, they continued until the middle of February, with Richard Howe offering his services as an intermediary with the cabinet.

But the admiral's intervention was just as hopeless as that of the Quakers. On reading Franklin's seventeen terms for a settlement, Howe "lamented," the American recalled, "that my propositions were not such as probably could be accepted." By now no small group of human beings in the metropolis, however well-intentioned, could stand in the way of what was about to happen. Too much had already occurred. In America, the people were already up in arms; and after all that they had said about submission by the colonies, the king and his cabinet dare not yield an inch.

Perhaps only two politicians in London truly understood how dire the situation had become. One was Charles Lennox, the indomitable Duke of Richmond, but even among his own Whig allies he was often regarded as too strange and too Frenchified to be listened to. The other was again Lord Barrington in the War Office. From his experience doing battle with the French, he knew just how difficult it would be to feed and supply an army in America against the will of the people who lived there. On Christmas Eve, Barrington wrote another memorandum calling for retreat from Massachusetts.

On land the British simply could not win. The province was too large, he told Lord Dartmouth, and too full of farmers used to bearing arms. Even if it were conquered, the cost would be appalling, involving what Barrington called "the horrors and bloodshed of civil war," followed by the burden of a long occupation. He agreed that Boston deserved to be punished, but not at such a price. Pull the army back to Canada, said

Barrington: then send more ships to patrol the coast until the Americans began to succumb and Britain could offer honorable terms with which both countries could be content.[5]

His argument, so strongly made, fell on deaf ears. A week later the schooner *St. Lawrence* arrived in England swiftly followed by a merchant vessel, the *Minerva* from Salem, and then a military transport, the *Charming Nancy*. After the snow and the storms of November, the skies had cleared to bring an unexpectedly mild winter on both sides of the Atlantic. After leaving Boston as recently as December 16, the *Charming Nancy* sped across the ocean in a mere twenty-four days. Suddenly, after so many long delays, the flow of official news became a torrent. At last the British cabinet need not rely on dispatches alone. All three ships brought passengers who could brief the ministers face-to-face. In the new year of 1775 the decision for war became impossible to avoid.

The News on the *Charming Nancy*

The crucial events at Westminster in January have rarely been explored in detail. Only two British historians have written about them at any length. Understandably, most American scholars focus far more closely on the revolutionary process on their side of the water. And when they do try to analyze the decisions taken by the British, they tend to veer toward one of two extremes. American writers either dismiss Lord North and his colleagues as fools or tyrants, who instinctively resorted to force against the uprising regardless of the blood that would be shed; or they lean too far in the other direction, arguing that the cabinet never seriously intended to begin a war but merely wanted General Gage to frighten the Americans until they ceased to resist authority.

As often, the surviving evidence lies open to more than one interpretation; but examined as a whole, it leads to the following conclusion. Believing that they were taking a calculated risk, North and the cabinet deliberately chose to begin what they thought would be a brief, local war in Massachusetts. In doing so, they allowed themselves to be deceived by the only precedent available, the defeat of the Jacobite insurgency of 1745. Its shadow fell across the table at every meeting the cabinet held. After the battle of Culloden, the Highlands had fallen quiet forever, and this seemed to prove the point that military action could bring about a lasting peace. As always, Alexander Wedderburn made the point with brutal candor. "The people of Scotland were better humoured ever since the rebellion," the solicitor general told Thomas Hutchinson on January 19. Under fire from their opponents and the press, the ministers felt obliged to act as firmly as their forebears had done against Charles Edward Stuart.

Once the government had chosen to use force, there could be no turning back, and this North and his colleagues knew full well. But they expected the fighting to be confined to the hinterland of Boston. They failed to realize that any armed clash in Massachusetts would inevitably raise the rest of the colonies against them too. Despite what they knew about the Continental Congress, they convinced themselves that John Hancock and his comrades spoke only for misguided zealots in New England. This was a terrible error, but again it came about with a fearful inevitability.

In the first week of January, the cabinet ministers received a stream of new evidence that they were staring treason in the face. In sailed the *St. Lawrence,* sending her papers straight up to London, where they reached Lord Dartmouth on the second. They included not only the request from General Gage for an army twenty thousand strong but also confirmation of the votes in Cambridge in late October that had formed a new militia and called for each town to withhold its taxes. The same day, the story appeared in the newspapers, which—as they had with the Tea Party—immediately recognized how grave its implications were.[6]

The affairs of Great Britain were "tumbling to the dogs," said the *Morning Post.* "America resists by force of arms." Delay would be disastrous, the paper cried, by giving the colonial militias time to train and equip. Worst of all, the government had failed to assess the scale of the military task that lay ahead. Soon this became a dominant theme, not only in the press, but among the politicians. For Burke and the opposition in Parliament, it opened a new line of attack against Lord North, for whom the reports were acutely embarrassing.

His own colleagues were exasperated, with Rochford still deeply upset by Dartmouth's lack of initiative, while Gower was apparently feeding the press with more tales of a change of leadership. By now even North was losing patience with Lord Dartmouth, sending him a note calling for new ideas. Under heavy pressure, the colonial secretary gradually abandoned his own hopes of peace. The ships from America brought the first eyewitness account of the uproar the previous summer. It left him with no room for doubt about the nature of the beast unleashed in Massachusetts.

Among her passengers, the *Minerva* carried Jonathan Bliss, a pro-British lawyer from Springfield, a town where his neighbors were especially fiery radicals. When a crowd three thousand strong gathered there in August to close the Hampshire County Court, they had forced Bliss to sign a paper in which he agreed not to take office under the new colonial regime. On January 4, he met Lord Dartmouth and gave him a firsthand description of the troubles in the region. Should the British offer concessions? the minister asked. No, Bliss replied: only the use of force would restore the province to order.[7]

Thomas Hutchinson witnessed the conversation and was struck by what seemed to be the idleness of Dartmouth's most senior aides. He found William Knox and John Pownall lounging at their desks, something he considered very odd, but there was an explanation. The British officials kept Hutchinson at bay, telling him little of what they had in mind. Their plans were far too sensitive to share with someone who talked and wrote so incessantly. The former governor left for a holiday in Bath, while the officials began to swap information with a new urgency.

From the Admiralty, word arrived the next day about the latest dispatch from its officer on the spot. According to Admiral Graves, the rebels intended to attack the army, take Boston by storm, and set it ablaze. Next there came a report from New York, saying that the radicals had gained control of the town and fallen in behind the Continental Congress. And with the newspapers pursuing every lead, the city of London had also begun to stir, placing still more pressure on Lord North.

Until now the business community had remained relatively quiet, but the latest stories from America led to intense activity. On January 3 the West India merchants, alarmed by the threat of a boycott that would ruin the commerce between the sugar islands and the mainland colonies, held an emergency meeting. The following day, John Hancock's friend George Hayley addressed a gathering of three hundred traders who dealt with Virginia and New England. They voted to draw up a petition calling on the government to find a peaceful resolution of the conflict. While petitions from the colonies could be ignored, a protest from the city would require a debate when the House of Commons reassembled. At that moment, or soon afterward, North would need to be ready with a new plan to satisfy his own backbenchers. Meanwhile, the press accused the government of incompetence and inertia. "America will triumph, and see her own independence the distant consequence of British policy," said the *Morning Post*. "Never was Great Britain in a situation so contemptible."

As yet, the political class remained mostly away in the country, where the frosty weather made the ground ideal for hunting, but soon enough London would be full again. In a fortnight's time Queen Charlotte would celebrate her official birthday, with the ball that marked the start of another social season. The day after that—January 19—Parliament was due to reopen, with Lord Chatham likely to reappear. To prepare themselves for the political fray, the cabinet ministers agreed to meet the previous week at Lord Rochford's office in Cleveland Row, facing St. James's Palace. By the time they gathered on January 13, they had received a dispatch from Boston that struck a new note of confidence and resolve.

Written less than a month earlier, the letter arrived on the *Charming Nancy* carried by a senior officer on Gage's staff, Colonel Richard Prescott of the Royal Fusiliers. This was very unusual—the general had never sent a personal envoy before—and not least because Prescott was a highly experienced man in his late forties, a veteran of the war in Germany and soon to be promoted to brigadier. Far from being merely a messenger, Prescott came under orders to meet the cabinet, answer any questions the ministers might have, and give them information too secret to be put in writing. Because no verbatim note survives, we will never know precisely what he told them, but his briefings removed their last lingering doubts about the military option.

The colonel brought a bundle of Boston newspapers containing a new word—"minuteman"—deriving from another act of treason by John

On the left, the office of the senior secretary of state, Lord Rochford, in Cleveland Row, St. James's, where the cabinet met to approve the use of force in New England, from a painting by Paul Sandby. On the right is St. James's Palace. *Crown Copyright: U.K. Government Art Collection*

Hancock. Meeting at Cambridge in December, the congress had told each town in Massachusetts to have its part-time soldiers ready to fight at a minute's notice, with each volunteer carrying a firearm, a bayonet, and thirty rounds. Something of the sort had been discussed in New England before, way back in August, but news of this had not crossed the ocean. Now the term appeared openly in the Boston papers in stories making it plain that the Provincial Congress saw itself as a legitimate government.

The Congress planned to meet again in Cambridge on February 1: a crucial piece of information that gave the cabinet no choice. Any assembly of the kind would be another act of rebellion, which had to be suppressed with whatever forces General Gage had under his command. He could not be given twenty thousand soldiers—time was far too short—but the tone of the general's dispatch suggested that if he acted firmly, the rebels would disperse. Gage's letter was calm and even quite optimistic, conveying the improvement in his morale since the dark days of the summer. It also contained a fateful prediction: that if the British were seen to be resolute, and put what Gage called "a respectable army" in the field, they would be joined by loyal Americans ready to defend the empire.

From what happened next, it is clear that Colonel Prescott said the same thing. The atmosphere became more ominous immediately after his appearance. Thomas Hutchinson was still away on holiday when he heard that the colonel was in London and that nine letters from America were awaiting his return. Filled with a new sense of alarm, he hurried back from Bristol. En route, he suffered a strange hallucination—"that part of my body was gone, which I now felt no more affection for, than if it had been the tooth of a stranger"—whose symbolism could not be more clear. America was being lost, like an amputated limb.

Meanwhile, another colonial visitor to London had noticed the same change in the political weather. It was of all people Josiah Quincy Jr., the radical lawyer from Boston, who had come to England on a bizarre personal mission to make peace. After landing in late November, he met Dartmouth and then Lord North, who listened patiently and then, when he had gone, dismissed him as a troublemaker. But Quincy still went on hoping for the best until suddenly, on the morning of January 13, he discovered that the crisis was irreparable. Impressed by the merchants' meetings in the city, up to that moment Quincy had convinced himself that public opinion had swung behind the American cause. But then he received a visit from Thomas Pownall, the brother of Lord Dartmouth's closest aide. "You will have terrible news from Boston soon," Thomas Pownall said. "The matter is decided."[8]

He would not tell Quincy exactly *what* decision had been made, but Pownall was correct. The colonel's briefings and the news carried by the *Charming Nancy* had put an end to hesitation. At eight o'clock that evening, the cabinet ministers assembled at Cleveland Row to draw up a new and vigorous policy to stamp out the insurgency. First, Parliament would be asked to declare that Massachusetts was in rebellion; and then, to reinforce General Gage, the cabinet would send three more regiments to Boston, two of foot and one of light dragoons, while Admiral Graves would be given more ships and marines. The cabinet also began to formulate a plan for a commercial embargo of its own, a retaliatory ban on American trade by sea, to be imposed on every colony that had signed the Association. Once again Lord Dartmouth suggested sending peace commissioners to negotiate with the Continental Congress. This idea was put aside, as something that would have to wait until after Massachusetts had surrendered to royal authority.

The Queen's Palace, where Colonel Prescott briefed the king about the situation in Boston, as it was in 1775 before the rebuilding that transformed it into Buckingham Palace, from a painting by Joseph Collyer.

On Saturday, January 14, Colonel Prescott went to see the king. Again we have no record of exactly what was said, but according to Hutchinson the news the colonel brought had "fixed those who were wavering." With every new dispatch the situation seemed to grow worse. The same day the

Admiralty circulated a report from Rhode Island, where the people of Providence had seized a battery of cannon belonging to the Crown. By Sunday night the talk of minutemen was all over London, reaching the ears of the diarist Horace Walpole. The press also knew the outcome of the cabinet's deliberations.[9]

The ministers convened again on Monday evening. Only two days were left before Queen Charlotte's ball, the city was filling fast, and, said the *Morning Post*, "the milliners of the West End were never more hurried." Across the capital the crisis in America had drowned out every other topic for conversation, as a pamphlet war broke out in which opposing writers put the case for appeasement or for severity. While the government looked for help from Thurlow's friend, Dr. Johnson, who began to pen his anti-American polemic, *Taxation No Tyranny*, Burke reprinted his finest speech from the previous year. Bookstores began to sell a pocket atlas of the colonies, with maps for readers to follow the campaign Gage was about to wage.

In this feverish atmosphere the cabinet assembled on January 16, with two urgent matters on its agenda: to decide what North should say to Parliament and to draw up new orders for the general. For weeks the navy had kept a sloop, the *Falcon*, standing by at Spithead to sail to Boston with cash for the army—another £10,000—and with whatever instructions the cabinet might issue. If Gage were to have his orders in time for an encounter in the spring with the Massachusetts militia, the *Falcon* would have to sail without delay. And so, at the meeting on the sixteenth, Lord North began to add the last element his new American policy required.

It came to be known as the Conciliatory Proposition. While its name suggests that Lord North wished to be amicable toward the colonies, the plan he outlined really had two objectives, only one of which was peaceful. Revisiting the problem of taxation, North reaffirmed the principle that the colonies had to contribute to the costs of empire. The army and the navy had to be financed, and so did the royal bureaucracy in America, tiny though it was. Great Britain would ask every colony to make a fixed annual grant to the Crown. In exchange, Parliament would surrender its right to levy any more taxes in each colony that agreed to do so.

This would provide, Lord North believed, the basis for a new and lasting settlement, but that was not his only motive. The Conciliatory Proposition was also a maneuver aimed at isolating New England and making it easier to reconquer. Far from replacing the military option, it would stand alongside it, as a means of discouraging the other colonies from rallying to defend Massachusetts. Crucially, however, the plan assumed that the other colonies contained a moderate majority who would abandon the defiant pose struck in Philadelphia; and for this assumption Lord North had not a shred of evidence.[10]

In any case, the plan was still vague and sketchy, the details would take a month or so to finalize, and some of his colleagues were skeptical. A more pressing matter had to be dealt with at once. It was at this meeting on the sixteenth that the cabinet finally crossed the Rubicon and formally decided to end the insurgency by force. This must be so, because at the end of that week Lord Suffolk said as much in debate in the House of Lords. Queen Charlotte's birthday ball came and went, with the usual ringing of bells and a display of fireworks at the French embassy. On Thursday, Parliament reopened, and at last Lord Chatham made his speech, so well trailed in the press. Britain should withdraw its troops from Boston, where Gage led only what he called "an army of impotence and contempt." On January 20 his motion went down to defeat by seventy-seven votes to eighteen. But in reply to Chatham, Lord Suffolk confirmed what everyone already suspected: he avowed, said a reporter, "the ministerial resolution of enforcing obedience by arms."

On the same day the cabinet asked the lawyers for a written opinion that Massachusetts had risen in revolt. Lord Dartmouth gave Thurlow and Wedderburn the *Boston Gazette* with its stories about the minutemen and the votes taken at Cambridge in October. Then he settled down to wait in a mood that swung back and forth between extremes. To Dartmouth's delight his wife, a woman now in her early forties, had recently given birth to a baby girl, while his friend the poet William Cowper was at last recovering from years of insanity. But while Dartmouth rejoiced in both happy events, the crisis in America left him exhausted and distraught. It fell to him to draft the new orders for the general; but as he did so, he found himself besieged by well-wishers and cranks who thrust upon him long letters of advice.

Somebody calling himself "ZYX" wrote four times, assuring him that all the talk of rebellion was nonsense: bar the lunatics in Boston, Americans remained devoted to the Crown, and resistance was about to fizzle out. "Depend upon it, sir," he told Lord Dartmouth, "that nothing less than a miracle could make the New Englanders the warlike people they pretend to be." Another writer took the opposite view, urging the government to occupy Long Island and make it an armed camp from which the British could put down the insurrection and allow loyal merchants to defy the colonial boycott. Self-proclaimed experts gave Dartmouth absurd suggestions. A ranting letter arrived from one of Scotland's richest men,

Richard Oswald, the owner of thousands of slaves, telling him to send an envoy to Virginia. The problems in New England were the work, he said, of "a confederacy of smugglers, narrow-minded bigots," but in the South the planters were still friendly. Win over what he called "the best families" with an offer of a monopoly over trade to the West Indies, and they would stop what he called "the pestilential blasts from the North." John Pownall was inclined to agree; but although there was a time when tactics such as these might have worked, that time had long since passed.[11]

And so Lord Dartmouth began to write his new instructions for General Gage. On January 26 the press ran the story that a dispatch was being prepared, and soon enough they guessed its contents. Marked "secret" and dated on the twenty-seventh, the letter can fairly be called the fatal dispatch. When it arrived in America in April, it sent the army marching out of Boston and up the road to Lexington and Concord.

This letter has received much less scrutiny than it deserves. Sometimes historians fail to mention it at all, and when they do they offer widely differing interpretations of its significance. Occasionally, they argue that General Gage received it reluctantly and would have preferred to sit out the spring secure behind his fortifications. It has also been suggested that Dartmouth wrote the dispatch dishonestly, filling it with caveats intended to make Gage bear the blame if military action ended in disaster. Another school of thought says that by the time the letter reached Boston, the cabinet ministers had already changed their minds in favor of a new attempt at reconciliation.

By way of evidence, all we have to go on are the words written or spoken at the time; and in this case they survive in their thousands. We have not only the text of the letter—which is unambiguous—but also debates in Parliament, diaries, private correspondence, and official papers that set out the political context in which the fatal dispatch was composed. The reality is this: the British—both General Gage and the politicians—had made a conscious choice to put down the rebellion by force in the spring, by breaking up the next session of the Provincial Congress. Gage had requested orders permitting him to take the field, sending Prescott as his emissary, and the cabinet ministers responded as he wished.

They knew—Lord Dartmouth said as much—that direct action against the Provincial Congress might be regarded as what he called "a signal for hostilities"; but if a civil war was looming in New England, then it was better to begin it now, before the rebels were fully armed, trained, and organized. All the time, the British were keeping close watch on the Americans trying to buy weapons and gunpowder in Holland.

Dartmouth's dispatch began by rapping the general's knuckles. Long before, when he sent word on the *Scarborough* about the events of late August, Gage had failed to show that they amounted to more than merely local incidents of riot. But that was history and the news received in early January had cast everything in a fresh light. There had been "proceedings"—by which Lord Dartmouth meant the votes at Cambridge—that amounted to outright rebellion.

"The king's dignity, & the honour and safety of the Empire, require," he wrote, "that, in such a situation, force should be repelled by force." Nothing could be clearer. If the rebels dispersed or surrendered, all well and good—the government hoped that they would—but if not, they had to be fought. And so Gage would be sent the regiments the British could spare. For the cavalry, the general was told to find two hundred horses as remounts.

With these reinforcements, Gage could take "a more active & determined part," Lord Dartmouth wrote. Not only in Massachusetts, but also in Rhode Island and Connecticut if necessary: Dartmouth said that too. He could not give Gage all his twenty thousand men, but then why should he? For the moment, the militia remained "a rude rabble," the cabinet believed. If it were hit soon and hard, then no larger army would be required. As for the Continental Congress and its boycott of trade, that challenge would be left to the navy, which would protect any loyal ships that ignored the ban. Gage was told to arrest the leaders of the Provincial Congress if and when it met again. They should be tried for treason, or if that proved impossible, they could be held without trial. As governor, Gage had the power to declare martial law. Of course Dartmouth gave the general the discretion to decide exactly how to execute his orders, since only the commander in the field could draw up a precise plan of action. But in every other respect, the dispatch was explicit, leaving not the slightest room for hesitation: the army must restore the colony to order.

Hundreds of letters survive from Lord Dartmouth, both private and official. Very few of them resemble this one. Mostly inclined to leave room for doubt where worldly matters were concerned, and always aware of the frailty of the human soul—whether the souls were those of poets, whores, or politicians—Dartmouth rarely wrote in terms so categorical. But his Christian faith had always been a compound of different elements, and on this occasion, its authoritarian side came to the fore. Coupled with his loyalty to his colleagues, it triumphed over his compassion.

But while Lord Dartmouth had to draft the letter, there remained a political battle to be waged before it could be sent. Before the dispatch could sail on the *Falcon*, Parliament had to agree that a state of rebellion existed in Massachusetts. The lawyers had yet to give their view in writing; but when they did, North would be ready to face the House of Commons.

The Final Act

In the closing days of January, as though the nation were staging a scene from *King Lear*, the wind began to rise and a storm swept in from the west. The tide came surging up beneath the fleet at Portsmouth, flooding the streets of the town, while in London chimneys fell on passersby. The Thames rose as well, so that the water appeared to steam as if it were boiling. To mark the anniversary on January 30 of the execution of King Charles I, Bishop Brownlow North gave a platitudinous sermon in Westminster Abbey on the evils of political discord. The following day his half brother read another of the endless letters about turmoil in America.

At a different place called Portsmouth, this time in New Hampshire, the rebels had struck again, under the leadership of Paul Revere, seizing a fort and a magazine full of gunpowder. On December 14, under the cover of falling snow, four hundred militiamen had come up the river and brushed aside the six redcoats on guard. Hauling down the British flag, they hid the powder safely miles inland. In the eyes of the king, this insult to the colors was the most outrageous incident of all, but each day brought forth some wretched new development. A belated dispatch even arrived from Maryland, from which so little had been heard, warning that radicals were stockpiling arms in that colony as well.

By now, many Londoners were convinced that a war had already commenced. The mood of Parliament became more somber but also more determined, with every sign that Lord North would win its support for the firmest measures of retribution. From out of the shadows, people emerged whose careers might benefit from an escalation of the crisis. The language of debate became ever harsher and more violent.

The previous year, when Charles Van called for Boston to be destroyed, he had stood out as a lonely extremist. But now he found new allies among more distinguished politicians with years of military service behind them. They included George Sackville Germain, who would, at the end of 1775, replace Lord Dartmouth as colonial secretary. In 1746, during the purge of the Highland clans after Culloden, Germain had led a regiment of foot, burning his way across the glens behind Ben Nevis, where his soldiers dealt in rape and murder. On January 26, as Parliament voted down the petition from the London merchants, he intervened, speaking up for the Coercive

Acts, and calling for their enforcement with "a Roman severity." A close friend of Wedderburn's, Germain evidently knew the contents of the legal opinion on its way from the Scottish lawyer and from Thurlow.[12]

Before it arrived, first the government had another obstacle to clear: Lord Chatham again, ready to reveal his own proposals for pacifying America. On February 1, after some discussions with Benjamin Franklin, whose own secret talks with Whitehall had all but broken down completely, Chatham took his plan to the House of Lords. He called on Parliament to recognize the Continental Congress, preserve the old colonial charters, and renounce the use of force. The peers chose not to debate his proposals.

And then, on February 2, with the newspapers still full of war, and with more floods and storms across the south of England, the attorney general and his deputy came back with their advice. Yes, said Thurlow and Wedderburn, the Provincial Congress had committed treason. At last Lord North had everything he needed. At a little after 4:00 p.m., with the chamber overflowing and the lobby and the corridor outside crammed with spectators, he rose to address the Commons, speaking for two hours.

The quarrel had begun with a protest against taxation, and so North gave the house the relevant figures. How much tax did the British pay to the Treasury? Twenty-five shillings per annum, per head. And the Americans? Just sixpence each. The cabinet had already placed before the house another great bundle of papers, including the letters from General Gage, and Lord North went through them, painting a picture of willful treachery in Massachusetts and then setting out the government's position. The army would be reinforced, and a new law would be passed to ban New England from any overseas trade and from the fishing grounds of Newfoundland. He would also ask the house to send an address to the king, declaring that the colony was in revolt. Soon afterward Wedderburn spoke, calling the rebels "an enemy in the bowels of the kingdom."

It was only the first of three debates, two in the Commons and one in the Lords, spread over a week while the *Falcon* strained at its anchor at Spithead. Although they lacked the eloquence seen the previous year, even so these were sessions of high drama, for which perhaps only one equivalent exists: the great parliamentary debate on the Munich Agreement in October 1938, when the question at issue was also one of war or peace. Although Lord North was bound to win the vote, just as Neville Chamberlain was sure to be victorious, the debate itself was far from one-sided. More than a hundred members of the Commons went through the lobby to vote against the government. They included the Rockinghams of course, the Wilkesites, and the friends of Chatham, but also dozens of independents fearful of the cost of war or the damage it would inflict on the economy, or opposed to the principles on which it would be fought.

Whether inside Parliament or on the streets, no one could doubt the gravity of what Lord North was proposing. The nation was plunging, said Edmund Burke, toward "a dreadful abyss." In poor health, he failed to shine at the first encounter: but with unaccustomed courage his fellow Rockinghams picked up the baton. In the words of Lord John Cavendish, the address to the king would constitute "a declaration of civil war," since it would leave General Gage no choice but to march against the rebels. With the phrase reechoing around the capital, Franklin came hurrying down to the Commons. There he was seen in the lobby, in a state close to desperation, trying in vain to gain admittance to the chamber.

Among the officials in Whitehall, these were days of high anxiety, not because they feared the loss of the debates, but because, if they won, they would have to find more troops and warships and then piece together a new order in the colonies after whatever transpired in Boston. Thomas Hutchinson spent an hour with John Pownall, whom he found a deeply worried man, poring over the history of Virginia, looking for precedents for dealing with the aftermath of a rebellion. At the Treasury another problem arose: the urgent need to find more money for the army as the cost of food and stores rose sharply in America.

Only George III seemed to be calm. Appalled by the theft of powder in New Hampshire—he urged Lord North to put this affront center stage—the king would hear no talk of compromise. In what he called "every candid and rational mind," the steps his cabinet was taking would be thought entirely right and proper. With this moral support from his sovereign, North won the two long debates in the Commons, on February 2 and 6, with three separate votes all taken after midnight. His majority varied slightly in each one, but even his narrowest victory saw him succeed by 288 to 106.[13]

For the opposition, the problem had been simply this: that in the debates in the spring and summer of 1774, the great question of British supremacy had already been discussed at great length and apparently settled for good. Unequivocally, Parliament had decided in favor of its right to make laws for America. How could it retreat now, when Americans challenged that right by force of arms? This left the opposition with only two alternatives. On the one hand, it might follow Lord Chatham—as John Wilkes did, branding Lord North a man "of injustice and cruelty"—and opt for a complete reversal of British policy. But this was something the Rockinghams simply could not do. For them it was out of the question, since they had drawn up the Declaratory Act and passed it into law nine years earlier.

On the other hand, they might argue that the general was to blame for the unrest. They could dispute his dispatches from the front and claim that no rebellion had actually occurred. The point was clearly made by George Johnstone on February 6: "It appears that General Gage has regularly deceived the administration. No event has turned out as he foretold." If, said Johnstone, the colonies were all now deeply disaffected, it was because they were victims, not rebels. If they were up in arms, Great Britain had to take the blame. The use of force would be wicked and doomed to fail.

The debates reached their climax in the House of Lords on February 7, with five hours of argument dominated by the Duke of Richmond. He made the same case as George Johnstone, added his own dire prediction of a war with France, and tried one last tactic, a personal attack on the bishops who sat in the chamber. Their white sleeves, he said, would be stained with American blood. Then he too went down to defeat. By ninety votes to twenty-four, the Lords declared that a rebellion had begun.

With that, the government had almost everything it needed. Lord North had still to produce his bill to ban New England from maritime trade, and soon he would also have to announce his Conciliatory Proposition. While he took the first bill to Parliament immediately, the latter could wait a week or so. In the meantime, the cabinet drifted along in a strange, unsettled state of mind, determined but also despondent. North sank into another fit of melancholy—he seemed "overborne with the weight of affairs," said Thomas Hutchinson—while Dartmouth's spirits also declined. While every new letter from America served to justify their actions, each story made the task ahead of them appear more daunting.

On February 10 a dispatch arrived at last from Lord Dunmore in Williamsburg. It was as bleak as it could be. Keen to defend his conduct in taking off to chastise the Shawnee, he wrote at enormous length. On his return to the provincial capital, he had found every county angry and disobedient, openly arming an independent militia. Blockade the Chesapeake, said the governor: no other option remained. And so early in March, North widened the scope of his bill to bar New England from overseas trade to encompass five more colonies. They would include Virginia and Maryland.[14]

Little remains to be said. There could be no turning back, and the cabi-

George III driving Britain over the wreckage of the constitution
and toward a chasm, while America burns in the distance and Lord
Sandwich bribes the public with a bag of cash, from the *Westminster
Magazine*, May 1775, before news arrived of the fighting at Lexington
and Concord. *Library of Congress*

net made no attempt to do so.* On February 20, North went to Parliament to present his conciliatory bill proposing a new deal for the taxation
of the colonies. Even though it was clearly intended to improve British
chances of success against New England, he found the Commons in no
mood for concessions to America. The house voted to approve the bill,
but only after backbench protests by members calling for still more punitive measures against the colonists.

Everything pointed to war; the papers were convinced of it, and the
government had decided to stiffen the resolve of General Gage by sending
out three generals to help him: William Howe, Henry Clinton, and John
Burgoyne. And then, on February 26, off the coast of Holland the naval
cutter *Speedwell* finally obtained the proof that Dutch and American ships
were leaving Amsterdam filled with gunpowder for the rebels. Her commander sent a message straight to Lord Suffolk.

Nine days later Benjamin Franklin drew a line beneath his confidential
talks with Fothergill, Barclay, and the Howes. Despite the memory of his

---

* Far from having any second thoughts, Lord Dartmouth sent Gage another four dispatches, the last dated April 15, reiterating the instructions from January 27.

shameful treatment at the Cockpit, Franklin had clung on and on, hoping for a change of heart in Whitehall. When the Conciliatory Proposition was published, it became obvious that further discussion would be futile. After one last conversation with Mrs. Howe, he began to pack his bags. On March 20, the cleverest man in England left for home. Quincy had already set sail, only to die at sea before he reached America.[15]

Meanwhile, the fatal dispatch from Lord Dartmouth was also crossing the ocean, but five weeks later than the government intended. Time and again as the war approached, the weather had played its influential part, sometimes accelerating the rhythm of events and sometimes slowing them down and creating a long hiatus. Early in February, the sloop *Falcon* had been entrusted with the dispatch and the opinion from the lawyers that Massachusetts was in rebellion. After the storms of late January, a gale had continued to blow up the English Channel from the west, leaving the *Falcon* trapped in the shallows off the Isle of Wight. She made it into the open sea on February 14, struggled and had to come back, and then she tried again, inching her way for weeks toward Land's End.

Not until the middle of March did the wind swing around to come from the east, allowing the *Falcon* to enter the Atlantic. Given the importance of the papers she carried, Dartmouth had made copies and placed them on another naval sloop, the *Nautilus*, which had fought the same battle with the elements. With the weather now firmly on their side, the two ships ran an ocean race to Massachusetts, with the *Nautilus* emerging as the victor. She sighted the tip of Cape Cod on April 14. At noon two days later, with a breeze blowing off the land, she came into Boston, where she saw the naval squadron and the flag of Admiral Graves. The dispatches had already gone ashore, carried by another boat while the *Nautilus* waited for a pilot.[16]

Every detail of the violence that followed has been chronicled at length, with all the sad accoutrements of slaughter and long debates about which side fired first and who showed greater efficiency in the violation of the sixth commandment. In the preceding weeks General Gage had made forays outside the town, gathered what intelligence he could, and come to the conclusion that Concord was the place to aim for. There, he believed, the rebels had concealed a cache of arms. Nearby his troops might also find Samuel Adams and John Hancock. Having first made the error of occupying Boston, he blundered again by trying to break out of it.

Equipped with orders that obliged him to take the offensive, General Gage sent his soldiers out on the highway that led through Lexington. On April 19 they met the rebels, and somebody pulled a trigger. Knowing far too little about the terrain, and without a screen of cavalry ahead of them—the light dragoons had yet to arrive—the British marched on to Concord regardless. They entered a trap laid by a topography that Gage had failed to survey in full. On they went, into the bend of a river that they could not ford, with hills to their right above the road providing ample cover for an enemy all too ready for a skirmish. Down through the woods came the militia, in numbers and at a speed that Gage did not anticipate. The battle followed at Concord Bridge, small but bloody, and then came a still more bloody retreat to Boston. And so the war began. At the end of May the news would reach England, where no one could honestly claim to be surprised, and yet they were, and horrified as well.

The war had been long in the making, the product of an empire and a system deeply flawed, the work of ignorance and prejudice and of men well-meaning but the prisoners of ideas that were obsolete and empty. "You cannot force a form of government upon a people," the Duke of Richmond had said in the House of Lords on January 20, but although the radical duke would be proved right, it would take long years of fighting before the nation could admit that this was so. Charles Lennox had spoken for his country; but the time had not yet come when England could listen.

THE NOBLE DEAD

Such honours Ilion to her hero paid,
And peaceful slept the mighty Hector's shade.

—ALEXANDER POPE, *The Iliad of Homer*, 1715–20

In search of the resting place of Frederick, Lord North, it is best to go to Wroxton in the autumn, when the rain brings out the beauty of the buildings at their finest. The village sits on a slope at the northern end of that great belt of limestone which, beginning on the coast of Dorset, sweeps up as far as Oxfordshire. The village has a pond, with a duck house on an island, and a sign that urges drivers to slow down and mind the ducks. It has two pubs, selling ales with names like Crazy Ox, but best of all it has the stone from which its cottages are made. As it weathers, tiny particles of iron give the stone a warm, deep color, a tawny yellow or a brown, like toast or butter left too long to simmer in a pan.

The village has a peaceful history in which the name of North takes pride of place. Eight centuries ago, a band of monks came here to build a monastery, which eventually became a Jacobean mansion with a deer park and an obelisk. For nearly three hundred years the Norths lived at Wroxton Abbey. When they died, they were taken to All Saints, the parish church, and the vault beneath the chancel where Lord North lies buried. The church has a tower whose stone turns in the wet to the same rich shade of nutty brown.

The bells still ring on Sundays; a yew tree sheds its needles on the path; and inside the church we find the old familiar things: the pews, the hassocks, and the font. If we know what to look for, we can also find the traces of the system that produced Lord North, with his flaws but also with his finer qualities. In the north aisle of the nave, only two small gray tablets remain from the eighteenth century, with nothing to explain why the names inscribed on them were worthy of commemoration. These were the agents who managed the North estates and collected the rent from his tenants.

Far away beside the Mississippi we encountered, in the fort that fell into the river, a symbol of the British Empire's frailty in America. But the deepest of its weaknesses lay at home in the mother country, in the old regime that had created North and his colleagues. In the church at Wroxton we can see the traces of the system they administered: a system that held rural England in a grip apparently far more secure. It was a system based on hierarchy and servitude, in which power remained the possession of a few, and it rested on the ownership of land. The Norths spoke for half the acres in the village, and their influence spread over all the rest. This is why their agents are remembered in the church.

There is a phrase, coined with his usual flair by Benjamin Disraeli, that perfectly describes the English system of the eighteenth century. The country had what he called "a territorial constitution." It lay embedded in the fabric of the nation, as deeply as the rust that stains the masonry in Oxfordshire. When Lord North led a meeting at the Treasury, he occupied the summit of the edifice of power, but its foundations lay in thousands of parishes like this, each with a local elite whose authority arose from their tenure of the soil.

The Norths were a dynasty of exactly such a kind. Of course the family had to perform the duties that their rank imposed, even when their own resources were slim. Despite the burden of debt they carried, they chose to be benevolent at Wroxton, providing the village with what it had by way of public welfare: the tower of All Saints, for example, which is rather less ancient than it might appear. In the 1740s a gale blew down the medieval tower, and so Lord North's father paid the cost of building the one we see today. There was a village school, with a master: his salary came from the Norths. The family gave the church its silver plate, they mended the roof of the chancel, and when the bill came in each year for the cost of poor relief, they paid the bulk of that as well.

Beneath their supervision, the village was quiet and orderly, but in exchange for their kindness the Norths demanded far more than just the rent. They expected obedience as well, in everything to do with God or politics. On another wall inside the church there hangs a list of Wroxton's clergy down the ages. Both here and nearby at Banbury, the Norths chose the vicar—the same man occupied both pulpits—and he served their interests faithfully. In 1774 it was the vicar of All Saints who arranged the reelection of Lord North to Parliament. Meanwhile, Brownlow North sat as bishop of the next diocese, keen to place tame clergymen in every parish.

Since the vicar also served as a magistrate, passing judgment on poachers and petty thieves, the power of the Norths reached into every little corner of their enclave. And while by nature they were easygoing, if they chose to be otherwise they had many ways to be harsh. If you vote against his lordship, said the vicar, expect to be struck off the list of suppliers of beer to the abbey. And whenever a tenancy at Wroxton fell due for renewal, only loyal supporters were encouraged to apply.

All of this was what Disraeli meant by a constitution based on property in land. Every one of Lord North's colleagues in the cabinet had Wroxtons of his own, places where as landlords they could dominate their neighborhood. So did most of their allies on the benches in the Commons and the House of Lords. While the system they administered had a vast superstructure—not only Parliament and the church, but also the army, the navy, and the universities—it could not survive without its rural base, in ten thousand parishes like Wroxton, each with its proprietors. The system could not endure forever, and in time it vanished, although it took another century or more to reach extinction.

While it lasted, the territorial constitution encouraged some men and women to be virtuous in public life. It might compel a politician to pay close attention to his roots and to behave with a nobility worthy of his status. Ambushed by a rioter or a highwayman, he would have to keep his nerve: that was what a gentleman did. As a matter of honor as well as out of ambition, he might feel obliged to work hard at Westminster in the service of what he took to be the national interest. At home in the shires, generosity would feel like a duty, requiring him to keep open house and support every new initiative—a workhouse, a canal, or a turnpike road—to improve the prospects of his area.

These were exactly the virtues that Lord North possessed, but the territorial constitution had its vices too, which far outweighed the benefits it yielded. Hypocrisy and pride were merely the most obvious. The crisis that led to the revolution in America had many causes, and ranking high among them was the narrowness of vision that afflicted North and his colleagues. Its origins lay in the system that a place like Wroxton epitomized. The system set mental boundaries that they could not transcend, raised as they were in a culture where the landscape and the parish church bore everywhere the signs of privilege.

They found the rebels in America unthinkable. Nothing in rural Oxfordshire could prepare Lord North for an encounter, at a distance of three thousand miles, with men like Boston's Thomas Young or his friend Ethan Allen of Vermont. For radicals like Young and Allen, the tenant was the equal of his landlord or even his moral superior; they would never pay a tithe to please a vicar or doff their hat in the street as he walked by; nor would they permit a magistrate to jail a laborer for poaching. An English country parish in the 1770s bore not the slightest resemblance to a township in the colonies. The attitudes that each engendered were profoundly different too.

Perhaps the deepest divide of all was the one that separated Lord North from John Hancock. In the eyes of the king and his ministers, a Bostonian so wealthy had a duty to defend the status quo. Since the empire had enriched his uncle, what right had he to question its authority? At best the man was deeply ungrateful, while at worst he was a traitor, which eventually he proved himself to be, becoming the rebel whom the British most wanted to hang. In reality, John Hancock shared some of the virtues of Lord North; but the citizen who endowed the church on Brattle Square came from a place where, although the wealthy expected to lord it over their neighbors, they had to ask their permission first.

A man with origins like those of Frederick North could never understand an enemy of Hancock's kind. Nor could he be creative in response to the challenge that the colonies threw down. The very qualities George III liked best about him—his devotion to his church, to his king, and to the landed gentry—were precisely those that rendered North incapable of governing America. And so what became of him and his friend and kinsman William Legge?

After the terrible casualties at Bunker Hill in the summer of 1775, Lord Dartmouth lost what appetite he still possessed for public life. The battle had occurred, on the slopes across the water from Boston, because of the error he and Gage had made: their attempt to hold the town as a way to force New England to submit. Deeply grieved by what had come to pass, hoping for peace but unable to achieve it, in November Lord Dartmouth resigned from his post as colonial secretary. The old soldier George Germain supplanted him, finally free to be severely Roman with the rebels. By this time General Gage was coming home at last, as the British prepared to withdraw to New York, which the army should have done so long before.

After that Dartmouth beat his own retreat into a quiet family life of prayers and the countryside. He continued to support the new evangelists inside the Church of England until his death in 1801. By the time he breathed his last, nearly ten years had gone by since Lord North preceded him to the grave, at the age of only sixty. North's career had not collapsed after Bunker Hill. Instead, North had survived, still a superb commander of the House of Commons and still the only man whom the king could really trust.

On he went, through triumph and disaster, but increasingly the latter, until the war was lost and his melancholy had become almost unbearable. The redcoats surrendered at Yorktown, and after a messy crisis in Parliament Lord North had to go as well. A year or so later he returned to office, in a coalition with his old antagonist Charles James Fox. Another crisis intervened, centering on India again, and the coalition lost a general election, defeated in a landslide by the younger William Pitt, Lord Chatham's son. Estranged from George III, Lord North left the government for good.

That was in 1784. His health began to fail, and his weight began to dwindle, suggesting—like his early death—that he suffered from a form

The monument to Lord North by John Flaxman, at All Saints Church, Wroxton, Oxfordshire.

of cancer. Never strong, his eyesight grew weaker with each passing season until he lost his vision altogether. Since his days at Eton and Oxford, North had never forgotten his Latin, and so, in his years of blindness, his daughters would read to him from Horace or Virgil. At dinnertime they would carve his meat, while Lady North stood by and fussed about the husband she loved. While North served his king, his life had been filled with toil and worry. With the cares of office cast aside and with friends like Edward Gibbon to amuse him, he was cheerful and funny to the last.

Among their social equals the Norths were renowned for their charm, their hospitality, and the pleasure they took in each other's company. When he died in 1792, the family gave him a monument whose grandeur conveys the depth of their affection. They chose the finest sculptor of the day, John Flaxman, to make a marble likeness of Lord North, his double chin, plump face, and flabby lips. His image can be seen in the chancel of All Saints, with his blind eyes staring upward and toward the east in search of the day of resurrection.

Beneath him the artist carved a tall, slim figure of Britannia with a spear, a shield, and a British lion reclining at her side. For more than two centuries the children of Wroxton have adored the lion, stroking his nose until the marble shines amid the gloom. Below the lion with the gleaming nose there lies the vault where Lord North sleeps forever.

Appendix One: The Meaning of Treason

It was a lawyers' war. On both sides of the Atlantic people made the decision to fight in the belief that they had the law on their side, whether they were Americans defending the civil liberties enshrined in their old colonial charters or British politicians convinced that Parliament was sovereign. This decision was never taken lightly. Before they resorted to force, the combatants in both nations took legal counsel from experts, however hurried and informal the process might appear if it occurred in a small town in New England or in the backcountry of Virginia.

American lawyers gave their opinions about the rights and wrongs of resistance in speeches in colonial assemblies or at the Congress in Philadelphia, in private letters and conversations, or in columns in the press, of which those written by John Adams are the most famous. In Great Britain the legal advice was brief or even terse. It was provided by just three officials: in writing by Thurlow and Wedderburn and then orally by the lord chief justice, William Murray, Lord Mansfield. He attended the crucial cabinet meetings in 1775.

The American view of the law is well-known. It was eloquently expressed in Thomas Jefferson's *Summary View*, in Adams's *Novanglus* essays, and then eventually in the Declaration of Independence. The British side of the story is far less familiar. From the cabinet ministers' perspective, it was essential to have a firm answer to the following question: had treason been committed in the northern colonies? If the answer was yes, then they had not only a right but also an obligation to punish the traitors and put a stop to any further crimes of the same kind.

Thurlow, Wedderburn, and Mansfield all agreed that treason had taken place in New England, not once, but at least three times. Try as he might, it would be very hard for any lawyer in London, whatever his political persuasion, to deny that this was so, although two or three—principally Franklin's barrister, John Dunning—made a valiant effort during the debates in Parliament. The relevant law was a statute from the reign of King Edward III, but far from being archaic or obsolete, it actually remains in force today. Used many times in the eighteenth century, it was clearly understood by judges and advocates alike.

First enacted in 1351, the statute against treason certainly used vivid language and dealt with some picturesque, Shakespearean types of treachery. It was high treason "to compass or imagine the death of our lord the king," his wife, or his son and heir, or to conspire to do so. Sex with the queen, the king's eldest daughter, or the consort of the monarch's eldest son: these also fell within the meaning of the crime. A man could also die as a traitor for counterfeiting the king's great seal, for making false coins, or for killing a judge in open court.

So far, so medieval, but the statute was readily adaptable to fit more up-to-date kinds of disloyalty. It contained an important clause that called it treason "to levy war against the king in his realm." This made treason and rebellion synonymous, and over time the judges extended the definition of the words to cover situations beyond the physical act of taking up arms. For example, after the Jacobite rebellions of 1715 and 1745, the courts sent people to the gallows for exporting gunpowder, knowing that it might find its way into rebel hands, for collecting money for the Stuart cause, or for encouraging other people to do so. It was also treasonable to write letters to the Stuarts in exile or to claim that they were still the rightful rulers of the kingdom.

As Scotsmen themselves, both Mansfield and Wedderburn were especially familiar with the cases from that era. Indeed Lord Mansfield had acted as one of the prosecuting counsel in the Jacobite treason trials of 1746. It was relatively easy for them and Edward Thurlow to take precedents such as these and apply them to the outrages perpetrated in America, starting with the sinking of the *Gaspée*.

Only two issues had to be addressed before John Brown and his accomplices could be described as traitors. First, did Rhode Island fall within the realm as the statute required? It certainly did, because the law defined the colonies as "dependent dominions," subject to the authority of the Crown and Parliament. Second, Thurlow and Wedderburn had to be sure that the raid itself was treasonous. It clearly was, because the *Gaspée*'s commander held the king's commission. By attacking his ship, the colonists had levied war against His Majesty. This was treason, for which the penalty was always death.

On the face of it the Boston Tea Party seems more complicated, but again the law of England left no room for doubt. Here the precedent came from the reign of Queen Anne. In 1710, during the so-called Sacheverell riots in London, a mob had attacked chapels belonging to Protestant dissenters. "Down with the Presbyterians!" the rioters cried. In Drury Lane a boatman called Daniel Damaree appeared at the head of the crowd and was heard to shout "Come on boys, I'll lead you, down with the meeting houses!" He was arrested, charged with high treason, put on trial, and hanged.

According to the court, Damaree's crime amounted to an act of war against the Crown and the legislature. A riot was a private thing, in which the mob attacked a particular person or place out of some local grievance or merely because they were drunk and disorderly. The crowd led by Damaree did something far worse. Far from being merely a riot, their rampage against the chapels was a public act of rebellion, aimed at destroying *all* the chapels in the city, not just one. Damaree wished to frustrate the will of Parliament, which had voted to allow Presbyterians to worship free from harm.

The mob at Griffin's Wharf were guilty of the same offense when they used force in an attempt to make the Tea Act unworkable. None of the culprits had a private grievance against the East India Company; instead, they were seeking to prevent by force the collection of a tax that had the full authority of the British House of Commons. If violent protests against the Tea Act occurred elsewhere on the coast of America, the rule of law would vanish altogether, and Parliament would be deprived of sovereignty. For this reason the men who destroyed the tea ought to be indicted as traitors, just like the wicked Damaree. Lord Mansfield said as much in a speech in the House of Lords.

In British eyes, the most flagrant cases of rebellion were those that occurred at Cambridge, Massachusetts, in late October 1774. When the Provincial Congress voted to create a new militia, to withhold the provincial taxes, and to pay them into a new fund under its control, it repeated acts of treason performed by the Jacobites. The new militia amounted to an independent army raised unlawfully: its creation was an act of war as English judges defined the word. The vote to divert the colony's taxes into rebel hands fell into the same category. In Glasgow the Jacobites in 1745 had appointed their own tax collector to take possession of excise duties payable to George II. The army arrested the man in question, and he met his end on the gallows on Kennington Common. Here again the principle was easy to state. Theft of the royal revenue amounted to an attack on the king. By the same token, John Hancock and his comrades were traitors too.

However, before the British put men and women to death for treason they had to gather the evidence required to satisfy a jury. In the case of the *Gaspée* raid this could not be done, because no reliable witnesses came forward. The Tea Party posed a similar problem: the men who sacked the ships could not be identified. According to Thurlow, the speeches made at the Old South Meeting House were also treason, and so was the riot against Richard Clarke on November 3, but although the names of the culprits were known, another difficulty arose. The evidence pointing to named individuals came from depositions taken in Boston. Before an English judge could issue warrants for their arrest, he would have to examine the witnesses himself. Thurlow dismissed this as impractical.

The votes at Cambridge were quite another matter. As the *Boston Gazette* reported at the time, John Hancock and his colleagues passed the resolutions under their own names. Under oath the secretary of the meeting could be forced to confirm the accuracy of the minutes. That would be enough to secure convictions. In addition, General Gage needed an assurance that he would be within the law if he opened fire on rebels in the field. For this reason Lord North asked Parliament for the formal declaration that a state of rebellion existed in Massachusetts, citing the congressional proceedings as his justification. Once the declaration had reached Boston on the *Nautilus,* General Gage could march his men to Concord.[1]

Appendix Two: The Value of Money in the 1770s

This book has frequently referred to sums of money in pounds sterling, such as the price of tea, the debts of Alexander Fordyce and the East India Company, or the incomes of the aristocracy. The author wishes it were possible to translate these figures into twenty-first-century equivalents by simply applying a standard multiplier to capture the effect of some 240 years of currency depreciation. Unfortunately, this would be highly misleading. The problem is, first, that prices and wages have risen very unevenly, with rates of inflation that vary widely from one item or one occupation to another, and, second, that the structure of household budgets and the British economy have changed out of all recognition.

Although economic historians can readily chart yearly movements in the prices of specific commodities, and also plot general trends in wages, no scholar has produced a robust and reliable aggregate consumer price index reaching back to the eighteenth century. Without such an index, it is impossible to produce a single multiplying factor to convey the overall rate of inflation. However, all is not lost. There is another way to give a meaning to sums of money from the period: we can simply give benchmarks that indicate what they meant to Britons at the time. For what follows, it needs to be borne in mind that a pound sterling consisted of twenty shillings, each of which was made up of twelve pennies.

Starting from the top, the average yearly output of Great Britain's domestic economy in the 1770s was about £130 million. If we divide that by the population, then output per head was about £17 per annum, roughly equivalent to the annual wage earned by farm workers, whose average weekly income was between six and seven shillings. In practice, wage rates varied widely from region to region, and—if they were lucky—a laboring family of five in a prosperous area could boost its weekly income to £1 or more by putting everyone to work. Even so, the British laboring classes endured a wretched standard of living. In the 1770s, a hearty breakfast for one at a market town's best inn cost one shilling, a good dinner cost about four shillings, and a pound of even the cheapest smuggled tea cost about two shillings and four pence.

Moving further up the social scale, outside London a skilled artisan such as a carpenter could probably earn at least twelve shillings a week or roughly £31 a year, but this was still only a tiny fraction of the incomes of the gentry. To live respectably in the capital, with a few dependent relatives and two or three domestic servants, a gentleman needed a minimum annual income of about £300. This was the amount of the pension awarded by George III to Samuel Johnson in 1762 in honor of his dictionary. A senior captain in the Royal Navy was paid £365 a year, and at the Colonial Office John Pownall's salary came to £1,650, roughly the same as an admiral's. This was still far less, however, than the £4,000 a year regarded as the minimum acceptable income for a peer of the realm. Ten or a dozen aristocratic families had incomes of more than £20,000. Queen Charlotte received an annual allowance of £50,000, a sum intended to maintain a household superior to that of the wealthiest duke.

As regards public spending by the central government, in 1773 it was about £11.3 million, or less than 10 percent of the economy, within which the largest items were interest payments on the national debt (£4.5 million), and the budget for the navy (£1.8 million) and the army (£1.6 million). And so when Fordyce vanished after his bank lost £500,000 and the East India Company came close to collapse with debts of £3 million, these were enormous numbers. If we assume that an American corporation became insolvent today with liabilities comparable to the East India Company's, amounting to about 2.3 percent of the U.S. economy, then its borrowings would come to $380 billion, four times greater than those of General Motors when it declared itself bankrupt in the summer of 2009.

Sources and Further Reading

An Empire on the Edge draws upon primary research undertaken by the author in more than twenty manuscript collections and record offices on both sides of the Atlantic, of which six were especially important.

At the National Archives at Kew in southwest London, the Colonial Office records contain a vast wealth of material from the years 1771–75, of which only a small proportion has been published. A few miles to the east at the Palace of Westminster, the Parliamentary Archives hold the American papers placed before the House of Lords in 1774 after the Boston Tea Party, preserved in rather better condition than those at Kew. At St. Pancras, the British Library makes available not only an important cache of documents created by Thomas Hutchinson but also the East India Company's files, perhaps the finest single archive collection in the United Kingdom. In Stafford, the county record office holds the papers of Lord Dartmouth, another treasure store, especially valuable for the correspondence that he received and for his affectionate letters to his son.

In America, the Bancroft Collection in the Forty-Second Street building of the New York Public Library includes the papers of the Boston Committee of Correspondence, essential for anybody trying to follow the unfolding of the revolution in New England. And finally, the Massachusetts Historical Society—the author's home away from home in the United States—stands guard over such superb assets as the Harbottle Dorr scrapbooks of contemporary newspapers, annotated by Mr. Dorr, a Boston shopkeeper of the revolutionary era. Since the research for this book was completed, these have been digitized and made available online with funding from the Richard Saltonstall Charitable Foundation.

The secondary literature relating to the American Revolution is immense. Any list of the best books about its origins is bound to be subjective and open to disagreement. From the point of view of the author of *An Empire on the Edge*, the ten most useful books are the following, in order of relevance.

At the top of the roster stands Merrill Jensen's *The Founding of a Nation: A History of the American Revolution, 1763–1776*, first published in 1968 but still the most reliable handbook for following the period's events. Next comes a much more recent work, Jack P. Greene's *The Constitutional Origins of the American Revolution*, a tour de force, concise and penetrating, that appeared in 2011. In third place, we have a British book, P. J. Marshall's *The Making and Unmaking of Empires: Britain, India, and America, c. 1750–1783* (2005), a wide-ranging analysis of Great Britain's imperial predicament.

The fourth item on the list is Gordon S. Wood's *The Radicalism of the American Revolution* from 1991, a winner of the Pulitzer Prize. Wood brilliantly elucidates the cultural divergence between the mother country and its colonies. Number five is T. H. Breen's *American Insurgents, American Patriots: The Revolution of the People* (2010), whose great merit is excitement. Breen conveys the passion of the uprisings in Massachusetts in 1774, as well as a persuasive understanding of their origins.

The sixth book is Fred Anderson's *Crucible of War* (2000) about the Seven Years' War of 1756–63 and its implications for British North America. After that, we have the sensitive account of British political and military failure in the colonies after Lexington by Andrew Jackson O'Shaughnessy, *The Men Who Lost America* (2013). Number eight is Jeremy Black's moving but fair-minded biography of George III, published in 2006.

Written in the most elegant language, the ninth book is Bernard Bailyn's *The Ordeal of Thomas Hutchinson*, which has acquired classic status since it appeared in 1974. But the finest account of the 1770s will always be James Boswell's biography of Dr. Johnson, a book that ranges far beyond the life of its subject. Once upon a time, nobody could claim to be educated without having read it. Today scarcely anyone outside a university opens its pages. Nevertheless Boswell remains, for all his wild emotions, his liquor, and his lechery, the indispensable guide to his era.

Notes

Abbreviations

ADM Official Papers of the Board of Admiralty at the National Archives, Kew, U.K.

BFP William B. Willcox et al., eds., *The Papers of Benjamin Franklin*, vols. 19–22 (New Haven, Conn., 1976–82)

BL British Library, London

BPL Boston Public Library

CGG Clarence E. Carter, ed., *The Correspondence of General Thomas Gage with the Secretaries of State, 1763–1775* (New Haven, Conn., 1931–33)

CG3 Sir John Fortescue, ed., *The Correspondence of King George the Third, 1760–1783* (London, 1927–28)

CO Records of the Colonial Office at the National Archives, Kew, U.K.

DAR K. G. Davies, ed., *Documents of the American Revolution, 1770–1783* (Shannon, Ire., 1972–81)

ESTC English Short Title Catalogue

IOR India Office Records, in the Asia, Pacific, and Africa Collections at the British Library, London

LMA London Metropolitan Archives

MHS Massachusetts Historical Society, Boston

NAK National Archives, Kew, U.K.

NAS National Archives of Scotland, Edinburgh

NLS National Library of Scotland, Edinburgh

NYPL New York Public Library

ODNB *Oxford Dictionary of National Biography*

PDNA R. C. Simmons and P. D. G. Thomas, eds., *Proceedings and Debates of the British Parliaments Respecting North America, 1754–1783* (Millwood, N.Y., 1982–87)

RIHS Rhode Island Historical Society, Providence

SCRO Staffordshire Record Office, Stafford, U.K.

WWM Wentworth Woodhouse Muniments (papers of Edmund Burke and Charles Watson-Wentworth, second Marquess of Rockingham), Sheffield Archives, Sheffield, U.K.

Epigraph

1. Adam Smith, *The Wealth of Nations* (London, 1999), vol. 2, bk. 5, p. 550.

Prologue

Chapter One: The Finest Country in the World

1. Gage to Lord Hillsborough, Nov. 10, 1770, in *CGG*, vol. 1, p. 278.

2. The British in the Illinois country: Gage's dispatches to Whitehall between 1764 and 1771, in *CGG*, vol. 1, esp. pp. 31–32, 65–67, 121–23, and his Nov. 1770 discussion of western policy, pp. 274–81.

3. For "the finest Country in the known World," see J. H. Schlarman, *From Quebec to New Orleans: The Story of the French in America, Fort de Chartres* (Belleville, Ill., 1929), p. 430. Fort de Chartres: Edward B. Jelks, Carl J. Ekberg, and Terrance J. Martin, *Excavations at the Laurens Site,* Studies in Illinois Archaeology 5 (Illinois Historic Preservation Agency, 1989), pp. 7–20; and David Keene, "Fort de Chartres: Archaeology in the Illinois Country," in *French Colonial Archaeology: The Illinois Country and the Western Great Lakes,* ed. John A. Walthall (Chicago, 1991), pp. 29–41. British accounts: Clarence W. Alvord and Clarence E. Carter, *The New Régime, 1765–1767* (Springfield, Ill., 1916), pp. 177, 297–99. "Your excellency knows": Lieutenant Colonel Wilkins to Gage, Sept. 13, 1768, D(W) 1778/II, 302, Dartmouth Papers, SCRO.

4. "We Carried out in a Cart": Schlarman, *From Quebec to New Orleans,* p. 432. Indian affairs: *CGG*, vol. 1, pp. 237–39, 244–45; and Add. MS 21,687, fols. 120–23, and Add. MS 21,730, fols. 27–29, Haldimand Papers, BL.

5. Withdrawal from the Illinois country: Gage to Hillsborough, Sept. 3 and Oct. 1, 1771, in *CGG*, vol. 1, pp. 307–12, and Hillsborough to Gage, Dec. 4, 1771, in *CGG*, vol. 2, pp. 136–38. Abandonment of forts: Gage to Hillsborough, June 4, 1771, in *CGG*, vol. 1, pp. 299–301; and John Shy, *Toward Lexington: The Role of the British Army in the Coming of the American Revolution* (Princeton, N.J., 1965), pp. 330–31. Ruinous state of Castle William: Colonel Montresor's report, Aug. 31, 1772, Add. MS 21,687, fols. 124–25, Haldimand Papers, BL.

6. From Franklin's satirical article "Rules by Which a Great Empire May Be Reduced to a Small One," *Public Advertiser,* Sept. 11, 1773.

7. Although every regiment in the British army kept muster rolls that recorded the names of dead soldiers, it seems that the government in London rarely collated them to give aggregate numbers of casualties. Indeed, it appears that only one official estimate survives, dated January 1781, in a document prepared by the War Office for the Treasury. It gives figures of 5,893 British deaths on active service in North America between 1774 and the end of 1779, and 3,795 deaths in the West Indies between 1774 and the end of 1780. If these numbers are grossed up to allow for two more years of fighting on the mainland and for further losses in the Caribbean, with (say) 500 more deaths in North America after the surrender at Yorktown, we can arrive at an estimate of about 14,250 deaths in the army. For lack of reliable data, this number excludes deaths from disease among British prisoners

in American hands, among women and children who traveled with the redcoats, and among American Loyalists or German soldiers fighting alongside the British. On the face of it figures for the navy are easier to come by, with official records showing 1,243 deaths in action and 18,545 from disease in the years 1776 to 1780; but these numbers include casualties in Europe and Asia and mortality that might have occurred in peacetime. Overall, it seems reasonable to say that the American war cost the British armed forces at least 20,000 dead, and possibly considerably more. For the evidence and some commentary: *An Account of the Men Lost & Disabled . . . from 1st November 1774*, at BL, Add Ms. 38,375 (Liverpool Papers, vol. 186), fols. 74–75; Christopher Lloyd and Jack S. Coulter, *Medicine and the Navy* (Edinburgh, 1961), vol. 3, pp. 131–37; and Stephen Conway, *The British Isles and the American War of Independence* (Oxford, 2000), pp. 26–27.

Chapter Two: THE OLD REGIME

1. Edmund Burke in the House of Commons, March 22, 1775, in *PDNA*, vol. 5, p. 608.

2. British colonial policy after 1740: Jack P. Greene, *The Constitutional Origins of the American Revolution* (Cambridge, U.K., 2011), pp. 28–35; and Jeremy Black, *Crisis of Empire: Britain and America in the Eighteenth Century* (London, 2008), pp. 51–68.

3. British public finance: House of Commons, *Accounts Relating to the Public Income and Expenditure of Great Britain and Ireland*, Parliamentary Papers, sess. 1868–69, vol. 35, pt. 1, pp. 122–93, 288–325, and (for the National Debt) pt. 2, pp. 302–5; and Patrick K. O'Brien, "The Political Economy of British Taxation, 1660–1815," *Economic History Review* 41, no. 1 (Feb. 1988). Every writer about British politics in the eighteenth century also owes a special debt to John Brewer, *The Sinews of Power: War, Money and the English State, 1688-1783* (London, 1989).

4. Royal officials: "A List of the Civil Establishment in Virginia," in a dispatch from Governor Dunmore, March 18, 1774, CO5/1352, fols. 14–15, NAK.

5. Edward Gibbon, "General Observations on the Fall of the Roman Empire in the West," in *The History of the Decline and Fall of the Roman Empire*, ed. David Womersley (London, 1994), vol. 2, pp. 513–14. For "the law of nations" and Gibbon on European politics, see his *Mémoire justificatif*, written in French in 1778 to defend Britain's sovereignty in America, in *Miscellaneous Works of Edward Gibbon*, ed. John, Lord Sheffield (London, 1814), vol. 5, pp. 1–3, 25.

6. The global trade in commodities: Carole Shammas, "The Revolutionary Impact of European Demand for Tropical Goods," in *The Early Modern Atlantic Economy*, ed. John J. McCusker and Kenneth Morgan (Cambridge, U.K., 2000), chap. 7; T. H. Breen, *The Marketplace of Revolution* (Oxford, U.K., 2004), esp. pp. 59–64; Jacob M. Price, "The Economic Growth of the Chesapeake and the European Market, 1697–1775" in *Journal of Economic History* 24, no. 4 (Dec. 1964), pp. 496–511; and for statistical data on colonial trade on the eve of the American Revolution, James F. Shepherd and Gary M. Walton, *Shipping, Maritime Trade and the Economic Development of Colonial North America* (Cambridge, U.K., 1972), especially pp. 36–42 and pp. 156–66.

PART ONE: THE EMPIRE OF SPECULATION

Chapter One: THE TIGER'S MOUTH

1. Zhuang Guotu, *Tea, Silver, Opium, and War: The International Tea Trade and Western Commercial Expansion into China in 1740–1840* (Xiamen, China, 1993), p. 21.

2. Voyage of the *Calcutta:* From the ship's log, Oct. 1770–Sept. 1772, L/MAR/B/308/E, IOR. Approaches to China: Alexander Dalrymple, *Chart of the China Sea* (April 1771), Maps 62710 (1), BL; James Horsburgh, *Directions for Sailing to and from the East Indies, China,* . . . (London, 1811), vol. 2, pp. 192–203; and William Milburn, *Oriental Commerce* (London, 1813), vol. 2, pp. 462–65. This chapter's opening section also draws upon the logs of other ships that sailed to China that year, especially the *Vansittart* and the *Cruttenden,* in the same L/MAR series, and Alfred Spencer, ed., *Memoirs of William Hickey* (London, 1948), vol. 1 , chaps. 16–18. Data on cargoes to China: *East India Company Journal of Commerce,* 1769–1773 at L/AG/1/6/16, IOR.

3. Burke on tea: Speech in the House of Commons on American taxation, April 19, 1774.

4. British tea trade to 1772: Louis Dermigny, *La Chine et l'Occident: Le commerce à Canton au XVIIIᵉ siècle, 1719–1833* (Paris, 1964), vol. 2, pp. 521–25, 621–28; and House of Commons, *Return Showing the Number of Pounds Weight of Tea Sold by the East India Company, 1740–1837* (Feb. 11, 1845), in *Parliamentary Papers (Commons),* 1845 (191).

5. Profit made on sales of tea: Calculated by the author, using data taken from House of Commons, *3rd Report of the Committee of Secrecy,* Feb. 9, 1773, reprinted in *Reports from Committees of the House of Commons* (1804), vol. 4 (East Indies), pp. 68–69, containing a profit-and-loss account for the China trade for the years 1762–72; and from the same volume, p. 278, an account of shipping costs, in the *5th Report* of the same committee, March 30, 1773.

6. Size of the smuggling trade: Author's estimate, calculated by taking total Chinese tea exports, given in tables in Dermigny, *La Chine et l'Occident,* and then deducting the tea imported legally into European markets with duty paid. Also see Hoh-Cheung and Lorna H. Mui, "Smuggling and the British Tea Trade Before 1784," *American Historical Review* 74, no. 1 (1968), pp. 51–55.

7. China under Qianlong: Evelyn Rawski, "Re-envisioning the Qing: The Significance of the Qing Period in Chinese History," *Journal of Asian Studies* 55, no. 4 (Nov. 1996), pp. 829–42; and Ramon H. Myers and Yeh-Chien Wang, "Economic Developments, 1644–1800," in *The Cambridge History of China,* vol. 9, pt. 1, *The Ch'ing Empire to 1800,* ed. Willard J. Peterson (Cambridge, U.K., 2002). However, perhaps the most vivid illustration of China's economic achievements in this period can be found in a masterpiece of Chinese art, the vast panoramic townscape *Prosperous Suzhou,* commissioned by Qianlong from the artist Xu Yang and painted between 1756 and 1759. Some forty feet long, and intended to be kept in the emperor's private apartments for his eyes only, this painting of the town of Suzhou near Shanghai celebrates Chinese commerce and agriculture and depicts them in exquisite detail. Usually on display at the Liaoning Provincial Museum in China, it was exhibited at the Victoria and Albert Museum in London in the winter of 2013–14. Canton trading system and the Flint case: Guotu, *Tea, Silver, Opium, and War,* pp. 2–6, 12–13, 22–23; and Paul A. Van Dyke, *The Canton Trade: Life and Enterprise on the China Coast, 1700–1845* (Hong Kong, 2005), pp. 9–16.

8. Tax revenues from Canton: Preston M. Torbert, *The Ch'ing Imperial Household Department* (Cambridge, Mass., 1977), pp. 97–103; and H. T. Huang, "Tea Processing and Utilisation," in *Science and Civilisation in China*, vol. 6, *Biology and Biological Technology*, ed. Joseph Needham (Cambridge, U.K., 2000), pp. 538–48.

9. Tea planting in Fukien: Guotu, *Tea, Silver, Opium, and War*, pp. 53–74; and Robert Gardella, *Harvesting Mountains: Fujian and the China Tea Trade, 1757–1937* (Berkeley, Calif., 1994), pp. 14–31, 38–48.

10. Role and remuneration of the supercargoes at Canton: File D/27, EIC Correspondence Reports, 1771–77, pp. 47–48 (entry for Nov. 5, 1771), IOR; and the supercargoes' diaries, in the Canton Factory Records, R/10/5 (1761–69), and R/10/9 (1771–77), IOR. For the career of a typical supercargo: The cash book of John Searle, relating to a trip to the East between 1769 and 1771, Chancery Masters' Exhibits, file C107/154, NAK. He invested £788 on his own account and came home with commission income of about £4,000, together with trading profits from selling the tea, rhubarb, spices, and cloth that he acquired. British activities in China in the 1760s and 1770s, see H. B. Morse, *Chronicles of the East India Company Trading to China* (Oxford, 1929), vol. 5, pp. 144–46.

11. The shipping interest: *5th Report of the Committee of Secrecy of 1772–73*, pp. 279–85; Lucy S. Sutherland, *A London Merchant, 1695–1774* (Oxford, 1933), chap. 4; and Anonymous, *Observations on East India Shipping* (London, 1774). On Captain Thomson: Entries relating to Thomson, his brother David, his father, George, and his uncle George Willson, in Anthony Farrington, *Biographical Index of East India Company Maritime Service Officers, 1600–1834* (London, 1999).

12. Dutch tea trade: Yong Liu, *The Dutch East India Company's Tea Trade with China, 1757–1781* (Leiden, 2007), pp. 44–48, 146–52. Smuggling: Dermigny, *La Chine et l'Occident*, vol. 2, pp. 660–66. Corruption in Guernsey: Documented in Treasury correspondence for 1772, T1/489/118–42, NAK.

13. Credit and the Hongs: Van Dyke, *Canton Trade*, pp. 96–97; and balance sheet for the Canton factory, March 9, 1772, R/10/9, IOR and Morse (1929), vol. 5, pp. 165–73.

14. London tea auctions: Data from a pamphlet published in 1780 by the Committee of Fair Trade Tea Dealers, *Advice to the Unwary; or, An Abstract of Certain Penal Laws Now in Force Against Smuggling.*

15. Indian background: C. A. Bayly, *Indian Society and the Making of the British Empire* (Cambridge, U.K., 1988), pp. 45–55. For an excellent account of the way the East India Company functioned at home and abroad, see H. V. Bowen, *The Business of Empire: The East India Company and Imperial Britain, 1756–1833* (Cambridge, U.K., 2006), esp. chaps. 5 and 8.

16. Colebrooke and his colleagues: Biographical sketches in James Gordon Parker, "The Directors of the East India Company, 1754–1790" (PhD thesis, University of Edinburgh, 1977), and also see note 12 on p. 395 herein.

17. The company's deteriorating finances: *8th Report of the Secrecy Committee*, pp. 356–58, 374–89, 401–23. Also see Sulivan's very revealing letter to Henry Vansittart, May 28, 1770, MS Eng.Hist.b.190, Sulivan Papers, Bodleian Library. Bengal famine: Rajat Datta, *Society, Economy, and the Market: Commercialization in Rural Bengal, c. 1760–1800* (Manohar, 2000), pp. 285–315, 238–56. For a clear and cogent narrative of the company's relation-

ship with the politicians of the day, see H. V. Bowen, *Revenue and Reform: The Indian Problem in British Politics, 1757–1773* (Cambridge, U.K., 1991); but also Lucy S. Sutherland, *The East India Company in Eighteenth-Century Politics* (Oxford, 1962), chaps. 7–8.

Chapter Two: "This Dark Affair": The *Gaspée* Incident

1. Conversation between George III and Thomas Hutchinson, July 1, 1774: Peter Orlando Hutchinson, *The Diary and Letters of His Excellency Thomas Hutchinson* (London, 1886), vol. 1, p. 172.

2. Winter of 1771–72: *Massachusetts Gazette and Boston News-Letter*, Dec. 26, 1771; entries for Jan. 27–30, 1772, in Donald Jackson, ed., *The Diaries of George Washington* (Charlottesville, Va., 1978), vol. 3, pp. 86–87; *Connecticut Journal*, Feb. 21, 1772; and *Providence Gazette*, Feb. 22, 1772. Generally, for daily notes on weather in southern New England: Farm journals (1752–87) of Joseph Andrews of Hingham, Massachusetts, microfilm P-363, MHS. Tea smuggling and Royal Navy response: daily entries in Journal of Rear Admiral John Montagu, "Remarks on the Squadron in North America (1771–1774)," (hereafter cited as "Montagu's journal"), ADM 50/17, NAK.

3. Admiral Montagu: *ODNB*; and Diary of John Adams, Dec. 29, 1772, digitized by the Massachusetts Historical Society at www. masshist.org/digitaladams/archive/diary. Montagu's orders: Letter from Lord Sandwich, May 27, 1771, ADM 2/97 (Admiralty Letters), pp. 73–88, NAK. Naval role in the colonies: Neil R. Stout, *The Royal Navy in America, 1760–1775: A Study of Enforcement of British Colonial Policy on the Eve of the Revolution* (Annapolis, Md., 1973), pp. 165–70.

4. Opinions of Dudingston: Henry Marchant to Benjamin Franklin, Nov. 21, 1772, in *BFP*, vol. 19, p. 379; and Charles Stedman, *History of the Origins, Progress, and Termination of the American War* (London, 1794), vol. 1, p. 80. The Dudingstons of Fife: Walter Wood, *The East Neuk of Fife: Its History and Antiquities* (Edinburgh, 1887), pp. 175–77. Three boxes of Dudingston family papers are in the special collections at the University of St. Andrews in Scotland, MS dep 114 (Dudingston of St. Fort). The most relevant document is box 1, number 4, containing schedules of family debts, including those owed by the lieutenant.

5. Laws of trade: His Majesty's Customs Commissioners, *Instructions to John Mascarene, Comptroller at Salem* (1769), reprinted in *Sources and Documents Illustrating the American Revolution, 1764–1788*, ed. Samuel E. Morison (Oxford, 1923), pp. 74–83. Dissenting opinions in Whitehall: "Observations on the Trade & Revenue of North America, with . . . a Plan for the Prevention of Smuggling" (1771), D(W) 1778/II, 494, esp. pp. 27–31, Dartmouth Papers. For the figure of £47,000, the gross revenue from customs duties in North America: Colonial tax receipts, T1/504, f.71, Treasury Board Papers, NAK. Cost of imperial administration: Julian Gwyn, "British Government Spending and the North American Colonies, 1740–1775," *Journal of Imperial and Commonwealth History* 8, no. 2 (1980), pp. 77–81.

6. Stedman, *History of the Origins, Progress, and Termination of the American War*, vol. 1, pp. 11–17.

7. Dudingston's reputation: Story in *Virginia Gazette* (Rind's edition), July 27, 1769, describing his fracas at sea with Davis Bevan of Chester, Pennsylvania.

8. The *Canceaux*: Montagu's journal, Feb. 19, 1772; proclamation by Governor Hutchin-

son, *Boston News-Letter,* March 19, 1772, and *Boston Post-Boy,* March 22, 1772; *Newport Mercury,* Feb. 22, 1772, and *Providence Gazette,* Feb. 22, 1772; and Montagu to the Admiralty, April 18, 1772, in *DAR,* vol. 5, pp. 73—74.

9. Seizure at Tarpaulin Cove: Montagu's journal, Feb. 20, 1772. Meeting with Governor Joseph Wanton, and reference to the *Swanzey:* J. R. Bartlett, ed., *Records of the Colony of Rhode Island* (Providence, 1862), vol. 7, pp. 64—66. *Fortune* incident: Dudingston to Boston customs commissioners, Feb. 22, 1772, TI/491, fol. 125, Treasury Board Papers, and March 9–31, 1772, TI/491, fols. 127—28, Boston Admiralty Court Papers, NAK. Also see the *Newport Mercury,* story datelined Feb. 24, 1772, cutting preserved inside Admiral Montagu's letter of Sept. 1, fol. 393, TI/491, NAK. American sources: Bartlett, *Records of the Colony of Rhode Island,* vol. 7, pp. 145—46; and Richard K. Showman et al., eds., *The Papers of General Nathanael Greene* (Chapel Hill, N.C., 1976), vol. 1, pp. 29–35.

10. The Greenes: David McCullough, *1776* (New York, 2005), pp. 20–22. For "such a Spirit of Resentment," see Greene to Samuel Ward, April? 1772, in Showman, *Papers of General Nathanael Greene,* p. 26.

11. Colonial Rhode Island: David S. Lovejoy, *Rhode Island Politics and the American Revolution, 1760–1776* (Providence, 1958), esp. pp. 6–11, 15–18; and Sydney V. James, *Colonial Rhode Island: A History* (New York, 1975). Volume of shipping: *Accounts of Vessels Entering American Ports, 1772,* among Lord North's papers, MS North a.12, Bodleian Library.

12. Rebuilding of Providence: John Hutchins Cady, *The Civic and Architectural Development of Providence, 1636–1950* (Providence, 1957), chaps. 4 and 5. Candle factory: Caroline Frank, "John Brown's India Point," *Rhode Island History* 61 (Fall 2003), pp. 54–57.

13. Rhode Island charter: David A. Weir, *Early New England: A Covenanted Society* (Grand Rapids, Mich., 2005), pp. 51–56.

14. Stephen Hopkins: *American National Biography;* and Jack P. Greene, *The Constitutional Origins of the American Revolution* (Cambridge, U.K., 2011), pp. 40, 83–84, 186. Also see note 23 below.

15. College of Rhode Island, first commencement: *Newport Mercury,* Sept. 11, 1769. Also see Reuben Aldridge Guild, *Early History of Brown University* (Providence, 1897), p. 85.

16. The increase in smuggling in the British Isles: House of Commons, *First Report from the Committee on Illicit Practices Used in Defrauding the Revenue,* Dec. 24, 1783, app. 4; and Treasury Board Papers for March to June 1772, TI/505 pt. 1, NAK.

17. The Browns: James B. Hedges, *The Browns of Providence Plantation: The Colonial Years* (Providence, 1968), esp. chap. 8 and p. 208. Charles Rappleye vividly describes the Browns in his *Sons of Providence: The Brown Brothers, the Slave Trade, and the American Revolution* (New York, 2006), esp. pp. 24–28.

18. Dudingston in Narragansett Bay: *Providence Gazette,* March 21 and 28, 1772.

19. Rhode Island rum and molasses trade: John J. McCusker, *Rum and the American Revolution: The Rum Trade and the Balance of Payments in the Thirteen Continental Colonies* (New York, 1989), pp. 397–99, 439–40. John Adams on molasses: Adams to William Tudor, Aug. 11, 1818, in *The Works of John Adams* (Boston, 1856), vol. 10, p. 345.

20. Governor Wanton: J. R. Bartlett, *History of the Wanton Family of Newport, Rhode Island* (Providence, 1878), pp. 78–80; and Hedges, *Browns of Providence Plantation,* pp. 32–33, 81. Wanton's exchanges with Dudingston and Montagu, and John Brown's petition: Bartlett, *Records of the Colony of Rhode Island,* vol. 7, pp. 60–68, 174–75.

21. Principal sources for the destruction of the *Gaspée*: Bartlett, *Records of the Colony of Rhode Island*, pp. 58–190; and Dudingston's court-martial, reprinted in Samuel W. Bryant, "HMS *Gaspée*—the Court Martial," *Rhode Island History* 25, no. 3 (July 1966), pp. 65–72. There is a useful discussion of inconsistencies in the sources in Neil L. York, "The Uses of Law and the *Gaspée* Affair," Rhode Island History 50, no. 1 (Feb. 1992), pp. 3–21.

22. *Gaspée* raid participants: Abraham Whipple, John B. Hopkins, Joseph Tillinghast, and Samuel Dunn (sea captains); Ephraim Bowen (son of Ephraim Bowen, MD); and Joseph Bucklin. Whipple and Bucklin were schoolhouse trustees: Providence Town Papers, MS 214, vol. 2 (1761–75), fol. 35, RIHS. Celebrations in 1826: *Rhode Island American*, July 4, 1826; and *Newport Mercury*, July 8, 1826.

23. For an expanded discussion of this point, see John Phillip Reid, *In a Defiant Stance: The Conditions of Law in Massachusetts Bay, the Irish Comparison, and the Coming of the Revolution* (University Park, Pa., 1977), chaps. 7 and 8 and pp. 85–87.

24. Response to the *Gaspée* incident: Hutchinson to Lord Hillsborough, June 12, 1772, in Hutchinson Letter Books, typescript copy, MHS; Dudley to Admiral Montagu, July 23, 1772, T1/491, NAK; and Montagu's journal, June 12, 1772. For "confusion, dismay and distress," see James Boswell, *Reflections on the Late Alarming Bankruptcies in Scotland* (Edinburgh, 1772), p. 1.

Chapter Three: A BANKRUPT AGE

1. George F. Norton of Yorktown, Virginia, to John Hatley Norton, July 8, 1772, in *John Norton and Sons: Merchants of London and Virginia*, ed. Frances Norton Mason (New York, 1968), p. 254.

2. For "the greatest speculator in London," *see* Robert Orme to William Ridge, July 1, 1772, MS Eur/Orme OV 202, pp. 90–91, IOR. Alexander Fordyce: Press reports in *Middlesex Journal*, June 11–15 and 20–23, 1772, and *Morning Chronicle*, June 24, 1772; his examination in bankruptcy, in the *Morning Chronicle*, Sept. 26, 1772; and "Memoirs of a Late Celebrated Banker," *Scots Magazine*, Aug. 1772. The figure of £500,000 represented the total trading losses of the Fordyce bank. The net deficiency in its accounts was £150,000, of which £100,000 was owed by Fordyce himself.

3. *Memoir of the Late Mrs. Henrietta Fordyce* (London, 1823), pp. 53–55.

4. For "a bankrupt age," see prologue to Samuel Foote, *The Bankrupt* (London, 1773). Gambling culture of the period: Paul Langford, *Public Life and the Propertied Englishman, 1689–1798* (Oxford, 1991), p. 558. Lord North on Britain as a gambling nation: 1774 budget speech, *General Evening Post*, May 19.

5. Economic acceleration after 1760: Joel Mokyr, *The Enlightened Economy: An Economic History of Britain, 1700–1850* (New Haven, Conn., 2009), pp. 84–85.; and Robert C. Allen, *The British Industrial Revolution in Global Perspective* (Cambridge UK, 2009), chaps. 3 to 6.

6. Boswell, *Reflections on the Late Alarming Bankruptcies in Scotland*, p. 7. Crash of 1772 and America: Richard B. Sheridan, "The British Credit Crisis of 1772 and the American Colonies," *Journal of Economic History* 20, no. 2 (June 1960), pp. 172–76, 185–86. European dimension of the crash: Frank C. Spooner, *Risks at Sea: Amsterdam Insurance and Maritime Europe, 1766–1780* (Cambridge, U.K., 1983), pp. 86–96.

7. British economy in the 1770s: Mokyr, *Enlightened Economy,* chiefly chap. 9 (agriculture), pp. 177–86, and chap. 12 (productivity), pp. 255–60. Economic output: Stephen Broadberry and Bas van Leeuwen, "British Economic Growth and the Business Cycle, 1700–1850," online from the Department of Economics, University of Warwick, Nov. 25, 2008, www2.warwick.ac.uk.

8. Perhaps the most successful defense contractor was Sir Lawrence Dundas (1712–81), a Scottish banker commonly known as the Nabob of the North. His profits during the Seven Years' War came to at least £600,000. Dundas led the financing of two great construction projects of the 1760s and 1770s: the Edinburgh New Town and the Forth and Clyde Canal. For a perceptive analysis of the connection between military contractors and the speculative boom of the 1760s and early 1770s: David Hancock, *Citizens of the World: London Merchants and the Integration of the British Atlantic Community, 1735–1785* (Cambridge, U.K., 1995), chap. 9. Business conditions after 1763: T. S. Ashton, *Economic Fluctuations in England, 1700–1800* (Oxford, 1959), pp. 61–62, 98–100, 127–30, 151–60.

9. Number of banks: F. G. Hilton Price, *Handbook of London Bankers* (London, 1876), pp. 160–65; and T. S. Ashton, *An Economic History of England: The 18th Century* (London, 1955), pp. 179–84.

10. For "every member of the cabinet," see Sir George Colebrooke, *Retrospection; or, Reminiscences Addressed to My Son, Henry Thomas Colebrooke, Esq.* (London, 1898–99), pt. 1, p. 53. Alexander Fordyce: Sources cited in note 2 above, but also *Public Advertiser,* Aug. 7 and Dec. 10, 1772, and Jan. 8, 1773; *Glasgow Journal,* June 18–25, 1772; M. G. Buist, *At Spes Non Fracta: Hope & Co., 1770–1815* (The Hague, 1974), pp. 20–22; and East India Company Stock Ledger, 1769–74, L/AG/14/5/18, IOR.

11. Rents and the price of land in England: M. E. Turner, J. V. Beckett, and E. Afton, *Agricultural Rent in England, 1690–1914* (Cambridge, U.K., 1997), chap. 11.

12. The Adam brothers: Charles Saumarez Smith, *Eighteenth-Century Decoration: Design and the Domestic Interior in England* (London, 1993), pp. 215–21; and Arthur T. Bolton, *The Architecture of Robert and James Adam, 1758–1794* (London, 1922), vol. 1, p. 72, and vol. 2, "Appendix: Index of Clients."

13. For "The English are now," see John Gwynn, *London and Westminster Improved* (London, 1766), p. xv. Gwynn's significance: Sir John Summerson, *Georgian London* (London, 1988), chap. 9. The Adelphi: Bolton, *Architecture of Robert and James Adam,* vol. 2, pp. 18–47; and Alastair J. Rowan, "After the Adelphi: Forgotten Years in the Adam Brothers' Practice," *Journal of the Royal Society of Arts* 122 (Sept. 1974), pp. 661–67. Garrick at the Adelphi: Entry for May 3, 1772, in travel journal of Henry Marchant (1770–72), microfilm copy, F82 M37, RIHS.

14. Scottish banks: Adam Smith, *The Wealth of Nations* (London, 1986), vol. 1, pp. 406–12.

15. Role of the Bank of England: *Public Advertiser,* April 10, 1772; *Virginia Gazette* (Purdie and Dixon), July 2, 1772, reprinting a London newspaper report dated April 14; and Sir John Clapham, *The Bank of England: A History* (Cambridge, U.K., 1944), vol. 1, pp. 244–46.

16. Douglas, Heron: The principal secondary sources are A. W. Kerr, *History of Banking in Scotland* (London, 1926), pp. 83–94; and Henry Hamilton, "The Failure of the Ayr Bank, 1772," *Economic History Review,* n.s., 8, no. 3 (1956), pp. 405–17. But the best mate-

rial can be found in the report of the Ayr Bank committee of inquiry, *The Precipitation and Fall of Messrs. Douglas, Heron and Company* (Edinburgh, 1778) (ESTC T107205), which refers to "abuse and irregularity" on p. 28. List of the partners and other revealing documents relating to the Ayr Bank can be found in GD 224/178/1–2, Buccleuch Papers, NAS. For "a black swarm of projects," see Richard Glover, *The Substance of the Evidence Delivered to . . . the House of Commons* (London, 1774), p. 9.

17. Events of June 22: *General Evening Post*, June 27–30, 1772; *Middlesex Journal*, June 27–30; and Richard Glover to Earl Temple, July 12, 1772, in *The Grenville Papers*, ed. W. J. Smith (London, 1853), vol. 4, pp. 539–43. The precise course of events can be reconstructed from the Bank of England's archives, at G4/21, minute book of the Court of Directors, 1769–74, and ADM9/55, banking department general ledger for 1772, pp. 146–71. On the recession, see Ashton, *Economic Fluctuations in England*, pp. 156–58.

18. For "Were I to recount," see note 2. Marchant's visit to Britain: His journal at RIHS (note 13 above).

19. For "the Luxury and Folly," see Marchant's journal, entry for June 22; for "a mad and foolish act," see John N. Cole, "Henry Marchant's Journal, 1771–1772," *Rhode Island History* 57, no. 1 (May 1999), p. 47.

Chapter Four: THE UNHAPPINESS OF LORD NORTH

1. Lord North to his father, Lord Guilford, May 6, 1772, after delivering his budget speech, MSS North adds.c.4, fol. 158, Bodleian Library.

2. Norths at Bushy Park: North to Guilford, Aug. 18, 1772, MSS North adds.c.4, fols. 161–62, Bodleian Library. The North Papers at the Bodleian contain not only a wealth of material about the North family, but also some important working papers from the treasury of a kind that rarely survive. The finest published sketch of his personality is John Brooke's biographical essay in *The History of Parliament: The House of Commons, 1754–1790*, ed. Sir Lewis Namier and John Brooke (London, 1964). The best political biography is P. D. G. Thomas, *Lord North* (London, 1976). For anecdotes about the North family by his son-in-law, see the many references in Francis Bickley, ed., *The Diaries of Sylvester Douglas* (London, 1928), vol. 1.

3. Frederick the Great to the Prussian ambassador in London, May 18, 1772, in *Politische Korrespondenz des Friedrichs des Grossen*, ed. J. G. Droysen (Berlin, 1908), vol. 33, p. 205.

4. Gibbon on North: J. E. Norton, ed., *Letters of Edward Gibbon* (London, 1956), vol. 2, p. 66. North's kindness: Entries for Oct. 4, 1768, and Aug. 13, 1769, in the diary of Thomas Beedall, file T/PH/WSN 2, Somerset Heritage Centre, Taunton.

5. North's blustering elocution and the ugliness of the Norths: Colebrooke, *Retrospection*, part 2, pp. 275–76; and C. W. Everett, ed., *The Letters of Junius* (London, 1927), pp. 162–63.

6. The quotations in this paragraph come from the letter cited in note 1.

7. For "No rain," see entry for July 17, 1772, in *The Letters and Journals of Lady Mary Coke*, ed. James A. Hume (Edinburgh, 1896), vol. 4, p. 99. For weather conditions in England during the 1770s, the best sources are John Kington, ed., *The Weather Journals of a Rutland Squire: Thomas Barker of Lyndon Hall* (Oakham, U.K., 1988), pp. 78–81, covering the years 1771 to 1775; and John Kington, *Climate and Weather* (London, 2010), pp. 161–63, 308–10.

For detailed daily observations of the drought of 1772, see Francesca Greenoak, ed., *The Journals of Gilbert White* (London, 1986), vol. 1, pp. 412–14.

8. Newspaper reports: *Berrow's Worcester Journal*, April 30 and May 28, 1772. Food prices: D. G. Barnes, *The History of the English Corn Laws from 1600 to 1846* (London, 1930), pp. 38–45.

9. Riots in East Anglia: R. A. Roberts, ed., *Calendar of Home Office Papers, 1770–1772* (London, 1881), pp. 486–88. Disturbances in Somerset: James Street, *The Mynster of the Ile* (Taunton, U.K., 1904), pp. 259–60. The Ilminster workhouse: Ilminster vestry minutes, Aug. 6, 1771, D/P/ilm/9/1/1, Somerset Heritage Centre.

10. *Hearts of Steel*: James R. Donnelly Jr., "Hearts of Oak, Hearts of Steel," *Studia Hibernica*, no. 21 (1981), pp. 62–66.

11. Smuggling in 1772: Minute book of the Treasury Board, T29/42, with accompanying papers in T1/489, Jan. 8, April 5, April 9, and Aug. 18, 1772, NAK. Dunkirk: Letter dated March 31, 1772, from the papers of John Robinson, Treasury Board secretary, in Historical Manuscripts Commission, 10th report, app. 6, *The Manuscripts of the Marquess of Abergavenny* (London, 1887), p. 5.

12. News from America: T29/42, July 28, NAK. Montagu's letter: CO5 761, fol. 110, NAK.

13. For the figure of £200,000, and for an analysis of British public finance and the need for American revenues, see Thomas Whately, *Considerations on the Trade and Finances of the Kingdom* (London, 1766), esp. pp. 69–74. A close friend of Grenville's, Whately served as a junior minister in Lord North's government, and his views can be taken to represent official attitudes. Whately quotes figures of £100,000 for the revenue originally expected from the Stamp Act and another £60,000 for the anticipated yield from other duties introduced by Grenville, principally on sugar and molasses. To this we need to add some £40,000 for the estimated product of the Townshend duties, which came into force in 1767.

14. On Lord Hillsborough, see James Kelly, "Wills Hill, 1st Marquess of Downshire and 2nd Viscount Hillsborough," in *Dictionary of Irish Biography*, ed. James McGuire and James Quinn (Cambridge, U.K., 2009).

15. For "unlucky business," see North to Lord Gower, June 30, 1772, Gower Papers, PRO 30/29/1/14, fols. 635–38, NAK.

16. Cabinet paper by Lord Rochford, Nov. 12, 1772, D(W) 1778/II, 460, Dartmouth Papers. On Rochford and British foreign policy, see *ODNB*; Michael Roberts, "Great Britain and the Swedish Revolution, 1772–73," *Historical Journal* 7, no. 1 (1964), pp. 17–18; and H. M. Scott, *British Foreign Policy in the Age of the American Revolution* (Oxford, 1990), chap. 7.

17. North and Sandwich: Exchange of letters in Sept. 1772, in *The Private Papers of John, Earl of Sandwich* (London, 1932), vol. 1, pp. 19–26. On Sandwich: N. A. M. Rodger, *The Insatiable Earl: A Life of John Montagu, 4th Earl of Sandwich* (London, 1993).

18. Suffolk's verses: Suffolk to Rochford, April 6, 1775, file PRO 30/29/1/15, fols. 701–3, NAK. Suffolk in office: Roberts, "Great Britain and the Swedish Revolution," pp. 10–11; and *ODNB*. Lord Suffolk was also close to Thomas Whately, who served under him at the Northern Department: On Whately, see note 13 above.

19. Repeal of the Stamp Act: For the views of Sandwich and Suffolk, see the report of the debate on March 11, 1766, in *PDNA*, vol. 2, pp. 338–42.

20. On the Grand Ohio Company, see Jack M. Sosin, *Whitehall and the Wilderness* (Lincoln, Neb., 1961), pp. 186–206.

21. The shareholders: Clarence E. Alvord, *The Mississippi Valley in British Politics* (Cleveland, 1917), vol. 2, pp. 98–103. Besides Wharton, Benjamin Franklin, and the English banker Thomas Walpole, the principal investors included Robert Trevor, whose daughter was married to Lord Suffolk from 1764 until her death in 1767.

22. Hillsborough's memorandum: April 29, 1772, from the Commissioners for Trade and Plantations, in *DAR*, vol. 5, pp. 79–89.

23. On Dartmouth's appointment: North to Lord Dartmouth, Aug. 3, 1772, D(W) 1778/ II, 373, SCRO; for "good nature and love of indecision," see George III to Lord Suffolk, July 22, 1772, in *CG3*, vol. 2, pp. 369–70, 376.

Chapter Five: IGNORANCE AND BAD POLICY

1. Hutchinson to Samuel Hood, Sept. 2, 1772, letterbook copy, *Thomas Hutchinson Letter Books* (transcripts), microfilm edition, reel 3, MHS.

2. Staff in the Colonial Office: List of salaries and allowances, 1772, D(W) 1778/II, 1080, Dartmouth Papers. For "I consider my race," see Pownall to Dartmouth, Aug. 8, 1772, D(W) 1778/II, 377, SCRO. John Pownall: Franklin B. Wickwire, "John Pownall and British Colonial Policy," *William and Mary Quarterly*, 3rd ser., 20, no. 4 (Oct. 1963), pp. 543–54.

3. For "Such savage degeneracy," see John Pownall to Dartmouth, Sept. 19, 1772, D(W) 1778/II, 420, SCRO.

4. South Carolina: Jack P. Greene, "Bridge to Revolution: The Wilkes Fund Controversy in South Carolina, 1769–1775," *Journal of Southern History* 29, no. 1 (Feb. 1963), pp. 53–70.

5. William Knox: Patrick Geoghegan's essay in McGuire and Quinn, *Dictionary of Irish Biography*. Knox and the conversion of slaves in Georgia: William Piercy to Selina, Countess of Huntingdon, Jan. 6, 1775, file A4/2 (no. 12), Cheshunt College Papers, Westminster College, Cambridge. For "It was with no small degree," see William Knox, *Extra Official State Papers Addressed to the Lord Rawdon* (London, 1789), vol. 2, p. 11; for "neglect, Ignorance," see Jack P. Greene, "William Knox's Explanation for the American Revolution," *William and Mary Quarterly*, 3rd ser., 30, no. 2 (April 1973), pp. 305–6.

6. Greene, "William Knox's Explanation for the American Revolution," p. 295.

7. Brownlow North's marriage to Henrietta Bannister: Vere Langford Oliver, *History of Antigua* (London, 1894), pp. 31–33. West Indies in 1772: Andrew Jackson O'Shaughnessy, *An Empire Divided: The American Revolution and the British Caribbean* (Philadelphia, 2000), chap. 4.

8. "You can never": Frederick Montagu to Dartmouth, Aug. 10, 1772, D(W) 1778/II, 378, SCRO.

9. "In the progress": Lord Dunmore to Lord Hillsborough, March 1772, in *DAR*, vol. 5, p. 53.

10. Dartmouth sent the questionnaires to America in the first week of July 1773. Uncom-

municative as ever, Connecticut did not reply until late in 1774, and its response did not reach London until February 1775. This is a good example of the difficulties the British faced in obtaining information from the colonies: See Governor Trumbull of Connecticut to Lord Dartmouth, Nov. 23, 1774, CO5/1285, fols. 116–36, NAK.

11. Lord Rochford to Lord Gower, Aug. 15, 1772, file PRO 30/29/1/14. *Five times worse than the Stamp Act*: John Pownall to Dartmouth, Aug. 29, 1772, in Historical Manuscripts Commission, 14th report, *The Manuscripts of the Earl of Dartmouth, Vol. 2, American Papers* (London, 1895), pp. 91–92.

12. Jurisdiction of King's Bench: Lord Mansfield's judgment in the case of *Rex v. Cowle* (1759), in Sir James Burrow, *Reports of Cases Argued and Adjudged in the Court of King's Bench, 1756–1772* (London, 1790), vol. 2, pp. 856–57. Important for understanding British lawyers' attitudes to America, Cowle's case involved issues similar to those raised by the *Gaspée* incident: Mansfield was giving reasons for his decision to move the venue of a criminal trial in order to ensure an impartial jury. American implications of the *Gaspée* raid: William R. Leslie, "The *Gaspée* Affair: A Study of Its Constitutional Significance," *Mississippi Valley Historical Review* 39, no. 2 (1952).

13. Dartmouth to Wanton, Sept. 4, 1772, in *DAR*, vol. 5, p. 187.

14. For "a truly good man," see Benjamin Franklin to William Franklin, July 14, 1773, in *BFP*, vol. 20, p. 308. There is only one full-length study of Lord Dartmouth: B. D. Bargar, *Lord Dartmouth and the American Revolution* (Columbia, S.C., 1965).

15. For "the melancholy loss," see Dartmouth to his son Lord Lewisham, Aug. 14, 1775, from the bundle of more than thirty letters between them dated between 1772 and 1796, D(W) 1778/V, 853, SCRO.

16. Dartmouth's letters: See note 15. The passages come from letters dated Sept. 13, 1774, and May 12, 1775.

17. For "universally acknowledged," see *Public Advertiser*, Aug. 24, 1772.

18. For "ill-delivered and formal," see debate on Jan. 14, 1766, in *PDNA*, vol. 2, p. 72.

19. The Legges and the Norths: See *ODNB*, for Francis North, first Baron Guilford (1637–85), and George Legge, first Baron Dartmouth (ca. 1647–91). Financial affairs of Lord and Lady Dartmouth: Bargar, *Lord Dartmouth and the American Revolution*, pp. 5–8; and their marriage settlement and valuation of their estates in 1756, D1501/A/1/1-6 and D564/13/2/2, SCRO. The tortuous finances of Lord North and his family can be unraveled from the North Papers at the Bodleian Library. The principal sources are the account book of Lord Guilford (1756–75), MSS North.b.15, and the assortment of papers in MSS North.b.29, esp. fols. 152–55. Lord North's financial embarrassment arose from the terms of his marriage settlement with Anne Speke, dated May 20, 1756. Her principal asset was the Ilminster estate, made up of more than three thousand acres centered on Dillington Park, though much of it consisted of woods, orchards, and pasture rather than prime arable land. Including a house in Piccadilly, her fortune had a capital value of at least £80,000 (based on the rent roll of about £3,000 a year). However, because North's father, Lord Guilford, was struggling with his own inherited obligations, North agreed to pay him a sum of £15,400 in seven annual installments. It was assumed that this could be financed from the Ilminster property, but the burden proved too onerous, partly because some of the land at Ilminster was mortgaged, and partly because an annuity had to be paid to Anne Speke's unmarried half sister. At the

end of the 1760s, North began a program of improvements to the estate, but even so and despite the benefit of his official salary he ran chronically into debt until eventually, in 1777, George III agreed to pay off North's borrowings from the king's own pocket. On the Norths and the Spekes in Somerset, and the marriage settlement, see the Dillington estate papers, files DD/CA 2 (the 1756 deed of settlement), DD/CA/164, DD/CA/165, and T/AH/sro/89 (maps and surveys, 1768–69), Somerset Heritage Centre.

20. The Brudenell connection: North Papers at the Bodleian, many references, and Joan Wake, *The Brudenells of Deene* (London, 1953), pp. 287–95.

21. Dartmouth's Christianity: Edwin Sidney, *The Life of Richard Hill* (London, 1839), pp. 80–95; and D. Bruce Hindmarsh, *John Newton, and the English Evangelical Tradition* (Oxford, 1996), pp. 106–111. His conversion and relationship with Whitefield: Luke Tyerman, *The Life of the Reverend George Whitefield* (London, 1877), vol. 2, pp. 399–401, 414–16; and G. C. B. Davies, *The Early Cornish Evangelicals, 1735–1760* (London, 1951), pp. 117–19. On the evangelical movement, see D. W. Bebbington, *Evangelicalism in Modern Britain* (London, 1989), esp. pp. 5–17; and the entries in the *ODNB* for Martin Madan, William Romaine, and Henry Venn.

22. For "Beware of the general corruption," see Charles de Coetlogon's eulogy for Baron Smythe, *The Death of the Righteous: A Public Loss* (London, 1778), p. 29. Lord Dartmouth secured de Coetlogon's appointment as an assistant chaplain at the Lock Hospital. His Calvinist sermon *The Divine Message* (London, 1773) conveys a clear idea of Dartmouth's own beliefs. It was intended, said the author, "as an antidote to the dangerous and spreading evils of infidelity, Arianism and immorality."

23. Baron Smythe: Entry in the *ODNB* and de Coetlogon's eulogy, pp. 24–25.

Part Two: The Sending of the Tea
Chapter Six: The East India Crisis

1. *Public Advertiser,* Oct. 13, 1772.

2. Lord North in September and October 1772: MSS North d.24, fols. 170–78, Bodleian Library.

3. For "Things both at home and abroad," see Burke to William Dowdeswell, Oct. 27, 1772, in *The Correspondence of Edmund Burke,* vol. 2, July 1768–June 1774, ed. Lucy S. Sutherland (Cambridge, U.K., 1960), p. 349.

4. For "this immense, unruly town," see Lord Hardwicke to Sir Stanier Porten (Lord Rochford's deputy), Jan. 28, 1773, in *Calendar of Home Office Papers of the Reign of George III, 1773–1775,* ed. Richard Arthur Roberts (London, 1899), p. 9.

5. Public opinion: Tim Blanning, *The Pursuit of Glory: Europe, 1648–1815* (London, 2008), pp. 332–35. For a comprehensive account of the political role of newspapers and their use by John Wilkes and his supporters, see another pioneering book by John Brewer, *Party Ideology and Popular Politics at the Accession of George III* (Cambridge, U.K., 1976), chap. 8. Newspaper circulation and readership: Hannah Barker, *Newspapers, Politics, and English Society, 1695–1855* (Harlow, U.K., 2000), pp. 47–48; and Brewer, *Party Ideology and Popular Politics,* pp. 142–43.

6. For "a Senate composed," see speech by John Wilkes at the Guildhall, Oct. 8, 1772,

Public Advertiser, Oct. 9, 1772. London politics in 1772–73: George Rudé, *Wilkes and Liberty* (Oxford, 1962), pp. 168–70; and Reginald R. Sharpe, *London and the Kingdom* (London, 1895), vol. 3, pp. 130–35. Wilkesite critique of Parliament: John Cannon, *Parliamentary Reform, 1640–1832* (Cambridge, U.K., 1973), pp. 64–66.

7. Hayley served as an MP for London from 1774 to 1781. Despite his importance as an intermediary between the Boston patriots and the Wilkesites in London and as one of the leading merchants trading with America, Hayley's career remains obscure. For what little is known about his business career, see Katherine A. Kellock, "London Merchants and the Pre-1776 Debts," *Guildhall Studies in London History* 1, no. 3 (Oct. 1974), pp. 120, 129. My own research suggests that Hayley probably originated from a Presbyterian family in the Kidderminster and Bewdley area of Worcestershire, an old Presbyterian stronghold, before joining the London mercantile firm run from Aldgate by the Storke family, who had been trading with New England since the late seventeenth century.

8. On the financial plight of the East India Company, and for the sequence of events between September 1772 and February 1773, see the Secrecy Committee reports, cited above in note 17 of chapter 1; the board minutes of the Bank of England, at the Bank of England Archives, G4/21; and the minutes of the General Court of the East India Company, B/258, pp. 53–103, IOR. For the negotiations with Lord North, see official minute book of the Treasury Board, file T29/42, NAK. Also see Lucy S. Sutherland, *East India Company in Eighteenth-Century Politics* (Oxford, 1962), chaps. 8 and 9.

9. September 23 meeting: *General Evening Post,* Sept. 24, 1772.

10. For "The damned East India Company," *see* Rochford to Gower, Oct. 10, 1772, PRO 30/29/1/14, fol. 667, NAK.

11. Ownership of the East India Company: Huw Bowen, *The Business of Empire: The East India Company and Imperial Britain, 1756–1833* (Cambridge, U.K., 2005), chap. 4, esp. pp. 102–4.

12. Mrs. Thrale on Colebrooke: Katharine C. Balderston, ed., *Thraliana* (Oxford, 1942), vol. 1, pp. 333–35. On Colebrooke's activities in 1771–73: Lucy S. Sutherland, "Sir George Colebrooke's World Corner in Alum," in *Economic History: A Supplement to the Economic Journal,* vol. 3 (1934–37), pp. 236–58; letters to Baron Mure of Caldwell relating to Colebrooke in *Selections from the Family Papers Preserved at Caldwell* (Maitland Club, Glasgow, 1854), vol. 3; and newspaper reports of his bankruptcy, in the *Morning Chronicle,* April 3 and April 13, 1773, and the *Daily Advertiser,* April 8.

13. George III on the "rapine and ill-conduct" of the East India Company: George III to Lord North, March 9, 1773, in *CG3,* vol. 2, p. 459.

14. For "Papers are ordered everyday," see Burke to Dowdeswell, Oct. 27, 1772: See note 3 above.

15. November riot: Rudé, *Wilkes and Liberty;* and Sharpe, *London and the Kingdom.*

16. "The Fair Consumer": His letter appeared in several newspapers, but the earliest publication seems to have been in *The Gazetteer and New Daily Advertiser,* Sept. 26, 1772.

Chapter Seven: WHIGS, WEST INDIANS, AND THOMAS HUTCHINSON

1. The king's speech at the opening of Parliament, *London Gazette,* Nov. 24–28, 1772.

2. For "poor dumb creature," see *ODNB,* life of Rockingham by S. M. Farrell.

3. Makeup of Parliament : Sir Lewis Namier and John Brooke, ed., *The History of Parliament 1754–1790* (London, 1964), General Introduction.

4. For "I never felt more distress," *see* Rockingham to William Dowdeswell, Nov. 17, 1772, file WWM/R/I/1412 (a).

5. For "Many men of tender feelings," see Rockingham to Burke, Oct. 28, 1772, in Sutherland, *East India Company in Eighteenth-Century Politics,* p. 242.

6. For "spoke incomparably," see Frederick Montagu to Rockingham, Dec. 8, 1772, WWM/R/I/1416; for "panic struck," see Dowdeswell to Rockingham, Dec. 20, 1772, WWM/R/I/1419.

7. For the career of William Crichton, the principal published source is Huw Bowen's sketch in the *ODNB*. His business activities can be pieced together from the records of Alexander Houston & Company, MS 8793, foreign letter book, 1776–78, NLS. Also see Vere Langford Oliver, ed., *Caribbeana* (London, 1912), vol. 2, pp. 236, 349.

8. Society of West India Merchants: Microfilm of minute books (1769–79), M915, reel 1.1, Special Collections, Senate House Library, University of London.

9. For "Irascible, intemperate," see Nathaniel Wraxall, quoted in I. R. Christie, "George Johnstone," in Namier and Brooke (1964).

10. Hurricane: *London Gazette,* Nov. 24–28, 1772; and Oliver, *Caribbeana,* vol. 2, pp. 322–23.

11. Robert Herries is another rather elusive character. He can be pursued by way of Jacob M. Price's *France and the Chesapeake* (Ann Arbor, Mich., 1973), vol. 1, pp. 620–48; *Scots Magazine,* June 1773, pp. 292–94; and Sir William Forbes, *Memoirs of a Banking House* (London, 1860), pp. 29–30. His brother's tea smuggling: Dermigny, *La Chine et l'Occident,* vol. 2, p. 643. Scottish connection between the Herries and Johnstone families: C. L. Johnstone, *History of the Johnstones* (Edinburgh, 1909), pp. 243–44.

12. Hutchinson's family: Bernard Bailyn, *The Ordeal of Thomas Hutchinson* (Cambridge, Mass., 1974), pp. 11–15, 154–55.

13. Hutchinson and the Palmers: Biography of Eliakim Palmer, in *Sibley's Harvard Graduates,* ed. Clifford K. Shipton (Boston, 1951), vol. 8, pp. 239–45. William Palmer: *Burke's Landed Gentry* (1879), vol. 2, pp. 1227–28; and W. R. Powell, ed., *A History of the County of Essex* (London, 1966), vol. 5, pp. 140–50, with details of Palmer's country estate at Nazeing Park. William Palmer's holdings in East India stock can be found in the company's share register, IOR, L/AG/14/5/18. This also gives his London address in Devonshire Square, where Thomas Hutchinson visited Palmer several times in 1775.

14. Thomas Hutchinson Jr. to John Wendell of Portsmouth, N.H., Sept. 14, 1769, b. MS Am 1907 (191), Wendell Papers, Houghton Library, Harvard University.

15. Thomas Hutchinson, private letter to Lord Hillsborough, Sept. 10, 1771, Hutchinson Letter Books on microfilm, vol. 27, p. 225, MHS. Altogether, during 1772 and 1773 Hutchinson wrote eleven letters to William Palmer, almost all of them concerned with their dealings in tea.

To understand the competitive dynamics of the tea trade in America between 1769 and 1772—when, because of the Townshend duty, Americans were boycotting tea imported from England—we need to know why the smugglers enjoyed such a clear advantage. The arithmetic was as follows. Purchased wholesale from the East India Company in London, a pound of Bohea cost about thirty-three pence, including the customs duties already paid by the company. On top of that, the dealer had to pay an excise duty that brought the total to about forty-one pence. If he intended to export the tea to America, he received a rebate of the customs and excise, bringing his cost per pound back down to about twenty-eight pence. However, in Amsterdam, a smuggler could buy the same Bohea more cheaply, at about twenty-four pence, because the Dutch had smaller overheads and lower costs of finance and used larger, more efficient ships to sail to China. So the smuggler from Holland to America had an advantage of four pence per pound, or seven pence when we include the effect of the Townshend duty payable in the colonies on legally imported tea. In other words, American smugglers could afford to undercut the legal traders by as much as 25 percent. Hence the need for Palmer, Hutchinson, and the East India Company to come up with a ploy to close the competitive gap.

16. Thomas Hutchinson to William Palmer, Sept. 11, 1772, Hutchinson Letter Books, vol. 27, pp. 388–89, MHS.

17. Palmer's objections: Minutes of the East India Company Committee of Correspondence, Jan. 5–6, 1772, D/27, pp. 195–96, IOR.

18. East India Company letter to the Hopes: Reply from Hope & Company, Jan. 12, 1773, E/1/57, fols. 21–22, IOR.

19. Meeting of the General Court of the East India Company, Jan. 7, 1773, B/258, General Court Minute Book, 1770–73, pp. 100–101, IOR; and *Craftsman; or, Say's Weekly Journal*, Jan. 16, 1773.

20. For "pelted at & disavowed," see Augustus Keppel to the Marquess of Rockingham, March 15, 1773, WWM/R/1/1428.

21. North's approval for shipping of surplus tea to America: Note of a conversation between Sulivan and Lord North, Jan. 14, 1773, WWM/R/1/1423(a).

22. Colebrooke, *Retrospection*, part 2, pp. 45-47.

23. Treasury paper on tea sales to America, January 18, 1773: Add. MSS 38398, vol. 209, fols. 1–5, Liverpool Papers, BL.

24. "All depends upon Circumstances": BFP, Vol. 20, p.147.

Chapter Eight: MASSACHUSETTS ON THE EVE

1. Samuel Adams to Darius Sessions (deputy governor of Rhode Island), Jan. 2, 1773, in *The Writings of Samuel Adams*, ed. Harry Alonzo Cushing (New York, 1904–8), vol. 2, p. 398.

2. These comments about East Germany are based partly on the author's personal recollections of his visits to Berlin, Weimar, and Leipzig in 1989–90 and partly on David Childs, *The Fall of the GDR* (Harlow, U.K., 2001), pp. 28–32.

3. Pownalborough: Richard D. Brown, *Revolutionary Politics in Massachusetts: The Boston Committee of Correspondence and the Towns, 1772–1774* (Cambridge, Mass., 1970), p. 106; and James S. Leamon, "Maine in the American Revolution, 1763–1787," in *Maine: The Pine Tree State from Prehistory to the Present*, ed. Richard W. Judd et al. (Orono, Maine, 1995), pp. 144–52.

4. Local government and public opinion in Massachusetts: Benjamin W. Labaree, *Colonial Massachusetts: A History* (Millwood, N.Y., 1979), esp. chap. 8; and Brown, *Revolutionary Politics in Massachusetts*.

5. Topography and appearance of Boston: Thomas Pemberton's description in *Collections of the Massachusetts Historical Society* 3 (1794), pp. 241–304; Nathaniel B. Shurtleff, *A Topographical and Historical Description of Boston* (Boston, 1890), esp. pp. 66–70, 77–90; and Annie Haven Thwing, *The Crooked and Narrow Streets of the Town of Boston, 1630–1822* (Boston, 1920). For anyone studying the subject, the best place to start is the excellent local history section on the open shelves in the Bates Hall in the Boston Public Library.

6. Cotton Mather, in his *Magnalia Christi Americana* of 1702, in *The Puritans: A Sourcebook of Their Writings*, ed. Perry Miller and Thomas H. Johnson (Mineola, N.Y., 2001), p. 173.

7. Trade statistics: HM Customs, *Accounts of Vessels Entering American Ports, 1772*, MS North a.12, Bodleian Library; and Jacob M. Price, "New Time Series for Scotland's and Britain's Trade with the Thirteen Colonies and States, 1740 to 1791," *William and Mary Quarterly*, 3rd ser., 32, no. 2 (April 1975), pp. 307–25. Social and economic conditions: Richard Archer, *As If an Enemy's Country: The British Occupation of Boston and the Origins of Revolution* (Oxford, 2010), pp. 7–9, 21; Allan Kulikoff, "The Progress of Inequality in Revolutionary Boston," *William and Mary Quarterly*, 3rd ser., 28, no. 3 (July 1971); and William Pencak and Ralph J. Crandall, "Metropolitan Boston Before the American Revolution: An Urban Interpretation of the Imperial Crisis," in *Proceedings of the Bostonian Society* (1977–83), pp. 57–79.

8. The countryside: Robert A. Gross, *The Minutemen and Their World* (New York, 1976), chap. 4; and Brian Donahue, *The Great Meadow: Farmers and the Land in Colonial Concord* (New Haven, Conn., 2004), esp. chap. 8.

9. Brattle Square: Samuel K. Lothrop, *A History of the Church in Brattle Street* (Boston, 1851), esp. pp. 20–26, with the manifesto of 1699, and 92–102, concerning its rebuilding in 1772–73. Also see *Boston Post-Boy*, Feb. 24, 1772, and *Massachusetts Gazette*, Feb. 27 and Oct. 15, 1772.

10. Samuel Cooper: Charles W. Akers, *The Divine Politician: Samuel Cooper and the American Revolution in Boston* (Boston, 1982), pp. 20–22. For more about the flavor of religious thinking in Boston, see Edward M. Griffin, *Old Brick: Charles Chauncy of Boston, 1705–1787* (Minneapolis, 1980), esp. pp. 109–25, 172–75, dealing with the cooperation between Chauncy and Cooper.

11. John Adams on John Hancock: Adams to William Tudor, June 1, 1817, in *Works of John Adams*, vol. 10, pp. 260–61. The best Hancock biographies are William M. Fowler, *The Baron of Beacon Hill* (Boston, 1980) and W. T. Baxter, *The House of Hancock: Business in Boston, 1724–1775* (Cambridge, Mass., 1945).

12. Johnny Dupe: Quoted by Shipton, in his strangely hostile biography of Hancock in *Sibley's Harvard Graduates*, pp. 422–23.

13. Hancock the public man: Fowler, *Baron of Beacon Hill*, p. 143. Hancock, Palfrey, and Wilkes: the William Palfrey Papers in the Houghton Library at Harvard University, and esp. the 1774 inventory of Palfrey's home, in bMS Am 1704.18 (14), folder 18; and his entertaining journal of his visit to London in 1771, at bMS Am 1704.18 (46).

14. Hancock's donation of books: UA III 50.15.30, *Gifts of Books Presented by Mr. Hancock*, Harvard University Archives.

15. Decline of Hancock's business: Hancock letter book (1762–83) on microfilm at the Baker Library of the Harvard Business School, vol. JH-6, pp. 392–420; also, in the Hancock Papers at the Baker Library, letters from London, 1772–74, box 16,

folder 5; and in the Palfrey Papers at the Houghton Library, a letter from Hayley & Hopkins, June 25, 1773, at MS Am 1704.3 (93). This period is discussed by Baxter, *House of Hancock*, pp. 281–82. My quotation comes from the letter book, JH-6, pp. 409 and 411, letter from Hancock to Hayley, Nov. 4, 1772.

16. Adams, writing as *Candidus*, in *Boston Gazette*, Oct. 7, 1771.

17. The Boston pamphlet: *The Votes and Proceedings of the Freeholders and Other Inhabitants of the Town of Boston, in Town Meeting Assembled* (Boston, 1772). For the context in which it appeared, see Brown, *Revolutionary Politics in Massachusetts*, pp. 65–74.

18. Hutchinson's reply: Bailyn, *Ordeal of Thomas Hutchinson*, pp. 202–11.

19. Adams to Lee, April 9, 1773, in Cushing, *Writings of Samuel Adams*, vol. 3, p. 24.

Chapter Nine: THE BOSTON TEA PARTY: PRELUDE

1. George III to Lord North, May 22, 1773, in *CG3*, vol. 2, p. 491.

2. The debate on the Tea Act, April 26, 1773: *PDNA*, vol. 3, pp. 487–92.

3. Diplomatic situation in 1773: Roberts, *"Great Britain and the Swedish Revolution,"* pp. 1–46. For a more general account of British foreign policy at the period, see H. M. Scott, *"Britain as a European Great Power in the Age of the American Revolution,"* in *Britain and the American Revolution*, ed. H. T. Dickinson (London, 1998), pp. 180–96.

4. For "If I sail," see Roberts (1964) p. 40n, and the life of Saunders in *ODNB*. The navy's monitoring of the situation at Toulon and the plan to use fireships: Sandwich's letter of April 24, 1773, to the commanding officer in Gibraltar, Secret Letters, ADM2/1333, fols. 7–8, NAK. Strength of the Royal Navy relative to France and Spain and problems of mobilization: Nicholas Tracy, *Navies, Deterrence, and Independence: Britain and Seapower in the 1760s and 1770s* (Vancouver, 1988), pp. 31–33, 40–42; and N. A. M. Rodger, *The Insatiable Earl* (London, 1993), pp. 131–45.

5. Spithead review: George Marsh, "An Account of the Preparation Made for the Entertainment of the King at Portsmouth in June 1773," *Colburn's United Service Magazine* (1887), pt. 1, pp. 433–49, 517–30; and *Annual Register for 1773* (London, 1793), vol. 1, pp. 202–7.

6. Lord Suffolk: Roberts, "Great Britain and the Swedish Revolution," p. 40.

7. British diplomatic isolation: Scott, "Britain as a European Great Power," and the wide-ranging, provocative analysis by Brendan Simms, *Three Victories and a Defeat: The Rise and Fall of the First British Empire, 1714–1783* (London, 2007), chaps. 20 and 21.

8. Dunmore: *ODNB*; and *DAR*, vol. 4.

9. Smith's letter: D.1778.II/592, SCRO.

10. Dartmouth's comment to Franklin: Franklin to Cushing, May 4, 1773, in *BFP*, vol. 20, pp. 200–203. Dartmouth's "veil of error" letter to Hutchinson: From the Colonial Office, Dec. 9, 1772, in *DAR*, vol. 5, pp. 238–41.

11. George III and the Massachusetts petition: *BFP*, vol. 20, pp. 222–24.

12. Dartmouth's letter to Cushing, and Cushing's August letter in reply: Ibid., pp. 376f–79.

13. On the role of William Palmer and the other London dealers in the sending of the tea: the evidence from London was transcribed and published in America in the nineteenth century by Francis S. Drake, *Tea Leaves: Being a Collection of the Documents Relating to*

the Shipment of the Tea to the American Colonies in 1773 (Boston, 1884), pp. 189–247. However, the picture only becomes complete with Hutchinson's letters to William Palmer, Nov. 15 and 16, 1772, Feb. 25, April 21, June 26, and Aug. 7, 1773, Letter Book 27, Hutchinson Letter Books, MHS.

14. In December—this is hard to believe, but it is true—John Pownall had to write to a Whitehall colleague for confirmation that the Treasury had issued the export license: HMC Dartmouth, 14th report, app. 10, vol. 2 (London, 1895), p. 184.

15. Franklin to Cushing, Sept. 12, 1773, in *BFP*, vol. 20, pp. 400–401.

16. Franklin to Cooper, July 7, 1773, in *BFP*, vol. 20, pp. 268–71, with other letters of the same date to Cushing and the Massachusetts House of Representatives, pp. 271–86.

17. Text of the Hutchinson letters: *BFP*, vol. 20, app., pp. 539–80. Thomas Whately: *ODNB*, and above, note 13 to chapter 4.

18. For "a gentleman of character and distinction," see Bailyn, *Ordeal of Thomas Hutchinson*, pp. 224–38, for a full discussion of the affair. Professor Bailyn makes an excellent case for identifying John Pownall's brother Thomas, the ex-governor of Massachusetts, as the gentleman in question.

19. Whiteford and the *Advertiser:* W. A. S. Hewins, ed., *The Whiteford Papers* (Oxford, 1898), pp. 143–44.

20. The columns ran in the *Public Advertiser*, Sept. 8, 11, 14, and 22, 1773. Apart from the *Edict*, the most famous was "Rules by Which a Great Empire May Be Reduced to a Small One," Sept. 11, 1773. They can be found reprinted in *BFP*, vol. 20.

21. John, Lord Campbell, *Lives of the Lord Chancellors* (London, 1856–57), vol. 8, p. 8.

Chapter Ten: THE BOSTON TEA PARTY: CLIMAX

1. Alexander Leslie, letter from Boston, Dec. 6, 1773, GD26/9/512/5, Leslie-Melville Papers, NAS.

2. Montagu's journal, entry for Nov. 18, 1773, ADM 50/17, NAK.

3. Sixty-Fourth Regiment of Foot at Castle William: Regimental muster roll (June–Dec. 1773), WO12/7312, NAK. Comments on Alexander Leslie: Major James Wemyss, *Sketches of the Character of General Staff Officers*, file HOU b MS Sparks 22, p. 215, Jared Sparks Collection, Houghton Library. Leslie's letter: See note 1 above.

4. Early stages of American resistance to the tea: Benjamin W. Labaree, *The Boston Tea Party* (Oxford, 1964), chap. 5; Benjamin Carp, *Defiance of the Patriots: The Boston Tea Party and the Making of America* (New Haven, Conn., 2010), chaps. 4–6; and the American papers from the House of Lords referred to below in note 8.

5. Pigou and Booth: Kellock, "London Merchants and the Pre-1776 American Debts," pp. 140–41.

6. Adams's letters to Hawley, October 4 and 13, 1773: Cushing, *Writings of Samuel Adams*, vol. 3, pp. 52–62.

7. Thomas Young: Pauline Maier, "Reason and Revolution: The Radicalism of Dr. Thomas Young," *American Quarterly* 28, no. 2 (Summer 1976). Importation to Boston in 1773 of duty paid tea on Hancock's ships: Davison & Newman Papers, London Metropolitan Archives, Gl.Ms. 8633.

8. Hannah Fayerweather Winthrop to Mercy Otis Warren, November 10, 1773, *Correspondence with Mercy Otis Warren*, microfilm edition, reel 1, MHS.

9. Archive repositories in Great Britain contain a wealth of source material relating to the Boston Tea Party. The most important collections are the Parliamentary Archives at Westminster, which contain the House of Lords copies of the documents laid before Parliament by Lord Dartmouth in March 1774, HL/PO/JO/10/7/406–8; and the Colonial Office records in the National Archives, where the relevant files are CO5/160 and CO5/763. These include all the witness statements taken in London and Boston, the official dispatches from Hutchinson, Montagu, and Leslie, and some American newspapers and pamphlets such as *The Alarm* of October 1773. Some of these papers have been transcribed and published, first in *Tea Leaves* by Francis S. Drake in 1884 (see above, note 13 to chapter 9) and then in *DAR*, vol. 6, in the 1970s. However, it is unwise to rely on selectively printed material because the various accounts of the destruction of the tea and the events leading up to it contain many discrepancies that become apparent only when the sources are compared. Typescripts of the relevant letters of Thomas Hutchinson are on microfilm at the Massachusetts Historical Society, in Letter Book 17, pp. 1077–1165, covering the period November 12, 1773–January 4, 1774.

10. The meetings on November 29 and 30: L. F. S. Upton, "Proceedings of Ye Body Respecting the Tea," *William and Mary Quarterly*, 3rd ser., 22, no. 2 (April 1965), pp. 287–300.

11. John Adams's reading of Rousseau's *Social Contract* and its influence in Massachusetts: R. R. Palmer, *The Age of Democratic Revolution* (Princeton, N.J., 1959), vol. 1, *The Challenge*, pp. 223–24.

12. Alexander Leslie: See note 1 above. This comment appears in a postscript, dated Dec. 11, to his letter of Dec. 6.

13. Alexander Leslie to General Haldimand, Dec. 16, in "The Montresor Journals," ed. G. D. Scull, in *Collections of the New-York Historical Society* 14 (1881), pp. 531–32.

14. For the meeting on the sixteenth, Upton, *"Proceedings of Ye Body Respecting the Tea,"* pp. 297–300, seems to be the most reliable source, when checked against the witness statements preserved in London and against the accounts of the Tea Party given by Labaree, *Boston Tea Party*, and Carp, *Defiance of the Patriots*.

15. Two lists of names of the Tea Party's participants survive from the nineteenth century. The first, containing 58 names, appeared in 1835 in *Traits of the Tea Party*, whose author was a young lawyer, journalist, and antislavery activist from Boston, Benjamin Bussey Thatcher. A second, much longer list of 113 names was printed by Francis S. Drake in *Tea Leaves*. Dealing first with Drake: While much of his book remains extremely useful, his list of the men who destroyed the tea has to be treated with caution. For example, it contains the name of David Kinnison, who died in Chicago in 1852, allegedly aged 115. Although Kinnison was clearly an impostor—centenarian or not, no trace of him survives in Boston town records from the eighteenth or nineteenth century—Drake did not question his story. Indeed, in general Drake's methods were less than rigorous. He took Thatcher's list and then added 55 names, but he seems to have collected these from hearsay without attempting to verify what he was told. This is apparent from a

file of Drake's working papers at the New England Historic Genealogical Society in Boston (11.D.3 [Dr.24], Special Collections).

In 1871, Drake was commissioned to produce a biographical dictionary for the Massachusetts Sons of the Cincinnati, a society of descendants of officers in George Washington's army. Drake circulated a questionnaire to the members and asked them for information about their forebears. Then word for word he copied what they told him into the dictionary, published in 1873, without any further authentication. In those cases where his respondents claimed that their forebears had been at Griffin's Wharf, he incorporated the material into *Tea Leaves* when it appeared a decade later. Drake's handwritten notes suggest that for the rest of the names he relied on press reports and earlier books, all of which had first appeared long after the revolution.

We are on much safer ground with the 1835 list from Thatcher. None of his names are absurd, like that of David Kinnison, and most check out well against the archive material that survives from revolutionary Boston. Moreover, Thatcher had ready access to men and women with firsthand information about the period. Starting in 1825, at the time of the fiftieth anniversary of the outbreak of the war, a few of the last survivors of the Tea Party had begun to give press interviews, including the Boston shoemaker George R. T. Hewes, whom Thatcher met and with whom he cooperated on another book. Indeed, Thatcher's own family had played a prominent role in the events of 1773–75. His grandfather Reuben Brown was a minuteman at Concord, and his great-uncle was Henry Knox, Washington's chief of artillery.

Thatcher said that he took his list from "an aged Bostonian, well-acquainted with the history of our subject." This might well have been the veteran journalist Benjamin Russell (1761–1845), the son of John Russell, who is known to have been a Tea Party participant. Benjamin Russell knew Paul Revere well, he also befriended George Hewes, and during the 1830s he remained very active in Boston politics at a time when Thatcher was making his name in the town. In the light of all this, Thatcher's list appears to be sound, as far as it goes, even though it cannot be complete. All the eyewitnesses suggest that far more than 58 men were involved. I am grateful to J. L. Bell for his suggestion that Russell was the source of the list, which he and I discussed in Cambridge, Massachusetts, in the fall of 2011.

16. Sir Lewis Namier, *England in the Age of the American Revolution* (London, 1930), p. 32. For an incisive American interpretation: chaps. 12 and 13 of Robert W. Tucker and James C. Hendrickson, *The Fall of the First British Empire: Origins of the American War of Independence* (Baltimore, Md., 1982).

17. North's speech on April 18, 1785, in *Parliamentary History of England* (London, 1815), vol. 25, cols. 456–61.

PART THREE: DOWN THE SLOPE

Chapter Eleven: THE CABINET IN WINTER

1. For the political debates about America in London in 1774–75, the most reliable scholarly studies are two fine works by British historians: Bernard Donoughue, *British Politics and the American Revolution: The Path to War, 1773-1775* (London, 1964) and P. D. G.

Thomas, *Tea Party to Independence: The Third Phase of the American Revolution, 1773–1776* (Oxford, 1991). However, these are Anglocentric books, focused on high politics at Westminster, and they tend to neglect not only the American dimension of the story but also its military and economic elements. The approach adopted in *An Empire on the Edge* has involved not only a re-examination of the British political papers used by Donoughue and Thomas and the addition of new ones, but also a close reading of the newspapers of the period. In order to trace the interaction of events on each side of the ocean as the war drew near, one has to reconstruct the flow of news as accurately as possible: and this can be done using the press reports that survive. On the British side, the most useful coverage can be found in the *London Evening Post* (very anti-government); the *Public Advertiser* (mildly anti-government); the *Lloyd's Evening Post* (pro-government); and the *Morning Post* (non-aligned but scurrilous). In the 1770s, British political journalists left no stone unturned in their pursuit of a story and they were just as funny, irreverent and well-informed as they are in the twenty-first century. The American papers tended to be less entertaining, but they were very thorough and—which is still the case today—more reliable about numbers and quotations. As for British official material, *An Empire on the Edge* also makes extensive use of Admiralty and Treasury documents, which fell outside Donoughue's and Thomas's field of interest. These records are exceptionally valuable because of their precision in matters of detail and chronology.

2. Alexander Wedderburn, later Lord Loughborough: The best source is the biography by John, Lord Campbell in vols. 7 and 8 of his *Lives of the Lord Chancellors*, with the quotation from Thurlow on p. 206 of vol. 8.

3. Whitehall and the Cockpit: *London and Its Environs Described* (London, 1761), vol. 2, pp. 154–55; and *London in Miniature* (London, 1755), pp. 109–10. Accounts of the Privy Council meeting on January 29: Campbell, *Lives of the Lord Chancellors*, vol. 8, pp. 15–21; William Temple Franklin, *Memoirs of the Life and Writings of Benjamin Franklin* (London, 1817–18), vol. 1, pp. 427–28, and app. 7; and John Bowring, ed., *The Works of Jeremy Bentham* (Edinburgh, 1838–43), vol. 10, pp. 59–60. Wedderburn's speech: *BFP*, vol. 21, pp. 37–70.

4. For "all the licensed scurrility," see *Public Advertiser*, Feb. 2, 1774.

5. *Public Advertiser*, Feb. 4, 1774.

6. The American business: Lord John Cavendish to the Marquess of Rockingham, Jan. 29, 1774, WWM R/I/1479.

7. For "a witling, a punster and a prig," see *Public Advertiser*, Feb. 7, 1774.

8. Buckinghamshire's motion, February 1, 1774: *PDNA*, vol. 4, p. 8. For cabinet meetings and Dartmouth's conduct of affairs, the principal sources are the Dartmouth Papers, calendared by the Historical Manuscripts Commission, 14th Report, app. pt. 10 (London, 1895), vol. 2, pp. 192–213, covering the period January to June 1774.

9. Gage on colonial disobedience: Gage to Lord Barrington, June 28, 1768, and Sept. 8, 1770, in *CGG*, pp. 479–80, 556–57. His meeting with the king: George III to Lord North, Feb. 4, 1774, in *CG3*, vol. 3, p. 59.

10. Estimate of eighty thousand militiamen: *General Evening Post*, Feb. 12–15, 1774, quoting the *Newport (R.I.) Mercury*.

11. Charles Van: *Morning Post*, Jan. 31, 1774; and P. D. G. Thomas, "A Monmouthshire Politician of Character: Charles Van (d. 1776) of Llanwern," *Monmouthshire Antiquary* 18 (2002), pp. 85–89.

12. Edward Thurlow: Arthur Polson, *Law and Lawyers; or, Sketches of Legal History and Biography* (London, 1840), vol. 1, pp. 100–116; and Lord Campbell, *Lives of the Lord Chancellors*, vol. 7, esp. pp. 173–86.

13. *BFP*, vol. 20, pp. 106–15.

14. From the Dartmouth Papers: See note 8 above. The letter is calendared on p. 197.

15. On the legal obstacles to closure of a port, see William Blackstone, "Of the King's Prerogative," in *Commentaries on the Law of England* (London, 1765–69), bk. 1, chap. 7, as corrected in the second edition.

16. Thurlow's outburst: Historical Manuscripts Commission, *Manuscripts of Captain H. V. Knox* (Dublin, 1909), p. 270.

17. *CG3*, vol. 3, pp. 71–76.

Chapter Twelve: "Boston Must Be Destroyed"

1. *Public Advertiser*, March 4, 1774.

2. The House of Commons: Orlo Williams, "The Topography of the Old House of Commons" (Ministry of Works, 1953; unpublished monograph in the Parliamentary Archives, London); and for an account of the interior and the behavior of members, see P. D. G. Thomas, *The House of Commons in the Eighteenth Century* (Oxford, 1971), pp. 1–7.

3. On the career and personality of Edmund Burke: The superb biographical sketch by Paul Langford in the *ODNB*. Verses by Goldsmith: From his poem "Retaliation" (1774). Comment from a Frenchman: The Abbé Morellet, who met Burke early in 1773, in Sutherland, *Correspondence of Edmund Burke*, vol. 2, July 1768–June 1774, p. 425n.

4. The debate on March 7: *PDNA*, vol. 4, pp. 36–51, with Wedderburn on pp. 39–41 and Burke on pp. 41–44.

5. Debate on March 14: Ibid., pp. 55–82, with the "coldest proceedings" comment on pp. 77–78.

6. Merchants' deputation: *London Evening Post*, March 17–19, 1774. For data about the London firms that dealt with the colonies, see Kellock, "London Merchants and the Pre-1776 American Debts," with material about Hayley on p. 129. Weakness of the colonial lobby in Great Britain: Jacob M. Price, "Who Cared About the Colonies? The Impact of the Thirteen Colonies on British Society and Politics, 1714–1775," in *Strangers Within the Realm: Cultural Margins of the First British Empire*, eds. Bernard Bailyn and Philip D. Morgan (Chapel Hill, N.C., 1991), pp. 395–436.

7. Leaked story: By "Crito," *Morning Post*, March 17, 1774.

8. Debate on March 23: *PDNA*, pp. 87–112, with Charles Van on pp. 102, 106–7, 112. John Wilkes and the Tea Party: His appointment diary, Add. MSS 30,866 (No. 2), BL, shows him dining on January 20, 1774, with "several American gentlemen." This was the night when the news arrived from Boston. On March 25, he dined at William Lee's house with guests including Hugh Williamson, a physician from Philadelphia who had been in Boston and seen the tea destroyed. And then, on March 28, at George

Hayley's house, Wilkes met John Hancock's sea captain James Scott and also Captain Hall of the tea ship *Dartmouth*. The *London Evening Post*, its publisher, John Miller, and his relationship with Wilkes: Lucyle Werkmeister, *The London Daily Press, 1772–1792* (Lincoln, Neb., 1963), pp. 112–14. Also see a letter from Wilkes, Jan. 15, 1772, in Everett, *Letters of Junius*, pp. 358–59.

9. The Duke of Richmond: The only full-length study is Alison Olson, *The Radical Duke: Career and Correspondence of Charles Lennox, 3rd Duke of Richmond* (Oxford, 1961). My quotations come from pp. 4 and 12.

10. Richmond and resistance in Boston: A. F. Steuart, ed., *Last Journals of Horace Walpole* (London, 1910), vol. 1, p. 344.

11. *PDNA*, vol. 4, pp. 172–73, 177–78.

12. Debate on May 2, including Burke's speech on American taxation: *PDNA*, vol. 4, pp. 329–83. For the best edition of Burke's speech, see Paul Langford, ed., *The Writings and Speeches of Edmund Burke* (Oxford, 1981), vol. 2, pp. 406–63, with preface and notes.

13. Remark by George III: Steuart, *Last Journals of Horace Walpole*, vol. 1, p. 346.

14. Richard Rigby: *ODNB*.

15. *CG3*, vol. 3, pp. 102–3.

16. The dissenting motions: *PDNA*, vol. 4, pp. 417–19, 431–33.

17. Waning of anti-Catholicism among the ruling elite: Colin Haydon, *Anti-Catholicism in Eighteenth-Century England* (Manchester, U.K., 1993), chap. 5, esp. pp. 187–92. Another reason for animosity against Catholics to diminish was simply this: the fact that there were so few in England. A census of their numbers in 1767 produced a total of only 69,376.

18. Wedderburn on the Quebec Act: *PDNA*, vol. 4, p. 469.

19. The politics of London in the 1770s remain a murky subject, partly because so many of the personalities involved, including Frederick Bull, left very few letters and papers to posterity. The surviving correspondence of John Wilkes is also quite thin. For their political activities more generally, the principal sources are the newspapers, especially the *London Evening Post* and the *Public Advertiser;* the printed poll books, which list the voters for each candidate in parliamentary elections; and the collections from the Corporation of London and from some livery companies at the London Metropolitan Archives. We also have the benefit of scholarly research by John Sainsbury, *Disaffected Patriots: London Supporters of Revolutionary America, 1769–1782* (Kingston, Ont., 1987), and Julie Flavell, *When London Was Capital of America* (New Haven, Conn., 2010), with the latter dealing extensively with Stephen Sayre and the Lees.

   With regard to Bull: Box C.78, Noble Collection, LMA; and *Public Advertiser*, Jan. 2, 1772, and Dec. 2, 1773. There is a brief sketch in J. Parsons (publisher), *City Biography: Anecdotes and Memoirs* (London, 1800), pp. 84–87. Property deals in the West Indies by Stephen Sayre and William Lee: Dominica land sales register, April 1770, CO 106/11, fols. 58–59, and a printed list of proprietors, ca. 1772, CO 76/9, NAK. Electoral activities of the radical caucus in London: Records of the Framework Knitters' company, MSS 3445/2 and 3447, LMA; *Journal of the Court of Common Council*, microfilm X109/100, LMA; and Common Hall Papers, 1770–74, COL/CN/056-060, LMA. The last mentioned include material relating to the choice of Sayre and Lee as sheriffs, and drafts in Bull's handwriting of a Wilkesite manifesto for his 1773 election to

Parliament. Lists of the votes cast in the city: *A Corrected List of the Persons Who Have Polled for Frederick Bull* (London, 1773). This supports an estimate that 60 percent of the city's electorate supported Bull and the other radicals.

20. Events of June 18–22: *CG3*, vol. 3, pp. 112–13; Steuart, *Last Journals of Horace Walpole*, pp. 358–60; and Haydon, *Anti-Catholicism in Eighteenth-Century England*, pp. 193–203.

21. American reports of English opposition to the act, including the riot on June 22: *Boston Post-Boy*, Aug. 15 and 22, 1774; *Connecticut Journal*, Aug. 25, 1774; *New York Journal*, Aug. 25, 1774; *New Hampshire Gazette*, Aug. 26, 1774; and *Pennsylvania Packet*, Aug. 29, 1774.

22. Walpole on Dartmouth: Steuart, *Last Journals of Horace Walpole*, p. 322. Dartmouth to Gage: *DAR*, vol. 8, pp. 122–25.

Chapter Thirteen: THE REVOLUTION BEGINS

1. Greene to Samuel Ward Jr., July 10, 1774, in Showman et al., *Papers of General Nathanael Greene*, vol. 1, p. 65.

2. Elbridge Gerry and the militia: Gerry to the Boston Committee of Correspondence, April 4, 1774, in the committee's papers, microfilm reel ZL-231-2, Bancroft Collection. Gerry and Pickering: Clifford K. Shipton, ed., *Sibley's Harvard Graduates* (Boston, 1970), vol. 15, pp. 239–42, 448–51.

3. On the *Centinel*: Neil L. York, "Tag-Team Polemics: The 'Centinel' and His Allies in the Massachusetts Spy," *Proceedings of the Massachusetts Historical Society*, 3rd ser., 107 (1995), pp. 85–114. Hancock on the militia: *An Oration Delivered March 5, 1774* (Boston, 1774), printed text annotated by Harbottle Dorr at MHS.

4. Hutchinson, ed., *Diary and Letters of Thomas Hutchinson*, vol. 1, pp. 112–17.

5. The *Minerva: Boston Newsletter*, May 2, 1774.

6. Town meeting on May 13: *Massachusetts Gazette and Boston Post-Boy*, May 9–16, 1774.

7. Strategic significance of the Hudson valley: Gage to Lord Barrington, Feb. 7, 1766, quoted in John Richard Alden, *General Gage in America* (Baton Rouge, La., 1948), pp. 132–33; and Piers Mackesy, *The War for America 1775–83* (London, 1964), pp. 58–59 and 143–44.

8. Criticisms of General Gage: Major (later Lieutenant Colonel) James Wemyss, "Sketches of the Character of the General Staff Officers . . . That Served in America," transcript, file Hou.b. MS Sparks 22, Sparks Collection; and John Montresor, *Journals*, in *Collections of the New-York Historical Society* (New York, 1881), pp. 135–39. Also see John Shy's incisive account of the general, in his *A People Numerous and Armed* (New York, 1976).

9. Gage's swearing-in: *Boston Evening-Post*, May 23, 1774.

10. Gage to Lord Dartmouth, May 19, 1774, in *CGG*, vol. 1, p. 355.

11. Josiah Quincy Jr., *Observations on the Act of Parliament Commonly Called the Boston Port Bill* (Boston, 1774), pp. 10–19.

12. Alexander Leslie to the Earl of Leven, June 17–July 2, 1774, GD26/9/512/6, Leslie-Melville Papers, NAS.

13. The army in Boston: Details from the order book of General Gage, July 10–Dec. 9, 1774, microfilm, Lamont Library, Harvard University, photographed from the originals in the New York Historical Society.

14. Gage to Dartmouth, July 20, 1774, in *CGG*, vol. 1, pp. 361–62.

15. Charleston in July: Dispatch from Lieutenant Governor William Bull, July 31, 1774, in *DAR*, vol. 8, pp. 153–54.

16. For "A throne cannot be established," see Marblehead Committee of Correspondence to the Boston committee, July 28, 1774, ZL-231-2, pp. 499–502, Boston Committee of Correspondence Papers, Bancroft Collection. *Essex Gazette* story: Aug. 2–9, 1774.

17. For "I hope the acts," see Gage to Dartmouth, July 27, 1774, in *CGG*, vol. 1, p. 364; for "frenzy . . . of Popular rage," see Gage to Dartmouth, Aug. 27, 1774, in ibid., p. 366.

18. Cooper to Franklin, Aug. 15, 1774, in *BFP*, vol. 21, pp. 273–76. In general, for the events of August–September 1774 in Massachusetts, see T. H. Breen, *American Insurgents, American Patriots: The Revolution of the People* (New York, 2010), chaps. 3–5; and Roy Raphael, *The First American Revolution: Before Lexington and Concord* (New York, 2002).

19. Calley and the *Molly*: For Calley's background, see *Essex Gazette*, Aug. 9–16, 1768, and June 4–11, 1771; for his role in August 1774, see *Massachusetts Spy*, Aug. 25, 1774; *New York Journal*, Aug. 25, 1774; *New Hampshire Gazette*, Aug. 26, 1774; and *Connecticut Courant*, Aug. 30, 1774.

20. The Salem town meeting: Ronald M. Tagney, *A County in Revolution: Essex County at the Dawning of Independence* (Manchester, Mass., 1976), pp. 92–93.

21. General Gage's order book, note 12 above.

22. The Boston conference: Minutes of the meeting, microfilm reel ZL-231-1, pp. 702–5, Boston Committee of Correspondence Papers.

23. For "Popular fury," see Gage to Dartmouth, Aug. 27, 1774, in *CGG*, vol. 1, pp. 365–68. William Brattle and the gunpowder: Lucius R. Paige, *History of Cambridge, Massachusetts, 1630–1877* (Boston, 1877), pp. 404–7, 499–500; Robert P. Richmond, *Powder Alarm 1774* (Princeton, N.J., 1971), pp. 6–26; and General Gage's order book. Brattle's letter was printed in the *Boston Gazette*, Sept. 5, 1774.

24. For "When once the sword is drawn," see letter from Marblehead, Aug. 31, 1774, microfilm reel ZL-231-2, p. 507, Boston Committee of Correspondence Papers.

25. Gage to Dartmouth, Sept. 2, 1774, in *CGG*, vol. 1, pp. 369–72.

26. For "Civil government," see ibid.

27. Fortification of Boston: Gage's order book, note 12 above, entries for Sept. 1774; and John R. Galvin, *The Minute Men: The First Fight: Myths and Realities of the American Revolution* (Washington, D.C., 2006), pp. 68–72.

Chapter Fourteen: AN ELECTION IN ARCADIA

1. The party at the Oaks: Brownlow North to Lord Guilford, June 11, 1774, MS North.d.25, North Papers; *Morning Chronicle*, June 15, 1774; *London Magazine*, June 1774, pp. 299–300; and Alistair Rowan, "*Lord Derby's Reconstruction of the Oaks*," *Burlington Magazine*, Oct. 1985, pp. 678–87. For the text of the play as performed at Drury Lane, see John Burgoyne and David Garrick, *The Maid of the Oaks: A Dramatic Entertainment* (London, 1775). Stories in the American press: *Rivington's New York Gazetteer*, Aug. 25, 1774, reporting comments by Edmund Burke and others on June 8.

2. For "smothered in roses," see *St. James's Chronicle*, June 7–9, 1774.

3. For "extraordinary," see Dartmouth to Lord Dunmore, July 6, 1774, in *DAR*, vol. VIIII, p. 145.

4. Hutchinson's meetings in July with George III and Lord North: Hutchinson, *Diary and Letters of His Excellency Thomas Hutchinson*, vol. 1, pp. 157–82. Except where stated, this is the source for all quotations from Hutchinson.

5. For "cheerful, affable and easy," see Ralph S. Walker, ed., *James Beattie's London Diary, 1773* (Aberdeen, 1946), pp. 86–88.

6. George III to Lord North, July 1, 1774, in *CG3*, vol. 3, p. 116.

7. Sir Lewis Namier, "King George III: A Study of Personality" (1953), in *Crossroads of Power* (London, 1962), p. 129.

8. For the quotations, see entry for Aug. 3, in Hutchinson, *Diary and Letters of His Excellency Thomas Hutchinson*, pp. 203–4.

9. For "I am not a little perplexed," *see* Rockingham to the Duke of Portland, Oct. 1, 1774, quoted in Donoughue, *British Politics and the American Revolution*, p. 180. Lord Suffolk and the election: His speech in the House of Lords, Jan. 20, 1775, in *PDNA*, vol. 5, p. 271.

10. George III and the election: George III to Lord North, Aug. 24, 1774, in *CG3*, vol. 3, pp. 125–26.

11. Generally, on the election of 1774: Namier and Brooke, *History of Parliament*, vol. 1, pp. 73–80. I have also drawn heavily on press coverage, especially from the *Public Advertiser*, the *London Evening Post*, and *Berrow's Worcester Journal*.

12. Hume, *Letters and Journals of Lady Mary Coke*, vol. 4, pp. 407–8.

13. Entry for Oct. 10, 1774, in Hutchinson, *Diary and Letters of His Excellency Thomas Hutchinson*, p. 259.

14. Gower and Rochford: Quoted in Donoughue, *British Politics and the American Revolution*, p. 205.

15. Entry for Oct. 14, 1774, in Hutchinson, *Diary and Letters of His Excellency Thomas Hutchinson*, p. 261.

16. North and the highwaymen: North to Grey Cooper and John Robinson, Oct. 5, 1774, in Historical Manuscripts Commission, *Manuscripts of the Marquess of Abergavenny*, pp. 6–7.

17. Banbury election: Matthew Lamb (vicar of Banbury) to Lord Guilford, Oct. 3–18, 1774, MS North.d.15, fols. 199–215, North Papers.

18. Rockingham to the Duke of Portland, Oct. 1, 1774, file PwF 9084/2, Portland Papers, University of Nottingham Manuscripts and Special Collections.

19. Bull and the Catholics: *London Evening Post*, Sept. 24, 1774.

20. Politics in Worcester: From the files of *Berrow's Worcester Journal*, Sept.–Nov. 1774; and Valentine Green, *The History and Antiquities of the Town of Worcester* (London, 1796), vol. 2, pp. 18–22, 43–44, 66–67, 290–91.

21. Boswell to Johnson, Jan. 27, 1775, in James Boswell, *The Life of Samuel Johnson* (Oxford, 1946), vol. 1, p. 546. British public opinion in 1774–5: the leading authority is the American historian James E. Bradley, in two books, *Popular Politics and the American Revolution in England* (Macon, Ga., 1986) and *Religion, Revolution and English Radicalism* (Cambridge, 1990).

22. George III to Lord North, Sept. 11, 1774, in *CG3*, vol. 3, pp. 130–31.

Chapter Fifteen: THE ARMING OF AMERICA

1. Hugh Percy, second Duke of Northumberland, Sept. 12, 1774, quoted in his entry in the *ODNB*.

2. Yorke's dispatches from The Hague and Lord Suffolk's replies: From the British State Papers (Holland), June–Dec. 1774, SP84/543, NAK; and the Amsterdam intelligence reports at SP82/93. On Yorke: *ODNB*.

3. Benjamin Page, his role in the *Gaspée* incident, and the departure date of the *Smack*: *Newport Mercury*, Aug. 22, 1774, and Feb. 13, 1775; *Rhode Island Republican*, Aug. 26, 1824; and Page's file, S.3629, Revolutionary War Records, U.S. National Archives.

4. The Suffolk Resolves: *Middlesex Chronicle*, Oct. 27–29, 1774, and *Say's Weekly Journal*, Nov. 5, 1774. Text of the resolves and of the Continental Congress's motion supporting them: Worthington Chauncey Ford, ed., *Journals of the Continental Congress* (Washington, D.C., 1904), vol. 1, pp. 32–40.

5. Governor Robert Eden: *ODNB*; and Bernard C. Steiner, *Life and Administration of Robert Eden* (Baltimore, 1898), pp. 82–88.

6. Barrington's letter: Shute Barrington, *Political Life of William Wildman, Viscount Barrington* (London, 1815), pp. 148–50.

7. Hume, *Letters and Journals of Lady Mary Coke*, vol. 4, p. 441.

8. William Smith, quoted in Joseph S. Tiedemann, *Reluctant Revolutionaries: New York City and the Road to Independence* (Ithaca, N.Y., 1997), p. 200.

9. For "raised a universal flame," see William Fitzhugh, Oct. 18, 1774, quoted in David Ammerman, *In the Common Cause: American Response to the Coercive Acts of 1774* (Charlottesville, Va., 1974), p. 12.

10. The Continental Congress: Ibid., esp. chaps. 3 and 4, and Jack Rakove's review in *New England Quarterly* 48, no. 1 (May 1975).

11. Text of the Cambridge resolutions: *Boston Gazette*, Oct. 31, 1774.

12. For "I hope you will be firm," *CGG*, vol. 2, pp. 663–64; his earlier letter to Barrington, asking for twenty thousand men, is on pp. 655–56, dated Oct. 3. For Gage's order book, up to December 9, 1774, see note 12 to chapter 13 above. His order book for December 10, 1774–June 6, 1775, is in the manuscript collection at the Boston Public Library, file MS R 1.4.

13. All of these details come from Gage's order book.

Chapter Sixteen: THE FATAL DISPATCH

1. The Druids: *Morning Post*, Jan. 3 and 9, 1775.

2. Debate on the army estimates, Dec. 16, 1774, in *PDNA*, vol. 5, p. 252. For the estimates themselves, see *Journal of the House of Commons* 35 (Dec. 12, 1775), and (for the navy) *Parliamentary History of England* (London, 1813), vol. 18, pp. 54–59. Reports from France: dispatches from Lord Stormont, Nov.–Dec. 1774, State Papers Foreign (France) SP 78/294, NAK, especially fols. 45, 53, and 165–71.

3. Burke on General Gage: In the Commons, Dec. 20, 1774, in *PDNA*, vol. 5, pp. 258–60. Rumors about Gage's dismissal: *London Evening Post*, Nov. 29–Dec. 1, 1774, but also *Morning Post*, Jan. 1, 1775. Gower, Hillsborough, and Chatham: *London Evening Post*, Dec. 23, 1774.

4. For Franklin's talks with Fothergill and Barclay, all the sources are collected in *BFP*, vol. 21, with the "Hints" on pp. 365–68. For a reference to the rumors in the stock market on December 23, see p. 405.

5. Barrington to Dartmouth, Dec. 24, 1774, D 1778 II.1035, SCRO.

6. The principal sources for the rest of this chapter are the reports of the parliamentary debates in *PDNA*; Thomas Hutchinson's diary and letter book, not only the edition published by Peter Orlando Hutchinson in 1884, but also the unpublished letters in MS 2661, Egerton Manuscripts, British Library; the official papers of Sir Joseph Yorke and Lord Suffolk, including dispatches from the Royal Navy patrol off Amsterdam, SP84/546, State Papers Foreign (Holland), NAK; and the very extensive coverage in the London newspapers.

7. Jonathan Bliss: *Boston Evening-Post*, Sept. 12, 1774, reporting events at Springfield on August 30.

8. Quincy's change of mood and the visit from Thomas Pownall: George H. Nash III, "From Radicalism to Revolution: The Political Career of Josiah Quincy Jr.," *Proceedings of the American Antiquarian Society* 79, pt. 2 (1969), pp. 279–80.

9. For "fixed those who were wavering," see Thomas Hutchinson to Jonathan Sewall, Jan. 27, 1775, from Hutchinson's letter book, MS 2668, fol. 115, Egerton Manuscripts. Hutchinson also comments on the importance of the *Charming Nancy* dispatches in a letter to Thomas Flucker, Jan. 29, 1775, MS 2661, fol. 116, Egerton Manuscripts: "I am told that the last advices by Deverson . . . have removed all hopes of any terms of reconciliation & that something effectual is to be done." Deverson was the *Charming Nancy*'s captain: *Essex Gazette*, Dec. 13–20, 1774. Prescott's audience with the king was reported in *Lloyd's Evening Post*, Jan. 13–16, 1775. From his dispatch to Dartmouth dated December 15, it seems clear that Gage wanted Prescott to brief the king and his ministers with an appraisal of the situation in Massachusetts that was too frank to be put down in writing: *CGG*, vol. 1, p. 388.

10. The interpretation of the Conciliatory Proposition given here follows that of Thomas, *Tea Party to Independence*, pp. 178–79, 198–206.

11. Letters to Dartmouth: All from his papers at SCRO. From "ZYX," Jan. 13, 1775, file D(W) 1778/II, 1103; from Corbyn Morris, "A Systematical Plan," Jan. 1775, D(W) 1778/II, 1096; and from Richard Oswald, "Thoughts on the State of America," Feb. 9, 1775, D(W) 1778/II, 1139.

12. Germain in 1746: John Prebble, *Culloden* (London, 1996), pp. 198–202.

13. Attitude of George III: Letters to Lord North, Feb. 3 and 8, in *CG3*, vol. 3, pp. 170–71. The stepping up of military preparations can be followed through the minutes of the Treasury Board, T29/44, fols. 61–95 (Jan. 19–March 14 1775), NAK, and the accompanying memoranda at T1/513/8.

14. Dunmore's dispatch: Dec. 24, 1774, CO 5/1353, NAK.

15. For the intelligence gathered by the navy in Holland, the key document is a letter from Captain Pearson of the sloop *Speedwell*, Feb. 26, 1775, and covering letter from the Admiralty, March 6, 1775, SP 84/546, NAK.

16. *Falcon* and *Nautilus*: Their captain's logs, ADM 51/336 (*Falcon*) and ADM 51/629 (*Nautilus*), NAK; and *St. James's Chronicle*, Feb. 21–23, 1775. We know from Gage's own papers that he received the fatal dispatch on April 14, the day the *Nautilus* first saw

Cape Cod, which means that she must have sent it on by small boat before entering harbor two days later. For the events that followed, the principal recent accounts are John Galvin's *The Minutemen* (2006), David Hackett Fischer's *Paul Revere's Ride* (Oxford, 1994), and Nathaniel Philbrick's *Bunker Hill* (New York, 2013), although J. L. Bell's insightful and entertaining website www.boston1775.blogspot.com has established itself as the most accessible source.

Appendix One: THE MEANING OF TREASON

1. Contemporary definitions of treason: Giles Jacob, *New Law Dictionary* (Dublin, 1773); Edward Hyde East, *A Treatise of the Pleas of the Crown* (London, 1806), vol. 1, pp. 37–141; and W. G. Holdsworth, *A History of English Law* (London, 1925), vol. 8, pp. 318–21. East deals with the Damaree case on pp. 73–75. Also helpful is E. N. Williams, *The Eighteenth-Century Constitution* (Cambridge, U.K., 1960), pp. 408–19. Lord Mansfield referred to Damaree's case in the House of Lords on Feb. 7, 1775, in *PDNA*, vol. 10, pp. 388–89, 401.

Acknowledgments

Often it can be hard to fix the exact date at which a book begins to take shape, but in the case of *An Empire on the Edge* the moment took place in the autumn of 2011 at the top of the steeple of the First Baptist Church in Providence, Rhode Island. I owe a special debt of thanks to the sexton, Peter Forsstrom, a retired firefighter with a head for heights. Peter led me up the ladders inside the great wooden structure erected in 1774–75 by shipwrights and carpenters from Boston, some of whom probably took part in the destruction of the East India Company's tea. I find it impossible to think about history without having in mind the precise physical setting in which events unfolded. That trip up the steeple kindled my enthusiasm to begin writing.

Elsewhere in Rhode Island, I am very grateful to two latter-day members of the Brown dynasty, Alice Westervelt and Henry A. L. Brown, and to Pam Cole and Paul Dimeo of Dimeo Properties, for giving me a tour of Namquid Point, the site of the *Gaspée* raid; and to Lee Teverow and her colleagues at the Rhode Island Historical Society, who found for me the microfilm of Henry Marchant's journal. In Boston, my thanks are due to Jane Kamensky; to Jayne Gordon and Peter Drummey and their colleagues—especially Anna Clutterbuck-Cook—at the Massachusetts Historical Society; to Brenton Simons and his staff at the New England Historic Genealogical Society; to Ann Kardos of Heritage New England, Catharina Slautterback of the Boston Athenaeum, and Elizabeth Roscio of The Bostonian Society, for helping me find images of the pre-revolutionary town; to J. L. Bell; and to Walter Ferme, my landlord on Tremont Street, and his colleague Mike Eruzione.

As always, the Boston Public Library and the Houghton, Lamont, and Widener libraries at Harvard gave me free and courteous access to everything I required, including the unpublished order books of General Gage, which I was allowed to digitize and bring home to England in electronic form. I also have to thank the Harvard University Archives and the Baker Library at the Harvard Business School for permitting me to read manuscript materials connected with John Hancock. Two discussions over dinner with Maya Jasanoff helped me to clarify my thinking, but we had to agree to differ about John Wilkes, a subject on which I tend to concur with Benjamin Franklin. Elsewhere in the United States, I am grateful to Jasminn Winters of the Library of Congress in Washington, D.C.; to Dawn

Braasch of the Bunch of Grapes Bookstore on Martha's Vineyard; to Sandra Hewlett, for genealogical advice; and in New York to Sherida Paulsen, Steve Margulis and the Margulis family, and to Didi and Andrew Hunter. I also wish to thank John Demos, who over lunch at his home in Tyringham, Massachusetts, encouraged me to carry on with the book.

In the United Kingdom, I am greatly indebted to William Legge, the tenth Earl of Dartmouth, his brother Rupert Legge, and the Dartmouth Heirloom Trust for kindly permitting me to reproduce Gainsborough's portrait of their ancestor and to quote from the Dartmouth papers. My thanks are also due to Joanna Terry, head of Archives and Heritage at the Staffordshire Record Office, and her predecessor, Thea Randall, county archivist. Elsewhere in the U.K., I am grateful to John Moffett, librarian of the East Asian History of Science Library at the Needham Research Institute, Cambridge; to the Fitzwilliam Estates for permitting the publication of material from the Burke and Rockingham papers held as part of the Wentworth Woodhouse Muniments at the Sheffield Archives; to Maia Sheridan, manuscripts archivist at the Department of Special Collections, University of St. Andrews; and to the staff of all the other libraries and record repositories referred to in the endnotes, especially Sarah Millard of the Bank of England Archives, Hugh Alexander of the National Archives at Kew, and Annie Pinder and Simon Gough of the Parliamentary Archives at the House of Lords. While visiting Lord North's old estate in Somerset, I received a friendly welcome from Wayne Bennett, the manager of Dillington House, and from Lady Caroline Cameron of Whitelackington Manor, to both of whom I extend my thanks.

Like its predecessor, *Making Haste from Babylon*, *An Empire on the Edge* was commissioned in America by Carol Brown Janeway of Alfred A. Knopf, without whose editorial support, encouragement, and wisdom neither project could have come to fruition. I am deeply grateful to Carol; to Will Sulkin, her opposite number at Random House in London, who commissioned the British editions of both books for The Bodley Head and examined the first draft of *An Empire on the Edge* with an athletic attention to detail; and to my agents, Bill Hamilton of A. M. Heath in London and George Lucas of Inkwell Management in New York. At Knopf, my thanks are also due to Victoria Pearson, Lisa Montebello, Joshua LaMorey, and Erica Hinsley; and at The Bodley Head, to Stuart Williams and Katherine Ailes.

This book is dedicated to my wife, Sue Temple, with my heartfelt thanks for her love and companionship, and for her frequent advice to pause for a while at moments when work on the book threatened to become overwhelming. Sue was ably assisted by our otterhound, Champion Teckelgarth Quintus, a tower of canine strength.

Index

Page numbers in *italics* refer to illustrations.

absentee land tax of 1773, Irish, 200, 258
Adam, Robert: architectural style and
    cultural significance, 78–9, 181, *313*;
    designs for the fête champêtre of 1774,
    310–12; finances, 79–80; relationship
    with politicians, 79, 147, 314
Adams, John, 49; on molasses, 64; political
    ideas and the Novanglus essays, 166,
    373; and the Tea Party, 230; *see also*
    Braintree Instructions
Adams, Samuel, 21, 130, 164–5, 184–5, 196,
    202, 254, 287, 292–3, 337; aptitude for
    politics, 223–4; British opinions of,
    207, 225–6, 316, 332, 364; connections
    in London, 192, 277, 303; letter to
    Joseph Hawley (1773), 212–13; quoted,
    162, 183; relationship with Elbridge
    Gerry, 283; relationship with John
    Hancock, 180, 182, 186, 219; Tea Party
    meetings and, 213, 216, 220, 222–3,
    228–30, 250; *see also* Committees of
    Correspondence, Boston; Solemn
    League and Covenant

Adelphi Project: see Adam, Robert,
    finances
Alarm, The, 209–10
Alexander Houston & Company, 145
Alice's coffee house, Westminster, 256–7,
    265
Allahabad, treaty of, 44
Allen, Ethan, 105–6, 214–15, 335, 359
Amelia, Princess, 334
American colonies: see colonies,
    American
Andros, Governor Edmund, 14, 16, 260
Annapolis, Maryland, 101, 295, 335
Anti-catholicism, 168, 275–8, 323, 336
Antigua, 75, 108, 134, 147
army, British, 14, 18, 68, 97, 182, 216;
    attitude to colonists, 56, 205–9,
    225, 249; casualties in America
    and the West Indies in 1775–83, 12;
    finances and logistics, 75, 264,
    282, 300, 322, 347, 355, 378; in
    Ireland, 9; occupation of
    Boston, 21; in Seven Years' War, 75;

army, British (*continued*)
    shortcomings, 9, 10, 166–7; size and
    strength, 9, 19, 20, 25n, 273, 290, 308,
    350; in the western wilderness, 7–11.
    See also regiments of foot, British
army, French, 25n
army, Russian, 25n, 96
Association, the, 334, 338–40, 343, 354.
    See also Continental Congress of
    1774
Ayr Bank. *See* Douglas, Heron (bank)

balance of power, European, 23–4, 96
banks, Dutch, 41, 70–1, 77, 137, 147, 153
banks, English, 75–6, 80–1, 128
banks, Scottish 76, 80–2
Bankrupt, The (play by Samuel Foote), 71
Bank of England, 14, 70, 188; as lender to
    the East India Company, 42, 133–4,
    136, 149, 155; role in financial crisis of
    1772, 80–2
Barbados, 13, 75
Barclay, David, 346–8, 363
Barkley, Gilbert, 210
Barré, Colonel Isaac, 269, 272–3, 282
Barrington, Lord, 333, 341, 344, 348
Bedford, Dukes of, 36, 97
Bengal, 24; British annexation of, 43–4;
    British régime in, 44–5, 107, 135, 144,
    146–7, 188, 210, 319; famine, 46–7, 136;
    Nawab, 43; population, 38n
"Bengal bills," 47–8, 132, 136
Berkshire Hills, Massachusetts 286, 301–2,
    339
Bigelow, Joshua, 340
Bigelow, Timothy, 302, 304–5
Blackstone, William, 224
Black Watch. *See* regiments of foot,
    British
Bliss, Jonathan, 350–1
Bloomsbury Gang, 97–102, 141, 246,
    262
Bocca Tigris, 33–4, 38
Bohea. *See* tea, varieties of
Booth, Benjamin, 210

Boston, 50–1, 54, 56; appearance and
    buildings, 170–3; Beacon Hill, 172,
    177–8, 182; Common, 292, 298,
    301, 303, 306–7; early radicalism, 16;
    economy in 1770s, 174–6; education,
    175; fortification by General Gage,
    309; massacre of 1770, 21, 94, 167;
    mood in summer and autumn of
    1774, 302–4, 341–2; political debate
    in 1772–3, 63–4, 68, 109, 130–1, 161,
    164–9, 177–8, 183–6; population, 57;
    religion in, 177–8; response to Gage's
    arrival, 287–8; waits for news from
    London after Tea Party, 285–6; *also*
    Castle William; Dorchester Heights;
    Faneuil Hall; Fort Hill
Boston Pamphlet, 1772, 184–5
Boston Port Act, 253, 260, 284, 287, 295,
    301
Boston Tea Party, narrative, 225–30; origins,
    145–9, 151–7, 231–5; public meetings
    preceding, 217–18, 221–4, 226–9;
    reaction in London, 239–41, 245–55
Boswell, James, 69, 72–3, 83, 233, 250, 324,
    380
Boulton, Henry Crabb, 189, 199
Boulton, Matthew, 75, 82, 119, 136
boundary disputes, colonial, 106, 111, 166,
    201, 245
Bowdoin, James, 177, 217, 219, 316
Bowen, Ephraim, 67
Braintree Instructions, 166
Brattle, William, 306–7
Brattle Square Church, 177–8, 182, 186, 201,
    217, 369
Brecon, Wales, 248, 263
Brest, French naval base at, 297
Brown University. *See* Rhode Island,
    College of
Browns of Providence, 62–3, 71–2, 93, 114,
    157; John, 64–8, 111, 161
Brudenell, James, 120
Buccleuch, Duke of, 82
Buckinghamshire, Lord, 246, 252
Bull, Frederick, 246, 276–7, 323

Bunker Hill, Battle of, 56, 114, 162, 171, 177, 288, 324, 369

Burgoyne, General John, 310–12, 363

Burke, Edmund, 159, 181, 232, 255, 317, 319, 322; character sketch, 257–8; at the Cockpit, 249; inattention to colonial affairs, 188, 200, 233; interventions in American debates of 1774–75, 258–60, 263, 265, 269–733, 350, 355; political philosophy and *Thoughts on the Causes of the Present Discontents*, 142–3, 275–6; quoted, 14, 32, 127, 136, 270, 273, 312, 345, 361; relationship with Marquess of Rockingham, 141

Burma, 37

Bushy Park (granted by George III to Lord North), 85, 103

Bute, Lord, 242

Byron, Lieutenant Richard, 170–1

cabinet, British: 21, 23; composition in 1770s, 95–9; functioning, 197–8; notion of collective responsibility, 279–80; opts for coercion of Massachusetts, 246–7; sense of disarray in autumn and winter of 1774–75, 320–2, 327, 329–32, 339–40, 343–4; takes decision for war, 349–50, 352–6. *See also* Dartmouth, Lord; North, Frederick Lord; Rochford, Lord; Sandwich, Lord; Suffolk, Lord

Calcutta, Black Hole of, 44

Calcutta, British officials at, 46–7

Calley, Captain Benjamin, 302–3

Calvert family, Maryland proprietors, 15, 331

Camden, Lord, 269

Canada, role in the British Empire, 220–1

Canton: approaches to, 31–3; Chinese authorities, 34, 37–8; English factory, 34, 39–40, 43; trading system, 40–3

Cardigan, earls of, 120

Caribs of St. Vincent, 108, 157

Castle William, 10, 170, 196, 207, 216, 220, 223–6, 288, 292, 333

casualties, British in Revolutionary War, 12, 382

Catherine the Great, 24, 96, 112, 189, 192

Cavendish, Fort. *See* Fort de Chartres

Cavendish, Lord John, 246, 361

Channel Islands, British, as center of smuggling trade, 41

Charles I, King, 13

Charles II, King, 59, 118, 226

Charleston, South Carolina, 27, 101, 106, 130, 161, 175, 199, 233, 240, 261, 293, 299–300, 303

Charlotte, Queen, 119, 173, 239, 316; birthday balls, 231, 351, 355

charters, colonial, 14–5, 94, 143–4, 253, 290, 313, 338, 360, 373

Chartres, Fort de: abandonment, 10; appearance, 3–6; surrendered by the French, 7–8; weakness of British at, 8–9

Chatham, Lord, 142, 265, 269, 274–6. *See also* Quebec Act of 1774

China: agriculture and commerce, 38–40; imperial regime under Qianlong, 37–8; population, 37n. *See also* tea

Christie, Mr (of the Royal Navy), 54

Clarke, Richard: riots against, 216–18

Cleveley, John (the elder), 33

Cleveley, John (the younger), 190

Clinton, General Henry, 363

Clive, Robert, 44, 132, 134, 242

Cockpit, the, 243

Coercive Acts. *See* Boston Port Act; Massachusetts Government Act; Impartial Administration of Justice Act; Quartering Act (1774)

Coffin, Hezekiah, 229

Coke, Lady Mary, 319, 334

Colebrooke, Sir George, 75, 158, 188; appearance and character, 134–5; memoirs, 156; political ambitions, 36; role in East India Company's affairs, 45–6, 48, 133–4, 137; speculative dealings by, 76, 80, 154

Colonial Office, Whitehall: "official mind"
of, 105–9; procedures, 105; staff, 104,
194n

colonial system in America: American
critique of, 165–8, 176, 184–5, 336–9;
Benjamin Franklin's view of, 11, 13, 61,
201; weaknesses in early 1770s, 107–11,
122, 335. *See also* Jefferson, Thomas

colonies, American: British attitudes
toward, 22–3, 231–4; development pre-
1740s, 13–16; first British steps toward
reform, 16–17; response to Coercive
Acts, 280, 299–303. *See also* colonial
system in America

committees of correspondence: Boston,
185, 196, 202, 213, 220, 227, 282–4, 296;
conference in Boston (August 1774),
304–5; Marblehead, 300, 306; Salem,
304; Virginia, 192–3

commodities, global trade in, 26–7, 32

Common Sense. See Paine, Thomas

Conciliatory Proposition (Lord North's),
355–6, 362–4

Concord, Battle of, 12, 115, 140, 291, 365

Connecticut (colony), 105, 107, 110, 301, 308,
316, 331, 340, 358

Connecticut River, 105, 175

constitutional ideas, American, 60–1,
165–9, 183–6, 338. *See also* Adams,
John; Jefferson, Thomas; Quincy Jr.,
Josiah

constitutional ideas, British. *See* Parliament,
British

Continental Congress of 1774, 201, 295–6,
298–9, 300, 303, 312, 314, 318, 329, 331–3,
334, 336–8, 343, 350–1, 358, 360

Cooke Jr., Elisha, 16, 19, 21, 161

Cooper, Samuel, 177–8, 201, 230, 287, 302,
316

Cooper, William, 177, 287

Copley, John Singleton, 178–9, 222, 224,
289

Corsica, annexed by France, 191

Cowper, William: and Edward Thurlow,
250; and Lord Dartmouth, 115, 356

Crash of 1772, 70–2, 147–8, 232–3;
causes, 75–8; extent, 80–2; impact in
America, 73, 82–3, 167; recovery from,
in Great Britain, 272

Crichton, William, 47–8, 133, 136, 148,
149, 199; background and business
career, 145–6; political ambitions, 145;
suggests shipment of surplus tea to
America, 153–5

Crimea, 192

Crime wave in London area, 1774, 322, 333

Crown Point, 11

Cruger, Henry, 180–1, 323

Culloden, Battle of, 289, 324, 349, 359

Cushing, Speaker Thomas, 196–7, 200–2,
251, 269, 287, 316

Customs duties. *See* taxation, British

Customs service, British: activities on
American coast, 51–3, 92–3; in Great
Britain, 92

Dacca, 146

Dance, Nathaniel, 87

Danvers, Massachusetts, 298, 300, 304

Dartmouth College, 117

Dartmouth, William Legge, Second Earl
of, 26, 95n, 102–4, 109–11, 136, 191, 207,
359; American policies, 114–5, 117, 164,
185, 195, 314–5, 321, 330, 332; colleagues'
views of, 254, 340; correspondence
with Joseph Galloway, 329;
correspondence with Speaker
Cushing, 196–7; correspondence
with Thomas Hutchinson, 185, 195;
early life and family background,
117–19; finances, 119, 140; letters to his
son, 115; life after 1775, 369; London
home, 252; newspaper comments
about, 116–17, 303; portrait by
Gainsborough, *116*; relationship and
correspondence with General Gage,
274, 279–80, 293, 296, 298, 300, 305,
307–8, 330; relationship with Benjamin
Franklin, 160, 194–5, 200, 203, 346–9;
relationship with George III, 119–20,

316–17; relationship with Lord North, 117–18, 160–1; religious beliefs, 115–16, 120–3, 194–5n, 314; response to Boston Tea Party, 240–1, 246–7, 249–51, 267; takes part in decision for war, 350–1, 353–7, 362, 369; warned about unrest in America, 193; writes "fatal dispatch" to Gage, 357–9, 364–5

Declaratory Act for America (1766), 20–1, 140, 142, 184, 260, 269, 271, 321, 338, 362

Declaratory Act for Ireland (1720), 19–20

Devonshire, Duke of, 36, 200, 258

Disraeli, Benjamin, 258, 367–8

Diwan, 44–5, 132, 136

Dominica, 78, 109, 277

Dorchester Heights, 171; British failure to fortify, 298

Douglas, Heron (bank), 77, 80–2

Dowdeswell, William, 187, 265

Dudingston, Lieutenant William: background and family, 51–2; early affrays with Americans, 54–5; meets Governor Wanton; seizure of the *Fortune*, 55–6. *See also* Gaspée incident of 1772

Dudley, Charles, 62, 68

Dunkirk, smuggling at, 41, 92

Dunmore, Lord, 110, 113, 192–4, 291, 295, 331, 362

Dunning, John, 243–4, 269, 272, 275, 373

East Germany, 162–3, 165

East India Company, British, 24, 26–7, 261, 269, 295; Canton trade, 34–6, 40–43; criticisms of, 132–3, 135, 143–4; dividends ramped up by, 45–6; early history and subsequent transformation into territorial power in India, 43–4; finances in disarray, 71, 82, 90, 131–4, 153–5; governance, 45–6; Lord North's proposed reforms, 136–7, 186, 199, 253; schemes for its rescue, 147–53; shareholder base, 134;

ships and shipping interest, 40–1; tactics in tea trade, 41–2; Treasury's intervention, 153–7

East India Company, Dutch: business tactics, 41

East India Company, French, 34, 41

economy, British: characteristics and growth rate, 26–7, 73–6; recession of 1772–3, 82–3, 128, 131, 167, 272; statistics, 377–8. *See also* Crash of 1772

Eden, Governor Robert, 331

Edgartown, Massachusetts, 54

Edinburgh: New Town, 77

elections, British: at Banbury, 322, 367–8; general (1774), 318–325; Middlesex (1768–9), 85; Worcester, 323–4

elections, Massachusetts, 287

England, Bank of. *See* Bank of England

England, Church of, 72, 108, 120, 158–9, 178, 262, 275; evangelical movement, 121–2, 194n

Erie, Lake, 10

evangelicals. *See* England, Church of

Exeter, England, 90

Falklands Crisis of 1770–1, 32, 53, 189

Falmouth, England, as port for official mail, 302

Falmouth, Maine, 93

Faneuil, Benjamin, 213, 217

Faneuil Hall, Boston, 173, 184, 221, 287, 293

fête champêtre at the Oaks (1774), 310–13

Fifeshire, Scotland, 52–3, 207

Flaxman, John, *370*, 371

Flint, James, 37

Fordyce, Alexander: background and origins, 76–7; business dealings, 70–1, 77, 81

Fordyce, John, 80–1

Fort Hill, Boston, 225

Fothergill, John, 346–8, 363

Fox, Charles James, 261, 272, 370

Framework Knitters, Company of, 277

France: defeat in Seven Years' War, 3, 7,
      17, 35; foreign policy, 37, 112; scares
      about war with, 24, 53, 69, 90, 96, 160,
      189–92, 212–13, 362; threat to India,
      135; unrest in countryside 128, 344
Franklin, Benjamin, 159, 175, 177, 233, 281,
      361; attitudes toward Great Britain
      and the empire, 61, 83, 108, 161, 164;
      circle of friends, 158–9; at Craven
      Street, Westminster, 78; departure
      for America, 364; Hutchinson letters
      and, 200–2; mistakes by, 114, 158–60,
      167, 188, 213; Ohio country and,
      100–1, 209, 275; *Public Advertiser*
      columns, 203–4; quoted, 11, 13;
      relationship with Lord Dartmouth,
      160, 194–5, 200, 203, 346–9; secret
      talks in 1774–5 with British
      government, 345–8, 360, 363–4;
      response to Tea Party and Coercive
      Acts, 250–1, 261, 269, 293; summer
      travels in British Isles, 83, 91;
      vilification by Wedderburn, 241–5,
      264, 286, 314
Frederick the Great: foreign policy, 24, 96;
      opinion of Great Britain, 21, 86, 89,
      96, 190; opinion of Lord North, 86
frontier policy, British: *see* Seven Years' War,
      consequences in America *and* western
      wilderness
Fukien, China, 38–9
Fuller, Rose, 263, 270

Gage, General Thomas, 52, 109, 163, 166,
      184, 206, 264, 268, 272, 274, 282,
      295, 314, 325, 327, 349; appointed
      governor of Massachusetts, 259–60,
      263, 267; arrival at Boston, 282, 287–8;
      character, early career, and military
      record, 267, 288–91; contemporary
      criticisms of, 288–9, 297, 330, 332,
      345; enforcement of Coercive Acts,
      300–304; errors made by, 291–3, 296,
      298–9, 330–1; frontier policy, 3, 8–11,
      95, 100, 105, 157; interview with

George III, 247–8, 253, 317, 321; orders
      seizure of gunpowder store, 306–7;
      panics after the powder alarm, 308–9,
      320; recovers his nerve in winter of
      1774–5, 340–2; requests army 20,000
      strong, 350, 358; sends Colonel
      Prescott to London as emissary,
      352–3; sends redcoats out to Concord,
      364–5; termination of his command,
      369. *See also* Gage, Margaret
Gage, Margaret (née Kemble), 289
Gainsborough, Thomas, 115–16
Galloway, Joseph, and the Galloway Plan,
      329, 331, 337
gambling craze, British, 71–2, 133–4
Garrick, David, 79, 83, 191, 311, 313, 333
Gaspée incident of 1772: narrative, 63–9;
      origins, 49–54; political and legal
      significance, 68, 83, 113, 141, 157, 168–9,
      192, 196, 206–7, 209, 221, 231, 262;
      raiders, 327–8; response by Great
      Britain, 92–4, 111–14, 160–1, 183–4,
      244–5, 289; treasonous, 111–2, 204,
      374. *See also* gun running in 1774 by
      Americans
"General Observations on the Fall of
      the Roman Empire in the West"
      (Gibbon), 23
George II, King, 17
George III, King, 3n, 6, 18, 19, 23, 37, 48,
      76, 115, 144, 149, 162, 166, 186, 195,
      197, 253; appearance and character,
      119, 317–18; attitude toward American
      colonies, 21, 188, 247–8, 325, 333–4,
      343, 347; attitude toward East India
      Company, 135, 139; caricatures of, 24,
      363; Christian beliefs, 120, 315–16; loss
      of confidence in General Gage, 330;
      meeting with Thomas Hutchinson,
      315–17; portrait, *88*; relationship
      with Lord Dartmouth, 119–20;
      relationship with Lord North, 21,
      84–6, 119, 128, 187, 273, 277, 340,
      369–7; respect for British constitution,
      61, 196; on Rhode Island, 50; role in

general election of 1774, 319–20; role
in onset of war, 361–2; at Spithead
naval review, 190–1

Germain, George Sackville, Lord, 359–60,
369

Gerry, Elbridge, 283–4, 286, 296, 303–5,
329, 339

Gibbon, Edward, 23, 25, 72, 86, 88, 233, 256,
313, 317, 371

Glasgow: in 1745 Jacobite rebellion, 375;
journey times via, 320n; tobacco trade,
27, 73–4, 101, 148, 320; West Indies
connections, 145

Glorious Revolution of 1688–89, 14

Golden Hill, Battle of (New York), 211

Gordon, Reverend William, 251

Gower, Lord, 140–1, 246, 262, 321;
background, character, and finances,
97–8, 136; at the Cockpit, 243; hawkish
views about America, 240, 248, 265,
324; involvement in Ohio scheme,
100–1; rival to Lord North, 350

Graves, Admiral Samuel, 297, 308, 330, 351,
354, 364

Great Britain: diplomatic isolation, 24–5,
96, 111–2, 191–2; naval strategy, 97,
189–90, 297, 333; public finances,
13, 17–18, 27, 35–6, 91–3, 86, 89, 188,
282, 377–8. *See also* economy, British;
colonial system in America

Green Dragon Tavern, Boston, 213, 215

Greene, Nathanael, 56, 65, 69, 281; as
militia officer, 308

Greene family of Warwick, Rhode Island,
56, 65

Grenville, George: colonial policies and
new taxes, 18–22, 52, 61, 93; personal
influence on other British politicians,
141, 156, 201, 242, 254

Guernsey, 41

guerre des farines (flour war), 344

gun running in 1774–5 by Americans,
326–9, 357, 363

Gustav III, king of Sweden, 112, 189

Gwynn, John, 79

Haldimand, Major-General Frederick, 292

Halifax, Nova Scotia: British base at, 51,
199, 291

Hall, Captain James, 222, 225, 227, 250

Hallowell, Benjamin, 307

Hamilton, Lady Betty, 310, 312

Hancock, John, 178, 192, 206, 217, 228, 241,
251, 300, 327–8; background and early
career, 178–81; Beacon Hill estate, 178;
Boston Massacre oration, 1774, 285;
Brattle Square Church membership,
178; British attitudes toward, 207,
247, 296, 300, 316, 318, 332, 350, 369;
business dealings, 131, 182, 221, 239, 316;
connections in England, 131, 323, 351;
literary tastes, 181; political activities
and ideas, 182, 184, 186, 212, 219;
portrait by John Singleton Copley,
179; president of Provincial Congress,
1774, 334, 339, 342, 352–3, 375;
relationship with Samuel Adams, 182,
219, 292–3, 364; Tea Party meetings
and 216–7, 222, 224–5, 228–30, 250n.
See also Palfrey, William

Hancock, Lydia, 180

Hancock, Thomas, 181–2

Hanover, New Hampshire, 47

Harvard College, 149, 175, 177, 180–1, 185,
215, 283–4, 300, 307

harvests, British, 89–90; 1772, 128, 139;
1774, 313, 319, 344

Hatch, Mr., magistrate from Dorchester,
Massachusetts, 216–17

Hawley, Joseph, 212, 215

Hayley, George, 131, 180–1, 262, 277, 323, 351

Hearts of Steel rebellion, 91, 94

Henry, Patrick, 192

Herries, Robert, and the Herries Plan,
145–9

Hillsborough, Lord, 183, 275; background
in Ulster, 94; memorandum of
April 1772, 99–102; policy toward
New England, 21, 94–5, 151–2, 160;
policy toward South Carolina, 106;
relationship with Benjamin Franklin,

Hillsborough, Lord (*continued*)
158; resignation, 103; response to
Gaspée incident, 111–12; rumor of his
return to office, 345; unpopularity in
America, 94, 101
Hodges, William, 78
Hodson, Mr., Amsterdam merchant,
326
Holmes Hole, 54–5
Honecker, Erich, 163, 165
Hongs, 37–8, 40–2
Hope & Company, bankers, 77–8, 80, 153,
155
Hopkins, Chief Justice Stephen, 60–2, 64,
67–8, 114, 177, 214, 229
Howe, Mrs. Caroline, 347–8, 364
Howe, Admiral Richard, 195, 347–8
Howe, General William, 363
Hudson River and valley, 101, 105, 209, 331;
rural unrest, 214; strategic importance,
11, 110, 291, 308, 333
Hurricane of 1772, Caribbean, 147
Hutchinson, Thomas, 50, 104, 176, 180,
207, 243–4, 300, 379; background
and character, 149–50; conflict with
Massachusetts General Court, 164,
170, 182–3, 185–6, 192, 201; in England (1774–75), 203, 313–318, 321;
family business, 150–3, 199; Benjamin
Franklin and, 201, 204–5; letters to
Thomas Whately, 201–5; relationship
with British government, 109–11,
194–6, 240–1; relationship with
William Palmer, 151–3, 198;
response to *Gaspée* affair, 68; role in
Massachusetts after the Tea Party,
282, 285–8, 301; role in Tea Party
crisis, November–December 1773,
207–9, 211–13, 226–7; witnesses British
decision-making on the eve of war,
350–1, 353–4, 361–2

Illinois Country, 3, 6–10
Ilminster, Somerset, 91, 127

Impartial Administration of Justice Act
(1774), 264
independence, American: early ideas about,
16; talked about in Rhode Island,
60–2; viewed by British politicians as
the goal of colonial resistance, 107,
110, 186, 244, 271, 285, 317, 351
India. *See* Bengal; East India Company,
British
Industrial Revolution, 25, 72, 167
inflation since eighteenth century, 377–8
Intolerable Acts. *See* Coercive Acts
Ireland: British army in, 9, 266, 321, 341;
comparisons with America, 18–19;
conditions, 91, 158; population, 38n,
rebellions, 25, 68, 92, 193; smuggling,
92; union with Great Britain, 347

Jacobite Rebellion (1745–46), 146–7, 187,
207, 275, 278; influence on British
official thinking, 68, 95, 326, 342, 349,
374–5
James, Henry, 176
James I, King, 13
Jamestown, Virginia, 13
Jefferson, Thomas, 113, 192, 295; *Summary
View of the Rights of British America*,
298–9, 315, 323, 330, 332, 336, 373
Jenkinson, Charles, 156–7, 198
Johnson, Samuel, 79, 324, 378; attitude to
America, 233; friendship with Edward
Thurlow, 250; *Taxation No Tyranny*,
336, 355
Johnstone, George, 147–8, 153–5; against
Tea Act, 187, 199; opposes Coercive
Acts, 269; opposes war, 344, 362
Johnstone, John, 146
Johnstone family, 146–7. *See also* Crichton,
William; Pulteney, Sir William
Jones, Sir William, 34
jurisdiction of English judges in the
colonies, 112–13
jury trial: political significance in America,
113

Keene, Mr. Whitshed, 120

Kerouaille, Louise de, first Duchess of Richmond, 266

Kew Palace, 139, 191

King's Bench, Court of, 85, 112, 268

Knox, William: background, 106–7; critique of empire in America, 107, 111; role in 1775, 351

"law of nations," 23

law, rule of, 55, 91, 93, 98, 106, 207, 217, 235, 286, 374–5

Lee, Arthur, 130–1, 186, 210, 220, 277, 345

Lee, Richard Henry, 192

Lee, William, 130–1, 264, 277, 303

Leipzig, 163, 170

Lennox, Charles. *See* Richmond, Charles Lennox, Duke of

Leslie, Lt-Col Alexander: meets General Gage at Castle Williams, 288; seeks toughest measures against Massachusetts radicals, 300, 304, 306, 308, 341; in Tea Party crisis, 206–7, 219, 223, 225–6, 247

Lewes, Sir Watkins, 324

Lexington, Massachusetts, 12, 25, 57, 115, 161, 171, 174, 209, 267, 357, 363–4

Liberty Boys of New York, 209, 211

Li Shiyao, 38

Liverpool, England, 27, 156, 170, 320

Locke, John, 143, 184

Lock Hospital, 121–2

London: city government and Lord Mayor, 123, 128–9, 137–8, 212, 276–7; newspapers, 129; political climate in 1770s, 129–31; population, 170; real estate boom, 78–9

Lorient, France, 41, 149

Lott, Abraham, 210

Lotteries: British national, 71–2, 333; Robert Adam's Adelphi, 82

Louis XV, King, 7, 189; death, 297

Louis XVI, King, 213, 297; economic problems, 324

Macao, 32–3, 37

Macklin, Charles, 241

Madan, Martin, 121

Maddison, Colonel George, 306–7

Madras, 43–4, 46–7

Magna Carta, 224

Maine, Gulf of, 51

Malaya, 41

Malcolm, John, tarred and feathered, 260, 262, 271, 285, 307

mandamus councillors, 253, 279, 304–5, 308

"Manifesto Church." *See* Brattle Square Church

Mansfield, Lord, 262, 314; definition of treason, 373

Marathas, 47

Marblehead, Massachusetts, 227, 283; role in revolution, 300, 302, 304, 306

Marchant, Henry, 83

Marines, Royal, 206, 219, 321

Martha's Vineyard, 51, 54, 211

Maryland: governor, 15, 110, 351–2; role in revolution, 293, 295, 299, 335, 359, 362; tobacco trade, 15, 27, 74

Massachusetts, 68; charter of 1691, 62, 94, 165, 183, 247, 253, 257; early history, 13; government (pre-1774), 15, 19, 109–10, 149–51; population, 57; public opinion in, 161–4, 211–12, 215, 230, 264, 268; revolutionary movement in, 11, 165–70, 183–6, 195–7, 243–4, 260, 281–6, 300–13, 334–5, 338–9

Massachusetts Government Act (1774), 253, 301–2

Mather, Cotton, quoted, 174

Mauritius, 46

McDougall, Alexander, 209–10, 213

Melvill, Thomas, 230

Middlesex, England: courts of law, 128; parliamentary elections of 1768–69, 85, 195

Middlesex County, Massachusetts, 227, 305

Miller, John, 264

militia, colonial, 15, 60, 107–8, 110, 169,
248, 327, 355, 358; Boston, 260, 293;
legal status, 375; New Hampshire, 359;
revolutionary plans for reform, 284–5,
329, 339, 350, 365; Rhode Island, 308,
328, 340; Virginia, 362
Minutemen, 343, 352–3, 355–6. *See also*
militia, colonial
Mississippi valley: role in British official
thinking, 6–10, 108
Mobile, Alabama, 10
Mohawks, 60; name taken by protestors
against Tea Act, 209, 211, 240, 250n,
251
Molasses trade, 15, 18, 49, 52–3, 57, 61, 63–4,
146, 181, 232–3, 298
Molineux, William: as possible smuggler,
213–14; role in Clarke riot, 216–17; role
in Tea Party meetings, 230, 247, 281
Montagu, Admiral John: anti-smuggling
campaign, 50–1, 152, 252; attitude
toward Americans, 55; letters to
London about the *Gaspée*, 63, 68,
93, 114, 170; role in Tea Party crisis,
206–7, 225, 227
Montagu, John. *See* Sandwich, Lord
Montresor, Colonel John, 292
Murshidabad, 44, 47
Mysore, Sultan of, 46
Mystic River, 306

Namier, Sir Lewis, 231
Namquit Point, 66, 68
Narragansett Bay, 48, 55–7, 58–9, 63, 65
Natick, Massachusetts, 175
Navigation Acts, 15, 52
Navy, French: perceived threat from,
189–90, 297, 344
Navy, Royal, 16, 24–5; role in America
pre-1775, 49–56, 252, 297; size and
strength, 189–90; Spithead review,
189–91, *190*; Tea Party and, 206–8,
225–6. *See also* Great Britain, naval
strategy; Ships
Neale, James, Fordyce and Down, 70

Netherlands: gun running from, 326–9; tea
smuggling from, 37, 49. *See also*
banks, Dutch; East India Company,
Dutch
Nevis, 75, 145
Newcastle, England, 130, 277
Newfoundland fisheries, 101, 181, 360
Newgate Prison, 128, 137
New Hampshire: claims to Vermont, 105;
market for tea, 151; role in revolution,
197, 286, 359, 361
newspaper titles, American: *Boston Gazette*,
164, 303, 339–40, 356, 375; *Essex Gazette*,
225, 300–1; *Massachusetts Spy*, 173, 218,
282; *Newport Mercury*, 63; *Pennsylvania
Gazette*, 251; *Pennsylvania Journal*, 209;
Pennsylvania Packet, 336; *Providence Gazette*,
60, 143; *South Carolina Gazette*, 303;
Virginia Gazette, 73
newspaper titles, British: *London Evening Post*,
264–5, 268, 270, 273, 277, 299, 310,
320, 323; *Morning Post*, 203, 248, 262–3,
350–1, 355; *Public Advertiser*, 80, 135,
202–3, 286, 340
New York, province: claim to Vermont,
205; political divisions, 110, 197; rural
disorders, 214, 298. *See* Hudson Valley
New York City: Liberty Boys, 20, 68, 247;
as military base, 6, 8, 10, 92, 157, 207,
226, 290–2, 308, 369; smuggling, 152;
tea ships and protests against them,
199, 209–10, 213, 215, 281, 225, 227,
240, 271n
nonconformity in Britain, religious, 130,
158, 262, 267
North, Frederick, Lord, 23–5, 61, 163,
169, 173, 178–9, 200, 213, 279, 337–8;
appearance, 86–8; background, early
life and personal finances, 86, 117–19;
becomes prime minister, 21; cartoon
images, *278*, *363*; character traits,
88–9, 205; colonial policies, 21–2, 48,
73, 98–9, 108, 212, 281, 314, 317–18;
criticized in the press, 240–1, 262–3,
340, 345; expertise as a politician, 26,

84–6, 128–9, 140–1, 143–5, 192, 197–8, 309; financial policies, 27, 71, 91–3, 282, 344; illness and death, 370–1; learns of *Gaspée* affair, 92; negotiations for rescue of East India Company, 133–7, 139, 146, 148–9, 153, 199; plan to ship tea to America, 156–8, 161, 187–9, 195, 198, 230; portrait by Nathanael Dance, 87; reaction to Boston Tea Party, 241, 245, 248–9, 252, 254–5; speeches in Parliament (1774–5), 263–5, 267–8, 271, 287, 334; takes decision for war, 330–2, 349–50, 355–6; ties to George III, 84–5, 119–20; views about British constitution, 232–4, 367–9. *See also* Conciliatory Proposition; Dartmouth, Lord

Northampton, Massachusetts, 212

North Carolina, 110, 218

Ohio Country: political debate in London, 99–102, 166, 201, 209, 275

Ohio River, 7, 99

O'Reilly, Alejandro, Spanish governor and captain general, 297

Ostend smugglers, 41, 147

Oswald, Richard, 356–7

Ottoman Empire, 96

Oxford University, 115, 117, 120, 134, 191, 279

Page, Benjamin, 326–8

Paine, Thomas, 337

Palashi (Plassey), battle of, 44

Palfrey, William, 181

Palmer, Thomas, 151

Palmer, William, 151–3, 157; role in tea shipments to Boston, 198–9, 211, 219, 226

Panshan (tea cultivation), 39

Pantheon, London, 313

paper money, colonial, 17–18, 245

Paris, 1763 treaty of, 7, 9, 44, 76–7

Parliament, British: doctrine of supremacy, 98–9, 186, 222, 234–5, 317, 330, 361, 375; reform proposals, 234, 267

Pays d'en haut (high country), 8

Pearl River, 33

Pennsylvania: economy, 175; government, 15, 158; role in revolutionary movement, 295; tea protests, 211, 218; western expansion, 9, 99, 276

Percy, Brigadier-General Hugh, 301, 326, 341

Petersham, Massachusetts, 244

petitions to George III, 186, 195–6, 202, 212, 243–4, 277–8, 285

Philadelphia: tea protests, 210–11, 217–18, 225–6, 240

Pickering, Timothy, 284, 304

Pigou, Frederick, 210

Pitt the Elder, William. *See* Chatham, Lord

Pitt the Younger, William, 234, 370

Plymouth, Massachusetts, 174

Poland, 1772 partition of, 24, 96, 111, 128, 191

Pontiac's war, 7

Pope, Alexander, 35, 60

Portsmouth, England, 191, 359

Portsmouth, New Hampshire, 152, 359

Powder Alarm, 306–8, 330, 336

Pownalborough, Maine, 163

Pownall, John: background and early career, 104–7; response to *Gaspée* affair, 111, 114; role in events of 1774–5, 254, 319–21, 331, 357, 361; role in tea shipments, 197, 200

Pownall, Thomas, 105, 353–4

Pownall, Vermont, 105

Prescott, Colonel Richard: mission to London, 352–3, 354, 357

press, American: 19, 54, 63, 164, 166. *See also* newspaper titles, American

press, British, 22, 197; political role, 102, 123, 128–9, 136, 173. *See also* newspaper titles, British

Price, Richard, 167

Proclamation of 1763, 3, 4–5, 10, 101, 105

Proctor, Edward, 250n

Providence, Rhode Island, 49; appearance in 1772, 56–7; industry, 57–9, 62–3; political complexion, 59–61, 67–8

Provincial Congress of 1774, Massachusetts, 169, 305, 329, 341, 353, 357–8; seen as treasonous by British, 358, 360, 375

Prudence Island, 58, 61

Prussia: foreign policy and relations with Britain, 86, 89, 96, 190

Puankhequa, 38, 42

public opinion, British: in early 1770s, 86, 128–9, 203; regarding East India Company, 144; regarding Tea Party and its aftermath, 262, 303, 324, 353

Pulteney, Sir William, 147–8, 187

Purling, John, 45, 48, 133

Qianlong, emperor, 31, 37–8. *See also* China

Quartering Act (1774), 274

Quebec Act of 1774, 275–9, 278

Queensberry, Duke of, 82

Quincy Jr., Josiah: as *Centinel*, 282; attendance at Tea Party meetings, 228–9; pamphlet against Boston Port Act, 294–5, 297–8, 330; visit to London and death, 353–4, 364

Rakove, Jack, 281

Raleigh Tavern, 295, 314

regiments of foot, British: Black Watch, 7–8, 12; Fourth, 293; Fifth, 298; Forty-Third, 293; Fifty-Ninth, 304; Sixty-Fourth, 207, 292

Revere, Paul, 171, 174–6; Quebec Act and, 278; role in Tea Party, 213–14, 230; role in revolutionary movement, 288, 334, 339, 359

Reynolds, Sir Joshua, *142*, 193, 242, 313n

Rhode Island: charter of 1662, 60–1; College of, 60–1; culture and ideas in, 48–9; economy, 48; government, 50, 59–60; population, 56–7. *See also* gun running in 1774–75 by Americans; Providence, Rhode Island

Richmond, Charles Lennox, Duke of, 255; background, character and political views, 266–7, 322; portrait, *266*; pro-American campaign, 269, 273–5, 279, 303, 334, 348, 362, 365

Robespierre, Maximilien, 214

Robinson, John, 156

Rochford, Lord, 91, 108; character sketch, 95–6; death of wife, 153; on the East India Company, 134; foreign policy, 96, 128, 134, 191; office in Cleveland Row, 352; response to *Gaspée* affair, 111–12; role in decision for war, 321, 344, 350, 352

Rockingham, Marquess of: 20, 117, 140–1, 245–6, 258, 274, 318–9, 322. *See also* Whigs, Rockingham

Romaine, Reverend William, 121, 194n

Romney, George, *249*, 266

Rotch, Francis, and Rotch family, 221–2, 226, 227; in London, 250

Rousseau, Jean-Jacques, 221, 267

Rowe, John, 224, 227

rum, colonial trade in, 64. *See also* molasses trade

Russia: army, 23n; foreign policy and relations with Great Britain, 24, 96, 98, 111–12, 189; threat of war involving, 319, 326

Saint Croix, 328

Saint Eustatius, 328

Saint Vincent, 108, 157

Salem, Massachusetts: importance, after Boston Port Act, 261, 283, 287, 293, 300–1; role in revolutionary movement, 296, 298, 304; smuggling, 50

Sandby, Paul, *352*

Sandwich, Lord: cartoon, *363*; character sketch, 95–7; and *Gaspée* affair, 51, 93; hawkish views about America, 98–9, 117, 140–1, 164, 169, 196, 240, 248, 265, 289, 324; libel action against *London Evening Post*, 264; role in 1773

French war scare, 189–91. *See also* Great Britain, naval strategy; Navy, Royal

Saunders, Admiral Charles, 190

Sayre, Stephen, 277

Scott, Captain James, 241, 250

Serle, Ambrose, 194–5n

Seven Years' War: consequences in America, 3, 4–5, 7, 17; economic consequences, 17–8, 75–6, 203

Sewall, Jonathan, 307

Siraj-ud-Daula, 44

Shelburne, Lord, 99

Ships: *Active*, HMS, 225; *Beaver*, HMS, 65; *Beaver*, tea ship, 200, 225, 229; *Calcutta*, 31–4, 41, 131; *Canceaux*, HMS, 54; *Captain*, HMS, 206, 219–20; *Charming Nancy*, 349, 352, 354; *Dartmouth*, tea ship, 200, 225; *Eleanor*, tea ship, 200, 224–5; *Falcon*, HMS, 335, 359–60, 364; *Fortune*, 55–6; *Gaspée*, HMS (*see* Gaspée affair); *Hannah*, 66, 68; *Harmony*, 287; *Hayley*, 206; *Liberty*, 180–1; *Lively*, HMS, 267, 288, 292; *Minerva*, 287, 349–50; *Molly*, 302–3; *Nautilus*, HMS, 364; *St. Lawrence*, 340, 349–50; *Scarborough*, HMS, 300–1, 320–1, 358; *Smack*, 326–8; *Speedwell*, HMS, 363; *Swanzey*, 54–5

Slavery: British attitudes toward, 122, 262, 319, 331

Smith, Adam: epigraph; 53, 187, 221, 233

Smith, Charles, 193

smuggling, 37; American, 49–50, 53–4, 62, 92–4, 146, 153, 181–2, 210, 214, 297; British, 62, 81n, 92, 147–8

Smythe, Baron Stafford, 122

Solemn League and Covenant, 296

South, American: British ignorance about, 101, 290, 299, 316, 331: *see also* Maryland; South Carolina; Virginia

South Carolina: disputes with Great Britain pre-1774, 105–6, 188, 197, 212; role in revolutionary movement of 1774–5, 299, 303, 335. *See also* Charleston

Springfield, Massachusetts, 301, 350–1

Staffordshire, 97, 118

Stamp Act, 20, 22, 26, 61, 93, 105, 117, 161; American protests against, 20, 62, 111, 166–7, 180, 210, 219; repeal, and its political legacy in Britain, 98–9, 140, 156, 225, 240, 246–8, 270, 291, 304

Stanley, Edward Lord, 310–12

Stanwix, Fort and Treaty, 99

Stedman, Charles, 53

Suffolk, Lord: character sketch, 98; close to Thomas Whately, 201; hawkish views about America, 98–9, 140–1, 196, 243, 324, 332; response to Tea Party, 246; role in decision for war, 356; role in 1774 general election, 319, 321; surveillance of Dutch coast, 326, 363

Suffolk County, Massachusetts: *see* Suffolk Resolves

Suffolk Resolves, 329, 331, 337

sugar. *See* commodities, global trade in; West Indies, British

Sulivan, Laurence: background and early career, 46; role in East India crisis, 133, 137

Summary View of the Rights of British America (Jefferson). *See* Jefferson, Thomas

Swedish revolution of 1772, 112, 128, 189

tariff of 1789, U.S. federal, 176

Taunton, England, 130

taxation, American, 20, 61, 113, 166, 184, 209, 355, 360; Edmund Burke on, 270–1. *See also* Conciliatory Proposition (Lord North's), Townshend Duties

taxation, British, 17–18, 36–7, 232, 360

Taxation No Tyranny (Johnson). *See* Johnson, Samuel

tea, 21–2; from China, 35–7, 39–42, 46; economic significance, 26–7, 32, 135; glut in western Europe, 42, 48–9, 50, 71, 131–2; see also East India Company; Herries, Robert, and the Herries Plan; smuggling; Palmer, William

tea, varieties of: Bohea, 35, 39, 41, 131, 137,
    148, 151, 152–5, 199, 220, 229; Hyson,
    41; Singlo, 155, 220
Temple, John, 204–5
"territorial constitution" (Disraeli), 367–8
Thomson, Captain William, and the
    Thomson family, 31–7, 40–1, 131
Thornton, John, 251
Thrale, Mrs., 134–5
Thurlow, Edward: character and
    temperament, 249–50; opinion about
    Gaspée raid, 111–12, 204; opinion of
    Lord Dartmouth and Lord North,
    254; role as attorney-general in British
    response to the Tea Party and the
    decision for war, 254, 275, 321, 356,
    360; view of Alexander Wedderburn,
    242. *See also* treason, law of
Tobacco: fiscal importance, 15–6, 36,
    52, 293; Glasgow merchants, 145,
    148; planters, and their role in
    revolutionary movement, 73, 110, 192,
    314, 332; trade, expansion of, 14–15, 27,
    32, 63, 65, 74–6, 101, 232, 263
Tobago, 78, 109
Toulon, 189, 297
Townshend Duties, 21–2, 26, 105, 151–3,
    155–7, 160, 167, 183, 270, 339
treason, law of, 55, 65, 111–12, 204, 216,
    249–50, 254–5, 281, 284, 305–6, 332,
    373–5
Treasury, His Majesty's: boardroom,
    92; fiscal policy, 17, 27, 42, 72, 97;
    reaction to smuggling and *Gaspée*
    affair, 62, 92–3, 152, 260; response
    to East India crisis, 131–3, 135–7, 188;
    role in Massachusetts judges' salaries
    dispute, 183; seniority in British
    government, 198; Tea Act devised by,
    152, 158, 161, 195, 198–9, 219, 333. *See also*
    elections, British
Tryon, Governor William, 110, 194, 210–11,
    219–20
Turgot, Anne-Robert-Jacques, 344
Turkey. *See* Ottoman Empire

Ulster: rural unrest in, 25, 91, 94
Unitarians, 120, 267

Van, Charles, 248–9, 254–5, 263–4, 268,
    272, 359
Venn, Henry, 121
Vermont: disputes over, 101, 105–6; in
    rebellion, 335. *See also* Allen, Ethan
Vineyard Haven. *See* Holmes Hole
Virginia: early history, 13; government,
    15, 19, 110, 192; role in revolutionary
    movement, 113, 161, 197, 201, 233, 287,
    291, 293, 295–6, 299, 314, 362; westward
    expansion, 9, 99, 101, 110, 276
Virginia, West, 100
Voltaire, 181, 267

Walpole, Horace: quoted, 267, 274, 279,
    343
Wanton, Governor Joseph, 64–5, 113–14
Warren, Joseph, 177, 184, 192, 213, 216–17,
    220, 250n, 305, 329, 332
Warren, Mercy Otis, 215
Washington, George, 50, 56, 107, 167n, 251,
    281, 314
Watt, James, 72, 75, 82
Wedderburn, Alexander, 204–5, 241,
    246; background and early career,
    241–3; debate with Edmund Burke,
    258–9; defends Coercive Acts, 268–70;
    denounced in America, 286–7, 296;
    legal opinions on treason in New
    England, 249, 314, 356, 360, 373; refers
    to Jacobite rebellion, 349–50; speech
    at the Cockpit, 243–5, 264, 286; views
    about western wilderness and Quebec
    Act, 275–6
Wedgwood, Josiah, 72, 75, 272
Wemyss, Major James, 288, 290
Wesley, John, 115, 120–1
western wilderness: British policy
    regarding, 9–11, 99–102, 275–6. *See
    also* Ohio Country; Proclamation of
    1763
West India Merchants, Society of, 145–6

West Indies, British, 12, 157, 181, 262, 282, 287–8, 357; colonial assemblies in, 107; economy, 74–5, 101, 108, 232, 331; real estate speculation, ca. 1770, 77–8, 100, 145, 147, 277

West Indies, Dutch, 54, 328

West Indies, French, 55, 145

Whampoa Roads, 34, 37

Wharton family: Isaac, 210–11; Samuel, 209; Thomas, 210–11

Whately, Thomas, 201–4

Whately, William, 204–5

Whigs, Rockingham: background, membership and ideas, 139–46, 260; in government (1765–66), 20–1; response to East India crisis, 187, 199–200; response to 1774 general election, 318–19, 322–3; response to Tea Party and Coercive Acts, 245–6, 255, 260–1, 265, 267–71, 273–4; role in 1775, 361–2. *See also* Burke, Edmund; Richmond, Charles Lennox, Duke of; Rockingham, Marquess of

White, Henry, 210

Whitefield, George, 120–1

Whitefoord, Caleb, 203

Wilberforce, William, 122

Wilkes, John, 95–6, 99, 123, 204, 242, 248, 267; background and character, 129–30; connections and influence in America, 130–1, 150, 181, 186, 193, 197, 209, 212, 214, 262; distrusted by Franklin, 159; mayoral election campaign of 1772, 128, 134, 137; Middlesex elections and, 85–6, 195; supported by South Carolina Assembly, 106; West Indies connections, 108, 145, 264

Wilkesite movement: anti-Catholic, 276–8; electoral strength, 322–4; geographical reach, 130; ideas behind, 130; support for American liberty, 246, 261–2

Williams, Roger 48, 59

Winslow, Joshua, 213

Winthrop, Hannah Fayerweather, 215

Worcester, England, 90; Wilkesites in: 323–4

Worcester, Massachusetts, 163, 244, 301–2, 304–6, 308, 328, 332, 339–40

Wroxton, Oxfordshire: North estate at 86, 118–19, 366–9; parish church of All Saints 366–8, 371

Wu Yi Mountains, 38–9

Yorke, Sir Joseph, 326–7, 329

Yorkshire, and Marquess of Rockingham, 140–1, 143, 245

Yorktown: surrender at, 56, 370

Young, Thomas: political ideas, 213–14, 369; role in Tea Party meetings, 222–4, 228–9, 250n; speaks of a "perfect crisis," 287–8

Zhejiang, 37

Zoffany, Johann, 8

TO THE
Commiſſioners
APPOINTED by the *EAST-INDIA* COMPANY, for the SALE of
TEA, in America.

GENTLEMEN,

YOUR Appointment, which is notoriouſly deſigned to enforce the Act of 7th G. III. *for raiſing a Revenue in America*, juſtly claims the Attention of every Man, who wiſhes well to this Country: And you need not be ſurprized to find the Eyes of ALL now fixed on you; as on Men, who have it in their Power to ward off the moſt dangerous Stroke, that has been ever meditated againſt the Liberties of America.

You have before you the Examples of many of your unhappy Countrymen, I mean *ſome* of the STAMP MASTERS; Examples, which, if properly attended to, may convince you, how fooliſh, how dangerous it is, to undertake to force the loathſome Pills of Slavery and Oppreſſion down the Throats of a free, independent and determined People.——Your *Appointment* is exactly ſimilar to that of our late STAMP MASTERS—They were commiſſioned to enforce one Revenue Act; you to execute another—The Stamp and Tea Laws were both deſigned to raiſe a Revenue, and to eſtabliſh *Parliamentary Deſpotiſm* in America.

There cannot therefore be any Difference in your Appointments; except in this; that their Office as *Stamp Men* favoured ſtrongly of the Nature of *Exciſe Officers*; whilſt you, in the Execution of your *Duty*, may retain ſome feint Reſemblance of the decent Characters of *Factors*. But let not Names deceive you :—Your Characters as Stamp Maſters and Tea Commiſſioners have a ſtrong and near Affinity.—They and you could boaſt, that you were our Brethren; they and you owe at leaſt SUPPORT, if not LIFE, to America; and what characteriſes the two Employments in the ſtrongeſt Manner, they and you were marked out, by the Conſpirators againſt our Rights, to give the laſt, the finiſhing Stroke to Freedom in this Country.—Strange indeed! that Americans ſhould be pitched on to violate the Privileges of Americans!

You cannot believe, that the *Tea Act*, with Reſpect to its Deſign and Tendency, differs in one ſingle Point from the *Stamp Act*.—If there be any Difference, the *Tea Act* is the *more dangerous*.—The *Stamp Act* was ſenſibly felt by all Ranks of People; and was therefore oppoſed by all—But the *Tea Act*, more inſidious in its Operation, required ſome Pains to diſcover its Malignity.—Under the *Firſt*, no Man could transfer his Property; he could not even read a News-Paper, without ſeeing and feeling the deteſtable Impoſition; it was therefore too glaring to paſs unnoticed and unoppoſed.—But under the *Tea Law*, the Duty being paid on Importation, is afterwards laid on the *Article*, and becomes ſo blended with the Price of it, that although every Man who purchaſes Tea, imported from Britain, *muſt of Courſe pay the Duty*; yet every Man does not know it, and may therefore not object to it. It is in Vain then to ſeek for any Diſtinction between the two Employments.—To Americans it muſt be a Matter of Indifference, by what Stile or Title you may think proper to demean yourſelves; whether STAMP MASTERS or TEA COMMISSIONERS.—If you are appointed to enforce the Revenue Act in America, any Titles you may aſſume to yourſelves, in the Execution of your Office, will prove deteſtable and infamous.

If Parliament can of Right tax us Ten Pounds for any Purpoſe; they may of Right tax us Ten Thouſand, and ſo on, without End.—And if we allow them a fair Opportunity of pleading Precedent by a ſucceſsful Execution of the Tea Act under your Auſpices, we may bid Adieu to all that is dear and valuable amongſt Men.

Ireland has long groaned under the Weight of Parliamentary Reſtrictions and Impoſitions—She was once a rich and flouriſhing Iſle; but being charged beyond her Abilities with the Payment of exceſſive Sums to worn out Panders and Whores, ſhe is now ſinking beneath the infamous Load; and muſt, ere long, be a Martyr to the *abſolute Controul of the Parliament of Great-Britain*.

To this miſerable Situation America will in Time be reduced, if you are determined and allowed to execute the ſcandalous Office to which you are appointed. You are marked out as political Bombardiers to demoliſh the fair Structure of American Liberty: and much, very much depends on your Conduct at this Time. For be aſſured, reſolute and ſucceſsful as you may prove in the Execution of your Office, AMERICANS *will not part with the PALLADIUM OF AMERICA without a hard STRUGGLE*; a Struggle which it is your Duty, and the Duty of every Man, who wiſhes the Proſperity of Great-Britain and America to prevent. The Perquiſites of your Office cannot prove ſuch faſcinating Objects, as to tempt you to fly in the Face of your Country—What Appointments at Home or Abroad can ever make up to you the Loſs of your Brethren's Affections? What Appointments can atone to your Children, for the cruel, moſt horrid, Predicament to which you may ſubject them ?—You have given them a Birth-Right in America; which you found a Land of Liberty and ſocial Enjoyment—Let them therefore peaceably and happily inherit it.—You can have no Proſpect of ſubjugating America, that you or they may become ſovereign Princes; if you have, your Proſpect indeed muſt be extenſive; and in my Opinion, productive of every Miſchief to them and you : Beſides, if you mean to eſtabliſh your Children happily, they will derive more real Satisfaction as PRIMI INTER PARES; to which their Virtue may entitle them in a free Country; than they can ever enjoy as TYRANTS over a Band of Slaves.—But ſuch I truſt cannot be your Motives.—You have already filled ſome of the moſt important Offices in the American State;—you have hitherto acted on the broad and ſafe Baſis of diſintereſted Virtue; by diſcharging many public Duties without Fee or Reward : And you cannot now act ſo directly repugnant to your former virtuous Actions; ſo contrary to the Sentiments of your watchful Countrymen, as to be induced by the paltry Bribe of a petty Commiſſion, to rivet the Shackles of Slavery on your American Brethren.

If the Eaſt India Company can eſtabliſh Warehouſes in America for the Sale of TEA *on which a Duty is impoſed for the Purpoſe of raiſing a Revenue in America*, they may vend, in like Manner, any other Articles of their Trade. On ſuch other Articles, Parliament may impoſe a Duty to be paid in America; and the Company's Commiſſioners will no doubt take ſpecial Care to pay ſuch Duty: and *reimburſe their Conſtituents, by fleecing it from the People.*—Thus the Impoſition may be encreaſed at Pleaſure; and America be ſubjugated without the Poſſibility of Redemption.

It has been alledged *by ſome* that your Friends in England, to whoſe ſpecial Grace and Favor you are entitled for the important Commiſſion, *have given Security, in very high Sums for the faithful Execution of the Truſt repoſed in you ;* and that, therefore, you cannot, in Honour or good Conſcience, leave your Friends in the Lurch; by neglecting or refuſing to comply literally with the Tenor of your Commiſſion. So much, Gentlemen, has been advanced in Favor of your Employment; let us now examine the Force of it.

It cannot be meant that your Friends in England have engaged *that you ſhall execute the* TEA ACT *in America;* this would be a raſh Engagement indeed: For it was well known in London what Confuſion your Appointment would occaſion in America: And no Man would be ſo fooliſh as to ſet you up for Quixotes; and give Security for your poſitive Execution of any whimſical Schemes the Miniſtry or the Eaſt India Company might chalk out for you: All the Security given amounts to no more than this, that, if you ſhould *undertake and be permitted to enforce the* REVENUE ACT *in America*, you would diſcharge faithfully all Duties appertaining to your Commiſſion: the principal of which was, the regular accounting for and payment of ſuch Money as might ariſe from the Sale of the *dutied Article.*

It is then evident that *you cannot injure your Friends in England* by rejecting the hazardous Employment to which you are nominated; but on the Contrary, *by ſo doing*, you will teſtify your Regard for the Rights and Privileges of your American Brethren; and prove to the World that you are not ſuch Men as your Friends in England preſumed you were; Men who, for the Sake of a paltry Emolument, would impiouſly ſheath the Dagger of Oppreſſion in the Bowels of your Country.

The Claim of Parliament to Tax America has been too well examined, for you to doubt, at this Time, to which Side Right and Juſtice have given the Palm.—Do not, therefore, heſitate at the Courſe you ought to purſue.—If you deliberate, you are loſt,—loſt to Virtue, loſt to your Country. It is in Vain to expect that AMERICANS can give a Sanction *to your Office.* —FREEMEN,—AMERICAN FREEMEN can never Approve it. You are abundantly capable to Judge for yourſelves : And I ſincerely wiſh that your Conduct, on the preſent alarming Occaſion, may be ſuch as will promote your future Peace and Welfare; anſwer, fully anſwer the anxious Expectations of your Brethren, who ſincerely believe it is in your Power to ſave them much Trouble : And laſtly, that your Conduct may be ſuch as will ſecure your Native Country from the deadly Stroke now aimed in your Perſons againſt her.—If you refuſe, no one elſe will dare to execute the diabolical Commiſſion.

SCÆVOLA.